Corporate Governance & Corporate Control

Edited by
Dr Saleem Sheikh
and
Professor William Rees

First published in Great Britain 1995 by Cavendish Publishing Limited, The Glass House, Wharton Street, London WC1X 9PX
Telephone: 0171-278 8000   Facsimile: 0171-278 8080

British Library Cataloguing in Publication Data

Sheikh S
Corporate Governance & Corporate Control
I Title II
344.20666

ISBN 1 874241 48 1

Printed and bound in Great Britain

Acknowledgments

We are grateful to the many people and institutions who assisted us in the preparation of this work. The inspiration in preparing this work derives largely from the Cadbury Committee Report on *The Financial Aspects of Corporate Governance* and the growing developments in the US on corporate governance, especially the recent publication by the American Law Institute on *Corporate Governance*. We are grateful to the American Law Institute for providing us with their recent publication at short notice.

In particular, we are very grateful to the contributors of this volume for their hard work, enthusiasm, patience and invaluable suggestions in the development of this work.

We also wish to express our thanks to Frances Burton of London Guildhall University for introducing us to Sir Peter Walters who kindly contributed a chapter during the later stages in the preparation of this work; to John Spelman (of Avalon Associates) worked exceedingly hard in the word processing of some of the manuscripts, and in assisting us in the technical layout, and proof reading, and we are very grateful to him for his contribution; and to Gee Publishing Ltd which kindly to allowed us to publish the Cadbury Committee's Code of Best Practice, which is set out in the appendix of this work.

Finally, we also wish to acknowledge our considerable appreciation of the patience, encouragement and enthusiasm shown by our publishers Cavendish Publishing Ltd and, in particular, to Jo Reddy, Sonny Leong, and Kate Nicol for all the assistance they have given us in the preparation and development of this work.

Saleem Sheikh and William Rees
London
1 May 1995

Introduction

In 1960, Berle wrote 'The curse of the bigness is still with us'. He referred to the large modern corporations wielding unassailable economic power adversely affecting the interests of the community. Since management powers are vested in directors, who are the main controllers of the corporation, Berle feared that they might abuse their powers and neglect the interests of shareholders and beneficiaries. To some extent, Berle's fears have not been ill-founded. In the UK, for example, corporate scandals such as BCCI, the collapse of the Maxwell empire, Polly Peck, and directors' excessive remuneration have heightened concerns about the role of directors within the corporate governance system. Corporations have been facing growing criticism from consumers, interest groups, shareholders and the broader community on issues such as abuse of directors' powers, how the corporate system is structured, the corporation's legitimacy as an economic as well as a social institution, including the extent of duties and responsibilities of directors, shareholders and employees in corporate decision-making.

The role of corporate governance is to ensure that directors are subject to their duties, obligations and responsibilities to act in the best interests of their company, to give direction and to remain accountable to their shareholders and other beneficiaries for their actions. Until the 1980s, the concept of 'corporate governance' received little attention in the UK. English company law was largely restricted to delineating the constitutional relationship between directors, shareholders and a company's auditors. Demands for an extension of corporate responsibility towards wider constituents was largely neglected by companies legislation. Attempts to remedy corporate abuse and corporate irresponsibility were largely of a casual nature. This failure of company law to address these issues is attributable to lack of clarity as to the role, responsibilities and duties of directors and shareholders. English companies legislation has failed to provide a clear direction in this regard, and the need for law reform in this area is now overdue.

The traditional narrow perception that directors just owe duties towards their shareholders can no longer remain sustainable. Advocates of the corporate governance debate have argued for a wider dimension to the concept of corporate governance. They have proposed various reforms ranging from greater 'shareholder democracy' to appointing non-executive directors on company boards. This work argues, *inter alia*, that the debate on corporate governance should be concerned with reforming the corporate governance structure. At the heart of the reforms should be a serious attempt to identify clearly the roles, responsibilities and accountabilities of directors, and how the reforms themselves may appropriately be implemented in practice.

It will be argued that the concept of 'corporate governance' should not be limited to the narrower confines of the duties and relationships between directors and shareholders. It also embraces wider constituents in relation to the corporation who include employees, creditors, consumers, suppliers and the broader community. These so called 'stakeholders' should also be addressed in the corporate governance debate.

These wider aspects of corporate governance should also be concerned with the role of shareholders and their broader participation with reference to the concept of 'shareholder democracy'. Shareholders too must accept their part in the responsibilities and duties carried by a corporation. They must also give their company effective direction.

The other component of corporate governance is 'corporate social responsibility', which is explained in detail in this work. Unless appropriate pressures are brought to bear upon a corporate management by the broader community, what may be necessary changes may not take place in a corporate governance system. It is for the wider community to ensure that there is a growing awareness of corporate activities within society and then to ensure that their representatives interact with governmental authorities in an attempt to attain a humane, caring and progressive corporate governance system. This work has emphasised that the role of law has its own limitations in the system and it is by strengthening the corporate social responsibility principle, to which the broader community subscribes, that appropriate changes can be made in what has been a narrow corporate governance system.

This work consists of 18 chapters. Chapter 1 establishes the foundations of the concept of 'corporate governance'. It considers the growth and development of the corporate governance debate in the UK. The causal connection between corporate governance and 'corporate social responsibilities' is also examined. This is followed by a consideration of the corporate governance debate in Australia, New Zealand and the USA.

Chapter 2 considers issues of the Governance of 'Shareholding and Public Companies'. Particular consideration is given to the role of shareholders in the corporate governance system.

The role of directors and shareholders is further elucidated in Chapter 3 by examining the 'Role of "Exit" and "Voice" in Corporate Governance'. This chapter examines the background to the corporate governance debate and critically examines various theories on corporate governance and the key concept of 'corporate social responsibility'.

Given that the subject of directors' responsibilities towards other 'stakeholders' is an important feature of the corporate governance debate, Chapter 4, in particular, considers 'Creditor Interests and Directors' Obligations' with an insightful examination of the recent cases in this area.

Chapter 5 on 'Corporate Governance – Great Expectations' discusses the various problems associated with corporate governance, including the growth in size and the international nature of corporations today; the widening separation of ownership from control; and the perceived inadequacies in the administration of laws governing the corporate world.

Chapter 6 critically examines 'Ownership and Accountability in Corporate Governance' with particular reference to 'management choice theory', and offers some suggestions for reform of the corporate governance system in the UK.

Chapter 7, is devoted to the special subject of 'Governance of Co-operative Societies', with particular reference to the role of the Co-operative Union and the role of the corporate governance working group, established by the Co-operative Union, to report on the direction and control of co-operative societies in the UK.

The issue of directors' excessive remuneration has provoked controversy and was the subject of some consideration by the Cadbury Committee. Chapter 8 addresses the issue of 'Directors' Remuneration: Towards Some Principles of Substantive and Procedural Review' with an examination of its quantum and structure. Suggestions are made for reforms in this area.

Reforms of the corporate board structure need to take account of non-executive directors. Chapter 9 thus examines 'The Role of the Non-Executive Director' and offers views on the impact of the non-executive director within the corporate governance system.

The roles of Chairman and Chief Executive are essential in the effective governance of the corporation and for ensuring that all directors, executive and non-executive, are both enabled and encouraged to play their full part in the corporation's activities. Chapter 10 provides 'The Roles of Company Chairman and Chief Executive: An Industrialist's View'.

In Chapter 11, the theme of 'Reform of the General Meetings' is addressed. The history of general meetings is analysed as well as the impact which shareholders could make by suggested reform to general meetings.

An important question is whether most corporations will voluntarily comply with some form of code of conduct or ethics to govern their relationship internally with shareholders and employees and externally with stakeholders such as consumers, suppliers and the general community. Chapter 12 examines the 'Codes of Conduct and Their Impact on Corporate Governance'. Various types of code are examined and particular consideration is given to the Cadbury Committee's Code of Best Practice and its implementation in practice.

The theme of codes of conduct is further developed in Chapter 13 by examining 'Ethical Codes of Conduct', which includes consideration of issues such as individual morals and corporate ethics. A framework is provided for examining the concept of 'ethical governance'.

Consideration of the role of shareholders' committees is an essential step towards shaping the future direction of corporations. This was recognised by the Cadbury Committee. In Chapter 14, 'The Role of the Institutional Shareholders' Committee' is considered by examining its composition and function.

This work argues that corporate governance also embraces the concept of 'corporate social responsibilities'. This concept is examined in Chapter 15 in 'Three Faces of "Corporate Social Responsibility": Three Sociological Approaches'.

The Cadbury Committee was particularly concerned with the financial aspects of corporate governance and the system of disclosure of corporate financial information. Chapter 16 addresses the issue of the 'Going Concern and Internal Control' and provides an accountancy perspective.

Since the Cadbury Committee published its final report in 1992, its role has been to monitor implementation of its recommendations and in particular to consider the extent to which public companies are complying with the Code of Best Practice. In Chapter 17, consideration is given to 'The Cadbury Report – Implementation and Influence', by examining how public companies are implementing the Code of Best Practice as part of their obligations under the Listing Rules.

Finally, before we give the last word to Sir Adrian Cadbury himself in the Postscript, our Chapter 18 examines the theme of 'Corporate Governance and Corporate Control – Self-Regulation or Statutory Codification?' It considers the recommendations made by the Cadbury Committee in its Final Report and examines whether self-regulation or statutory codification of the recommendations provided by the Cadbury Committee in particular would be the best way forward in the UK system of corporate governance. Interestingly in this specific context Pensions Investments Research Consultants (PIRC) in their recently published *Corporate Governance Review: a Company Health Check* has found that whilst the Cadbury Code has had a major impact on boardroom practice, just 47% of the top 190 Companies had fully complied with Cadbury so far. This Chapter 18 thus reflects on some of the reforms suggested by the contributors to this work and considers how their suggestions could perhaps best be implemented in practice possibly by the successor to the Cadbury Committee, which is to be established in mid-1995. The appointment and terms of reference of 'Cadbury Mark 2' or 'The Son of Cadbury' (as it is sometimes popularly called) are expected to be announced this Summer (most probably now in June) with its serious work starting in early 1996.

The sponsorship for the new Committee has been widened quite significantly with Sir Sydney Lipworth (the Deputy non-executive Chairman of National Westminster Bank) in the key role as chair of the sponsors' steering group as well as Chairman of the Financial Reporting Council (FRC). The sponsors now notably include the FRC, the Stock Exchange, the CBI, the Institute of Directors, the National Association of Pension Funds (NAPF), the Association of British Insurers (ABI) and the CCAB (the accountants body). It appears that Sir Adrian Cadbury will not continue in the role of Chairman when the new Committee is appointed by the sponsors, although the new membership listing of about 12 people is not yet in the public domain. The new Committee will decide its own priorities and agenda, although the Cadbury Committee has helpfully prepared a list of items for the new Committee's possible consideration. The Cadbury Committee's own recent (as yet unpublished) research, undertaken with the ABI, apparently shows that whilst the larger PLCs, including the so called 'Top 100', have substantially complied with the Committee's recommendations, this certainly cannot be said for all smaller PLCs. Interestingly also the Coopers and Lybrand survey of November 1993 of medium sized and smaller listed companies suggested that only 45% of such companies agreed that all listed companies should have the objective of fully complying with the Cadbury Code (although some 80% of their representatives agreed with Cadbury's general thrust).

Sir Sydney Lipworth has recently been quoted (see *The FT*, 29 April 1995) as saying (at the annual conference of NAPF) that the new Committee is likely to review the following matters: the Cadbury Code at large; the relationship between executive and non-executive directors; the rules regarding disclosure of directors' remuneration; the role of shareholders; whether companies should be required to include information on cash flow in interim reports; developments concerning the nature and extent of auditor liability; and procedures for putting forward resolutions at company meetings.

The 'Son of Cadbury' (or should it be the 'Daughter of Cadbury) will also have to take on board the thinking of the Greenbury Committee, set up under CBI auspices, under the Chairmanship of Sir Richard Greenbury of Marks & Spencer PLC on executive remuneration as well as the work of the Corporate Governance Sub-Committee of the City Group for Smaller Companies (CISCO) and the Myners Committee Report of February 1995. The rather forthright latter report was the fruit of the work of a joint Industry/City Committee, chaired by Paul Myners, the Chairman of Gartmore, and officially sponsored by the Department of Trade and Industry's (DTI's) Innovation Unit. This Committee's terms of reference were to find how to improve the key relationship between industry and institutional shareholders with a view to helping to stimulate both investment and development.

The new Committee will, *inter alia*, have to get to grips with the key issue of the relationship between boards and their shareholders. Although John Major, as Prime Minister, announced at the end of February 1995 that he would be prepared to consider introducing legislation on executive pay in the light of the Greenbury Committee Report (due out at the end of June 1995), it is clear that the present Government is reluctant to have to legislate in this whole area of Corporate Governance. For example, a recent formal proposal made to the President of the Board of Trade, Michael Heseltine, that directors duties should be codified (and indeed simplified) was not acted upon. Mr Heseltine, it appears, would wish to encourage institutional shareholders in particular to become more activist and thereby seek to avoid the need for legislation. But there is plainly an inherent difficulty in meeting Cadbury's requirements for transparency when the institutional shareholders may be acting 'behind closed doors'. On the other hand, should a Labour Government be elected after the next General Election (which must take place no later than the Summer of 1997), there is evidence that it would be 'poised to legislate' (see further Rupert Morris, 'Cracking the Cadbury Code', (1995) Management Today (April)). Stuart Bell, Labour's shadow DTI spokesperson on corporate affairs, is quoted by Morris as stating that the thrust of Labour's work is towards legislation and the introduction of two-tier boards, ie executive and supervisory boards, albeit preferably on a voluntary basis but with fiscal incentives for companies to go for the two-tier system. Thus the 'New' Labour Party will be looking closely at the work of the new Committee and will make judgments in due course about the practical effectiveness of its recommendations.

We would agree with the judgment of Jonathan Charkham of the Cadbury Committee in quoting (in his comparative work *Keeping Good Company*) with apparent approval George Goyder's strong statement of eight years ago from his book *The Just Enterprise*:

> 'It is absurd that a law [the Companies Act] designed for a family business a century ago should continue to apply without substantial change to the whole of industry today, regardless of the size and purpose of the Company. This represents the abdication of the state from its responsibility to create responsible institutions.'

A common theme that runs through the Chapters of our book is the promotion of a better and more effective corporate governance system than the current one, in the general belief that governance of a corporate body cannot be isolated from the interests of the community at large and the constituents within the corporation too. This work seeks to support these ideas by comparing the corporate governance system prevalent in other jurisdictions such as within Australia, the EC, New Zealand, and the US. It is evident now that the corporate governance system currently operational in the UK is, in many ways, different from that which exists in most other jurisdictions that have received attention in this work. There is, however, no need to take a theoretically radical approach to this concept of corporate governance in that any such approach might not have real practical utility if it cannot build upon and be properly integrated into our present system. What, therefore, is most needed is that the current corporate governance system in the UK be critically reviewed to accommodate the concerns of the wider community in a gradual way and by changing some of the key elements of the system which this work addresses.

This book does not set out to establish that total abolition of the unitary board system *per se* – and indeed the current corporate governance system generally – are overdue. What we aim much more to achieve is full recognition that the current corporate governance system is lagging behind the aspirations of many in the community and that at the heart of the corporate governance system should be the principle of profit optimisation rather than simple profit maximisation.

This work should cater for those who are interested in corporate law and practice, its aims and future objectives. It is extensively based on primary sources of information whilst references to secondary sources of information have also been made where necessary or appropriate.

Finally, we should just emphasise as the editors that the opinions expressed by the contributors to this work do not necessarily represent those of their institutions or organisations, and are best regarded as expressions of their own personal views.

Saleem Sheikh and William Rees
London,
1 May 1995

The Contributors

DONALD BUTCHER is a chartered engineer, Fellow of the Institution of Civil Engineers, Fellow of the Institute of Management Consultants and Fellow of the Royal Society of Arts. He spent the first half of his career designing engineering structures and management construction projects, in the UK and overseas. He then worked as a management consultant on over 100 international assignments in strategic planning, investment appraisal and industrial feasibility study. Latterly, he has specialised in consultancy for small businesses under the DTI Enterprise Initiative Scheme. In 1992, prompted by the recommendations of the Cadbury Committee, he founded, together with a small group of shareholders, the United Kingdom Shareholders' Association, the first organisation aimed at representing the UK's 10 million private shareholders. He is chairman of the Association.

SIR ADRIAN CADBURY has been a director of the Bank of England since 1970. He studied at Eton College and at the University of Cambridge. Between 1969-1974, he was Deputy Chairman and Managing Director of Cadbury Schweppes. Between 1975-1989 he was a director of Cadbury Bros Ltd. He has also held directorships in other companies and served as a member on the Panel on Takeovers and Mergers, as well as on West Midlands Council Committees. In 1991, Sir Adrian was appointed Chairman of the Committee on the Financial Aspects of Corporate Governance which prepared its final report in December 1992. In 1979, he was appointed Chancellor of the University of Aston in Birmingham. Sir Adrian was President of the Birmingham Chambers of Industry and Commerce during 1988-1989.

PROFESSOR SK CHATTERJEE PhD, who studied law at the University of Cambridge and the University of London, is Professor of International Commercial and Criminal Law at London Guildhall University. He has frequently worked as a legal consultant with the World Health Organisation and the International Labour Office. He is also a legal consultant with the Commonwealth Secretariat. Professor Chatterjee has published extensively in the form of books and articles on various aspects of public international law, international commercial law and health law. He was also the General Editor of Lloyd's Arbitration Reports for five years (1988-1992). Professor Chatterjee is also a barrister in England and Wales.

GINA COLE trained as a tri-lingual secretary working at the Foreign and Commonwealth Office, the Department of Trade and Industry and for various other private sector organisations. She was a recruitment officer with the Crown Agents for Overseas Governments and Administrations, specialising in appointments in the Asia and Pacific Region. After a career break, she rejoined the DTI, initially in the Equal Opportunities Division promoting alternative working patterns and, since January 1993, she has been on secondment as Secretary to the Cadbury Committee on the Financial Aspects of Corporate Governance working in the London Stock Exchange buildings.

PROFESSOR JANET DINE was called to the bar in 1973. She practised at the bar for five years, during which time she also completed her PhD thesis.

In 1978, she became a lecturer at King's College London University, an appointment she held until 1992 when she took up a Readership at Essex University. From 1987-1989 she was on leave from King's College having been appointed Law Society Senior Research Fellow at the Institute of Advanced Legal Studies, London University. During her tenure of this post, she concentrated on research into EC company law, publishing EC Company Law (Law Chancery) in 1991. Janet has published widely in the fields of criminal law, company law, EC law and insolvency law. In 1992 she was appointed a Commissioner for Friendly Societies and in 1994 became Professor at Essex University and Head of the Department of Law.

VANESSA FINCH LLB, LLM lectures in law at the London School of Economics and Political Science, specialising in Company Law and Insolvency Law. She has published widely in these areas in learned journals. Her most recent article in the Modern Law Review discussed the implications of Directors' and Officers' Liability Insurance for corporate governance and law. She is currently writing a book on Corporate Directors and Company Law.

SIR OWEN GREEN is former Chairman of BTR plc. He was born in Stockton-on-Tees (then County Durham) in 1925, qualified as a Chartered Accountant following Royal Naval war service (1943/46) in UK waters and in the Indian Ocean. He practised in a small City partnership until 1956 when he entered industry as Financial Director of Oil Feed Engineering, later acquired by BTR. After holding a number of positions in BTR's manufacturing operations, he was Managing Director from 1967 to 1986, and Chairman from 1984 to 1993. His leadership of a team which transformed a small industrial rubber company into a very large, highly profitable multi-national group is probably unparalleled in British industry. In 1982, Sir Owen received the 'Businessman of the Year Award'. In recognition of his services to British industry and management he received his knighthood from Her Majesty the Queen in 1984. The Institute of Chartered Accountants awarded Sir Owen the Founding Societies Centenary Award from 1985 for 'an outstanding contribution to British industry'. In the same year he also received the 1984 Gold Medal from the British Institute of Management. In 1986, Sir Owen was appointed a Trustee of the Natural History Museum. Between 1987 and 1992, he was a founder member of the Listed Companies Advisory Committee to the London Stock Exchange. In 1990, he received the National Free Enterprise Award. Sir Owen is married with three children and four grandchildren. His current pursuits include exploring the merits of senior citizenship.

ANDREW GRIFFITHS MA, Solicitor, studied law at Oxford University. He then practised as a solicitor in London before moving to Manchester. He is presently a lecturer in law at Manchester University and has published a number of articles on company law.

DR PAUL GRISERI is the director of the MBA programme at London Guildhall University. He took an upper second class external degree in philosophy from London University. His doctorate, obtained from the University of Kent, was in the philosophy of action. In addition, Dr Griseri has professional qualifications in education, public sector management, and personnel management, and is a member of the Institute of Management and the Institute of Personnel and Development. Dr Griseri has had extensive experience in the education sector, as well as having worked in shipping, telecommunications and consultancy. He has published articles on ethics and business ethics in international journals. He is currently researching into measurement and information in business ethics, and has a particular concern with implementation of ethical and philosophical concepts in the business environment.

PROFESSOR BRIAN HARVEY is The Co-operative Bank Professor of Corporate Responsibility at Manchester Business School. His book *Managers and Corporate Social Policy: Private Solutions to Public Problems?* was published by Macmillan in 1984. He was a member of the British Institute of Management's Working Party whose report Business Social Policy was published in 1987, and Chairman of the Co-operative Union's Working Party on Corporate Governance and co-editor of the books *Market Morality and Company Size* (1991 Kluwer Academic Publishers), and *European Casebook on Business Ethics* (1994 Prentice Hall). He was editor of *Business Ethics: A European Approach* (1994 Prentice Hall). Other publications include articles such as 'Business Ethics in Britain'; 'Business Success and Social Progress: What Role for Managers?'; and 'Managing in the Public Interest'. He is joint editor of the book series Issues in Business Ethics (with Dr Patricia Werhane) and a member of the editorial boards of the Journal of Business Ethics Quarterly; Business Ethics Quarterly; Business Ethics: A European Review. He was guest editor of the Journal of Business Ethics Vol 8 No 8, 1989. He is Honourary Secretary of the European Business Ethics Network, was Programme Committee Chairman of the 1990 annual conference in Milan, a member of the 1991 London annual conference Programme Committee, the theme of which is 'Values, Standards and the Globalisation of Financial Markets'. Professor Harvey is a Fellow of the Royal Society of Arts.

JOHN PARKINSON MA(Oxon) is Reader in Law at the University of Bristol, where he teaches company law and contract. Before moving to Bristol, he qualified as a solicitor in a major city of London law firm. He is the author of *Corporate Power and Responsibility: Issues in the Theory of Company Law* (1993 OUP). He is author of various articles on Company law.

JULIAN POTTER studied at Oxford University. From 1976-1986, he was the Partnership Secretary for a well-known accountancy firm. In 1991, he was appointed Secretary-General to the Institutional Shareholders' Committee until his recent retirement from this committee. He is currently secretary to the 'Co-operation for the Long Term' Committee.

PROFESSOR WILLIAM REES MA, Barrister, studied law at the University of Cambridge and qualified as a barrister in 1973. His academic career began with his undertaking research and teaching at Cambridge before moving to the Cardiff Law School, the University of Durham, and a visiting fellowship at the Centre for Socio-Legal Studies, Wolfson College, University of Oxford. He has worked in senior managerial positions with several leading City of London law firms. He is a former Tribunal Chairman and has held a number of visiting professorial appointments, namely at the University of Iowa, Brunel University and currently at the University of Hertfordshire sponsored by Pictons, Solicitors. Since 1991, he has also been Senior Visiting Fellow at the Centre for Commercial Law Studies, Queen Mary and Westfield College, University of London. Until recently he was Professor of Law at London Guildhall University. He is now The Stephenson Harwood Professor of Comparative Law and Head of the new Law School at the University of Greenwich. He is on the editorial boards of The International Company and Commercial Law Review and of the Journal of Financial Crime. He is a Consultant Editor of The Company Lawyer and has been a consultant to the Law Society and the EC Commission. He has published extensively in the fields of company law, labour and social security law, financial services regulation, public law, EC law and on the legal profession.

CHRISTOPHER RILEY LLB worked as a solicitor in a commercial, provincial practice from 1985-1987. He is currently a lecturer in law at Hull University. His recent research has focused on non-executive directors, directors' remuneration and a comparative study on Cadbury and the American Law Institute's Corporate Governance Project.

DIANE RYLAND LLB, LLM is currently a research assistant at the Law School, Hull University. Her recent research has focused upon corporate governance and directors' pay, European environmental laws and the legal regime governing non-executive directors.

TONY SCOTT BCom, BCompt (Hons), CA(SA), ACMA, FCCA was educated in South Africa where he trained as a chartered accountant and a management accountant with an international firm. He settled in England in 1978. Tony is managing director of VFL Limited, a company based in London. The company provides technical and training services to its parent company Littlejohn Frazer (Chartered Accountants), other independent firms of accountants and their clients. He has a wide range of practical experience in the financial services and business sectors. One of Tony's main areas of professional work is providing a consultancy service on financial and management accounting and auditing including quality control. He also writes and edits his company's regular newsletter on accounting, auditing and business-related matters.

Dr SALEEM SHEIKH LLB, LLM, PhD (Lond) is a solicitor and senior lecturer in law at London Guildhall University. He has worked for several City of London law firms, specialising in commercial conveyancing and company commercial work. In 1991, he joined London Guildhall University where he specialises in company and partnership law, employment law, insolvency law and corporate finance. He presented joint written evidence (with Professor William Rees) to the Cadbury Committee on the Financial Aspects of Corporate Governance. He is currently researching into the relationship between corporate governance and the social responsibilities of companies by comparing the American and European positions. He has written several articles in this area in The Company Lawyer and The International Company and Commercial Law Review.

DR STEPHEN LLOYD SMITH BSc (Econ) (Wales), PhD (Kent) was formerly a research fellow at Nottingham University, Department of Adult Education and research fellow at the Open University, Faculty of Technology which entailed research into social and technical changes in banking and retailing. He is currently senior lecturer at the School of Social Sciences at Kingston University. He is also a consultant to both the public and private sectors. He is the author of numerous articles on the social relations of technology, public and private issues. He is also joint author of Managers and Corporate Social Policy (Macmillan 1984).

SIR PETER WALTERS was appointed Chairman of Blue Circle Industries plc in June 1990, and Chairman of SmithKlineBeecham plc in April 1994. He is Deputy Chairman of Thorn EMI plc and HSBC Holdings plc, and a Director of Saatchi & Saatchi plc. Sir Peter was Chairman of British Petroleum Company plc from 1981 to 1990, having joined the company in 1954. He was Chairman of Midland Bank plc from 1991 to 1994. A former director of the Post Office and of the National Westminster Bank, Sir Peter is also a past-President of The General Council of British Shipping, The Society of Chemical Industry and the Institute of Manpower Studies. He is a former Chairman of the Governing Body of the London Business School of which he is now Chancellor and President of the Institute of Directors.

Born in Birmingham in March 1931, he was educated at King Edward's School and Birmingham University where he graduated B Comm in 1952. He is married with two sons and a daughter.

Sir Peter was knighted in the New Year Honours 1984, and was made a Commander of the Order of Leopold, Belgium, in May 1984. In March 1985, he was awarded the Society of Chemical Industry Centenary Medal and in July 1985 received an Honourary Fellowship Certificate from the Royal Society of Chemistry. In July 1986, Sir Peter received an Honourary Doctorate of Social Science from Birmingham University, and in 1987 the Honourary Degree of Doctor of Stirling University. Sir Peter received an Honourary Fellowship from the Institution of Chemical Engineers in May 1988. The Institute of Petroleum awarded the Cadman Medal to Sir Peter in October 1989, and in July 1991 he received an Honourary Fellowship from the London Business School.

STANLEY WRIGHT MA following graduation (1st class honours in philosophy, politics and economics at Oxford) spent nearly 20 years in government service at home and abroad. In 1972, when he was an under-secretary in HM Treasury, he left to become an executive director at Lazard Brothers. As a merchant banker, he was for some 10 years engaged in, or was close to, large numbers of takeover bids, mergers and issues of securities, and had extensive exposure at the top levels of UK business. He was subsequently chairman and chief executive of a consortium bank and a partner in a firm of international financial advisers. His experience of the corporate world also includes serving as a non-executive director of a number of quoted companies. He is currently treasurer of Queen Mary and Westfield College. He is also a director of a private company. Stanley is the author of *Two Cheers for the Institutions* published by the Social Market Foundation in April 1994.

Contents

Chapter

Table of Cases

Table of Statutes and Statutory Instruments

Chapter 1

Perspectives on Corporate Governance

Dr Saleem Sheikh and Professor SK Chatterjee
London Guildhall University

1.1   Introduction

Although the concept of corporate governance is well recognised in Australia,[1] New Zealand,[2] the USA[3] and in some European countries, it has hardly received any attention in the UK, primarily because of the traditional view maintained by the corporate governance system that directors are to maximise profits for their shareholders, as the interests of the latter are of paramount concern to directors. The corporate governance system in the UK is rooted in the concept of profit maximisation rather than profit optimisation. Naturally, any initiative to change the system is hardly encouraged.

UK company law entails a tripartite system of corporate governance: directors, shareholders and auditors. Whereas the directors are regarded as leaders for a company's management, directed towards maximisation of company's profits, the role of shareholders is to ensure, *inter alia*, that their directors will maximise profits on their behalf. The company's auditors will wish to ensure that there are no financial irregularities in the company and that the directors provide a 'true and fair view' of the company's financial performance.[4] This tripartite system operates as a means of checks and balances to ensure that directors do not abuse their powers within the

---

1   The Cooney Report, *Report of the Australian Senate Standing Committee on Legal and Constitutional Affairs*, (November 1989). See too, Bean, 'Corporate Governance and Corporate Opportunities' [1994] 15 *The Company Lawyer*, 266-72, especially 268. The Australian perspective on corporate governance is considered in 1.10.

2   In New Zealand, the Law Commission has published its views on this subject in '*Company Law Reform and Restatement*', NZLC R9, June 1989. There is another later report by the commission entitled 'Company Law Reform: Transition and Revision', NZLC R16, September 1990. The New Zealand perspective on corporate governance is considered in 1.11.

3   In the USA, the American Law Institute has been working on a corporate governance project. For the latest version see, The American Law Institute, *Principles of Corporate Governance: Analysis and Recommendations* 13 May 1992. For a brief synopsis of the latest draft see Maw, *Corporate Governance* (1994), especially pp 131-9. A US perspective on corporate governance is considered further in 1.9.

4   Sections 226-227 of the Companies Act 1985 and section 235 of the Companies Act 1985.

corporation. Yet, UK company law has failed to identify and establish in coherent form the functions and duties of directors within the corporate governance system. Recently, a study by the Forum of Private Business revealed that 79 per cent of the respondents supported a proposal to clarify directors' duties. There was not only a call for clarification of directors' duties, but also great anxiety in relation to the lack of effective control of, and sanction for, unscrupulous behaviour by directors.[5] Further, the role of shareholders within a corporation has hardly been questioned. UK company law has portrayed shareholders as 'passive actors' within this system; they are the 'absentee owners' largely content to accept decisions made by their directors. Both the Cohen[6] and Jenkins[7] Committees, which were set up to investigate company law reform, reinforced the traditional tripartite relationship. Substantial reforms within the corporate governance system are overdue. As early as 1965, Wedderburn, in response to the apparent neglect of the Cohen and Jenkins Committees to consider the wider aspects of corporate governance, urged that company law was in need of reform.[8] He contended that directors should consider the interests of employees, creditors, consumers and the wider public interest. The corporate governance debate in the UK needs to address this wider issue of directors' duties towards other potential claimants on the corporation.

In the UK, corporate bodies are usually treated as inanimate objects, the primary function of which is to earn profits in an impersonal way by providing service of a material nature to the community. The modern corporation, however, is a private institution with public obligations. The traditional belief that corporations are solely profit maximisers is no longer sustainable. Corporations have 'souls'. The modern corporation is perceived as a 'caring corporation' which discharges social as well as economic obligations in society. The rise of professional managers and directors within the corporation has symbolised a new 'managerial revolution' within the corporate governance system.[9] Industrial leaders have often urged more participation by the business community to resolve some of the community's social problems. They believe that a company should be a good citizen and neighbour in society.

In the USA, the business community generally maintains a broader perception of 'corporate governance' which includes a consideration of the

---

5   Forum of Private Business, A *Report Into Business Legal Structures*, (1991); see too DTI, *The Law Applicable to Private Companies*, (November 1994) p 34.

6   Board of Trade, *Report of the Committee on Company Law Amendment* (1945) Cmnd 6659 ('Cohen Committee').

7   Board of Trade, *Report of the Company Law Committee* (1962) Cmnd 1749, ('Jenkins Committee').

8   Wedderburn, *Company Law Reform* (1965).

9   cf: Burnham, *The Managerial Revolution* (1962), and Nichols, *Ownership, Control and Ideology* (1969).

other stakeholders on the corporation. The notion of 'corporate social responsibilities' is an essential feature of the corporate governance structure in most US corporations. This notion has probably been influenced to a large extent by the consumer lobbyists in the USA.[10]

The privilege of incorporation with limited liability has established various duties and responsibilities upon corporate directors and shareholders.[11] UK company law, however, has never clearly identified the duties and responsibilities of directors in the corporate governance system. Directors' duties and responsibilities have been identified in random fashion in the form of the common law, the fiduciary duties of directors, the Takeovers and Mergers Code, the Listing Rules and some duties under the Companies Act 1985.[12] According to Allen:

> *'The whole basis of the granting by the State of the privileges of incorporation needs to be re-examined. There is a need for a redefining of the nature of a company: of its ownership and of its control. In broader terms, the responsibilities and obligations which a company owes to its shareholders, workers, creditors, consumers and the public at large need to be examined at length.'*[13]

The debate on corporate governance is concerned with the accountability, responsibilities and duties of directors within the corporation. It is also concerned with the role of shareholders in the system. The issues that need to be addressed in this regard are: Why have shareholders delegated their powers of management to directors? Why are shareholders passive actors within the corporate governance system? What role should shareholders play within the system? What are the duties and responsibilities of shareholders towards other potential claimants on the corporation? Is 'shareholder democracy' an effective mechanism to monitor the powers and duties of directors? These issues also have an impact on the wider community. Pressures from the community are now powerful forces which can require directors and shareholders to reflect on their policies before they are implemented. To this extent, the debate on corporate governance should be widened in scope. Corporate governance should also be perceived as a 'social contract' between the company and the wider constituencies of the corporation which morally obliges the corporation and its directors to take account of the interests of other 'stakeholders'.

---

10 See especially Nader, Green & Seligman, *Taming the Giant Corporation* (1976), and Nader, *The Consumer and Corporate Accountability* (1973).

11 For a brief historical account of incorporation and limited liability, see Gower, *Principles of Modern Company Law* (1992), 5th edn, chapters 1-3, pp.3-54; Farrar, Furey & Hannigan, *Farrar's Company Law* (1991), 3rd edn, chapter 2, pp 15-23 and chapter 7, pp 70-83.

12 See further 1.7 and chapter 16.

13 Allen, *Socialising the Company*, (1974) p 3.

Corporate governance is also concerned with the ethics, values and morals of a corporation and its directors. Do corporations care about their environment? Do corporations care about the atmosphere they pollute? Do corporations care about the adverse publicity they attract from various constituencies? Do corporations take account of the demands of consumer lobbyists? These are all issues of ethics and morals which must form part of corporate culture. They must form part of corporate decision making. They must be implemented by corporations in practice.[14]

There is, however, a growing perception that the powers vested in directors may be abused by them and that, as a result, corporations may become uncontrollable – that the giant corporations are functioning without any effective reins controlling them. Shareholders fear directors' uncontrollable powers because of their perceived threat that directors will not maximise profits for their shareholders and that shareholders' welfare will not be the main objective of corporations. Employees fear the uncontrollable powers of directors for fear that directors will not take account of employees' interests on major matters affecting the corporation. The creditors' fear is that directors may carry on business knowing that the company will be unable to pay off its debts as they fall due. The creditors' interests may thereby be diminished. One of the major issues of corporate governance is for corporate managers to be made more accountable for their actions. According to Chayes:

> '*But to the extent that we are prepared to recognise centres of significant non-governmental power, they too must be subjected to the rule of law. It is implicit in the ideal ... that the process and institutions of the society be organised so as to give reasonable assurance that significant power will be exercised not arbitrarily, but in a manner that can be rationally related to the legitimate purposes of the society.*'[15]

Mason has contended:

> '*What ... we are afraid of is that this powerful machine, which so successfully grinds out the goods we want, seems to be running without any discernible controls. The young lad mastering the technique of his bicycle may legitimately shout with pride, 'Look ma, no hands' but is this the appropriate motto for a corporate society?*'[16]

This chapter deals with the corporate governance debate, and in particular, it considers the concept of 'corporate governance' and the essential features of this concept. This is followed by an analysis of the growth and development of the concept in the UK. The legal aspects of the corporate governance

---

14 On the issue of ethics in corporate governance see *Griseri, Ethics in Corporate Governance*, chapter 13.

15 Chayes, 'The Modern Corporation and The Rule of Law' in *The Corporation in Modern Society* (1960), Mason (ed) p 31.

16 ibid, p 3.

debate are examined with particular reference to directors' duties and shareholders' rights to control the abuse of power by directors. The corporate governance debate in other jurisdictions, notably Australia, New Zealand and the USA, has also received attention. The causal connection between corporate governance and the social responsibilities of companies has also been examined.

1.2 The concept of 'corporate governance'

Corporate governance is concerned with establishing a system whereby directors are entrusted with responsibilities and duties in relation to the direction of a company's affairs. It is founded on a system of accountability primarily directed towards the shareholders in addition to maximising shareholders' welfare.

An effective corporate governance system should provide mechanisms for regulating directors' duties in order to restrain them from abusing their powers and to ensure that they act in the best interests of the company in its broad sense. There are various methods of regulating directors' duties. In UK company law, this is achieved in a somewhat random fashion by employing the following control mechanisms:

- By legislation: under the Companies Act 1985, certain safeguards (eg unfair prejudicial conduct[17]) exist for the protection of shareholders and creditors. The Insolvency Act 1986 provides further protection and safeguards for the company's creditors who invest in the company. Directors bear a high level of responsibility to the company's creditors, in order to ensure that a company is not involved in fraudulent[18] or wrongful trading.[19]

- Directors have the common law duty to act with reasonable care and skill.[20]

- Directors may be subject to civil liability for breaches of their fiduciary duties.[21]

- Self-regulation: compliance with Codes of Conduct is highly recommended. In particular, directors are subject to the City Code on Takeovers and Mergers and SARs; and the Listing Rules. Self-regulation serves as a useful

---

17 See section 459 of the Companies Act 1985, including the orders that the court could make under section 461 of the Act. These sections are considered in 1.7.

18 Section 213 of the Insolvency Act 1986.

19 Section 214 of the Insolvency Act 1986.

20 See 1.6.2.

21 See 1.6.2.

mechanism in ensuring directors comply with their obligations lest sanctions are imposed on them by the Takeovers and Mergers Panel or the London Stock Exchange.[22]

- Shareholders are given some rights to monitor directors' actions under the articles of association as well as some statutory rights under the Companies Act 1985.[23]

- Auditors ensure that the risk of financial irregularities is minimised by auditing the company's accounts and ensuring that a company's accounts provide a 'true and fair view' of its financial position.

Corporate governance is also concerned with wider accountability and the responsibility of directors towards other 'stakeholders' on the corporation. These stakeholders include the company's employees, consumers, suppliers, creditors and the wider community. It may be argued that the relationship with these potential claimants creates a 'social contract' whereby the company is morally obliged to take account of the interests of these groups. This aspect of corporate governance is considered later in the chapter.[24]

Tricker argues that some of the management literature has confused the distinction between 'management of a company' and the 'governance of a company'.[25] The management role is primarily perceived to be running the business operations efficiently and effectively which includes the product, design, procurement, personnel, management, production, marketing and finance functions within the boundaries of the company under which it trades.

By contrast, however, the governance role is not concerned with running the business of the company, per se, but with directors giving overall direction to the enterprise, with overseeing and controlling the executive actions of management and with satisfying legitimate expectations for accountability and regulation by interests beyond the corporate boundaries: 'If management is about running business; governance is about seeing that it is run properly. All companies need governing as well as managing.'[26]

Therefore, the process of corporate governance comprises four main principal activities, namely:

- direction, which is concerned with formulating the strategic direction for the future of the enterprise in the long term;

- executive action applies to involvement in crucial executive decisions;

- supervision involves the monitoring and oversight of management performance; and

---

22　For further consideration of codes of conduct, see chapter 12.

23　See in particular 1.7.

24　See 1.8 on the causal relationship between corporate governance and corporate social responsibilities.

25　Tricker, *Corporate Governance* (1984).

26　ibid, p 7.

- accountability is concerned with recognising responsibilities to those making a legitimate demand for accountability.

Tricker contends that in the UK there is some difficulty in applying the term 'governance' to corporate bodies. This is because some executives fear an attack on their perceived rights and duties to manage the company as an erosion of their managerial prerogative. Other executives, such as civil servants, would prefer to identify governance solely with the government at the state level.[27]

Maw suggests that some commentators take a very narrow view of the concept of corporate governance by referring to it as a 'fancy term' for the way in which directors and auditors handle their responsibilities towards shareholders.[28] Others, however, use the expression as if it were synonymous with shareholder democracy. According to Maw: 'Corporate governance is a topic recently conceived, as yet ill-defined, and consequently blurred at the edges.'[29]

Sheridan and Kendall have advocated another definition of the term 'corporate governance'. They believe that good corporate governance consists of a system of structuring, operating and controlling a company in order to achieve the following objectives:

- to fulfil the long-term strategic goals of the owners which, after survival, may consist of building shareholder value or establishing a dominant market share or maintaining a technical lead in a chosen sphere, or something else, but will certainly not be the same for all organisations;
- to consider and care for the interests of employees, past, present and future, which comprises the whole life-cycle including planning future needs, recruitment, training, working environment, severance and retirement procedures, through to looking after pensioners;
- to take account of the needs of the environment and the local community, both in terms of the physical effects of the company's operations on the surrounding area and the economic and cultural interaction with the local population;
- to work to maintain excellent relations with both customers and suppliers, in terms of such matters as quality of service provided, considerate ordering and account settlement procedures;
- to maintain proper compliance with all the applicable legal and regulatory requirements under which the company is carrying out its activities.

Sheridan and Kendall believe that a well-run organisation must be structured in such a way that all the above requirements are catered for and can be seen as operating effectively by all the interest groups concerned.

---

27 See further Tricker on the origins of the term 'governance', pp 8-9.
28 Maw et al, *Maw on Corporate Governance* (1994).
29 ibid, p 1.

The concept of corporate governance advocated by *Sheridan and Kendall* embraces a wide spectrum of responsibilities which directors have towards their shareholders and other 'stakeholders' in the company including employees, customers, creditors and suppliers. Corporate governance is also, therefore, a wider concept. It includes the financial aspects of corporate governance, namely directors' responsibility for the company's financial situation which in turn requires directors to have regard to the interests of the company's creditors and shareholders. Directors also have a broader responsibility concerning payment of excessive remuneration. It is maintained that the concepts of corporate governance also include the social responsibilities of companies towards other 'stakeholders', who are otherwise known as the potential claimants on the corporation.

1.3   The growth and development of corporate governance in the UK

In the UK, the concept of corporate governance is largely entrenched in the traditional theory of the firm which advocates that the only objective of companies is to maximise profits and to consider shareholders' welfare its paramount consideration.[30] This structure of corporate governance mandates directors to carry out the shareholders' directions. Directors are, therefore, perceived as agents for their shareholders.

Adam Smith believed that individual entrepreneurs, who relied on their own efforts and the market forces, would be led by the 'invisible hand' to achieve the rewards which the markets were prepared to offer. The success of the entrepreneur was conditional upon risk-taking. In his *Wealth of Nations*, Adam Smith was not complimentary to directors when he wrote:

> *'The directors of such companies, however, being the managers of other people's money than of their own, it cannot well be expected, that they should watch over it with the same anxious vigilance with which the partners in a private co-partnery frequently watch over their own ... Negligence and profusion, therefore, must always prevail more or less, in the management of the affairs of such a company.'*[31]

---

30 On profit maximisation, see in particular Lamberton, *The Theory of Profit* (1965); Simpson, 'Price theory and the theory of profit' (1919-20) vol XXXIV, *The Quarterly Journal of Economics*, especially pp 151-60; and Weston, 'Enterprise and Profit' (1949) Vol XXII, *The Journal of Business of the University of Chicago*, pp 141-59.

31 Smith, *An Inquiry into the Causes of the Wealth of Nations* (1937, Random House edition) p 31.

Smith also observed that directors:

'seldom pretend to understand anything of the business of the company; and when the spirit of faction happens not to avail among them, give themselves no trouble about it, but receive contentedly such half yearly or yearly dividend, as the directors think proper to make to them.'[32]

UK company law clearly reinforces the profit maximisation principle within the corporate governance system. In *North-West Transportation v Beatty*,[33] the plaintiff, Henry Beatty, sued the directors of the company, and claimed an order to set aside a sale made to the company by James Hughes Beatty, who was one of the directors, of his steamer *The United Empire*, of which he was the owner before she was sold. Sir Richard Baggallay stated that the resolution of a majority of the shareholders, duly adopted, upon any question coming under the pinnacle of a company's mandate was binding upon the majority, and consequently upon the company. Further, every shareholder had a right to vote upon any such question, although he might have a personal interest in the subject-matter opposed to, or different from, the general or particular interests of the company.

The rule in *North-West Transportation* seems to have gained solid ground in the UK as it is in conformity with the traditional notion on which UK company law is based. It is not, therefore, surprising that initiatives for amending companies legislation in the UK prior to 1980 were sporadic, unconstructed and akin to the traditional notion that social responsibilities must not enter the realm of the company's activities.

However, in 1945, the Cohen Committee was set up to consider whether company legislation needed to be amended.[34] Its terms of reference were 'to consider and report what major amendments were desirable in the Companies Act, 1929, and, in particular, to review the requirements prescribed in regard to the formation and affairs of companies and the safeguards afforded for investors and for the public interest'. The committee was satisfied that a large majority of limited companies, both public and private, were honestly and conscientiously managed, and that the system of limited liability companies was beneficial to trade and industry. The Cohen Committee also recommended disclosure of a company's activity. It emphasised the need for 'a wakening social consciousness.' The lack of active participation of shareholders within their corporations was clearly identified by the Cohen Committee when it stated that:

'The illusory nature of the control theoretically exercised by shareholders over directors has been accentuated by the dispersion of capital among an

---

32   ibid, p 699.
33   (1887) 12 App Cas 589.
34   Cohen Committee, op cit n 6.

increasing number of small shareholders who pay little attention to their investments, so long as satisfactory dividends are forthcoming, who lack sufficient time, money and experience to make full use of their rights as occasions arise and who are, in many cases, too numerous and too wide dispersed to be able to organise themselves.'[35]

The Cohen Committee believed that the separation of ownership from control was largely responsible for the lack of shareholder participation in corporate affairs:

'The growth of investment trust companies and of unit trusts in recent years has tended to divorce the investor still further from the management of his investments. Executive power must inevitably be vested in the directors and is generally used to the advantage of the shareholders. There are, however, exceptional cases in which directors of companies abuse their power and it is, therefore, desirable to devise provisions which will make it difficult for directors to secure the hurried passage of controversial measures, and as far as possible, to encourage shareholders carefully to consider any proposals required by law to be put before them by the directors.'[36]

It was the Cohen Committee that drew the attention of the business community in the UK to the need for a separation of ownership from control of a company. The directors were to be treated as mere managers of a company and they should manage in accordance with the policies adopted by the company's shareholders, although directors, as managers, should be required to advise their shareholders as to whether a particular investment or venture would be profitable and beneficial to their interests.

Reporting in 1962, the Jenkins Committee set out to consider, *inter alia*, '... in the light of modern conditions ... what should be the duties of directors and the rights of shareholders; and generally to recommend what changes in the law are desirable'.[37] Again, it recommended wider disclosure of information as a means of remedying abuse within a corporation. On the issue of corporate governance, the Jenkins Committee thought that the protection of shareholders, creditors, intending investors and those responsible for their management, should be subject to a considerable degree of statutory regulation and control. However, the committee warned that:

'controls and regulations carried to excess may defeat their own object; and we share the views of the Greene and Cohen Committees as to the undesirability of imposing restrictions which would seriously hamper the activities of honest men in order to defeat an occasional wrongdoer, and the importance of not placing unreasonable fetters upon business which is conducted in an efficient and honest manner.'[38]

---

35   ibid, p 135.
36   ibid.
37   Jenkins Committee, op cit n 7.
38   ibid, p 3, para 11.

The Committee considered proposals for giving shareholders closer control over their directors, in order to allow shareholders a more 'effective voice' in the management of their company's business. In other words, according to the Committee, a separation of control from ownership would be essential for the general good of the company.

The Jenkins Committee also addressed such issues as directors' duties and shareholder control, within a corporation. It recognised that although the Companies Act established certain duties for directors, a large part of them were still determined by case law. A number of proposals which were made by witnesses suggested that the directors' duties ought to be codified in a new Act. Some witnesses suggested that the law on directors' duties should be set out as simply as possible. The Committee felt that it would be impossible to define exhaustively the duties of directors.

With specific reference to directors' powers and shareholders' control, the Jenkins Committee argued that although the articles of association gave directors a wide degree of powers to manage a company's affairs, shareholders still had a reasonable degree of control over their companies. It stated that unless the affairs of the company had gone badly wrong, there would seldom be any controversy from the shareholders. It may be deduced, therefore, that corporate governance is primarily concerned with keeping the shareholders content in terms of monetary returns and this is precisely what, according to the Committee, should be avoided. The fact remains that it is the shareholders who may need directions from directors as to how the company's image and future profitability might be secured by being conscious of corporate social responsibilities. In other words, the Jenkins Committee was concerned with another issue, that is, whether shareholders who contribute the equity of a company should really be involved in the management of a company; they can simply guide the managers where necessary, but the directors should perform their duties without being involved in the ownership of a company, as this would give rise to a conflict of interest. The committee argued that if directors were to manage their company efficiently, they must, within broad limits, have a free hand to do what they may think best in the interests of the company.

In 1992, the Cadbury Committee on the Financial Aspects of Corporate Governance considered, *inter alia*, the concept of corporate governance.[39] It defined the concept as the system by which companies are directed and controlled. The Committee stated that boards of directors are responsible for the governance of their companies. The shareholders' role in governance is to appoint the directors and the auditors and to satisfy themselves that an

---

39 *The Cadbury Committee on the Financial Aspects of Corporate Governance* (1 December 1992). For further discussion of the Cadbury Committee's recommendations see chapters 12 and 18. A useful comparison between the draft and final reports of the Cadbury Committee is provided by Dine, 'The Governance of Governance' [1994] 15 *The Company Lawyer*, 73-9.

appropriate governance structure is in place. The responsibilities of the board include setting the company's strategic aims, providing the leadership to put them into effect, supervising the management of the business, and reporting to shareholders on their stewardship. The board's actions are subject to laws, regulations, and the plans shareholders may present at general meetings. The Cadbury Committee was, however, specifically concerned with the financial aspects of corporate governance. This includes the way in which the board sets financial policies and oversees their implementation, including the use of financial controls, and the process whereby they report on the activities and progress of the company to the shareholders. Within the corporate governance system, the role of the auditors is to provide shareholders with an external and objective account of the directors' financial statements which form the basis for the reporting system. Although the reports of the directors are addressed to the shareholders, they are important to a wider audience. However, the concept of 'corporate governance' identified by the Cadbury Committee was too narrowly defined being limited for its purposes to the financial aspects of corporate governance. The Committee did not appreciate the wider dimensions of the concept of corporate governance. As with previous committees, the Cadbury Committee reinforced the tripartite relationship that has long existed in the UK between a company's directors, its shareholders and the auditors, without considering the other 'stakeholders' in the company such as the employees, consumers, suppliers and the broader community.

1.3.1   The UK government's attitudes towards corporate governance

The UK government's response to the corporate governance debate was largely limited to a series of policy statements during the 1970s, some of which were never implemented in uniform legislation.

In 1973, the Conservative Government published a document entitled *Company Law Reform.*[40] The government argued that a healthy free enterprise system was essential to the success of the UK's mixed economy. The rules governing the system must relate to the changing social and economic conditions of a society. The government acknowledged that the corporate governance system required directors to discharge their responsibilities and obligations towards a wider society which would include shareholders. In other words, this is a means of identifying the needs of shareholders and those of the wider community. The report showed, *inter alia*, that:

---

40 Department of Trade and Industry, White Paper, *Company Law Reform*, Cmnd 5391, London: HMSO, 1973.

'... the government are specifically recognising in the context of company law, the generally accepted fact that ownership involves responsibilities as well as rights. This requires company directors, on behalf of the shareholders, to discharge their social responsibilities as well as to protect their legitimate interests. The boards of companies, and their managements, thus have a manifest obligation towards all those with whom they have dealings – and none so more than the employees of the company.'[41]

As part of the company law reform, the government proposed a new Companies Bill (which was never brought into force in any companies legislation in the 1970s) to implement many of the recommendations made by the Jenkins Committee that were not included in the Companies Act 1967. Further, there has been a growing appreciation of the need for fuller disclosure of information by companies both as a spur to efficiency and as a safeguard against malpractice. The government also proposed that issues of corporate social responsibilities both towards a company's employees and the wider community required some acknowledgment in the new Companies Bill.

The government believed that the corporate governance structure would work effectively if there were full disclosure of information. According to the government report, disclosure of information was an essential part of the working of a free and fair economic system. Openness in company affairs was the first principle in securing responsible behaviour. Some of the proposals on wider disclosure included a requirement for companies to report on a broader range of matters such as health and safety. The directors would also be required to include in the directors' report particulars of their own contracts of service, their other interests, and dealings they had in the company's shares.

In order to further strengthen the corporate governance system, the government proposed that more non-executive directors should be on a company board as they have a powerful and useful role to play, in particular to protect the legitimate interests of shareholders. Shareholders might reasonably expect to rely on the non-executive directors for their impartial view of the company's activities, past and future, which is part of their 'stewardship' role.

Shareholders also had an important role to play within the company. In particular, institutional shareholders had a duty to ensure that directors complied with their duties and responsibilities. Institutional shareholders had greater resources to assess the performance of companies in which they held an interest. They also had greater power to voice criticism of inadequate and inappropriate management and to secure the election of able non-executive directors to the company's board.

In 1977, the Labour Party produced a Green Paper on *The Community and the Company* which criticised the proposals made by the Conservative

---

41   ibid, p 5.

government in 1973 as inadequate.[42] This was largely because the law was still based on the rights of shareholders and creditors. There was a need to provide both for the public interest and the employees' interest.

At the heart of the Labour Party's recommendation was the requirement for companies legislation to protect the public interest. It argued that directors' duties were not clearly defined in the companies legislation. Further, there should be a recognition that directors should take account of the interests of shareholders as well as their employees. It recommended the appointment of a new public supervisory body known as the Companies Commission. The Commission would have a continuing role in the control and regulation of a company's activities, particularly with reference to the form and frequency of disclosure of information. Again, a large majority of the Labour Party's proposals were never implemented in the form of any legislation.[43]

In 1977, the Conservative government published a White Paper entitled *The Conduct of Company Directors*.[44] The government recommended some reforms in the corporate governance system. It suggested that a new Companies Bill should be introduced setting out the statutory definition of directors' duties. The government would introduce a provision requiring a director to observe the utmost good faith towards his company in all of his actions and to act honestly in the exercise of his powers and in the discharge of the duties of his office. The new legislation would also provide that a director shall not make use of any money or property belonging to his company to benefit himself, nor of any information acquired by him or opportunity afforded to him by virtue of his position as a director of the company, if by doing so he gains an advantage for himself where there may be a conflict with the interests of the company. On the issue of the director's standard of care and skill, the government proposed that the new legislation would require a director to exercise the degree of care and diligence that a prudent person would exercise in comparable circumstances, and the degree of skill which may reasonably be expected of a person of his knowledge and experience. Clause 44 of the Companies Bill 1978 proposed, *inter alia*, a statutory codification of some of these directors' duties, but due to a change of government this aspect of the Bill was never enacted.[45]

---

42 The Labour Party, The Community and the Company: Reform of Company Law (Report of a working group of the Labour Party Industrial Policy Sub-committee: Green Paper) (1974).

43 For a consideration of reforms on corporate governance see chapter 18.

44 Department of Trade, *The Conduct of Company Directors* (Cmnd 7037), London: HMSO, 1977.

45 For a consideration of clause 44 of the Companies Bill 1978 and on codifying directors' duties see chapter 18.

The government also believed that employees should be given legal recognition by company law.[46] The statutory definition of the duties of directors would require directors to take into account the interests of employees and shareholders. They would also be required to send annual reports and accounts to employees as well as shareholders. Although this would mean an additional financial and administrative burden for companies, nevertheless, the government believed that employees and shareholders were entitled to the information in the company reports and accounts.

1.4 The response of the business community to the challenge of corporate governance

Until the 1970s, the response of the business community to the challenges of the corporate governance debate was virtually non-existent in the UK. Instead, a large section of the business community held the traditional perception of corporate governance preferring as little regulation as possible. Most businesses operated on the basis that self-regulation was preferable to any statutory regime.

In 1973, the Confederation of British Industry (CBI) published a report entitled the *Responsibilities of the British Public Company*.[47] Its terms of reference were to examine the factors which might assist directors and controlling public companies and corporations; to examine the role, responsibilities and structure of the boards of public companies and corporations; and to consider the impact of corporate behaviour towards interests other than those of shareholders and providers of finance, including employees, creditors, customers and the community at large.

The CBI argued that self-reform in the area of corporate governance was the best way forward for businesses. According to it:

'Business today operates in a time of change; it must therefore show itself capable of the degree of evolution and self-reform necessary to cope efficiently with the new circumstances in which it has to cope.'[48]

It further maintained that according to the business community, a company's main objective was profit maximisation. Profit should be regarded as the principal yardstick by which to assess the success or failure of a company. However, it recognised that profitability alone could not be the only

---

46 See clause 46 of the Companies Bill 1978, which required directors to have regard to the interests of employees in the performance of their functions, but this duty would also be owed to shareholders. See also sections 309 and 719 of the Companies Act 1985 and section 187 of the Insolvency Act 1986.

47 Confederation of British Industry, *The Responsibilities of the British Public Company: Final Report of the Company Affairs Committee* (1973).

48 ibid, p 5.

yardstick by which to measure the success or failure of a company. Business had obligations other than profit maximisation; and this became manifest in the following passage:

> 'The law sets minimum standards of conduct. But it does not, and cannot embody the whole duty of man; and mere compliance with the law does not necessarily make a good citizen or a good company.'[49]

The CBI perceived the company as owing its existence to the will of the community. It argued that the roles and responsibilities of directors had significantly changed, although not by statutory prescription. Directors were now perceived as 'professional managers' whose responsibilities embraced both political and economic issues.

The CBI argued that there was a strong case for improving relationships between shareholders and their boards through a wider availability of information and more interchange of ideas to be achieved by relaxing the rules of disclosure. This would require the company to periodically publish a statement setting out the policy and financial position of the company in relation to all the various interests with which it was concerned. This could be achieved by issuing a statement with the preliminary profit figures for the year. It further argued that this information should be disclosed to shareholders as well as the employees.

On the issue of corporate governance, the CBI thought that the main functions of the board would be to direct and control the company's business, and in particular, to establish the company's long-term objectives and the policies to be followed in order to attain these objectives, and to review these policies and statements from time to time. The board would also be required to ensure that:

- appropriate arrangements were made to enable these policies to be carried out;
- chief executive, or executives, of the company were appointed to carry out the policies and to acquire adequate means of checking the company's performance and the results;
- the company was at all times led by a board which fulfilled its responsibilities; and
- provisions for continuity of effective leadership were made.

According to the CBI, the board would have the total and ultimate responsibility for the operations of the company and for its continued well-being, which would include the interests not only of shareholders as the owners of the company, but also of those who work for the company, including those who might be adversely affected by the operations of the company. In this sense, directors occupy the position of 'trustees' and they are

---

49   ibid, p 7.

in a fiduciary position towards other stakeholders in the company. Greater attention should be paid to the preparation for board membership. There is a pressing need for directors to be better informed, not only in their responsibilities as directors, but also in business affairs generally, administration, financial management and personnel relations.[50]

The CBI recommended that the chairman should be appointed for a period not exceeding five years and that it should be for each company to decide what period of appointment, not exceeding five years, would be appropriate. It recognised the important role which a chairman plays within the corporate governance system. The chairman has all the responsibilities which are held by other members of the board, but to a greater extent than any other director, the chairman must remain responsible for the performance of the board as a whole, and of each member of it. It is the function of the chairman to see that policies are initiated, to secure the agreement and approval of the board, and to ensure by appropriate instructions and continuous monitoring that the policies are put into effect by those with executive responsibility. The CBI argued that there had to be a clear distinction between responsibilities as chairman and responsibilities as chief executive. The two functions should not be combined in one person. This separation may only be achieved over a period of time in view of the financial difficulties which a company might encounter initially in implementing it.[51]

The CBI believed that the inclusion on the board of public companies of non-executive directors was highly desirable. The number of non-executive directors to be included on any particular board must be decided separately in each case. Non-executive directors could make a valuable contribution by reason of their ability to bring an independent, objective and detailed approach to policy matters; giving the board the benefit of their knowledge and experience gained in other relevant fields of activity. As non-executive directors are not directly involved in the day-to-day affairs of the company, they would be in a better position to see the company as a whole and to take a critical view of it without any bias.

The CBI's response to the challenges of corporate governance was largely limited to formulating Principles of Corporate Conduct. The principles

---

50 According to the Cadbury Committee, the weight of responsibility carried by all directors and the increasing commitment which their duties require emphasise the importance of the way in which they prepare themselves for the post. Therefore, given the varying backgrounds, qualifications and experience of directors, it was highly desirable that directors should undertake some form of internal or external training. This was particularly important for directors with no previous board experience. Further, the committee believed that newly-appointed board members were also entitled to expect a proper process of induction into the company's affairs. It was then up to directors to keep abreast of their legislative and broader responsibilities, see the Cadbury Committee, op cit n 39, especially paras 4.19-20.

51 See too the proposals made by the Cadbury Committee on the separation of the roles of chairman and chief executive at paras 4.7-4.9. See further chapter 18.

required, *inter alia*, that the company board should be required to develop a closer relationship with the company's shareholders. It must provide all shareholders with full corporate information about its progress. The principles also acknowledged that shareholders, as owners of the business, had a responsibility that extended beyond the buying and selling of shares. In order to allow them to exercise their responsibility, they should be provided with proper information on which they could form their own judgments. Institutional shareholders had expertise which was not usually available to private shareholders. It was essential that institutions should fulfil their full role as shareholders in the interests of all shareholders. The principles also recognised that directors' duties extended to other constituencies. These principles required that the board develop closer relationships with its employees towards a common purpose. The main purpose would be to secure a wider participation in the decision-making process which would include some participation of employees. Further, a company should be responsive to informed public opinion, such as that on the protection of the environment and the social consequences of its business activities.

In 1985, the Institute of Directors published a document entitled *Guidelines for Directors*, which was essentially a set of recommendations on good boardroom practice. The Institute believed that the way to prevent further extensions of the law was to enforce effective self-regulation which could be developed in boardrooms. It argued that a modern company should be regarded as part of a system which linked customers and all the parties and which contributed to the customer's satisfaction. These parties include the 'stakeholders' such as suppliers, employees, creditors and the community. With particular reference to employees, the guidelines provide that companies should involve their employees in some form of decision-making not necessarily at board level. There was evidence, according to the Institute, to show that companies which sought to involve employees in decision-making and consulted employees prior to taking decisions, achieved harmonious employee relations and high levels of productivity.

The Institute thought that a board of directors' responsibility was for determining the company's strategic objectives; ensuring that the company operated to satisfy the customers and all the providers of the resources necessary to achieve those objectives. The main functions of the board in carrying out its responsibilities to the company were to ensure a necessary balance between the interests of shareholders, employees, customers, suppliers and the community. The board must ensure that the company reviewed its business plans in the wider context, embracing the interests of all concerned.

The board also had a planning function. They were required to determine the extent and priority of the company's investment in relation to the opportunities and threats ahead, having regard to the available resources. This included, for example, reviewing and challenging the company's technological capacity in designing and manufacturing their employee relations policy, motivation and productivity. The Institute believed that the board had a function in deciding the direction of the company in addition to approving any specific major investment and policy proposals.

1.5 Legal problems arising from companies legislation in regard to the relationship between directors and shareholders

It is to be re-emphasised that this section deals only with the effect of the conflict that may arise from Article 70 of Table A Articles of Association[52] and not the nature of other relationships that may be identified between directors and shareholders which have received attention elsewhere.[53]

In UK company law, the managerial duties of directors are largely governed by the powers vested in them under the articles of association. Traditionally, directors were perceived as agents of their shareholders with whose directions they were required to comply. In *Isle of Wight Rly Co v Tahourdin*,[54] the Court of Appeal stated that the shareholders should not be prevented from holding company meetings if such meetings were the only way they could influence corporate policies and the future direction of the company. In that case, the court in interpreting section 90 of the Companies Clause Consolidation Act 1845 perceived directors as agents of their shareholders; any directions given by shareholders had to be complied with by the directors.

Section 90 was subsequently replaced by Article 80 of the Companies Act 1948 Table A articles of association, which gave directors all the powers of management:

'as are not by the Act or by these regulations, required to be exercised by the company in general meetings, subject nevertheless, to any of these regulations, to the provisions of the Act and to such regulations being not inconsistent with the aforesaid regulations or provisions as may be prescribed by the company in general meeting.'

Article 80, however, provoked legal problems as it did not define 'regulations'. Some cases decided that shareholders could only give directions to their directors by way of a special resolution.[55] Other commentators, however, argued that the term 'regulations' should be interpreted to mean that shareholders could give directions to directors by way of an ordinary

---

52   Companies (Tables A to F) Regulations SI 1985 No 1052.
53   See 1.6.
54   (1883) 25 Ch D 320.
55   See for example, *Automatic Self-Cleaning Filter Syndicate Ltd v Cunninghame* [1906] 2 Ch 34.

resolution.[56] The effect of Article 80 was considered in *Automatic Self-Cleansing Filter Syndicate Co Ltd v Cunninghame*.[57] Under Article 96 of the plaintiff's articles of association, the powers of management were vested in the directors who had the day-to-day conduct of the company's affairs. Article 97 give the directors powers to dispose of the company's property as they thought fit. A general meeting was convened at which the shareholders passed a resolution requiring the directors to sell the company's undertaking to a new company. The directors exercised their powers under articles 96 and 97 and declined to carry out the shareholders' directions. According to Collins MR, articles 96 and 97 gave directors all the powers of management except so far as those powers were subject to the Companies Act and subject to such 'regulations' as may from time to time be made by extraordinary resolution. Therefore, if the shareholders wished to alter the powers of directors, this must be done not by an ordinary resolution but by an extraordinary resolution. In the circumstances, it was not valid for the majority of shareholders to alter the mandate originally given to directors by the articles of association at an ordinary meeting. On the issue of whether directors were agents for their shareholders in carrying out shareholders' wishes, Collins MR stated:

> '*No doubt for some purposes directors are agents. But for whom are they agents? You have, no doubt, in theory and law one entity, the company, which might be a principal, but you have to go behind that when you look at the particular position of directors. It is by the consensus of all the individuals in the company that these directors become agents and hold their rights as agents. It is not fair to say that a majority at a meeting is for the purpose of this case the principal so as to alter the mandate of the agent. The minority must also be taken into account. There are provisions by which the minority must be overborne, but that can only be done by special resolution. Short of that the mandate which must be obeyed is not that of a majority - it is that of a whole entity made up of all the shareholders. If the mandate of directors is to be altered, it can only be under the machinery of the memorandum and the articles themselves.*'[58]

In *Breckland Group Holdings Ltd v London & Suffolk Properties Ltd*,[59] a shareholder who had 51 per cent interest in the company instituted proceedings in the company's name in contravention of article 80 (now article 70) which vested all powers of management in directors subject to certain

---

56   Goldberg (1970) 33 *MLR* 177; Sullivan (1977) 93 *LQR* 569; and Mackenzie (1983) 4 *Co Law* 99.

57   [1906] 2 Ch 34. This reasoning has been followed in *Gramophone and Typewriter Ltd v Stanley* [1908] 2 KB 89; *Quin & Axtens Ltd v Salmon* [1909] AC 442; and *John Shaw & Sons (Salford) Ltd v Shaw* [1935] 2 KB 113.

58   ibid, at pp 42-43.

59   [1989] BCLC 100 overruling *Marshall's Valve Gear Co Ltd v Manning, Wardle & Co Ltd* [1909] 1 Ch 267. See too Sealy (1989) *CLJ* 26, and Wedderburn (1989) 52 *MLR* 401.

exceptions. The court decided that the shareholder could not bring such proceedings in breach of article 80, as all powers of management were vested in directors and it was up to the directors to decide whether or not to bring an action in the company's name. His Lordship stated:

> *'The principle, as I see it, is that article 80 confides the management of the business to the directors and in such a case it is not for the general meeting to interfere ... If the board does not adopt it, a general meeting would have no power whatever to override that decision of the board and to adopt it for itself.'*[60]

The modern version of the articles of association perceives directors as controllers and managers of the corporation and the role of shareholders is relegated. Article 70 of Table A articles of association provides:

> *'Subject to the provisions of the Act, the memorandum and the articles and to any directions given by special resolutions, the business of the company shall be managed by the directors who may exercise all the powers of the company. No alteration of the memorandum or articles of association and no such direction shall invalidate any prior act of the directors which would have been valid if that alteration had not been made or that direction had not been given. The power given by this regulation shall not be limited by any special power given to the directors by the articles and a meeting of directors at which a quorum is present may exercise all the powers exercisable by the directors.'*

In UK law, therefore, directors have all the powers of management and to conduct the day-to-day activities of the company subject to the provisions of the Companies Acts, the memorandum, the articles and to any directions given by the shareholders by a special resolution. Shareholders can mandate directors to undertake a particular course of action by passing a special resolution. This view has been accepted in *John Shaw & Sons (Salford) Ltd v Shaw*[61] where Greer LJ stated:

> *'A company is an entity distinct alike from its shareholders and its directors. Some of its powers may, according to its articles, be exercised by directors, certain other powers may be reserved for the shareholders in general meeting. If powers of management are vested in the directors, they and they alone can exercise these powers. The only way in which the general body of the shareholders can control the exercise of the powers vested by the articles in the directors is by altering their articles, or, if opportunity arises under the articles, by refusing to re-elect the directors of whose actions they disapprove. They cannot themselves usurp the powers which by the articles are vested in the directors any more than the*

---

60   ibid, p 108.
61   [1935] 2 KB 113.

directors can usurp the powers vested by the articles in the general body of shareholders.'[62]

According to Gower, article 70 of Table A represents an affirmation of case law but with the qualification that it recognises that the general meeting may curtail the future powers of directors by passing a special resolution. Gower believes that the new article 70 will raise some issues which have not yet been resolved. For example, can a 'direction' by special resolution effectively compel directors to enter or not to enter into a transaction which is clearly part of the general management of the company's business? It would appear that article 70 would cover this type of situation. Would it make any difference if the board of directors had already resolved that the transaction should not or should be entered into? Would that resolution be a 'prior act' of the directors, which under article 70 the special resolution cannot invalidate? According to Gower, the directors' resolution would remain valid as a resolution of the directors; what the special resolution would direct is that the directors should not act upon it. If however the directors had already acted upon their resolution by entering into a contract on behalf of the company, the special resolution could not invalidate that. If a directors' resolution resolved that a transaction should not be entered into, the shareholders could pass a special resolution under article 70 and apparently compel the directors to enter into the transaction.[63]

Article 70 of Table A provokes legal controversy in that it has created a conflict between the powers of directors and the method by which these powers may be modified or enlarged. On the one hand, directors derive powers from statutory provisions in addition to powers conferred on them by the memorandum and the articles. On the other hand, according to article 70, shareholders can only give them directions by special resolution. Shareholders' directions may have the effect of modifying or enlarging the powers already given to directors. Article 70 does not state whether there exists any hierarchy between the powers derived by directors from statutory provisions, memorandum and articles, and those that may be given to them by shareholders on the basis of a special resolution. Article 70 may be interpreted as a provision based on the idea that a special resolution adopted by shareholders may reduce the powers given to directors by the memorandum and articles. Alternatively, such a resolution can enlarge directors' powers too. In other words, a non-legislative instrument can have the effect of modifying a legislative provision.

---

62 ibid, p 134.
63 Gower, op cit n 11, pp 147-52.

1.6   Directors' duties in UK company law

It has been argued that corporate governance is concerned, *inter alia*, with regulating and monitoring directors' duties. This section considers some of the mechanisms which are used for ensuring directors' accountability and responsibility. The duties of directors in UK company law can be shown in three main categories:

* The duty of care and skill;
* the fiduciary duties of directors; and
* the statutory duties.[64]

1.6.1   The duty of care and skill

At common law, directors are only required to exercise reasonable care and skill in the performance of their business duties. Some have criticised the common law duty as out of date and impracticable to apply in modern conditions.[65] This is illustrated by the case of *Re Brazilian Rubber Plantations & Estates*,[66] where the company's directors sustained heavy losses in the rubber industry. According to Neville J., a director:

'... is not bound to bring any special qualifications to his office. He may undertake the management of a rubber company in complete ignorance of everything connected with rubber, without incurring responsibility for the mistakes which may result from such ignorance ... He is not ... bound to take part in the conduct of the company's business, but so far as he does undertake it he must use reasonable care ...'[67]

The common law standards of reasonable care and skill were summarised by Romer J in *Re City Equitable Fire Assurance Co*,[68] as comprising three main propositions:

* a director need not exhibit in the performance of his duties a greater degree of skills than may reasonably be expected of a person of his knowledge and experience;[69]

---

64 This section does not address the statutory duties of directors, for which see Gower, op cit n 11 and Farrar, op cit n 11.

65 According to Farrar: 'This is an area where the common law has failed to keep pace with modern developments and instead presents a lamentably out of date view of directors' duties.' Farrar, op cit., n 11, p 396. Similarly, Gower states: 'This subject can be disposed of briefly, for there is a striking contrast between the directors' heavy duties of loyalty and good faith and their light obligations of skill and diligence.' op cit, n 11 p 585.

66 [1911] 1 Ch 425.

67 ibid, at 437. See too *Overend, Gurney & Co v Gibb and Gibb* (1872) LR 5 HL 480; and *Lagunas Nitrate Co v Lagunas Syndicate* [1899] 2 Ch 392.

68 [1925] Ch 407.

69 See *Re Brazilian Rubber Plantations and Estates*, op cit, n 67.

- a director is not bound to give continuous attention to the affairs of his company. His duties, which are of an intermittent nature, must be performed at periodical board meetings, and at meetings of any committee of the board upon which he happens to be placed. He is not, however, bound to attend all such meetings, though he ought to attend whenever, in the circumstances, he is reasonably able to do so;[70] and

- a director is allowed to delegate his duties to officials in whom he has placed trust.[71]

It is arguable that the common law duty of care and skill has been superseded by higher standards of care under the Insolvency Act 1986. Under s 212, where, *inter alia*, an officer of the company has misapplied or retained or become accountable for, any money or other property of the company, or has been guilty of any misfeasance or breach of any duty, fiduciary or otherwise, in relation to the company, the court may require the director to contribute such sum to the company's assets by way of compensation.

Section 213 of the Insolvency Act 1986 provides that if in the course of a company's winding up, it appears that any business of the company has been carried on with an intent to defraud creditors of the company or creditors of any other person, or for any fraudulent purpose, then the court may, on the application of the liquidator, declare that any person who is knowingly a party to the fraudulent business is liable to make such contribution to the company's assets as the court thinks proper.[72]

Section 214 of the Insolvency Act 1986 is concerned with wrongful trading. It provides that even before a company was wound up, if a director knew or ought to have concluded that there was no reasonable prospect that the company would avoid going into insolvent liquidation, the court may require the director to contribute to such losses incurred by the company as the court thinks just. There is a defence for the director if he took all reasonable steps to minimise losses to the company's creditors. The test for a director's knowledge is those facts and steps which would be known or ascertained or reached or taken by a reasonably diligent person having both:

- the general knowledge, skill and experience that may reasonably be expected of a person carrying out the same functions as are carried out by that director in relation to the company; and

---

70   Also, in *Re Cardiff Savings Bank, the Marquis of Bute's case* [1892] 2 Ch 100, a director had only attended one board meeting in 38 years. The court held that it could not be expected that each director attend board meetings, nor to take an active part in the board management. However, see *Dorchester Finance Co Ltd v Stebbings* [1989] BCLC 498.

71   For an illustration of this proposition, see *Dovey v Cory* [1901] AC 477.

72   On the interpretation of section 213 see in particular *Re Sarflax Ltd* [1979] Ch 592; *Re Cooper Chemicals Ltd* [1978] Ch 262; and *Re Augustus Barnett & Son Ltd* [1986] BCLC 170.

- the general knowledge, skill and experience that the director has.[73]

The common law duty of skill and care is based on the minimum level of efficiency and care that a director should possess and demonstrate in performing his duties as a director.

1.6.2 A modern perception of directors' duties – the fiduciary duties of directors

Under UK company law, the system of corporate governance regulates directors' actions by imposing fiduciary duties on them. These include:

- a duty to act in good faith;
- a duty not to act for improper purposes;
- a duty not to engage in 'corporate opportunities';
- a duty not to fetter future discretion.

These fiduciary duties have an impact on corporate governance. It will be argued that these fiduciary duties impose higher standards of conduct on directors than the common law duty of care and skill. They are a means of monitoring directors' actions to ensure that they do not abuse their powers or possess uncontrollable powers to the detriment of their shareholders.

1.6.2.1 The duty to act in good faith

There is a general equitable principle of company law which requires directors to act in the best interests of the company. Directors' primary obligations are towards their company. The term 'company' would clearly include its shareholders collectively as a group. This is illustrated by *Percival v Wright*[74] where Swinfen Eady J contended that directors of a company did not normally stand in a fiduciary position towards their shareholders individually. This case was concerned with shareholders who offered to sell their shares to the company's directors and chairman at a price of £12.50 per share. The directors and chairman, however, negotiated a higher price with a third party for the sale of those shares. Swinfen Eady J stated:

'The true rule is that shareholder is fixed with knowledge of all the directors' powers, and has no more reason to assume that they are not

---

73 See *Re Produce Marketing Consortium Ltd* (No 2) [1989] BCLC 520; *Re Purpoint Ltd* [1991] BCC 121; and *Re DKG Contractors Ltd* [1990] BCC 903. See also chapter 4 on directors' duties towards creditors' interests.

74 [1902] 2 Ch 421.

negotiating a sale of the undertaking than to assume that they are not exercising any other power.'[75]

In this case, the directors were under no obligation to disclose the negotiations which had taken place between themselves and the third party. There was no question of unfair dealing. Further, the directors did not approach the shareholders with a view to purchasing their shares. Instead, the shareholders approached the directors and named the price at which they would be prepared to sell their shares; the directors did not take any initiative to buy the shares.

Although directors owe a duty to the shareholders collectively, there are authorities for the view that directors can owe fiduciary duties towards shareholders individually. This is illustrated by *Allen v Hyatt*.[76] In this case, the directors undertook to act as agents of their shareholders in the sale of their shares. According to Viscount Haldane LC, directors presented themselves to the individual shareholders as acting for them on the same footing as they were acting for the company itself, that is, as agents of the shareholders. However, the case of *Coleman v Myers*[77] goes further than the agency approach. This case was concerned with a takeover bid whereby the minority shareholders were compelled to sell their shares to the ultimate controller of the company. The Court of Appeal held that there existed a fiduciary duty between directors and the shareholders in view of the 'special circumstances' which subsisted between them: the company was a private company with shares held largely by the members of the one family; the other members of the family had habitually looked to the defendants for business advice; and information affecting the true value of the shares had been withheld from the shareholders by the defendants. Woodhouse, J stated:

'In my opinion, it is not the law that anyone holding the office as a director of a limited liability company is for that reason alone to be released from what otherwise would be regarded as fiduciary responsibility owed to those in a position of shareholders of the same company.'[78]

One of the main fiduciary duties of directors is that they must act in good faith and in the 'best interests of the company as a whole'. This expression has been interpreted to mean the short-term and long-term interests of shareholders. This expression clearly reinforces the principle of profit maximisation for the company as well as maximisation of shareholders' welfare. In *Re Smith & Fawcett Ltd*,[79] Lord Greene MR stated that directors

---

75   ibid, at 426.
76   [1914] 30 TLR 444 (Privy Council).
77   [1977] 2 NZLR 225.
78   ibid, at 324.
79   (1942) Ch 304.

must 'exercise their discretion bona fide in what they consider – not what a court may consider – is in the interests of the company, and not for any collateral purpose'.[80]

It should be noted, however, that the expression 'bona fide for the benefit of the company as a whole' was used in connection with the transfer articles in the company's articles of association which gave an absolute power to directors to refuse registration on a transfer of shares. This principle of 'bona fide for the benefit of the company as a whole' now appears to be used as a general criterion of directors' duty of good faith. This expression also makes clear that the courts will not wish to second-guess directors' decisions. On many occasions, the courts have made it clear that they will be reluctant to interfere in directors' managerial decisions.[81] It is not the task of the courts to inform directors as to how to manage their businesses. The courts will only intervene where there has been an abuse of power by directors or where shareholders have been or are likely to be unfairly prejudiced.

The expression 'bona fide for the benefit of the company as a whole' is a subjective test. The courts will inquire into the directors' decisions and not into what a reasonable director would have done in the circumstances. In *Greenhalgh v Arderne Cinemas Ltd*,[82] Evershed MR stated that the expression did not mean the company as a commercial entity, distinct from the corporators:

'*it means the corporators as a general body. That is to say, a case may be taken of an individual hypothetical member and it may be asked whether what is proposed is, in the honest opinion of those who voted in its favour, for that person's benefit.*'[83]

The expression 'bona fide for the benefit of the company as a whole' has also been applied in the context of alteration of articles of association. The inconsistency of application of the expression was highlighted in the Australian case of *Peter's American Delicacy Co Ltd v Heath*.[84] Dixon J stated that reliance upon the general doctrine that powers shall be exercised bona fide and for no bye or sinister purpose brings its own difficulties. The power of alteration is not fiduciary. The shareholders are not trustees for one another, and unlike directors, they occupy no fiduciary position and are under no fiduciary duties. They vote in respect of their shares, which are property,

---

80   ibid, at 306.

81   See for example *Carlen v Drury* (1812) Ves & B 154 where Lord Eldon stated that 'the court could not undertake the management of every brewhouse and playhouse in the kingdom'; see too *Burland v Earle* [1902] AC 83 and the rule in *Foss v Harbottle* (1843) 2 Hare 461. The latter case is considered in 1.7.

82   (1951) Ch 286.

83   ibid, at 291.

84   (1939) 61 CLR 457.

and the right to vote is attached to the share itself as an incident of property to be enjoyed and exercised for the owner's personal advantage. Dixon J stated that the reference to 'benefit as a whole' was but a very general expression negativing purposes foreign to the company's operations, affairs and organisation. The 'company as a whole' is a corporate entity consisting of all the shareholders. He stated that the expression was not particularly helpful where there were conflicting interests within the company. In these situations, it would be necessary to resort to more general principles of fairness between various classes of shareholders.

The concept of 'good faith' seems to have been treated in the abstract. It is based on the presumption that directors, like parties to commercial contracts, will perform their contractual obligations in good faith, otherwise a breach will be established. In the context of company law, the concept of good faith has a broader meaning which encompasses not only issues that concern protecting the interests of a company's financial aims, but also in protecting the community's interests by not, for example, becoming a party to a project, the execution of which might jeopardise the environment. Traditionally, UK law has treated the concept of good faith only in the context of directors performing their obligations towards the shareholders of their company which, as stated earlier, requires modification. It is possible to apply the concept of good faith in relation to an acceptable corporate governance system by emphasising its role in protecting the interests of the community.[85]

1.6.3   A duty not to act for improper purposes

A duty not to act for improper purposes arises where directors have acted in breach of their contracted purposes, or in breach of purposes inherent in their duties. This can include situations where directors are forestalling a takeover in the belief that it would be contrary to the interests of the company, or issuing further shares to change the control structure of the company.

In *Punt v Symons & Co Ltd*,[86] in order to secure the passing of a special resolution, the directors had issued new shares to five additional shareholders. Byrne J held this to be an abuse of directors' powers. His Lordship stated that these shares were not issued bona fide for the general advantage of the company. They were issued with the immediate object of controlling the holders of the greater number of shares in the company and of obtaining the necessary statutory majority for passing the special resolution, while at the same time, not conferring upon the minority the power to demand a poll. He stated:

---

85   See Frost on the concept of 'good faith' in relation to section 35A of the Companies Act 1985.
86   [1903] 2 Ch 506.

'A power of the kind exercised by the directors in this case, is one which must be exercised for the benefit of the company; primarily it is given to them for the purpose of enabling them to raise capital when required for the purposes of the company.'[87]

In *Hogg v Cramphorn*,[88] the company's directors issued shares which carried special voting rights for the trustees of a scheme established for the benefit of the company's employees. The directors' aim was to prevent a takeover bid. They had acted in good faith throughout the transaction. Buckley J held that this was an improper purpose but that it could be ratified by shareholders at a general meeting. He stated:

'Unless a majority in a company is acting oppressively towards the minority, this court should not and will not itself interfere with the exercise by the majority of its constitutional rights or embark upon an inquiry into the respective merits of the views held or policies favoured by the majority and the minority. Nor will this court permit directors to exercise powers, which have been delegated to them by the company in circumstances which put the directors in a fiduciary position when exercising those powers, in such a way as to interfere with the exercise by the majority of its constitutional rights ... It is not, in my judgment, open to the directors in such a case to say: 'we genuinely believe that what we seek to prevent the majority from doing will harm the company and, therefore, our act in arming ourselves or our party with sufficient shares to outvote the majority, is a conscientious exercise of our powers under the articles, which should not be interfered with.'[89]

According to Buckley J, a majority of shareholders at a general meeting were entitled to pursue what course of action they chose within the company's powers, provided the majority did not unfairly oppress other members of the company.

The decision in *Hogg v Cramphorn* provokes further controversy in that it supported the view that an 'improper purpose' can be legitimised by means of a ratification initiated by shareholders at a general meeting. This is a disturbing phenomenon in that shareholders might thus indulge in ratifying improper purposes which would otherwise have been regarded as factors which formed the basis for illegal acts. Furthermore, the legitimisation process might be directed at disregarding the interests of the minority of shareholders. Buckley J referred to the fiduciary position that directors hold in respect of the shareholders, but he seems to have limited it to majority shareholders only. The fiduciary position of a director demands that there be no discriminatory factors in protecting the interests of shareholders whether they are a majority

---

87   ibid, at 515-16.
88   [1967] Ch 254.
89   ibid, at 268.

or a minority. The act of disregarding the interests of the minority shareholders may in itself be regarded as an act for an improper purpose.

Judicial authorities in Australia and Canada rejected the *Hogg v Cramphorn* approach and decided that directors' decisions to use their powers to thwart a threatened takeover could be upheld by the courts. In *Harlowe's Nominees Pty Ltd v Woodside (Lakes Entrance) Oil Co*[90] and *Teck Corp Ltd v Millar*,[91] the High Court of Australia and the Canadian Court respectively upheld directors' decisions to prevent a takeover. The issue of directors acting for improper purposes was reviewed by the *Privy Council* in *Howard Smith Ltd v Ampol Petroleum Ltd*[92] which also concerned attempts by directors to prevent a takeover. The court rejected as too narrow an approach to argue that the only valid purpose for which shares may be issued is to raise capital for the company. The law should not impose such limitations on directors' powers, as they should be assessed in the context of each particular case. Further, the test of 'bona fide for the benefit of the company as a whole' did not serve a useful purpose when considering whether directors had acted for improper purposes. In Lord Wilberforce's opinion, it was:

> '... *necessary to start with a consideration of the power whose exercise is in question; in this case, a power to issue shares. Having ascertained, on a fair view, the nature of this power, and having defined as can best be done in the light of modern conditions, the awesome limits within which it may be exercised, it is then necessary for the court, if a particular exercise of it is to be challenged, to examine the substantial purpose for which it was exercised, and to reach a conclusion whether that purpose was proper or not. In so doing, it will necessarily give credit to the bona fide opinion of the directors, if such is found to exist, and will respect their judgment as to the matters of the management. Having done this, the ultimate conclusion has to be as to the side of a fairly broad line on which the case falls.*'[93]

In determining whether directors have acted for improper purposes, the court will construe the powers conferred upon directors and the limitations placed upon them in the exercise of that power. The court will then consider the actual purpose for which the power was exercised. The court is entitled to:

> '... *look at the situation objectively in order to estimate how critical or pressing, or substantial, or per contra, insubstantial an alleged requirement may have been. If it finds that a particular requirement, though real, was not urgent or critical, at the relevant time, it may have reason to doubt or discount the assertions of individuals that they acted solely in order to deal with it, particularly when the action they took was unusual or even extreme.*'[94]

---

91 (1972) 33 DLR (3a) 288.

92 [1974] AC 821.

93 ibid, at 835.

94 ibid, at 832.

The propriety or impropriety of purposes should be determined by referring to:

- the interests of shareholders whether they are a majority or a minority; and
- the interests of the company as a whole and also with reference to the parameters of power allowed to directors.

1.6.4 A duty not to fetter future discretion

Directors must not anticipate in advance as to how they will vote in the future. They must seek the company's consent before they can seek to fetter their future discretion. However, provided directors act bona fide and enter into a contract as to how they will vote at future board meetings, the courts will uphold such a contract. In *Thorby v Goldberg*,[95] the Australian Court stated:

> '*There are many kinds of transaction in which the proper time for the exercise of the directors' discretion is the time of the negotiation of a contract and not the time at which the contract is to be performed ... if at the former time they are bona fide of the opinion that it is in the best interests of the company that the transaction should be entered into and carried into effect, I can see no reason in law why they should not bind themselves to do whatever under the transaction is to be done by the board.*' [96]

Recently in *Fulham Football Club Ltd v Cabra Estates plc*,[97] the undertakings given by directors to the shareholders to support a planning application were held to confer substantial benefits on the company. The Court of Appeal held that the directors had not improperly fettered the future exercise of their discretion by giving those undertakings.

The duty not to fetter future discretion is subject to the condition that it does not run counter to the fiduciary duties that a director owes to the company, which includes a duty towards the majority as well as the minority shareholders.

---

95 (1964) 112 CLR 597.
96 ibid, at 605.
97 [1994] 1 BCLC 363.

1.6.5   A duty not to engage in 'corporate opportunities'

Another method of regulating directors' duties is to impose a requirement whereby directors should not seize a corporate opportunity for themselves nor make a secret profit. In *Cook v Deeks*,[98] the company's directors diverted a contract which belonged to the company for their own purposes. They were held liable to account to the company for the profits made out of the contract. According to Lord Buckmaster, directors have a duty to protect the interests of the company because of their position of authority and the knowledge they have acquired as a result of the transaction. Similarly, in *Regal (Hastings) Ltd v Gulliver*,[99] Lord Russell decided that even where directors had acted bona fide throughout the transaction, they may be liable to account to the company for the profits they had made:

> *'The liability arises from the mere fact of a profit having, in the circumstances, been made. The profiteer, however honest and well-intentioned, cannot escape the risk of being called upon to account.'*[100]

However, there are cases which have suggested that, provided the director has declared the contract and the company rejected the opportunity to pursue the contract, the director may keep the profits made from the contract.[101]

1.7   Monitoring directors' duties

In UK company law, directors' managerial discretion can be constrained by shareholders in three main ways:

1   under the exceptions to the rule in *Foss v Harbottle*;
2   by section 459 of the Companies Act 1985; and
3   by sections 35, 35A and 35B of the Companies Act 1985.

Under the *Foss v Harbottle* rule,[102] only the company is the proper plaintiff in an action. It is also based on the majority rule; in other words, if

---

98   [1916] 1 AC 554.

99   [1942] 1 All ER 378.

100 ibid, at 386. See too *Industrial Development Consultants v Cooley* [1972] 1 WLR 443; and *Canadian Aero Service v O'Malley* [1973] 40 DLR (3a) 371.

101 *Queensland Mines Ltd v Hudson* [1978] 52 ALJR 379; *Island Export Finance Ltd v Umunna* [1986] BCLC 460; *Peso-Silver Mines Ltd v Cropper* (1966) 58 DLR (2d) 1; Brudney and Clark (1981) *Harv L Rev* 997; Wolfson (1980) 34 U *Miami L Rev* 959; and Prentice (1967) 30 *MLR* 450. For a consideration of reform of the 'corporate opportunities' doctrine see Bean, op cit n 1; see too Brudney and Clark 'A New Look at Corporate Opportunities' (1981) 94 *Harv L Rev* 997; Beck 'The Quickening of Fiduciary Obligation: Canaero v O'Malley' [1975] 53 *Can Bar Rev* 771; and Wardle, 'Post Employment Competition – Canaero Revisited' (1990) 69 *Can Bar Rev* 232.

102 (1843) 2 Hare 461. See generally Sealy [1989] 10 *Co Law* 52 for an Australian perspective in this area.

the majority decide bona fide upon a particular course of action, the minority must usually comply with that decision. The rule in *Foss v Harbottle* was amplified by Jenkins LJ in *Edwards v Halliwell* as follows:

> '*First, the proper plaintiff in an action in respect of a wrong alleged to be done to a company or association of persons is prima facie the company or association of persons itself. Secondly, where the alleged wrong is a transaction which might be made binding on the company or association and on all its members by a simple majority of the members, no individual member of the company is allowed to maintain an action in respect of the matter for the simple reason that if a mere majority of the members of the company or association is in favour of what has been done, then cadet quaestio.*'[103]

The rationale of this rule is that the business of a company should be managed by the directors who make the day to day decisions relating to the company's affairs and who are fully acquainted with them. The courts are, therefore, reluctant to interfere with managerial decisions, subject to certain exceptions explained in this section.

Another rationale for the rule is to restrain shareholders from bringing unnecessary actions against the company and to prevent wasteful depletion of corporate funds in pursuing what may otherwise be vexatious and futile litigation. In *MacDougall v Gardiner*, Mellish LJ stated:

> '... *if the thing complained of is a thing which in substance the majority of the company are entitled to do ... there can be no use in having litigation about it, the ultimate end of which is only that a meeting has to be called, and then ultimately the majority gets its wishes.*'[104]

The courts, however, recognised the harshness of this rule especially for minority shareholders who may be unfairly prejudiced by directors' actions, and, therefore, developed certain exceptions to the rule. However, where an action is brought by a shareholder, the courts will have regard to the views of independent shareholders who are not concerned with the question of whether the action should be pursued.[105] The exceptions to the rule in *Foss v Harbottle* are:

- where the transaction is illegal;[106] or
- where there has been a procedural irregularity;[107] or
- where the personal rights of a shareholder have been infringed;[108] or
- where there has been fraud on the minority.

---

103 [1950] 2 All ER 1064 at 1066.

104 (1875) 1 Ch D 13.

105 *Smith v Croft (No 2)* [1988] Ch 114.

106 See *Simpson v Westminster Palace Hotel Co* (1860) 8 HL Cas 712.

107 See for example *Quin & Axtens Ltd v Salmon* [1909] AC 442; and *Edwards v Halliwell*, op cit, n 102.

108 On this exception see Wedderburn (1957) *CLJ* 194; and (1958) *CLJ* 93; and Sealy, *Cases and Materials in Company Law* (4th edn, 1989), p 463. Some of the more notable cases include *Pender v Lushington* (1877) 6 Ch D 70; and *Wood v Odessa Waterworks Co* (1889) 42 Ch D 636.

In relation to 'fraud on the minority', it will be necessary to show that the wrongdoers were in control of the company which prevented the company from bringing an action in its own name. In *Prudential Assurance Co Ltd v Newman Industries Ltd (No 2)*, the Court of Appeal stated that 'control' embraced a broad spectrum extending from an overall absolute majority of votes at one end to a majority of votes at the other end, made up of those likely to be cast by the delinquent himself plus those voting with him as a result of influence or apathy.[109]

The procedural obstacles which need to be surmounted under the exceptions to the rule in *Foss v Harbottle*, often lead shareholders to pursue an action under section 459 of the Companies Act 1985.[110] This states:

> '*A member of a company may apply to the court by petition for an order ... on the ground that the company's affairs are being or have been conducted in a manner which is unfairly prejudicial to the interests of its members generally or of some part of its members including at least himself or that any actual or proposed act or omission of the company (including an act or omission on its behalf) is or would be so prejudicial.*'

Section 459, therefore, requires that unfair prejudicial conduct has been suffered by the members. There is no statutory definition of these words. However, according to some cases, it refers to oppression or discrimination against a shareholder(s).[111] The cases also suggest that a member(s) can petition to the court where directors are incompetent or where there has been gross mismanagement of the company's assets to the prejudice of shareholders.[112] A shareholder who can successfully show unfair prejudicial conduct may be entitled to one or more of the following orders, namely:

- an order regulating the future affairs of the company;[113] or

- an order requiring the company to do an act or to refrain from acting;[114] or

- an order authorising a shareholder to bring civil proceedings on behalf of the company;[115] or

---

109 [1982] Ch 204. On the issue of 'fraud' see *Atwool v Merryweather* (1867) LR 5 Eq 464. On 'wrongdoer control' see especially *Russell v Wakefield Waterworks Co* (1875) LR 20 Eq 474.

110 As amended by section 145, Sch 19, para 11 of the Companies Act 1989.

111 Re *Harmer (HR) Ltd* [1958] All ER 689.

112 Re *Elgindata* [1991] BCLC 959 and [1993] BCLC 119.

113 Re *Harmer*, op cit, n 112, where an 80-year-old president of the company was ordered by the court not to interfere in his company's management. See also *McGuinness v Bremner plc* [1988] BCLC 673.

114 See for example *Whyte, Petitioner* [1984] 1 BCC 99; and *Re a Company* (No 002612 of 1984) [1985] BCLC 80.

115 This is a useful action for shareholders who cannot come within one of the exceptions to the rule in *Foss v Harbottle*. However, the costs of litigation may prevent shareholders from seeking this order, and they may instead prefer the company to buy out their shares.

- an order compelling the company or another shareholder to purchase the complainant's shares.[116]

It is arguable that directors' freedom of managerial discretion could be restrained under sections, 35, 35A and 35B of the Companies Act 1985 (as amended).[117]

Section 35 states that the validity of an act done by a company shall not be called into question on the ground of lack of capacity by reason of anything in the company's memorandum. The effect of this section is that neither the company nor the third party to the transaction can rely on the *ultra vires* doctrine. However, section 35(3) provides that it remains the duty of directors to observe limitations on their powers flowing from the company's memorandum. Directors who exceed the company's capacity may, however, be excused by their shareholders by a double special resolution procedure. Shareholders passing the first special resolution will be ratifying directors' actions in exceeding the company's objects. The second special resolution indemnifies a director or any other person from personal liability incurred by that person as a result of entering into the transaction with the third party.

However, section 35(2) provides the shareholder with a right to apply to the court for an injunction to prevent the company from entering any future legal obligation which the company may enter into. A shareholder cannot apply for an injunction where a legal obligation has already been entered into by the company. In practice, it will be difficult for the shareholders to find out in advance about the future actions of directors *vis-à-vis* the company.

Section 35A, however, is concerned with the powers of directors. It states that in favour of a person dealing with the company in good faith, the power of the board of directors to bid the company or authorise others to do so shall be deemed to be free of any limitations under the company's constitution. A person will be dealing with the company if he or she is a party to the transaction or other act to which the company is a party. Section 35A provides that there is a presumption of good faith in favour of the third party.[118] Section 35A(2)(b) specifically provides that a person shall not be acting in bad faith by reason of his knowing that an act is beyond the powers of directors under the company's constitution. A third party dealing with the company is not,

---

116 As to valuation of shares, see *Re Bird Precision Bellows Ltd* [1985] 3 All ER 523; *Re Cumana Ltd* (1986) 2 BCC 99; and Hannigan [1987] *Bus L Rev* 21.

117 Replaced together with sections 35A and 35B by section 108 of the Companies Act 1989. For a consideration of the background to the reform of the *ultra vires* doctrine, see Department of Trade and Industry, *Reform of the Ultra Vires Rule* (1988) (this report was prepared by Dr Prentice as he was then). See too Pennington [1987] 8 *Co Law* 103; Hannigan [1987] *JBL* 173; and Frommel (1987) 8 *Co Law* 14.

118 As to the concept of 'good faith' under the original s 35 of the Companies Act 1985 before it was replaced by the Companies Act 1989, see *International Sales and Agencies Ltd v Marcus* [1982] 3 All ER 551; *Barclays Bank Ltd v TOSG Trust Fund Ltd* [1984] BCLC 1; *TCB Ltd v Gray* [1986] Ch 621 noted by Birds [1986] *Co Law* 104; and Collier [1986] *CLJ* 207.

therefore, concerned with any limitations on the powers of directors. Any limitations on directors' powers are a matter for the company, its directors and shareholders. Further, a person shall be presumed to have acted in good faith unless the contrary is proved. Transactions which are tainted with fraud or illegality or wrongful trading would amount to bad faith and the third party dealing with the company would not then be able to rely on section 35A.

The reference to 'limitations' under section 35A(1) on the directors' powers under the company's constitution includes limitations deriving from a resolution of the company in general meeting or a meeting of any class of shareholders or any agreement between the members of the company or of any class of shareholders. This definition would clearly include the company's memorandum, articles of association, resolutions of the company in general meeting and shareholders' agreements.

Section 35B deals with the abolition of the doctrine of constructive notice. A third party is no longer put on notice of any limitations of the powers of directors contained in the company's constitution.[119]

1.8   The causal connection between corporate governance and corporate social responsibilities

It is arguable whether the managerial discretion vested in directors under Article 70 Table A may lead directors to pursue objectives in addition to profit maximisation. Since shareholders delegate their management powers to directors, the latter may pursue social objectives for their corporation which would include 'corporate social responsibilities'.[120]

The term 'corporate social responsibilities' includes corporate activities such as cash donations to charities, secondments, sponsorship, job creation programmes and the like. The term originated in the USA, where companies have been actively engaged in social activities such as the protection of the environment.

---

119 Section 35B of the Companies Act 1985 (as amended) should be read together with section 711A of the Companies Act 1985 (as inserted by section 142 of the Companies Act 1989). Section 711A is concerned with the exclusion of deemed notice. It states that a person shall not be taken to have notice of any matter merely because of its being disclosed in any document kept by the registrar of companies (and thus available for inspection) or made available by the company for inspection. Section 711A(2) provides that this does not affect the question whether a person is affected by notice of any matter by reason of a failure to make such inquiries as ought reasonably to be made. This latter sub-section leaves the possibility of the third party acquiring actual knowledge or at least inferred knowledge concerning matters or lack of matters contained in the company's constitution.

120 On the concept of 'corporate social responsibilities' and its causal connection with corporate governance see Fogarty and Christie, *Companies and Communities: Promoting Business Involvement in the Community* (1990); see too the Directory of Social Change (1991); and various publications by Business in the Community, notably *The Business of Change* (1993) and *Direction for the Nineties* (1992).

The duty of companies to act responsibly towards the broader community has been commented by Goyder:

'The social role of the big company is becoming so important for the community that the way in which big companies discharge their social responsibilities is of immediate concern to all of us.'[121]

Goyder argued that the social responsibilities of companies also required them to consider the interest of other stakeholders in the company; in particular, the worker in the corporate governance system could not be neglected. Company law should make provision for the representation of the worker. He clearly maintained that:

'At present, he is not regarded as having any rights in, or duties to, the company. As a result the individual worker increasingly adopts the attitude of irresponsibility towards the company in which he spends his working life. One cannot complain if the worker's attitude is irresponsible so long as he is legally excluded in his capacity as a worker from membership of the company. But the result is not only to alienate the worker's sympathy; it is to bring about an irreconcilable conflict of interest between workers and shareholders, since management is required by law to put the interests of the shareholders first, no matter how important this may be to the worker.'

He further maintains that directors should not be required primarily to consider the interests of shareholders in the corporate governance system. Companies should also form a close relationship with the local communities in which they are situated. For example, in the form of contribution to various charities and academic institutions. The golden rule for companies is to act in relations with the community as if they were citizens of the community.

A growing awareness of social accountability for companies has become manifest in Australia, New Zealand, the USA and in the UK, but only in rudimentary form. It is, therefore, still difficult to identify the causal relationship between corporate governance and corporate social responsibilities in the UK. Nevertheless, as suggested in various parts of this work, the wave of awareness perhaps cannot be halted and company management and corporate ethics, therefore, need urgent review in their own interest. If this premise is accepted, then it is not difficult to see why a causal relationship between corporate governance and corporate social responsibilities should be developed.

---

121 Goyder, *The Responsible Company* (1961) p 7. For a detailed consideration of the social responsibilities of companies see Wedderburn 'Trust Corporation and The Worker' [1985] 23 *Osgoode Hall Law Journal* 1; Wedderburn 'The Social Responsibilities of Companies' [1982] 15 *Melbourne University Law Review* 1; and his 'The Legal Development of Corporate Responsibilities: For Whom Will Corporate Managers be Trustees?' in Hopt and Teubner (eds) *Corporate Governance and Directors' Liabilities* (1985); Parkinson, *Corporate Power and Responsibility* (1994); and Sheikh, *The Social Responsibilities of Companies* (October 1994, unpublished PhD thesis).

The fundamental obstacles to developing this causal relationship are two: the age-old concept of profit maximisation; and apathy on the part of management towards the needs of society, as corporate entities tend to live in their own self-created world. Corporate activities have direct impact on societies, not only in respect of issues such as protection of the environment, but also the democratisation of corporate life. In other words, if the interests of creditors, stakeholders, and workers are to be properly protected, then it becomes difficult to dissociate a company from the aspirations of society, *vis-à-vis* corporate ethics. The need for more effective disclosure provisions must be regarded as a signal for questioning the methods of corporate activities. Shareholders have the right to know in which sectors a corporation invests. The rights of consumers, workers, stakeholders and the corresponding duties of corporate bodies forms the basis for a causal relationship between corporate governance and corporate social responsibilities.

1.9   The US position on corporate governance

The concept of corporate governance owes its origins primarily to the pioneering work of Berle and Means during the 1930s.[122] They argued that corporations were not to be utilised solely for business transactions of individuals. Instead, they had acquired a much more meaningful purpose; becoming both a method of property tenure and a means of organising economic life: a new corporate system with powers and responsibilities vested in the managers of the corporation. A modern corporation was a social institution as well as an economic institution in which corporate managers should assume new powers and responsibilities. The power attendant upon such concentration had brought forth 'princes of industry', namely the controllers, whose position in the community had yet to be identified. The shareholders were steadily being lost in the creation of a series of huge industrial oligarchies.

Berle and Means argued that as a result of the separation of ownership from control, and the wide dispersion of share ownership, shareholders would no longer be able to control the direction of their corporation. The rise of professional managers resulted in directors acquiring wider powers in shaping the future direction of the corporation. As a result, a large body of security holders had been created who exercised virtually no control over the wealth of the enterprise. The rise of professional managers within the corporation had signified new responsibilities towards the shareholders as well as other stakeholders including the employees, consumers, creditors, suppliers and the general community. According to Berle and Means:

---

122 Berle and Means, *The Modern Corporation and Private Property* (1933).

'Economic power in terms of control over physical assets, is apparently responding to a centripetal force, tending more and more to concentrate in the hands of a few corporate managements. At the same time, beneficial ownership is centrifugal, tending to divide and sub-divide, to split into even smaller units and to pass freely from hand to hand. In other words, ownership continually becomes more dispersed: the power formerly joined to it becomes increasingly concentrated; and the corporate system is thereby more securely established.'[123]

Central to their theory of the apparent separation of ownership from control was the concept of 'control'. They believed that 'control' was located in the hands of the individual or group who had the actual power to select the board of directors (or its majority), either by mobilising the legal right to choose them or by exerting pressure which would influence the decision-making process. Control could be identified by determining who had the power to select directors. Berle and Means distinguished five types of control within the corporation. They were:

- Control through almost complete ownership. This was where a single individual or a small group of individuals owned all or practically all of the shares.

- Majority control involving the ownership of the significant part of the assets. This was considered by Berle and Means as the first step towards the separation of ownership from control.

- Control through a legal device. Berle and Means referred to the process of 'pyramiding' which would involve the ownership of a majority of shares in one company which, in turn, would hold a majority of shares in another.

- Minority control. This existed where an individual or a small group held sufficient stock interest so as to be in a position to dominate a corporation. Such a group is often said to have a working control of the company. In general, their control rests upon their ability to attract from scattered owners proxies sufficient, when combined with their substantial minority interest, to control a majority of the votes at the annual elections.

- Management control. This existed where ownership was so widely distributed that no individual or small group had a minority interest significant enough to dominate the affairs of the company.

Berle and Means conducted a survey between 1929 and 1930 of the 200 largest non-financial corporations from various sectors of industry. They found that 44 per cent of these companies by number and 58 per cent by wealth, were subject to management control. Further, 21 per cent by number and 22 per cent by wealth were found to be controlled by a legal device. This

---

123 ibid, p 15.

meant that the aggregate of non-ownership control of large companies was 65 per cent by number and 80 per cent by total wealth. Control was therefore located with the controllers of the company who were described as the 'new princes' of industry, for this revolution had transformed the company into one that was management controlled.

The divergence of interests between ownership and control had created a division of functions. Within the corporation, shareholders had only interests in the enterprise while the directors had power over it. The position of shareholders had been reduced to that of having a set of legal and factual interests in the enterprise.

In *Power Without Property*, Berle contended that *The Modern Corporation* and *Private Property* 'in no way broke new ground'.[124] For at least 20 years prior to that study, corporations and their size had been the subject of discussion and controversy. Berle and Means merely described a phenomenon with which everyone was familiar. In his book, Berle reiterated that the system of separation of ownership from control vested control in the directors:

> '*In terms of law, nothing apparently has changed. The corporation is still the familiar corporation. The stockholder is still the stockholder. His rights are the same as before. His vote is still a vote. The new element is that the stockholders' votes have now been more or less permanently concentrated in a relatively small number of institutions – pension trusts ... and insurance companies and mutual trusts. This means that the nuclei of power have emerged, so constructed that they cannot be readily challenged or changed.*'[125]

Berle maintained that property in its ultimate sense had been diffused. The power element had been separated from it and had been concentrated into relatively few hands. It is the evolution of a new 'socio-economic structure'.[126] 'Management control' was still the dominant form of control in the American industrial world. By this term, he meant that no large concentrated stockholding existed which maintained a close working relationship with the management or was capable of challenging it, so that the board of directors might regularly expect a majority, composed of small and scattered holdings, to follow their lead. Thus, directors were not required to consult with anyone when appointing additional directors. They selected their own successors. The shareholders though still politely called the 'owners', were passive. The condition of their existence in the company was that they would not interfere in management. Berle argued that management would safeguard abuse of its own power. 'Corporate conscience' and the 'public

---

124 Berle, *Power Without Property* (1959) p 19. See too his *The Twentieth-Century Capitalist Revolution* (1955).

125 ibid, p 53.

126 ibid, p 54.

consensus' were essential ingredients of corporate governance. By corporate conscience, he meant that management could be restrained from acting in its own self-interest in a socially irresponsible manner.

1.9.1 The effect of the separation of ownership from control of companies

Monsen and Downs argue that there has been dissatisfaction with the traditional theory of the firm and its basic axiom that firms maximise profits.[127] This is because the traditional theory of the firm only dealt with the small owner-managed firm. However, since the inception of this theory, several other types of firm have come into being. A distinction between these types of firms is important because the behaviour of each firm with respect to profits depends upon certain elements of its internal structure. In firms whose managers are not also their owners, there may be a divergence of interest between the managers and owners in certain situations. Such a divergence could cause firms to deviate from profit maximising behaviour. They identified the following types of firms:

- owner-managed firms are those managed by people who own controlling interests in the firm;
- managerial firms are those managed by persons who do not own anything near a controlling interest in them;
- non-ownership firms are those legally considered non-profit organisations; and
- fiduciary owned firms are those whose 'owners' are persons making capital payments into the firms primarily for purposes other than receiving income or capital gains therefrom.

Monsen and Downs' central hypothesis concerns the motivations of owners and managers. They believed that the traditional theory of the firm was correct in assuming that the people who operated the business firms were primarily motivated by their own self-interest. But pursuit of self-interest was a characteristic of human persons and not organisations. A firm was not a real person, even when incorporated. Therefore, it cannot really have motives or any tendency to maximise profits. When traditional theorists stated that firms maximise profits, they really meant that the people who run the business make decisions so as to maximise profits for the firm. However, in most of the large and most significant modern corporations, ownership and management were functions carried out by two entirely separate groups of people. Therefore, the entity which was referred to as the firm, had in fact become a number of

---

127 Monsen and Downs, 'A Theory of Large Managerial Firms' (June 1965) vol LXXIII *The Journal of Political Economy* 221.

distinct sub-entities. The people in each of these sub-groups within the firm were still primarily motivated by self-interest. However, their changed relationship with the firm as a whole had changed the way in which their self-interest led them to behave regarding the firm's profits. In practice, however, owners tend to act as 'satisficers' rather than maximisers because of their unfamiliarity with the policies pursued by the firm. The authors argue that as a result of separation of ownership from control, managers act towards maximisation of their own lifetime incomes. The persons who really control the firm are the professional managers. Although they may own some stock, their ownership is usually the result of their executive positions rather than the cause of their holding such positions. As a result, when managers act in their own self-interest, they do not always act in the interests of the owners.

The behaviour of large managerial firms, therefore, deviates from the profit maximisation posited by the traditional theory of the firm. This is because the large size of such firms requires them to develop bureaucratic management which cannot be perfectly controlled by the persons in charge of it. The separation of ownership from control limited owners to being satisficers instead of maximisers; hence managers aim at achieving steady growth of earnings in addition to gradually rising stock prices instead of maximising profits.[128]

However, Herman's findings reveal that managerialism has not triumphed and that the Berle-Means theory of the separation of ownership from control had not materialised.[129] His survey revealed that management companies were still devoted to profitable growth. The broad objective of both large managerial and owner-dominated firms tended to be profitable growth.

---

128 For further consideration of the effect of separation of ownership from control see Hall and Hitch, 'Price Theory and Business Behaviour' (May 1939) *Oxford Economic Papers* 15; Higgins, 'Elements of Indeterminacy in the Theory of Non-Profit Competition' (September 1939) *American Economic Review* 31; Katona, Psychological Analysis of Economic Behaviour (1951); Boulding, 'Implications For General Economics of More Realistic Theories of The Firm' (May 1952) *American Economic Review*, supplement 29; Scitvisky, 'A Note on Profit Maximisation And its Implications' in *Readings in Price Theory*, Irvin (ed) (1952); Marris, 'A Model of The "Managerial" Enterprise' (May 1963) *Quarterly Journal of Economics* 45; Williamson, *The Economics of Discretionary Behaviour: Managerial Objectives in a Theory of the Firm* (1964); and McGuire, Chiu and Elbring, 'Executive Incomes, Sales and Profits' (September 1962) *American Economic Review* 51. On the concept of 'satisficing' see Cyert and March, 'Organisational Factors in the Theory of Oligopoly' (1956) vol XX *Quarterly Journal of Economics* 15.

129 Herman, *Corporate Control, Corporate Power* (1981). For a critical analysis of the Berle and Means' work see too Beed 'The Separation of Ownership From Control' (1966) 1 J *Econ Studies* 29; Aaronovitch and Smith, *The Political Economy of British Capitalism* (1984); Demsetz and Lehn, 'The Structure of Corporate Ownership: Causes and Consequences' (1985) 93 *Journal of Political Economy* 1155; Leech, 'Corporate Ownership and Control: A New Look at The Evidence of Berle and Means' (1987) 39 *Oxford Economic Papers* 534; Alchian and Demsetz, 'Production, Information Costs And Economic Organisation' (1972) 62 *American Economic Review* 125; Cubin and Leech, 'The Effect of Shareholding Dispersion on The Degree of Control in British Companies: Theory and Measurement' (1983) 93 *Economic Journal* pp 351-69; and Demsetz, 'The Structure of Ownership and The Theory of The Firm' (1983) vol XXVI *Journal of Law and Economics* 375-90.

Herman argues that the basis of management control is 'strategic position'. This refers to the role and status of directors within the corporation to make key decisions. The concept of 'control' is related to power which refers to the capacity to initiate, constrain, circumscribe, or terminate action, either directly or by influence exercised on those with immediate decision-making authority. Directors exercised 'literal control' which gave them power to make major decisions affecting the corporation. Their powers may however be constrained by limiting their managerial discretion in the company's constitution.

In the USA, the debate on corporate governance has also centred around the work of the American Law Institute (ALI) project entitled *Principles of Corporate Governance: Analysis and Recommendations*.[130] ALI began its project in 1982 and it produced various drafts of its report. The latest draft report was published in March 1992. The final draft of the ALI report considers various aspects of the corporate governance debate including the objectives and conduct of the corporation; corporate structure; functions and powers of directors and officers; the role of audit committees in large publicly held corporations; recommendations of corporate practice concerning the board and the principal oversight committee; duty of care and the business judgment rule; duty of fair dealing; the role of directors and shareholders in transactions in control and tender offers; and remedies. According to this report, a corporation should have as its objective the conduct of business activities with a view to enhancing corporate profit and shareholder gain. This concept reinforces the traditional view that corporations should maximise shareholder welfare and that directors should act in the best interests of their company which means that they must act in the interests of shareholders collectively as a group.

---

130 *The American Law Institute, Principles of Corporate Governance: Analysis and recommendations* (13 May 1992). For a critical view of the previous ALI draft proposals on corporate governance, see especially National Legal Centre For The Public Interest, *The American Law Institute and Corporate Governance: An Analysis and Critique* (1987). An historical US perspective on corporate governance is provided by Loomis and Rubman, 'Corporate Governance in Historical Perspective' (1979) 8 *Hofstra Law Review* 141; Branson, 'Countertrends in Corporation Law: Model Business Corporation Act Revision, British Company Law Reform, And Principles of Corporate Governance and Structure' (1983) 68 *Minnesota Law Review* 53; Wolfson, 'A Critique of Corporate Law' (1979-80) 30 *University of Miami Law Review* 899; Pritchett, 'Corporate Ethics and Corporate Governance: A Critique of The ALI Statement on Corporate Governance Section 2.01(b)' (1983) 71 *California Law Review* 994; Fischel, 'The Corporate Governance Movement' (1982) 35 *Vanderbilt Law Review* 1259; Mofsky and Rubin, 'Introduction: A Symposium on The ALI Corporate Governance Project' (1983) 37 *University of Miami Law Review* 169; Eisenberg, 'The Modernisation of Corporate Law: An Essay For Bill Cary' (1983) 37 *University of Miami Law Review* 187; and Brudney, 'The Role of the Board of Directors: The ALI And Its Critics' (1983) 37 *University of Miami Law Review* 223. For a detailed US symposium on corporate governance see Williams 'Symposium on Corporate Governance' (1979-80) 8 *Hofstra Law Review* 1.

On the issue of the functions and powers of directors as well as non-executive directors, the report states that the board of directors of a publicly held corporation should perform the following functions:

- select, regularly evaluate, fix the compensation of, and, where appropriate, replace the principal senior executives;
- oversee the conduct of the corporation's business to evaluate whether the business is being properly managed;
- review and, where appropriate, approve the corporation's financial objectives and major corporate plans and actions;
- review and, where appropriate, approve major changes in, and determinations of other major questions of choice respecting, the appropriate auditing and accounting principles to be used in the preparing of the corporation's financial statements.

The board of directors also has the power to initiate and adopt corporate plans, commitments and actions; to initiate and adopt changes in accounting principles and practices; to provide advice and counsel to the principal senior executives; to instruct any committee, principal senior executive or other officer, and review the actions of any committee, principal senior executive or other officer; to make recommendations to shareholders; to manage the business of the corporation; to act as to all other corporate matters not requiring shareholder approval. Subject to the board's ultimate responsibility for oversight, the board may delegate to its committees authority to perform any of its functions and exercise any of its powers.

The ALI report makes express reference to the 'business judgment rule'. In the US, the courts have developed a 'business judgment rule' to provide special protection for directors' informed business decisions. The ALI has proposed that a director or an officer has a duty to the corporation to perform the director's or officer's functions in good faith, in a manner that he or she reasonably believes to be in the best interests of the company, and with the care that an ordinary prudent person would reasonably be expected to exercise in a like position and under similar circumstances. This duty includes the obligation to make or cause to be made an inquiry when the circumstances would require a director or an officer to do so. The extent of such inquiry shall be such as the director or officer reasonably believes to be necessary.

The policy behind the business judgment rule is that informed business judgments should be encouraged in order to stimulate innovation and risk-taking. It seeks to limit judicial intrusion in private sector decision-making. The following factors may be developed by the law which might be adopted to absolve directors from liability for ill-effects arising from the exercise of the business judgment rule, namely:

- the director acted in good faith and was not subject to a conflict of interests or duties;
- the director exercised an active discretion in the matter;
- the director took reasonable steps to inform himself/herself; and
- the director acted with a reasonable degree of care in the circumstances, taking consideration of any special skill, knowledge or acumen he or she possessed, and the degree of risk involved.

Recently, Lipton and Rosenblum argued that the concept of corporate governance should be identified by reference to its goals and objectives.[131] Much of the academic literature has assumed that directors seek to maximise shareholders' welfare and that this is the only objective of corporate governance. This view is known as the 'managerial discipline model'. This model seeks to conform managerial behaviour to the wishes of the company's shareholders and to prevent directors from forestalling a hostile takeover. In the past, the US courts reinforced the managerial discipline model by upholding the views of shareholders as paramount and thereby reinforcing the principle of profit maximisation.[132] The managerial discipline model rested on the assumption that the shareholders were owners of the corporation; since they were property owners within the corporation, they had absolute freedom to vote in any way they pleased at meetings. This led to the conclusion that shareholders' views were paramount in the corporation. Consequently, the primary objective of corporate managers was to ensure that they complied with the wishes of the shareholders.

The authors, however, reject the managerial discipline model which assumes that conformity to shareholders' wishes and protection of hostile takeovers are the principal objectives of corporate governance. They argue that the ultimate objective of corporate governance is the creation of a healthy economy through the development of business activities that operate for the long-term and compete successfully within the world economy. 'Corporate governance' should be regarded as a means of ordering the relationships and interests of the corporation's constituents, namely the shareholders, management, employees, customers, suppliers and other stockholders including the public. Each of these stakeholders has a competing claim on the corporation and the role of the modern corporation is to meet the claims of the claimants on the corporation. The legal rules that constitute a corporate governance system provides a framework for this ordering. The legal rules and the system of corporate governance should encourage the ordering of these relationships and interests around the long-term success of the corporation. The ideal system of corporate governance should place particular

---

131 Lipton and Rosenblum, 'A New System of Corporate Governance: The Quinquennial Election of Directors' (1991) *The University of Chicago Law Review* 187.

132 *Paramount Communications Inc v Time Inc*, 571 A2d 1140, 1153 (Del 1989).

emphasis on the need for co-operation between managers and their principal institutional shareholders. The authors believe that the relationship between managers and shareholders is a problematic one in the modern public corporation which is dominated by apathy and confrontation. A system is required whereby managers and stockholders work co-operatively together towards the corporation's long-term success. Recently, the American courts have given judicial recognition to the long-term interests of various stakeholders.[133] The modern corporation should consider the interests of other stockholders on the corporation:

> *'The corporation affects the destinies of employees, communities, suppliers and customers. All these constituencies contribute to, and have a stake in, the operation, success, and direction of the corporation. Moreover, the nation and the economy as a whole have a direct interest in ensuring an environment that will allow a private corporation to maintain its long term health and stability. Rules of corporate ownership and governance must take account of many more interests than do the rules governing less complex property.'*[134]

Lipton and Rosenblum further argue that the managerial discipline model assumes that managers are inherently self-interested and that they act selfishly and to the detriment of the corporation and its stakeholders. In their experience, most directors act diligently and in good faith to develop and maintain the business success of the corporations they manage and direct. They suggest an alternative model to the managerial discipline theory, which is based on the interest of the corporation in its long-term business success. This interest, multiplied by many individuals, is also society's interests and therefore supplies the proper organising system for corporate governance. The long-term health of the business enterprise is ultimately in the best interests of the shareholders, the corporation's other constituencies and the economy as a whole. Reform of corporate governance should have as its basis a 'quinquennial system' which seeks to make shareholders and managers rational decision-makers who act like long-term owners. The quinquennial system would permit the delegation of control of the corporation to its managers for sufficiently long periods of time to allow them to make the decisions necessary for the long-term health of their corporation. At the same time, it would force managers to develop and justify their long-term plans for the corporation, and would evaluate and compensate managers based on their ability to implement those plans successfully. The system would motivate shareholders, directors and managers to work in harmony towards the long-term business success of the corporation. It may also allow shareholders

---

133 *Unocal Corp v Mesa Petroleum Co* 493 A2d 946, 955 (Del 1985); and *TW Services Inc v SWT Acquisition Corp* (1989) Fed Secur L Rept (CCH) (Del Chanc).
134 Lipton and Rozenbaum, op cit, n 130 p 192. See too chapter 11.

to remove incompetent management and to force the restructuring of the company in its best interest.

The quinquennial system would convert every fifth annual meeting of shareholders into a meaningful referendum on essential questions of corporate strategy and control. It would also limit severely the ability of shareholders to effect changes in control between quinquennial meetings. Shareholders would elect directors for five-year terms. Directors seeking re-election would stand on the corporation's record for the past five years and its strategic plan for the next five years. Shareholders would base their determination of whether to oppose incumbent directors, and focus any challenge they were determined to mount, on the same issues. Between these quinquennial election meetings, shareholders could only remove directors if fraud or illegality or wilful misfeasance were established or if the corporation were guilty of such misconduct. After the quinquennial meeting, shareholders would be entitled to a detailed report from the directors on the corporation's performance over the prior five years compared to its strategic plan. The report would also detail the corporation's projections for the next five years, the assumptions underlying those projections, and the expected returns on shareholder investment. At the same time, an independent accounting firm would send the shareholders a detailed, independent evaluation of both the corporation's performance for the past five years and its projections for the next five years.

The authors suggest that the quinquennial system would strengthen the board's independence by requiring a majority of outside directors. The system would look to outside directors to provide an effective monitoring function over the operations of the corporation. The increased ability of shareholders to replace directors at the quinquennial meeting would lead directors to work closely with their shareholders. In order to avoid their removal, directors would carefully monitor the corporation's progress against its long-term business plan and maintain a close dialogue with shareholders in relation to the corporation's progress. This system would also benefit other stakeholders of the corporation who would prosper if the corporation worked effectively and was required to take account of wider interests than those of the shareholders.

1.10 An Australian perspective on corporate governance

The corporate governance debate in Australia centres primarily around the report by the Senate Standing Committee on Legal and Constitutional Affairs.[135] On 26 May 1988, the Senate referred the following terms to the Standing Committee on the Legal and Constitutional Affairs: 'the social and fiduciary duties and responsibilities of company directors'.

---

135 *The Senate Standing Committee on Legal and Constitutional Affairs*, op cit, n1.

These terms of reference were as a result of opinions expressed by Mr Jim Kennan MLC, then Attorney General for Victoria, that the modern company director should be required to take into account not only the shareholders and the company's creditors, but also groups, such as consumers, employees and the environment, when making decisions about the operations of the company. The Committee, in particular, paid attention to the following broad areas in its inquiry, namely:

- qualification of directors;
- multiplicity of directorship;
- the role of directors and composition of the board, including board committees;
- the nature of directors' existing duties and responsibilities and standards required, and to whom duties and responsibilities are owed and whether they should be widened;
- the enforcement of law insofar as it concerns other directors.

The Committee recognised that the balance between ownership and the control of companies has shifted towards the controllers. Management has great power over vast assets which it pursues through takeovers and mergers and buy-outs. However, the corporate culture within Australian companies seems to have changed. Companies have developed a 'corporate conscience'. They consider the interests of other potential claimants on the corporation. Society has expectations of the corporation. It wants ethical conduct on the part of a corporation with due regard to the rights of shareholders, employees, consumers and suppliers:

> '*Directors are the mind and soul of the corporate sector. They are critical to how it operates and how its great power is exercised. They determine the character of corporate culture. Their actions can have a profound effect on the lives of a great number of people, be they shareholders, employees, creditors, or the public generally. They can weaken or even suppress market forces. They can disturb or destroy an environment.*'[136]

Ideally, company directors' conduct should beheld to high ethical standards. Courts and legislatures will need to intervene where ethical standards are not met. The degree to which the law will need to intervene in the corporate sector beyond the provision of this framework depends on the degree to which the corporate sector can effectively regulate itself.

Manager-directors primarily owe a duty to consider the best interests of their shareholders. They also have a duty towards employees. This arises from the relationship the company has with its entities. The issue is whether directors' duties should be extended to embrace other interests of the

---

136 ibid, p 9.

corporation other than the shareholders and employees. Unfortunately, the law does not define directors' duties towards the wider community. According to Mr Kennan:

> '*In my view it is essential that we ... consider ways in which the law can respond to the demands of the modern corporation and can allow the interests of those who are affected by the decisions of corporations to be taken into account in the decision making process.*'[137]

The Committee believed that to be successful, a modern corporation is required to consider the interests of a company's employees, its creditors, its consumers, the environment, as well as the shareholders, in order to balance the competing forces of these potential interests in the corporation. The Committee considered that Australian corporations should be required to consider the values of the community and the environment and that directors and companies must aim to secure adherence to what the community considers are reasonable standards for business practice. Apart from statutory regulations, there was a case for a code of ethics for directors to comply with. The Committee thought that a code of ethics and strong peer pressure would guide the conduct of directors. Self-regulation is regarded as more effective with regulations imposed by law. An ethical code was an ideal guide for the activity of directors. The development of a corporate culture within which adherence to ethical conduct would grow is essential. Where directors fail to regulate themselves effectively, the courts and the legislature would be obliged to do so.

Australian law on directors' duties is based on the common law and statute law. The common law duties are based on skill, care and diligence. The courts have been concerned, however, to allow for flexibility and not to hamper directors' decision making unnecessarily. Directors' duties of skill and care are based on a subjective standard. There is no objective common law standard of the 'reasonably competent' person. The Committee thought that the present state of law is not satisfactory and that an objective duty of care for directors should be provided in the companies legislation. Some of the suggestions made by the Committee were:

- To consider implementing the 'business judgment' rule which is part of US corporation law. The Committee thought that so long as directors were within the bounds of the business judgment rule, they should not be held liable for the consequences of their business decisions. In the expectation of profits, shareholders must accept the risk of the directors' business judgments, unless incompetence could be established. The business judgment rule should include an obligation on directors to inform themselves of the matters relevant to the administration of the corporation.

---

137 ibid, p 10.

Directors should be required to show a reasonable degree of care in the circumstances.

- Attendance at meetings – There was little obligation on directors to attend meetings or to take responsibility for decisions made in their absence. The Committee recommended that a director who fails to attend board meetings without reasonable excuse, fails to meet the appropriate standards of conduct. Failure to attend board meetings without reasonable cause should be considered prima facie evidence of the lack of exercising reasonable skill, care and diligence in the discharge of his/her duties as a director. This provision should be incorporated in companies legislation.

- Delegation – The law allows directors to delegate some of their duties to persons they trust to perform those duties honestly. The Committee recommended that a director or an officer who acts in good faith and who reasonably believes that reliance is warranted, be entitled to rely on information, opinions, reports, statements from other directors, officers, employees under joint or common control, whom the director or officer reasonably believes merits confidence; or legal, counsel, public accountants, or other persons whom the director or officer reasonably believes merits confidence.

Directors' duties in Australia require directors to use due care and diligence in the exercise of their functions. The burden of responsibilities of directors of public companies is heavier than that of those managing small companies.

The Committee believed that corporate culture had changed. Directors were crucial to the success of large corporations. Regulation of directors should not unnecessarily restrict their powers of decision-making. Any regulation of directors' duties must be warranted and a sensible balance must be struck between measures necessary to promote corporate activity in a way which may benefit all, and measures necessary to protect the bona fide shareholder, worker, consumer and the wider community. Profitability was but one basis of good corporate citizenship. The community should be given a voice in the future direction of corporation activities:

'The corporate sector possesses most of Australia's assets, employs most of its workers, and is the sector most capable of injuring the environment. Given this, it is of vital concern to the community and the community is entitled to impose appropriate restrictions on it.'[138]

---

138 ibid, p 17.

1.10.1   Directors' fiduciary duties

Australian company law on directors' fiduciary duties is very much similar to the fiduciary duties of directors under UK law. These fiduciary duties include a duty to act in the best interests of the company; a duty not to fetter future discretion; not to make secret profits; and not to act for improper purposes. A director's fiduciary duty must be justified from the standpoint of ethics and/or good practice. Problems arise where the duty goes beyond the directors' perception of ethics and the director is unaware of what the fiduciary duty entails. The Committee recommended that the companies legislation be amended to set out the requirements which must be met for exoneration of directors from what would otherwise be breaches of their fiduciary duties.

The Committee also considered directors' wider duties towards other stockholders. They suggested that directors' duties could be widened within the ambit of company law in at least three ways:

* Directors could be *required* to have regard to the interests of certain non-shareholders, but the duty to do so would be owed only to the company. This would mean that only the company could sue for breach of the duty.

* Directors could be *permitted* to consider the interests of certain non-shareholders when making decisions. This would amount to a relaxation of the fairly strict rules as to when directors may confer benefits on non-shareholders.

* Directors could be made subject to a *duty owed directly* to certain non-shareholders said to have an interest in the outcome of the directors' actions. The person suffering harm could sue for breach of the duty.

The Committee recommended that matters such as the interests of consumers, or environmental protection should not be included in the ambit of the companies legislation, but in legislation aimed specifically at those matters. The Committee also recommended that the establishment of an Audit Committee to be made a requirement for public listing of a company. The chairperson and a majority or all of the members of the committee be non-executive directors. The audit committee should be required to meet regularly and to report to the board. It should have direct access to the company's auditors (internal and external) and senior managers and the ability to consult independent experts were necessary. The audit committee would have the following tasks: reviewing financial information to ensure its accuracy and timeliness and the inclusion of all appropriate disclosures; ensuring the existence and effective operation of accounting and financial controls; overseeing the audit of the company including nominating the auditors, approving the scope of the audit and examining the results; providing a link between the auditors and the board; and any other functions allocated to it by the company. Smaller unlisted companies should be encouraged to set up an audit committee or in the absence of an audit committee, have auditors present at board meetings which approve financial statements prior to their distribution to shareholders.

Further regulation of public companies would require a public company to state in the company's annual report, the particular skills and expertise that each director possesses in addition to including a statement of the particular skills and expertise that it considers desirable to be represented on the board. Directors should comply with a code of ethics which should be drafted. The law should be amended to make a director personally liable for complicity where he or she intentionally or recklessly encourages an act or becomes an accomplice to an act which constitutes an offence by the company. Finally, the Committee recommended that civil penalties be provided in the companies' legislation for breaches by directors where no criminal liability is involved and in appropriate circumstances, that people suffering loss as a result of the breach be allowed to bring a claim for damages.

1.10.2   Statutory provision

The main statutory provision governing the duties and obligations of company officers, including directors, is s 229 of the Companies Code.[139] It provides, *inter alia*:

[1] An officer[140] of a corporation shall at all times act honestly in the exercise of his powers and the discharge of the duties of his office.

[2] An officer of a corporation shall at all times exercise a reasonable degree of care and diligence in the exercise of his powers and the discharge of his duties.

[3] An officer ... of a corporation ... shall not make improper use of information acquired by virtue of his position as an officer ... to gain directly or indirectly, an advantage for himself or for any other person or to cause detriment to the corporation.

[4] An officer ... of a corporation shall not make improper use of his position as such an officer ... to gain directly or indirectly, an advantage for himself or for any other person or to cause detriment to the corporation.

Section 299 applies in addition to any other rule of law affecting directors' duties. It does not prevent civil proceedings being brought for breach of any other duty.

---

139 Corporation Act, s 232.
140 This includes directors, s 229(5).

1.11   Corporate governance in New Zealand

In June 1989, the New Zealand Law Commission produced a report entitled *'Company Law: Reform and Restatement'* which was in response to the mandate given to the Law Commission by the Minister of Justice in 1986.[141] The mandate required the Law Commission to examine and review the law relating to bodies incorporated under the Companies Act 1955 and to report on the form and content of a new Companies Act.

The Law Commission argued, *inter alia*, that the New Zealand law on the duties of directors was inaccessible, unclear and extremely difficult to enforce. It recommended an urgent reform in this area of law. New Zealand law on directors' duties is also based on the courts' view that directors must exercise their powers in good faith, in the best interests of the company. Directors become liable if they act without proper care and the standards applied by the courts to directors' duties have not been satisfactory. These duties were not reflected in the Companies Act 1955 and the Law Commission suggested that it was urgently required to incorporate them in the statute and to make the law more accessible. The Law Commission argued that it would be more helpful for directors to know what their duties were as well as their responsibilities and to have these obligations expressed as statements of general duty. The current area of law suffered from the major confusion as to what was 'in the best interests of the company'.

The Law Commission stated that the aim should be to provide a remedy for shareholders aggrieved by breaches of directors' duties. In some cases, the interests of shareholders did not coincide with those of the company and thus shareholders' interests needed special protection.

In relation to the role of shareholders in the corporate governance system, the Law Commission did not extend the concept of 'shareholder democracy' to enable them to enjoy a greater role in decision-making at the general meetings. It acknowledged that the general meetings had not historically operated to protect shareholders from directors' abuse of powers but rather have often been used as a cipher by directors to absolve themselves of the responsibility. Further, there were more effective methods of protecting shareholders from abuse of management powers than the mechanisms available at the general meeting. The Law Commission however observed that shareholders exercised control over directors' management in a number of ways, namely:

> *'they could vote with their shares to remove directors; they could sell their shares; they could use the general meeting as a forum for questioning director management; they could dissent and require but-out in matters of*

---

141 op cit, n 1.

fundamental change or variation of their class rights; they could apply to the court for inspection of company records and to enforce breaches of the Act or constitution; they could hold directors liable for any breaches of duty owed directly to them as shareholders, or could bring derivative action in the name of the company to enforce duties owed directly to the company, and they could seek relief of the court where unfairly treated, even though there has been no breach of the Act or the constitution.'[142]

The Law Commission indicated that the wider social objectives should be dealt with by company-specific Acts.

Under the Companies Act 1993, the business and affairs of a company are to be managed by or under the direction of the board of the company who will have powers necessary for that management. The Act prohibits a company from entering into a major transaction unless it is of a nature expressly permitted by the company's constitution, or approved by a special resolution, or contingent upon approval by special resolution. A 'major transaction' in relation to a company means the acquisition of or an agreement to acquire, whether contingent or otherwise, assets equivalent to the greater part of the assets of the company before the acquisition; or the disposition of (or an agreement to dispose of, whether contingent or otherwise) the whole or the greater part of the company's assets. The Act gives powers of delegation to directors subject to the Act and to any restrictions in the company's constitution. The board of directors may delegate formally or informally (including by course of conduct), to a committee of directors, any director or employee of the company, or any other person any one or more of its powers, except certain powers which would always be reserved to the board of directors.

The Act also addresses the duties of directors. It provides that the fundamental duty of every director of a company, when exercising powers or performing duties as a director, is to act in good faith and in a manner that he or she believes on reasonable grounds is in the best interests of the company.

The Companies Act 1993 specifically provides that a director of a company must not, when exercising or performing duties as a director, act or agree to the company acting in a manner that unfairly prejudices or discriminates against any existing shareholder of the company. There is an exception to this rule where the director believes on 'reasonable grounds' that he/she may act prejudicially or discriminatorily.

In performing their duties, the Act requires directors to have regard to the interests of the company's creditors and employees. As part of directors' general duties, they are required to exercise their powers and perform their

---

142 ibid, p 16.

duties with such care, diligence and skill reasonably to be expected of a director acting in the same circumstances. A director is expressly prohibited from entering into a contract or transaction unless he/she believes at that time, on reasonable grounds, that the contract or transaction will not involve an unreasonable risk of causing the company to fail to satisfy the solvency test.

1.12 Conclusions

Corporate governance has now become a matter of major concern in the UK. It is a concept, the implementation of which requires a two-way process: attitudinal changes on the part of management in the light of the concept of 'corporate social responsibilities'; and growing awareness on the part of shareholders which would constantly operate as a watchdog for the effective implementation of the concept.

An effective corporate governance system demands that directors provide an effective direction for the corporation. The roles of Chairman, Chief Executive and non-executive directors are essential to ensure checks and balances in any board structure.

In the 1990s, the concept of corporate governance will attain a wider significance within Europe and in other countries. There are likely to be proposals for greater accountability of directors towards the company and shareholders; a broader representation of 'stakeholder' interests; and an enhanced role for the board in strategic direction. According to a report in 1992 by *Oxford Analytica*, changes in the influence of corporate boards will be most marked in those countries where boards are currently most independent.[143] Boards will take on a more active role and their influences *vis-à-vis* management is likely to change most in the USA, followed by the UK and Canada, where boards already possess a high degree of independence. In Germany, the two-tiered system will remain intact, although within it certain changes will take place. Change will be more constrained in France and Italy by the influence of executive management and family and state interests. Change will be slowest of all in Japan, where management is virtually free of oversight from boards.

Oxford Analytica predicts that the internationalisation of business will multiply the demands placed on management. Management will be forced to become more flexible and less hierarchical, as well as more specialised. This is likely to create pressures and demands on corporate boards and directors. In particular, boards will need to show a higher degree of professionalism, and greater degree of familiarity with the functions of management, specifically financial, production, marketing and R&D. Boards will also need to

143 Oxford Analytica: *Board Directors and Corporate Governance: Trends in the G7 Countries Over the Next Ten Years* (August 1992).

demonstrate adherence to strict ethical standards and codes of conduct and increased familiarity with international markets. Boards will also become more reliant on independent external consulting and support services. This will include independent information on management performance and international business conditions; independent corporate assessment services related to financial as well as more general aspects of corporate performance.

The concept of 'corporate social responsibilities' will also attain wider significance in most countries, especially in the UK. 'Stakeholders', whether direct or indirect, active or passive, will achieve increased representation in systems of corporate governance. Some of the major factors which have contributed to this development include the increased importance of institutional shareholders and the decline in the relative influence of bankers, even in Germany and France, where bank interests have been closely tied to board affairs. Further, the rise in transnational merger and acquisition activity will increase the need for transnational board representation. There will also be greater pressure to respond to the interests of wider potential claimants on the corporation who include the company's employees, consumers, environmental groups, and local communities, all of whom will have a major impact in the future direction and policy-making function of the modern corporation.

Chapter 2

Shareholding and the Governance of Public Companies

Andrew Griffiths
University of Manchester

2.1   Introduction

The Cadbury Report[1] has recognised a public interest in the governance of
public companies requiring some form of accountability:

> *'The country's economy depends on the drive and efficiency of its
> companies. Thus the effectiveness with which their boards discharge their
> responsibilities determines Britain's competitive position. They must be
> free to drive their companies forward, but exercise that freedom within a
> framework of effective accountability. This is the essence of any system of
> good corporate governance.'*[2]

It has identified this accountability with accountability to shareholders and
regarded the issue for corporate governance as being 'how to strengthen the
accountability of boards of directors to shareholders'.[3] It has also suggested
that shareholders have some kind of duty to respond to this accountability and
to play an active role in their company's affairs rather than being mere passive
investors. 'The way forward is through ... an acceptance by all involved that
the highest standards of efficiency and integrity are expected of them.
Expectations of corporate behaviour are continually rising and a
corresponding response is looked for from shareholders, directors and auditors
... this will involve a sharper sense of accountability and responsibility all
round – accountability by boards to their shareholders, responsibility on the
part of all shareholders to the companies they own, and accountability by
professional officers and advisers to those who rely on their judgment. All
three groups have a common interest in combining to improve the working of
the corporate governance system.'[4]

---

1   *The Report of the Committee on the Financial Aspects of Corporate Governance* ('the Cadbury
     Report') (Chairman: Sir Adrian Cadbury) (London: Gee, 1992).
2   The Cadbury Report, para 1.1.
3   The Cadbury Report, para 6.1.
4   The Cadbury Report, paras 7.4 and 7.5.

The aim of this chapter is to explore the assumptions behind the attitude that the shareholders of public companies should behave like the owners of a business who have entrusted its management to agents and that their failure to do so is a major defect in the existing system of corporate governance. The idea that shareholding is essentially concerned with the provision of equity capital for businesses will be used as a basis for examining the legal position of shareholders. From this perspective, shareholding can be treated as a contractual relationship in which the original holders of shares in a company receive a perpetual claim on the company's profits in return for supplying equity capital and the overriding aim of shareholders is assumed to be the maximisation of their return from this claim.

It will be argued that shareholders' apparent lack of interest in corporate governance reflects the difference between their property rights in the company and the rights and liabilities of property owners in the usual sense and that the power possessed by corporate management raises wider issues than the shareholders' effectiveness as a source of constraint. Proposals for reforming corporate governance should acknowledge the significance of these factors and recognise that changing the legal structure on which shareholders' property rights are founded might be a more effective basis for reform than merely attempting to shift the balance of power within the existing structure.

2.2   Shareholding and equity investment in public companies

Holding shares in a company can perform two distinct functions: it is a means of controlling the company, or having some say in its control, and it is also a device for receiving a share in the profits of a business without the risk of unlimited liability. These two functions broadly correlate to the two main types of company. Thus, private companies tend to be used to obtain the various advantages associated with legal personality,[5] and their shares are more likely to be used as a source of control or influence. Public companies,[6]

---

5   Companies can be used in this way by small self-standing businesses, individuals and large organisations. A public company may be the apex of a corporate group or some other type of complex organisation consisting of a network of inter-related companies: see Hadden, *The Control of Corporate Groups* (London: IALS, 1983); Hadden, *'Regulating Corporate Groups: an International Perspective'* in McCahery, Picciotto & Scott (eds), Corporate Control and Accountability (Oxford: Clarendon, 1993); and Collins, 'Ascription of Legal Responsibility to Groups in Complex Patterns of Economic Integration' (1990) 53 *MLR* 731. The complex corporate structures featured in cases such as *Multinational Gas v Multinational Services* [1983] Ch 258 and *Adams v Cape Industries* [1990] Ch 433 provide good examples of how fiscal and legal benefits can be obtained from separate legal personality.

6   In most public companies, there are some shareholdings which are held to give the holder some influence over the company's affairs rather than for their investment potential. However, the predominant motive of most shareholders in public companies is financial and, in any event, the requirements of the investment function will limit the extent to which shares in a public company can be used as a source of power and influence.

however, tend to be used to facilitate equity investment and here the profit-sharing function of shareholding is more important.[7]

Company law treats public and private companies and their shareholders in much the same way despite these differences.[8] The legal structure of a public company has not been specifically designed to accommodate equity investors,[9] but it has many features which are ideally suited to this function.[10] Limited liability, for example, gives shares an objective and uniform value carrying a fixed and quantifiable risk and thus has facilitated the development of markets for trading these shares.[11] Shares are more attractive as an investment if they can be readily sold on a market and this should increase their yield of equity capital.[12]

The separation of management from shareholding through having the board of directors as a separate organ of the company also increases its effectiveness as a device for raising equity capital:[13] each function can be performed by specialists and the total number of shareholders does not have to be limited to what is optimal for a managerial body. In combination with limited liability, this enables a company to accommodate a large number of relatively small shareholdings, so that small investors can participate and large investors can diversify their holdings. A side effect of this process of risk-sharing and risk-spreading is to lower the level of interest which each

---

7   The issue of shares in a public company to the general public can be used to raise equity capital for a business or to enable the owner of a business to realise its value, as governments have been able to do through the 'privatisation' of publicly-owned enterprises.

8   The difference in function is, however, recognised in the shareholders' remedy for unfair prejudice under the Companies Act 1985, s 459. For discussions of this remedy, which take account of the economic perspective, see Prentice, *'The Theory of the Firm: Minority Shareholder Oppression: Sections 459–461 of the Companies Act 1985'* (1988) 8 OJLS 55; and Riley, *'Contracting Out of Company Law: Section 459 of the Companies Act 1985 and the Role of the Courts'* (1992) 55 MLR 782.

9   For example, most shareholders' powers are only exercisable at meetings, as though they were the members of a relatively small club, despite the fact that this would be physically impossible for many public companies.

10 The influence of this function is analysed in Manne, *'Our Two Corporation Systems: Law and Economics'* (1967) 53 Virginia LR 259.

11 The separate legal personality of a company provides the legal basis for the limited liability of its shareholders since one person cannot be held responsible for the debts and liabilities of another unless there is a distinct basis of liability: see the judgments of the Court of Appeal and House of Lords in *Rayner v DTI* [1989] Ch 77 and [1990] 2 AC 418. From this perspective, limited liability does not appear to be a special legal privilege conferred on shareholders.

12 The economic significance of limited liability is analysed in Halpern, Trebilcock & Turnbull, *'An Economic Analysis of Limited Liability in Corporation Law'* (1980) 30 Univ Toronto LJ 117 and Easterbrook & Fischel, *'Limited Liability and the Corporation'* (1985) 52 Univ Chic LR 89. Its significance in the context of groups of companies is discussed in Landers, *'A Unified Approach to Parent, Subsidiary and Affiliate Questions in Bankruptcy'* (1975) 42 Univ Chic LR 589; Posner, *'The Rights of Creditors of Affiliated Corporations'* (1976) 43 Univ Chic LR 499; and Landers, *'Another Word ...'* (1976) 43 Univ Chic LR 527.

13 The terms 'the board of directors' and 'the directors' are used inter-changeably. The Companies Act 1985, s 282 requires every company to have directors (or at least one director in the case of a private company). Directors have various statutory duties and responsibilities, but their powers depend on the terms of the company's constitution: see note 34 below and the accompanying text.

shareholder need have in its affairs. Shareholders are less likely to be active and vigilant when their holding is relatively small or their investments are spread through a diversified portfolio, especially when their risk of loss is limited: their response to any dissatisfaction with a particular company is more likely to be to change their investment than to take any kind of direct action against the management of the company.

2.3   Safeguarding shareholders' claims on the profits of public companies

Focusing on the public company as a vehicle for equity investment provides a basis for analysing its legal features, including the rights and liabilities of shareholders, and has been used as the basis of a distinctive economic theory of the company.[14] According to this theory, the relationship between shareholders and their company should be viewed as a form of contract, resulting from a voluntary transaction, whose subject-matter of the contract is not the ownership of the company as such but the supply of equity capital to the company in exchange for a claim on its profits. The size of the payment should reflect the quality of this claim, that is the balance of rights and liabilities enjoyed by the shareholders, with subsequent dealings in the relevant shares being mere assignments of the claim.[15]

If the overriding aim of those who supply equity capital to public companies is the maximisation of their financial return from the company (through their entitlement to dividends, participation in future issues of shares and any repayments of capital), their role in governance must be ancillary to that aim and can be construed as merely something which gives them some security in an unpredictable future. Agreeing a basis for future decision-making (eg by giving one party discretion over certain matters within specified limits or by requiring the approval of a specified majority for certain decisions) can be a more a efficient way of dealing with the uncertainty inherent in long term relationships than attempting to make detailed

---

14   Analysing shareholding in this way is a crucial aspect of a contractarian or 'new economic' theory of the company: see Jensen & Meckling, 'The Theory of the Firm: Managerial Behaviour, Agency Costs and Ownership Structure' (1976) 3 Jo Fin Econ 305. This theory and the various refinements and criticisms that have been made of it are reviewed in Bratton, 'The New Economic Theory of the Firm: Critical Perspectives from History' (1989) 41 Stanf LR 1471 and Bratton, 'The Nexus of Contracts Corporation: A Critical Appraisal' (1989) 74 Cornell LR 407.

15   Subsequent dealings in shares are thus extraneous to the relationship between the shareholders and their company, although their terms should reflect and be influenced by the terms of that relationship. This distinction has sometimes been blurred in analysis of the relationship: see the discussion of this point in Brudney, 'Corporate Governance, Agency Costs and the Rhetoric of Contract' (1985) 85 Colum LR 1403.

provisions to cover every contingency.[16] In the case of shareholding, giving discretionary power to management is far more cost-effective than making detailed plans in advance since the latter, even if possible, would be a time-consuming and expensive exercise and would contradict the economic value of leaving management to those with specialist expertise. However, the shareholders need safeguards to deter management from exploiting their discretion for their own benefit or at least to provide some compensating advantage.

The shareholders' role in the governance structure of a company can thus be viewed as ancillary to their claim on its resources. They have certain powers over the affairs of the company, exercisable by them collectively through their right to vote on resolutions at shareholders' meetings: of these, the most important is their ability to appoint and remove the members of the board of directors.[17] In a public company, the votes of any one shareholder are unlikely to carry much weight and shareholders face serious practical difficulties in acting collectively: a body as large and diverse as the shareholders of the typical public company cannot readily initiate activity and function as a decision-making organ, and this problem is compounded by each shareholder's lack of incentive to take the initiative: if dissatisfied, their most likely course of action is to sell their shares and invest the proceeds elsewhere.

However, shareholders' voting rights do provide them with some protection against the abuse of managerial discretion because management have to take account of the risk that these votes might be aggregated and used to cut down their discretion or even to remove them from office altogether.[18] Shareholders' powers may also have a negative value in that they cannot be exercised by anyone else so that management do not have to take account of anyone else in quite the same way.[19] The potential power comprised in the shareholders' voting rights is the basis of the so-called 'market in corporate control', which has been presented as an important counter-balance to the discretionary power of the management of a public company.[20] According to this theory, shareholders influence the board of directors and the management

---

16 This has been termed 'relational contracting': see Macneil, 'Contracts: Adjustment of Long-Term Economic Relations under Classical, Neo-Classical and Relational Contract Law' (1978) 72 NW Univ LR 854; and Williamson, The Economic Institutions Of Capitalism: Firms, Markets, Relational Contracting (New York: The Free Press, 1985).

17 Their right to appoint directors is usually set out in the articles of association: eg Table A, regs 73 to 80. Their right to remove directors is guaranteed by statute: the Companies Act 1985, s 303.

18 Voting rights have been portrayed as equivalent to a set of unspecified promises by management to the company's shareholders: see Easterbrook & Fischel, 'The Corporate Contract' (1989) 89 Colum LR 1416.

19 See Hansmann, 'Of the Firm' (1988) 4 Jo Law, Econ & Org 267. This reasoning can also be used to justify the unlimited term of the shareholders' claim on their company's resources: see note 26 below and the accompanying text.

20 See Manne, 'Mergers and the Market for Corporate Control' (1965) 73 Jo Pol Econ 110; and Manne, op cit note 10 above.

of their company through their ability to sell their shares and thereby affect the company's share price. If directors do not ensure that shareholders receive the maximum possible financial return from the company, they risk provoking a sub-optimal share price, with the consequent adverse publicity that would entail, and an increased vulnerability to a takeover bid. After a takeover, the shareholders' voting rights and powers are concentrated in the hands of an effective controller and can be used decisively.

The precise impact of the shareholders' powers on the conduct of directors and management is a matter of speculation and debate, and depends among other things on the quality of information available to the shareholders, including that provided by the company's auditors.[21] The deterrence of self-serving or inefficient behaviour by a fiduciary agent should require a penalty which is at least equal to the gain made by the agent or the loss suffered by the principal and which makes due allowance for the likelihood of detection.[22] Mere removal from office is unlikely to do this unless the new controller is also able and willing to take action in respect of previous misconduct.[23] Shareholders' voting rights do provide them with some countervailing advantage, whatever their precise impact, and this should be reflected in the issue price of the shares, as should the quality of any other safeguards.

Other features of shareholding can also be construed as safeguards counter-balancing managerial discretion. The importance of limited liability was noted earlier.[24] It acts as a safeguard by fixing the shareholders' risk of loss without limiting their chance of gain. Investors facing a limited risk of loss from slothful or delinquent management but an unlimited prospect of gain from diligent and enterprising management, need not scrutinise and supervise management in the same way as those who face unlimited liability.

---

21 Its significance is discussed in Bradley, 'Corporate Control: Markets and Rules' (1990) 53 MLR 170; Brudney, op cit note 15 above; Buxbaum, 'Corporate Legitimacy, Economic Theory and Legal Doctrine' (1984) 45 Ohio St LJ 515; and Parkinson, Corporate Power and Responsibility (Oxford: Clarendon, 1993).

22 See Fama & Jensen, 'Agency Problems and Residual Claims' (1983) 26 Jo Law & Econ 327; Cooter & Freedman, 'The Fiduciary Relationship: Its Economic Character and Legal Consequences' (1991) 66 NY Univ LR 1045; and Ogus, 'The Trust as Governance Structure' (1986) 36 Univ Toronto LJ 186.

23 A classic instance of this occurred in Regal (Hastings) Ltd v Gulliver [1967] 2 AC 134 (1942), where former directors were held liable to account to their company for secret profits made by them upon its acquisition by new controllers. However, in Runciman v Runciman (Walter) plc [1993] BCC 223, where a former director's service contract was challenged on the grounds, inter alia, that it had been extended in breach of the company's articles, Simon Brown J was unenthusiastic about the new controller behaving in this way: '[n]othing could be less just than that the new owners of the company after take-over should now benefit from their adventitious discovery of such breach. To allow them to do so would be to sacrifice the [former director's] legitimate interests on the altar of slavish adherence to ritualistic form.' This attitude, if adopted generally, would reduce the impact of the market in corporate control as a corrective to the shareholders' shortcomings as a decision-making body.

24 See note 12 above and the accompanying text.

Shareholders may indeed calculate that where management is left relatively free from constraint, it is likely to be more enterprising and to generate a higher return for them,[25] and they do not have to take full account of the losses which could occur if they prove to be wrong. The unlimited time-span of shareholding also acts as a safeguard for shareholders by reducing the danger of profits being concealed or delayed by management, without necessitating the cost of drafting detailed provisions. An indefinite claim on the company's resources is probably not necessary to induce the provision of equity capital, but the existence of a residual claim elsewhere would expose the shareholders to a risk which might be difficult to counter-balance efficiently.[26]

2.4   The risk and advantage for shareholders in managerial discretion

Case law dealing with directors' discretionary powers has acknowledged that the discretionary power of directors represents a calculated risk by shareholders acting in their own best interests. Thus, in *Imperial Mercantile Credit Association v Coleman*,[27] Lord Hatherley LC recognised that shareholders might gain financially by relaxing the fiduciary rule against self-dealing and empowering the board to make binding arrangements without having to refer the matter back to the shareholders for approval:

> '... *the question then remains, whether [the shareholders] cannot stipulate that [the rule against self-dealing] is a benefit of which they do not desire to avail themselves, and if they are competent so to stipulate, whether they may not think that in large financial matters of this description it is better to have directors who may advance the interests of the company by their connection, and by the part which they themselves take in large money dealings, than to have persons who would have no share in such transactions as those in which the company is concerned ... It must be left to persons to form their own contracts and engagements, and this court has only to sit here and construe them, and also to lay down certain general rules for the protection of persons who may not have been aware of what the consequences would be of entrusting their property to the management of others where nothing is expressed as to the implied arrangement. In this case it does appear to me that there was a distinct*

---

25   Thus, there is some empirical evidence to support the idea that boards without non-executive directors perform better than those which have them: see Hillmer, '*The Governance Research Agenda: A Practitioner's Perspective*' (1993) 1 Corporate Governance 26.

26   This justification for the residual claim on a company's profits being allocated to shareholders (and not to any other stakeholder) is developed in Hansmann, op cit note 19 above: the allocation may not be satisfactory, but, in terms of minimising transaction costs, is better than any alternative. See also notes 72 to 77 below and the accompanying text.

27   (1871) LR Ch App 558.

*contemplation of directors being interested in the concerns of the
company, and acting and voting when the matter came before the board of
directors, and that the shareholders took such precautions as they thought
necessary.* '28

Shareholders may thus calculate that they are likely to gain more by giving
control over the company's affairs to directors with conflicting personal
interests and rely on procedural conditions to limit the scope for abuse. Risk
calculation of this kind was also recognised by the House of Lords in
Guinness Plc v Saunders,[29] when considering whether a committee of
directors could award remuneration to a director when the relevant power had
been vested in the board:

> '*The shareholders of Guinness run the risk that the board may be too
> generous to an individual director at the expense of the shareholders but
> the shareholders have, by [the enabling article], chosen to run this risk
> and can protect themselves by the number, quality and impartiality of the
> members of the board who will consider whether an individual director
> deserves special reward. Under [the article] the shareholders of Guinness
> do not run the risk that a committee may value its own work and the
> contribution of its own members. [The article] authorises the board, and
> only the board, to grant special remuneration to a director who serves on
> a committee.*'[30]

2.5   The legal basis of the shareholders' role in governance

The safeguards available to shareholders for protecting their financial return
from a company are, however, determined by the legal features of the
company and these form the basis of the present system of governance. A
company has two organs of governance, its directors and its shareholders,
although it is possible for the company's constitution to vest specific
decision-making power elsewhere.[31] The directors tend to be portrayed as the
agents of the shareholders,[32] but this image oversimplifies their legal status
and does not capture the impact of the company's separate legal personality on
the relationship between the two organs. Shareholders have certain powers
over their company's affairs analogous to ownership, but the directors operate
as a separate decision-making organ of the company. The directors are agents

---

28   (1871) LR Ch App 558 at 568.

29   [1990] 2 AC 663.

30   Lord Templeman, [1990] 2 AC 663 at 686.

31   In *Southern Foundries v Shirlaw* [1940] AC 701, a company's constitution vested the power to
      remove directors in one of its shareholders and that shareholder could therefore act unilaterally as
      the company in this respect. In *Quin & Axtens v Salmon* [1909] AC 442, two named parties had the
      power to veto decisions of the board of directors in relation to certain specified matters.

32   The Cadbury Report, para 6.1.

in the sense that they owe their powers to appointment by others,[33] are liable to removal from office and purport to exercise their powers on behalf of another and for that other's benefit, but the source of their powers is the constitution of the company. The directors are entitled to exercise the powers vested in them in their own right, in effect acting as the company itself.[34] The law draws a clear distinction between a company and its shareholders,[35] even though the shareholders are usually the main beneficiaries of the company's activities and the interests of the company tend to be identified with the interests of the shareholders.[36]

The constraints on the directors' powers originate from both the company's constitution and external sources such as the Companies Act, the rules of The Stock Exchange,[37] and fiduciary duties and disabilities. Some of these constraints operate as standard terms which the parties are free to adopt, vary or reject, but others are compulsory and apply regardless of whether the shareholders would prefer their impact to be modified or might be prepared to exchange the constraint for a lower share price. A governance structure comprising a person or body with discretionary power subject to constraints in this way, gives rise to two distinct governance problems: first, the constraints require enforcement in the event of breach; and secondly, there may need to be an alternative or complementary decision-maker to approve action beyond the constraints. These problems are difficult to resolve in a public company because its directors could not perform these functions without contradicting the very point of the constraints, and its shareholders are unsuited to playing the active role required.

---

33 See note 17 above. In practice, the passivity of shareholders usually enables boards to nominate their own membership and operate as self-perpetuating bodies.

34 *Automatic Self-Cleansing Filter Syndicate v Cunninghame* [1906] 2 Ch 34 (CA); *Breckland v London & Suffolk Properties* [1989] BCLC 100. See also the Companies (Tables A to F) Regulations, Table A, reg 70. There is nothing to prevent the shareholders from adopting a more complex governance structure. Thus, in *Quin & Axtens v Salmon*, note 31 above, the House of Lords upheld a power of veto over decisions of the board, which had been vested in the joint managing directors of the company: since this power of veto had been enshrined in the constitution, it could only be overridden by the shareholders if they were able to exercise their power to amend the constitution. See also *Shirlaw v Southern Foundries*, note 31 above, and *Cumbria Newspapers Group v Cumberland & Westmorland Herald* [1987] Ch 1.

35 The legal significance of this distinction was highlighted in Re *Exchange Banking Company* (1882) 21 Ch D 519, where the directors of a company had paid an illegal dividend. The Court of Appeal rejected the argument that the receipt of the illegal payment by the shareholders meant that the company had not suffered any loss and held that the directors were personally liable to compensate the company.

36 Directors owe their company a fiduciary duty to act bona fide in its best interests and this has generally been regarded as requiring them to act in the best interests of the company's shareholders by maximising their financial return from the company: *Charterbridge v Lloyds Bank* [1970] Ch 62; *Multinational Gas v Multinational Services*, note 5 above. There are, however, circumstances in which the directors' duty to the company may require them to take account of the interests of creditors and employees as well: the Companies Act 1985, s 309; *West Mercia Safetywear v Dodd* [1988] BCLC 250; *Fulham FC v Cabra* [1992] BCC 863.

37 See, for example, the Companies Act 1985, ss 35(3), 80, 89, 319 and 320; and Admission of Securities to Listing.

2.6   The missing organ in the present system of governance

In company law, the constraints on the directors' discretion are treated as legal rights of the company itself and their enforcement is forms part of the directors' normal managerial responsibilities, despite the paradox involved.[38] This may be satisfactory for dealing with breaches of duty by individual directors, but not where the collective performance of the board is at issue or where the board is unwilling to deal with a misfeasant director for reasons which do not accord with the best interests of the company: a breach of duty may only be considered properly if a new board of directors is appointed, as may occur after a takeover,[39] or if the company goes into administration or liquidation. The ability of the shareholders to 'call the directors to book',[40] whether by instituting proceedings or changing the composition of the board, is further impaired by their shortcomings as a decision-making organ of the company.[41] Litigation involves activity and decision-making of some complexity, since there will be a range of possible responses to any perceived breach of the company's rights and taking action will involve costs to the company as well as benefits which will have to be weighed against each other to determine what is in the company's best interests. In the typical public

---

38 *Shaw & Sons v Shaw* [1935] 2 KB 113; *Breckland v London & Suffolk Properties*, note 34 above, noted in Wedderburn, '*Control of Corporate Actions*' (1989) 52 MLR 401. Decision-making power reverts to the shareholders when the directors are unable to act because of deadlock or when disqualification through self-interest precludes a quorum: *Barron v Potter* [1914] 1 Ch 895; *Foster v Foster* [1916] 1 Ch 532. However, it has also been suggested that shareholders have an independent power to institute litigation in the name of the company (see *Marshall's Valve v Manning* [1909] 1 Ch 267 and *Alexander Ward v Samyang Navigation* [1975] 1 All ER 608), although this would now be hard to reconcile with the decision in *Breckland* (above): see Wedderburn, '*Control of Corporate Litigation*' (1976) 39 MLR 327 and (1989) 52 MLR 401. In Breckland, Harman J said that when voting on litigation in which he had a personal interest, a director 'undoubtedly must consider the true interests of the company and not his own interests in exercising his vote at the board', which begs the question of what happens if he does not. In practice, if the majority of the shareholders in a company are sufficiently independent and well-organised to be able to act collectively and take a view on a director's breach of duty, they may be better advised to replace the relevant directors or to ensure that there is an independent majority on the board and to leave the matter to the board to deal rather than to deal with it entirely themselves as shareholders.

39 This adds to the significance of the market in corporate control as a constraining influence on management: see notes 20 to 23 above and the accompanying text.

40 The Cadbury Report, para 6.6.

41 In the absence of collective action by the shareholders, an individual shareholder may be able to bring a derivative action in respect of a breach of duty or violation of the company's constitution, although the conditions attached to its availability mean that it cannot be used to enforce every breach of duty. See *Prudential Assurance v Newman Industries* [1981] Ch 229 & [1982] Ch 204; *Smith v Croft (No 2)* [1988] Ch 114; and Prentice, '*Shareholder Actions: The Rule in Foss v Harbottle*' (1988) 104 LQR 341. The statutory remedy of a shareholder to petition for relief under the Companies Act 1985, s 459 may also provide some redress: s 461(2)(c)). However, apart from their other difficulties, individual shareholders lack much incentive to enforce the limits and constraints on directors. They will have to bear the costs of initiating the action (although they may be entitled to an indemnity from the company: *Wallersteiner v Moir (No 2)* [1975] QB 108; *Smith v Croft (No 1)* [1986] 1 WLR 580), but they will only benefit indirectly since anything recovered will go to the company, providing a 'free ride' for the other shareholders.

company, the shareholders' large number and the fact that their collective views can only be ascertained through cumbersome formal procedures makes them suitable for only the crudest kind of decision-making.[42] In the absence of a specific institutional arrangement, shareholders are unlikely to be able to perform their role in enforcing any constraints on directors except through the 'market in corporate control'.

The lack of any suitable organ for complementing the directors' powers is also an acute problem in the present system of corporate governance. Where it is in the company's best interests for the directors to act beyond a constraint on their discretion, they can only do so legitimately by obtaining the consent of the shareholders at a duly-convened meeting.[43] This provides little scope for the proposed course of action to be scrutinised or negotiated in any detail (although the directors may take informal soundings from major shareholders or their representatives) and in practice is likely to prove cumbersome and expensive. In *Rackham v Peek Foods*,[44] for example, the directors of a public company had negotiated the acquisition of a property development company, but had to make it conditional on the shareholders' approval to comply with Stock Exchange rules.[45] There was thus a delay before the contract could become binding on the company so that a meeting of the shareholders could be convened and held. The delay proved fortuitous since the property market collapsed in the interval and the directors were able to recommend that the contract be rejected by the shareholders.[46] However, the case shows how delay can undermine a commercial contract and, in practice, this is more likely to harm the interests of the company than to work in its favour, if only by making the other party more wary and necessitating the time and expense of drafting safeguards to minimise the uncertainty.

The lack of an effective alternative or complementary governance organ which can override constraints on the directors' discretion must increase the cost to the shareholders of using such constraints as a safeguard. Where free to do so, the shareholders might prefer to allow management a wider discretion

---

42 Decision-making by shareholders in public companies is usually confined to matters where a crude yes or no is sufficient, such as changes in the company's name or constitution, approving or removing directors, the ordinary business at the annual general meeting and endorsing decisions or actions of the board where this is required by the Companies Act or by Stock Exchange rules.

43 A limit on the activities of the company itself, and not just the powers of the directors to act on its behalf (as with the objects clause), can only be overridden with the sanction of a special resolution: the Companies Act 1985, s 35(3); *Boschoek v Fuke* [1906] 1 Ch 148; *Quin & Axtens v Salmon*, note 31 above.

44 [1990] BCLC 894 (1977).

45 Admission of Securities to Listing, s 6, chap 1.

46 The court's decision confirmed that the directors were free to advise the shareholders to reject the contract, despite having given an undertaking to use their endeavours to obtain the shareholders' approval. See also *Crowther v Carpets International* [1990] BCLC 460 (1985) which also concerned a contract which required the approval of the shareholders. The directors' duties to shareholders in this type of situation are analysed in Griffiths, *'The Best Interests of Fulham FC: Directors' Fiduciary Duties and Long-Term Contracts'* [1993] JBL 576.

and accept the greater risk of abuse: given a straight choice between no limits and limits which only they can override, shareholders might well judge that their interest would be better served by relaxing the constraints on management and seek compensation through a lower share price, which perhaps explains the comprehensive scope of most objects clauses and the fact that regulation rather than shareholder pressure has been the source of many restrictions on directors' powers.[47]

2.7 Compulsory constraints in the present system of governance

The compulsory constraining of directors' discretion may therefore have the paradoxical effect of contradicting the shareholders' own perceptions of what is in their interests and reduce the efficiency of shareholding in promoting the supply of equity capital. Shareholders' calculations might differ if there were a governance structure available to them with a specific organ for enforcing and overriding the constraints on directors' discretion which did not require their direct involvement, such as a supervisory board or corporate senate.[48] They could indicate their preference in this respect if there were a choice of structure.

The Cadbury Report did not address this deficiency, but appeared to accept that responsibility for the ancillary functions generated by the constraint of directors' managerial powers would have to be split somehow between the two existing organs: '[all] directors ... whether or not they have executive responsibilities, have a monitoring role and are responsible for ensuring that the necessary controls over the activities of their companies are in place - and working';[49] it looked to the directors' 'collective ability to provide both the leadership and the checks and balances which effective governance demands',[50] but also to the shareholders to 'call the directors to book if they appear to be failing in their stewardship ... [and] to insist on a high standard of corporate governance.'[51] From the perspective of the shareholders' own

---

47 See, for example, the restrictions referred to in note 37 above and the accompanying text.

48 The idea of a corporate senate is discussed in Turnbull, '*Improving Corporate Structure and Ethics: A Case for Corporate Senates*' (1993) 17 Directors' Monthly no.5. It can be argued that this kind of structure could be set up under the present system, if shareholders were to attach value to it, by building it into the company's constitution: see note 34 above. This would, however, involve greater transaction costs than if a suitable corporate structure were to be available. Moreover, company law generally envisages a governance structure involving a single unitary board complemented only by shareholders and many of the restrictions on directors' powers are expressly subject to the consent of the shareholders, regardless of whether there might be a separate organ: see, for example, those referred to in note 37 above.

49 The Cadbury Report, para 1.8.

50 The Cadbury Report, para 4.1.

51 The Cadbury Report, para 6.6.

interests, it would have been better to consider alternative governance structures or even the removal of the compulsory constraints on directors' discretion so that the shareholders' role is confined to whatever evolves from the competition for equity capital.

Reforming corporate governance by shifting power from directors to shareholders within the present system appears even more inappropriate if management's discretion is viewed in the wider context of all the relationships which underlie a public company. According to the new economic theory,[52] a company is an organising device which enables the inputs required for a collective economic enterprise (including, but not exclusively, equity capital) to be supplied through a set of bilateral contracts rather than one complex multilateral arrangement. The company's management performs the crucial function of co-ordinating the other inputs and settling the terms on which they are supplied, including their own terms as managers.[53] Their self-interest may lead them to maximising the discretionary power which this function gives them and using it for their own benefit, which in turn may influence the arrangements with the other input providers such as the shareholders. Management can in effect use the company as a device for enhancing their own utility. Their scope for doing so is limited by their need to obtain other inputs in competitive markets. Thus, to attract equity capital, management have to weigh their interest in maximising their discretion against its impact on the share price, settling for an optimal balance which usually includes the risk of subsequent removal from office.[54] They may also have to concede constraints to other input providers such as creditors, who face an increased risk due to the company's limited liability,[55] in order to keep down the price of credit.[56]

It is hard to justify shifting power in public companies from directors to shareholders if the only reason is to protect the shareholders from unfair prejudice: its failure to evolve through transactions in the market for equity capital suggests that shareholders do not value such changes or at least are

---

52 See note 14 above.

53 This 'entrepreneurial' role of management is discussed in Manne, op cit, note 10 above.

54 This liability can be compared with a similar one which may be incurred where finance has been raised through a secured loan and the creditor has the power to appoint a receiver and administrator in specified circumstances.

55 Directors owe no general duties to creditors (*Multinational Gas v Multinational Gas Services*, note 5 above), although the interests of creditors may determine the content of directors' duties when their company is actually or virtually insolvent (*West Mercia Safetywear v Dodd*, note 36 above). In a liquidation or administration, creditors may indirectly benefit from any outstanding claims which a company may have against its directors relating to their conduct of its affairs and which have not been effectively extinguished by the shareholders (cf *Multinational Gas and Fulham FC v Cabra*, note 36 above). The remedies available to liquidators and administrators under the Insolvency Act 1986 and the Company Directors' Disqualification Act 1986 also provide directors with incentives to take account of the interests of the company's creditors.

56 This opportunity would not be available to involuntary creditors of the company such as tort victims: see the studies of limited liability referred to in note 12 above.

prepared to forego them in exchange for a lower share price. Compulsory regulation would only then be necessary if shareholders were prevented from acting in their own best interests by some form of market failure such as lack of information or insuperable transaction costs. This would, however, justify reviewing the governance structure itself and not just the balance of power within it: the shareholders best interests might be better served if there were a specific organ for monitoring management (and enabling management to override their limits where appropriate) rather than by increasing the size of a role which they are unable or unwilling to play and which, by reducing the scope of the discretion which their company's managers have to respond to commercial opportunities, may undermine their own interests.

It may be, however, that a wider public interest is served by using shareholders to constrain the power of the management of public companies.[57] If that is the case, the relevant public interest should be acknowledged openly, and the shareholders' suitability and effectiveness as an instrument of the public interest should be addressed directly, and their deficiencies as an organ of governance taken into account.

2.8   Managerial discretion and the public interest in governance

The discretionary power of corporate management has been regarded as a matter of public concern because it is difficult to reconcile with traditional economic theory, which looks to the private ownership of resources and competitive markets to explain how the self-interested behaviour of individuals also serves the public good.[58] Individuals and firms are assumed to be motivated by utility or profit maximisation and subject to competition so that resources are deployed where they are most highly valued.[59] A company, however, will only maximise its profits if its managers are motivated or compelled to maximise the return to the company's shareholders.[60] If they are not, the managers' own self-interest may prevail and lead them to use the company's resources for other purposes such as increasing their remuneration

---

57   This is consistent with other comments made in the Cadbury Report: see notes 2 and 4 above and the accompanying text.

58   The perceived problem has been termed 'the separation of ownership and control'. The debate about its economic significance dates from the publication of Berle & Means, *The Modern Corporation and Private Property* (New York: Macmillan, 1932).

59   The economic concept of efficiency is discussed in Veljanovski, 'The New Law-and-Economics: A Research Review' in *Ogus & Veljanovski* (eds), *Readings in the Economics of Law and Regulation* (Oxford, 1984).

60   This has been termed the 'classical model' of the company: see Graham, '*Regulating the Corporate Form*' in Hancher & Moran (eds), Capitalism, Culture and Economic Regulation (Oxford: Clarendon, 1989).

and perquisites, or working with less diligence, or retaining profits within the company to finance growth and expansion designed to enhance their own prestige. Such behaviour does not ensure the most efficient deployment of resources.

This separation of ownership and control in public companies is a variant of a general economic problem associated with agents. Agency is an aspect of the economic division of labour and there are many instances where an agent can perform a task more efficiently because of superior skill, expertise, information or opportunities. Both the principal and the agent should gain from the arrangement, but agency also involves a conundrum which reduces the overall benefit. The *raison d'être* of agency requires the agent to have some discretion, but this creates an opportunity for the agent to serve their own interests or pursue an alternative agenda and the imbalance of skill and expertise or the like reduces the likelihood of the principal detecting this and adjusting the agent's remuneration accurately.[61]

In a public company, the agency problem is intensified at the level of the board of directors because the shareholders are unlikely to act as a cohesive and effective principal and their incentives are in any event different because of limited liability.[62] One way of responding to this apparent problem is to cajole shareholders into behaving more like the owners of private property through regulation, and this perhaps explains the tendency to increase the shareholders' powers over management compulsorily, although it has not (so far) led to shareholders facing greater liabilities.[63] This provides some justification for those statutory reforms of UK company law which have specified a role for shareholders, and reduced the power of directors, over such matters as the issue of shares,[64] directors' service contracts[65] and transactions involving a likely conflict of interest.[66]

---

61 See note 22 above. The nature of this problem and its significance for both corporate management and government is discussed in Frug, *'The Ideology of Bureaucracy in American Law'* (1984) 97 Harv LR 1276.

62 The underlying issues and the various responses which have been made to the problem of the separation of ownership and control in public companies are discussed in Bratton, op cit note 14 above; Farrar, *'Ownership and Control of Public Listed Companies: Revising or Rejecting the Concept of Control'* in Pettet (ed), Company Law in Change (London: Stevens & Sons, 1987); Graham, op cit note 60 above; Romano, *'Metapolitics and Corporate Law Reform'* (1984) 36 Stanf LR 923; and Stokes, *'Company Law and Legal Theory'* in Twining (ed), Legal Theory and the Common Law (Oxford: Basil Blackwell, 1986).

63 In this respect, the comments of Sir Owen Green on the Cadbury Report are pertinent: 'the concept of ownership, as distinct from membership, of a limited liability company is novel, untested and inappropriate. The expression "owner" does not appear in the Companies Act, and the normal obligations of a true owner are, except in respect of unpaid share capital, non-existent.' See Green, *'Why Cadbury Leaves a Bitter Taste'* Financial Times, 9 June 1992. See also Sir Owen's chapter 5 below.

64 The Companies Act 1985, ss 80 and 89.

65 The Companies Act 1985, s 319.

66 The Companies Act 1985, s 320. In a similar vein, The Stock Exchange has limited the power of directors to make substantial acquisitions or disposals: Admission of Securities to Listing, s 6, chap 1. The Cadbury Report also reflects this attitude.

2.9   The public interest in separate legal personality

The new economic theory of the company has been used to oppose the compulsory regulation of public companies,[67] but this is not a necessary corollary of its insights. What it does suggest is that the apparent problem of corporate governance is not the exclusive concern of the company's shareholders and that focusing on shareholders alone can be counter-productive. Management's discretion can be seen as the space retained by or left to management by the terms on which various inputs are supplied to the company rather than as the result of shareholder weakness.[68] Governance problems may relate to the impact of this discretion on the company's relationship with all or any of its input suppliers.[69] 'Ownership' of a company is not vested in the shareholders, but is fragmented and dispersed, involving management, creditors and other input suppliers as well as the shareholders in a complex arrangement reflecting their respective perceptions of their own best interests. This detracts from the view that the public interest in managerial discretion requires a more active role for shareholders.

The law has played a crucial role in facilitating the evolution of the economic power associated with public companies[70] by providing a facility which combines separate legal personality, unlimited life-span and limited liability.[71] This role gives rise to a public interest in the affairs of public companies and the discretionary power of their management, especially since the terms of availability of this facility influences the conduct and development of public companies. The impact of the company's unlimited life-span on the relationship between shareholders and management provides a useful insight into the law's significance in this respect. It was noted earlier how this safeguards shareholders against management's discretion,[72] but it has also been viewed as a source of inefficiency because the arrangement persists into perpetuity. While the arrangement may be essential in the short run to protect the original shareholders from unscrupulous management, in the

---

67   See, for example, *Easterbrook & Fischel*, op cit note 18 above; Fama & Jensen, op cit note 22 above; and Romano, op cit note 62 above.

68   See Stokes, op cit note 62 above, on the celebration of managerial 'space'.

69   The interest of creditors in the quality of corporate governance has been recognised in recent developments in insolvency law. See the recommendations of The Report of the Cork Committee (1982) Cmnd 8558; and the remedies available under the Insolvency Act 1986 (especially for wrongful trading under s 214) and the Company Directors' Disqualification Act 1986.

70   The Cadbury Report referred to the economic importance of public companies in para 1.1. See note 2 above and the accompanying text.

71   Public companies may involve a two-fold use of this legal facility. First, the public company itself functions as a basis for structuring the relationships involving the various contributors to its activities and especially the suppliers of equity capital. Secondly, the private company may prove a valuable device for organising the internal affairs of the public company or structuring its relationships with other parties, enabling it to operate as a group or as part of a network of companies: see *Collins and Hadden*, op cit, note 5 above.

72   See note 26 above and the accompanying text.

long-run these shareholders' successors are likely to receive surplus profits far in excess of what would have been necessary to induce the original investment of equity capital.[73] The safeguard becomes a source of 'windfall' profits and unwarranted shareholder strength in relation to management and other input suppliers.[74]

The problem is that, while the shareholding relationship is structured upon a legal facility with an infinite life-span, its terms are settled by parties who do not appear to attach significant value to profits arising in the distant future. The management responsible for settling the terms of shareholding do not attach enough value to distant profits to outweigh the immediate cost that would be incurred in providing alternative safeguards to protect the shareholders' shorter term interests. It might be better if the life-span of a company were to be limited, or if the law provided a standard basis on which the shareholders' claim could fade out, so that the shareholding relationship would have to be structured on a different basis.[75] This would be justified if it were recognised that there is a public interest in the long-term future of companies which should override governance structures set up by private contracting parties, motivated by short-term considerations and concerned with a one-off payment of equity capital.

2.10   Conclusion

The aim of this chapter has been to show that analysis of corporate governance should go beyond a narrow pre-occupation with the relationship between shareholders and directors and consider the economic function of shareholding and the relevance of the legal features of the company to this function. The public interest in the affairs of public companies requires more than regulating the existing system of governance, or shifting the balance of power within it. It would justify the consideration of alternative governance structures and perhaps also of exacting a more economic price for obtaining the benefits of separate legal personality.[76] The company, and the terms of its availability, should not be treated as a permanent and unchangeable fixture,

---

73   This argument has been used in particular by Shann Turnbull in his advocacy of time-limited corporations: see '*Re-inventing Corporations*' (1991) 10 Human Systems Management No 3 (Netherlands: IOS Press) and '*Should Ownership Last Forever?*' (1992: PO Box 266, Woollahra, NSW, Australia). The point is also made in Goyder, '*Ought Company Debt to be Permanent?*' in Sethi (ed), Trusteeship: The Gandhian Alternative (New Delhi: Gandhi Peace Foundation, 1986).

74   See Aoki, *The Co-operative Game Theory of the Firm* (Oxford: Clarendon, 1984); and Coffee, '*Shareholders versus Managers: The Strain in the Corporate Web*' (1986) 85 Mich LR 1.

75   A prescribed cycle of birth and death for companies might also accelerate the evolution of more efficient corporate structures.

76   See notes 5 and 71 above.

but should be reviewed as an integral part of the corporate governance problem. As Professor Sealy has remarked:

> *'what is amazing ... is that we in the United Kingdom have done virtually nothing to change or improve this important institution in any really creative way in the 140 years since [it began]. If the history of the steam engine had followed a pattern similar to that of the limited company over the same period, every train leaving Paddington station today would be restricted to a speed of four miles per hour, and would still be proceeded by the legendary man walking with his red flag.'*[77]

---

77   Sealy, Company Law and Commercial Reality (London: Sweet & Maxwell, 1984).

Chapter 3

The Role of 'Exit' and 'Voice' in Corporate Governance

John Parkinson
Reader in Law, University of Bristol

3.1   Introduction

The term 'corporate governance' will be used here, somewhat proscriptively, to refer to the various mechanisms that are imposed, or whose operation is facilitated by company law, that shape the way company managers exercise their discretion.[1] These mechanisms rely principally on shareholder voting, the powers of the board, fiduciary duties, and the play of market forces. The function of governance is to achieve compliance with whatever may be the company's proper objectives. The governance process operates on a different level from the process of managing the business. While senior executives (who may also be directors) run the business day-to-day, governance involves selecting and removing those executives and monitoring their performance. It might also involve collaboration with executive management in making fundamental decisions and formulating long-term strategy.[2]

A minimum condition of effective governance, or at least of the monitoring aspect of governance with which this chapter is concerned, is that those engaged in it be independent of management. It is generally assumed in relation to public companies in the UK that the shareholders, who possess the necessary element of independence, in the main lack the incentive to participate in the company's internal governance procedures. The board on the other hand, while better suited to the performance of a governance role, is not independent, since directors are either part of management or else are management appointees. There is therefore in practice no powerful counter to management within the constitutional structure. It is argued in some quarters

---

1   For a more expansive definition, see Demb and Neubauer, *The Corporate Board: Confronting the Paradoxes* (New York, 1992), at 2: identifying the role of governance as being to keep business activity and societal objectives congruent, the authors subsume within their definition all the mechanisms employed to achieve that end, including general-law regulation.

2   See Tricker, *Corporate Governance: Practices, Procedures and Powers in British Companies and Their Boards of Directors* (Aldershot, 1984), at 6-7; Hilmer, *'The Governance Research Agenda: A Practitioner's Perspective'* (1993) 1 Corporate Governance: an International Review 26.

nonetheless that this does not leave managers with a dangerously wide discretion, on the ground that the existence of an active market in control is a more than adequate substitute for fully functioning internal accountability. In other words governance in this country does not rely chiefly, in Hirschman's terminology,[3] on 'voice', or the processes of dialogue and decision-making within the company's administrative structure, but on the 'exit' of dissatisfied shareholders and the market mechanism of the hostile takeover.

Just how effective the threat of takeover is in disciplining management is controversial, but it cannot be doubted that the market for control is a crucial element in governance in the UK. The purpose of this chapter is to assess the relative merits of controlling management discretion by means of the market for control on the one hand, and through mechanisms dependent on voice, for example, some form of supervisory board, on the other. While no firm conclusions will be reached about whether the predominant role played by exit in this country is desirable, the chapter will present a survey of the main points bearing on this issue that have arisen in the recent literature.

The next section describes the background to the current governance debate. The objectives that governance is or might be required to serve are examined in 3.3. In 3.4 and 3.5 the capacity of systems of governance relying on exit and voice respectively to fulfil these objectives is investigated. The chapter concludes with a consideration of how the balance between exit and voice might be shifted in this country should that appear desirable.

3.2   The background

The subject of corporate governance is receiving considerable attention from lawyers, economists, and business writers and practitioners in much of the developed world. An important reason is that the increased vulnerability of domestic product markets to foreign suppliers has required consideration to be given to all aspects of corporate competitiveness, one determinant of which is the company's control structure. This has provoked in particular an interest in questions of comparative governance, with some writers in this country and the USA seeing attractions in the close supervision of management by the providers of finance found in the 'bank-based' economies, most notably of Germany and Japan. These systems are examples of governance mechanisms that make substantial use of voice, in Germany facilitated by an institutional structure involving a separate supervisory board. In addition to the possibility that such forms of control might result in greater managerial effectiveness,

---

3   See Hirschman, *Exit, Voice and Loyalty: Responses to Decline in Firms, Organisations, and States* (Cambridge, Mass, 1970).

dissatisfaction with the consequences of an active takeover market, for example, in the economic sphere 'short-termism' and in the social sphere unemployment and regional imbalance, has also focused attention on alternative systems of governance. The rival forms have not been free of criticism either. It is often argued, for instance, that the banks in Germany have too much power, and there are questions about the speed of response to market and technological change where management is subject to monitoring by those who may have too great an interest in the maintenance of the status quo.

Whatever the theoretical merits of the different approaches to governance, the growing internationalisation of capital markets, increased competition for capital, and regulatory reform are forcing changes in national governance practices. In the bank-based systems the movement is in the direction of the Anglo-American model. The foreign investments of American pension funds, for example, had risen from virtually nothing in 1979 to around US$100 billion by 1990, and it has been estimated that they will exceed $200 billion in 1994.[4] These institutions are beginning to take an interest in the governance arrangements of the overseas companies in which they invest, and, in the belief that insufficient priority is afforded to increasing 'shareholder value', are directing their efforts to reforming restrictive voting structures and dismantling other barriers to investor participation in decision-making and especially to takeover.[5] This process will be assisted if the proposed EC Thirteenth Directive[6] is implemented. Part of the aim of the latter is to facilitate mergers in order to create companies large enough to meet competition from firms of great size outside the Community, but an invocation of the market for control as a disciplinary mechanism is also intended.[7] It cannot be anticipated, however, that either investor pressure or regulatory change will cause hostile takeover activity to rise to anything like Anglo-American levels, bearing in mind that the ownership structure of many

4   Baldi, 'The Growing Role of Pension Funds in Shaping International Corporate Governance, Benefits and Compensation', *International Magazine*, 21(3), October 1991. An increase in the equity holdings of German pension funds and insurance companies from their present comparatively low level of under 10 per cent has also been predicted: see Oxford Analytica Ltd, *Board Directors and Corporate Governance*: Trends in the G7 Countries over the Next Ten Years (Oxford, 1992), p 81.

5   See Dickson, '*Ballot Box Crusaders Ride to Foreign Wars*', Financial Times 3 March 1993. See also Oxford Analytica, *Board Directors and Corporate Governance*, ibid, at 142: 'structures and practices which have been established over the years to favour domestic management within a country over foreign and non-managerial interests are now being threatened by the need to attract the capital of major international investors'.

6   Thirteenth Directive on Takeover and Other General Bids, OJ, Vol 32, C64, 14/4/1989, 8 and OJ C240/7 of 26/9/90. See also the amendments to the *Second Directive* (OJ 8/5 of 12/1/91) and to the proposed Fifth Directive (OJ 7/4 of 11/1/91).

7   See Franks and Mayer, '*European Capital Markets and Corporate Control*', in Bishop and Kay (eds), European Mergers and Merger Policy (Oxford, 1993), p 163.

Continental companies gives them substantial protection against unwelcome bids.[8] It is interesting to note that while the concern in Europe is with freeing up the market for control, development in America has been in the opposite direction. Worries about the impact of takeovers on the economies of states in which target operations are located have among other factors provoked an attitude antagonistic to takeovers.[9] Recent state legislation[10] and judicial rulings[11] now mean that managements of target companies are allowed a substantial discretion to defeat hostile bids, to the point that such steps have 'largely succeeded in eclipsing the hostile takeover as a mechanism of corporate accountability'.[12] Off-setting measures to stimulate voice have so far been modest,[13] though institutional involvement in portfolio companies is reported to be growing.[14]

In the UK, despite some concern about the impact of the takeover process,[15] there have been no attempts to fetter the market in control.[16] It has largely been assumed that the market is an effective way of securing the efficient operation of the corporate sector and the governance debate has instead been dominated by a narrower range of problems that are relatively immune to the market's effects. Attention has thus been focused on the collapse of a number of companies which from their published accounts were financially sound, cases of spectacular management fraud, and the level of directors' remuneration. These preoccupations are, for example, reflected in the terms of reference of the Cadbury committee on corporate governance and the committee's recommendations.[17] Part of the explanation of all three problems is a lack of independence on the part of those charged with monitoring management. In relation to auditors there has been a limited

---

8   For the statistics, see Coopers & Lybrand, *Barriers to Takeovers in the European Community*: a Study by Coopers & Lybrand for the DTI (London, 1989), vol 1, p 4, and see also 21-2.

9   The motives for these changes are complex: see generally Gordon, *'Corporations, Markets and Courts'*, (1991) 91 Column L Rev 1931. For an account stressing managerial self-interest, see *Monks and Minnow, Power and Accountability* (Glasgow, 1991), pp 140-52.

10 See Herzel and Shepro, *Bidders and Targets: Mergers and Acquisitions in the US* (Oxford, 1990) chapter 6.

11 See eg *Paramount Communications Inc v Time Inc* 571 A 2d 1140 (Del Sup Ct, 1990).

12 Coffee, *'Liquidity versus Control: The Institutional Investor as Corporate Monitor'*, (1991) 91 Colum L Rev 1277, at 1304.

13 See Lipton and Panner, *'Takeover Bids and United States Corporate Governance'*, in Prentice and Holland, Contemporary Issues in Corporate Governance (Oxford, 1993), pp 132-4.

14 Coffee, *'Liquidity versus Control'* (above, note 12), at 1288-9.

15 See Peacock and Bannock, *Corporate Takeovers and the Public Interest* (Aberdeen, 1991), chapters 4 and 5.

16 Indeed, existing controls have not been fully utilised: see Fairburn, *'The Evolution of Merger Policy in Britain'*, in Fairburn and Kay (eds), Mergers and Merger Policy (Oxford, 1989), pp 204-5 (policy on referral of mergers to the Monopolies Commission on non-competition grounds).

17 The Committee on the Financial Aspects of Corporate Governance, Report (London, 1992).

response to the perception that their impartiality is compromised by the lucrative non-audit services they perform for their company clients, in the form of an obligation to disclose non-audit fees.[18] As far as internal monitoring is concerned, the Cadbury committee's recommendations for strengthening the controls chiefly rely on the appointment of more non-executive directors, with, for example, the creation of audit and remuneration committees made up wholly or mainly of non-executives. Not only is compliance voluntary,[19] however, but also these requirements suffer from the fundamental defect that the non-executives remain management appointees. There are no proposals for assigning responsibility in these sensitive areas to truly independent directors, and consideration of whether the absence of an independent monitoring function has adverse consequences for corporate efficiency in general falls outside the committee's brief. Aside from these structural changes, calls for increased involvement by the institutions in the affairs of the companies in which they invest are a regular, though seemingly largely unheeded,[20] feature of the corporate landscape.

Returning to the debate internationally, corporate governance is not only about different ways of improving financial performance. In their study of the operation of boards of directors in eight countries, for example, Demb and Neubauer predict that in the next decade there will be a marked shift in emphasis in the functions performed by the board from the purely economic to those concerned with social welfare more broadly understood.[21] Impending ecological crisis and the perceived inability of governments to solve on their own other problems such as unemployment and the decay of the inner city are, for instance, prompting demands for some form of corporate response. A distinction can be drawn here between strengthening the constraints on the way companies pursue their regular commercial activities, and extending the role of companies into the social sphere.[22] A consideration of the latter will not be undertaken in this chapter,[23] as giving rise to issues that extend beyond

---

18 Companies Act 1989 (Disclosure of Remuneration for Non-Audit Work) Regulations 1991, SI 1991/2128. There has also been a wide-ranging review of accounting standards, under the auspices of the Accounting Standards Board, with a view to reducing the discretion of management to present the accounts in an unduly flattering way.

19 A company must disclose in its annual report those respects in which it has not complied with the Cadbury committee's Code of Best Practice: Stock Exchange Listing Rules (1993), chapter 12.43.

20 See Davies, 'Institutional Investors in the United Kingdom', in Prentice and Holland, Contemporary Issues in Corporate Governance (above, note 13), pp 81-90.

21 Demb and Neubauer, The Corporate Board (above, note 1), chapter 8. See also the same authors, 'Corporate Governance – A Burning Issue', in Sutton (ed), The Legitimate Corporation: Essential Readings in Business Ethics and Corporate Governance (Oxford, 1993), 201.

22 For an elaboration of this distinction, see Simon, Powers, and Gunneman, The Ethical Investor: Universities and Corporate Responsibility (New Haven, 1972), chapter 2; Preston and Post, Private Management and Public Policy: The Principle of Public Responsibility (Eaglewood Cliffs, 1975), pp 4, 95-7.

23 For a discussion of the merits of such 'social activism' see Parkinson, Corporate Power and Responsibility: Issues in the Theory of Company Law (Oxford, 1993), pp 337-44.

the merits of different techniques of corporate control. As to the former, it may not be sufficient simply to allow the changes mentioned by Demb and Neubauer to evolve as a reaction to public opinion or market pressure. Political intervention may also be required if governance mechanisms are to be effective in securing an acceptable level of congruence between company conduct and the interests of groups affected by that conduct and society more generally.

Much of the interest in governance reform in this area arises from perceived weaknesses in regulatory techniques. Thus it is argued that for regulation to be effective it may be necessary to pay attention to company decision-making processes and not just the content of 'external' regulatory rules.[24] Moreover a more satisfactory balancing of affected interests may require a movement beyond conventional regulation: the latter tightens the constraints on profit making but does not seek to amend profit maximisation as the company's defining objective. From this alternative perspective the task in designing governance mechanisms is therefore to make company 'command and control' structures more responsive to the signals transmitted by the regulatory apparatus and, going beyond mere conformity with law, to 'force the organisation to internalise outside conflicts in the decision structure itself in order to take into account the non-economic interests of workers, consumers, and the general public'.[25] None of this means that the economic goal of the large public company ceases to be of central importance. The challenge is rather to construct a governance system that minimises inefficiency but does not at the same time impose on the organisation an unyielding commitment to maximum profits.

Having sketched some of the background to the corporate governance debate, the aim in the next section is to identify more clearly the objectives that governance is intended to serve, or more strictly the corporate objectives that governance is intended to enforce or promote. The result of this enquiry will provide a standard for evaluating exit and voice as governance techniques in 3.4 and 3.5 respectively.

---

24 See eg Stone, *Where the Law Ends: The Social Control of Corporate Behaviour* (New York, 1975), Part IV; Fisse and Braithwaite, *'The Allocation of Responsibility for Corporate Crime: Individualism, Collectivism and Accountability'* (1988) 11 Sydney L Rev 468.

25 Teubner, *'Corporate Fiduciary Duties and Their Beneficiaries: a Functional Approach to the Legal Institutionalisation of Corporate Responsibility'*, in Hopt and Teubner (eds), Corporate Governance and Directors' Liabilities (Berlin, 1985), p 165.

3.3   The objectives of corporate governance

3.3.1   Controlling agency costs

Most of the legal literature on governance (in the Anglo-Saxon economies) views the role of governance exclusively in terms of agency-cost reduction. The expression 'agency costs', which originated in economics[26] but is now used more widely, refers to the loss incurred by the shareholders as a result of management behaviour which deviates from the maximisation of shareholder wealth plus the cost of the mechanisms employed to control such behaviour, for instance the monitoring of management by the members or independent directors. An efficient governance structure is one which minimises the sum of these two costs. It is either explicit in this literature or an implicit assumption, that the proper function of management is the maximisation of shareholder wealth.[27] The existence of agency costs in public companies is often attributed to the separation of ownership and control, though in fact they must be borne in any agency relationship since the interests of principal and agent are unlikely ever entirely to coincide. Accordingly they will be incurred in the corporate context even where the company is subject to majority shareholder control, given the ability of managers to conceal self-serving behaviour. The idea that agency costs are particularly a problem in public companies is nevertheless strongly related to the state of control in the company, since in the absence of owner control, one of the principal mechanisms designed to limit divergent managerial conduct, shareholder supervision, is liable to break down.

The search for effective governance provisions is therefore largely a search for ways of overcoming the consequences of the separation of ownership and control. Not all writers agree, however, that the separation of ownership and control poses a threat to corporate efficiency, or certainly one that requires regulatory intervention by way of governance reform. That the managements of public companies pursue non-profit-maximising goals on a significant scale or otherwise fail to maximise shareholder wealth through 'shirking' (the 'managerialist thesis') depends on three propositions, each of them to a greater or lesser extent controversial. The first is that there has actually been a separation of ownership and control, in effect, that the directors have become self-appointing. As to this, the dominant view since the publication of Berle

---

26 See eg Jensen and Meckling, *'Theory of the Firm: Managerial Behavior, Agency Costs and Ownership Structure'* (1976) 3 J Fin Econ 305.

27 See eg Romano, *'A Cautionary Note on Drawing Lessons from Comparative Corporate Law'* (1993) 102 Yale L J 2021, at 2033, defining governance in terms of 'institutional arrangements that maximise the value of the firm'.

and Means' The Modern Corporation and Private Property[28] in 1932 is, first, that shareholdings in large public companies are typically widely dispersed, and, secondly, that in consequence of shareholders' very small proportionate stakes, it is not economically rational for them to incur the costs, including the costs of obtaining information and co-operating with other members, necessary to exercise their control rights.[29] Some evidence that the latter assumption of rational apathy is borne out in practice is afforded by the tiny proportion of shares voted in general meetings.[30] It is true that shareholders, particularly the institutions, may bring their influence to bear on management in other ways, but this does not appear to occur to an extent that undermines the argument that control is essentially located in management.[31] The second proposition on which the thesis depends is that the weakness of competition in companies' product markets frees managers from the requirement to maximise profits. In a perfectly competitive market profit maximisation is a survival condition, and in such circumstances the absence of shareholder control would not in itself enable managers to pursue non-profit goals. In reality, however, even with the growing internationalisation of markets, in many industries market imperfections permit substantial deviations from profit maximisation without forcing the firm into bankruptcy, though there are of course limits to management discretion imposed by the market.

The final proposition is that the interests of managers diverge significantly from those of shareholders, supplying a motive for managers to exploit their relative freedom from shareholder and competitive constraints. Management utility is often argued to depend on growth rather than profit maximisation,[32]

---

28 Berle and Means, *The Modern Corporation and Private Property* (New York: revised edn 1967).

29 See Easterbrook and Fischel, *The Economic Structure of Corporate Law* (Cambridge: Mass, 1991), pp 66-7. There are some countervailing strands in the literature which argue that the number of companies has been exaggerated in which there is no shareholder or group of shareholders with an interest sufficient to give control (see eg Zeitlin, 'Corporate Ownership and Control: the Large Corporation and the Capitalist Class', (1973-4) 79 Am J Sociology 1073, and for the UK, Nyman and Silberston, 'The Ownership and Control of Industry', (1978) 30 Oxford Economic Papers 74; Cubbin and Leech, 'The Effect of Shareholder Dispersion on the Degree of Control in British Companies: Theory and Measurement', (1983) 93 Econ J 351, or that the proportionate holding necessary for ownership control has been overstated (see Beed, 'The Separation of Ownership from Control', (1966) 1 J Economic Studies 29). These revisionist accounts tend to exaggerate the practical significance of relatively small shareholder stakes, however, and while members undoubtedly possess a degree of constraining power, it seems safe to assume that in the majority of listed companies management enjoys a considerable degree of autonomy: for a convincing exposition of this view, see Herman, *Corporate Control, Corporate Power* (Cambridge, 1981), chapters 2 and 3.

30 For some statistics, see Midgley, *Companies and Their Shareholders - The Uneasy Relationship* (London, 1975), at 37-58; CBI, *Pension Fund Investment Management* (London, 1988), pp 64-6.

31 See note 20 above.

32 See eg Marris, *The Economic Theory of 'Managerial' Capitalism* (London, 1964); Baumol, *Business Behaviour, Value and Growth* (New York, revised edn 1966).

and other suggested managerial characteristics include 'expense preference'[33] and a tendency to 'satisfice'.[34] The evidence on whether managers in management-controlled firms do pursue sub-profit-maximising goals or otherwise fail to maximise shareholder wealth is somewhat inconclusive.[35] To this evidence may be added, however, the recent experience with management buy-outs. The substantial increases in profitability that have been achieved where ownership and control have coalesced as a result of a buy-out is, to put it at its lowest, consistent with the managerialist thesis.[36]

The most important objection to the managerialist position is that it ignores the recent work on the 'secondary' markets which constrain management discretion, namely the market for managers,[37] the capital market, and the market for corporate control.[38] It is the last of these that is widely regarded as having the most significant effect in aligning management and shareholder interests and attention will be confined here to this form of market discipline. The basic idea is that if a company is badly managed this will be reflected in its share price. The company's low market valuation will act as a signal to rival managements that its assets are being under-utilised and that there is a gain to be made by taking control of the company and operating it at a level closer to its true potential. By making an offer to buy the company's shares at a premium above their current market value the existing shareholders are persuaded to exit and control is thereby transferred to the bidder. In this way inefficient managements are 'selected out' by the market, but more importantly the threat that this might happen provides managers with a strong incentive to keep profits, and therefore share price, as high as possible.

The evidence on the efficiency effects of consummated mergers is rather mixed, with studies based on relative accounting profits showing that takeovers have not on balance led to an increase in profitability, while those

---

33   The idea is that managers derive utility from spending the company's funds (eg on luxurious office accommodation) in excess of what is necessary for profit maximisation: see Williamson, *The Economics of Discretionary Behavior: Management Objectives in a Theory of the Firm* (Eaglewood Cliffs, 1964).

34   ie managers do not seek out the best possible outcome but settle for an option that will produce a merely satisfactory return, serving to appease the various interest groups within the organisation: see Simon, '*Theories of Decision-Making Behavior in Economic and Behavioral Sciences*' (1959) 49 Am Econ Rev 253.

35   See the review of a number of studies in Herman, *Corporate Control, Corporate Power* (above, note 29), pp 111-2.

36   See Thompson, Wright, and Robbie, '*Buy-Outs, Divestment, and Leverage: Restructuring Transactions and Corporate Governance*' (1992) Vol 8 No 3 Oxford Review of Economic Policy: Corporate Governance and Corporate Control, pp 65-6.

37   See Fama, '*Agency Problems and the Theory of the Firm*' (1980) 88 J Pol Econ 288.

38   There is an enormous literature. For an early exploration, see Manne, '*Mergers and the Market for Corporate Control*' (1965) 73 J Pol Econ 693. See also Easterbrook and Fischel, *The Economic Structure of Corporate Law* (above, note 29), chapter 7 and Coffee, '*Regulating the Market for Corporate Control: a Critical Assessment of the Tender Offer's Role in Corporate Governance*', (1984) 84 Colum L Rev 1145.

based on share-price movements are a little more positive.[39] The impact of the threat of takeover, which is the point at issue here, is of course less susceptible to systematic analysis, but the market for control is subject to substantial imperfections and it is inevitable that these will place a limit on its effectiveness. Thus in order to obtain control a hostile bidder must bear significant transaction costs in the form of professional and underwriting fees.[40] To make an acquisition worthwhile a raider must be confident of recouping these costs, together with what is likely to be a substantial control premium,[41] through improvements in efficiency or other gains. Poor managements are able to shelter behind these costs and it has been suggested that the price of obtaining control is so high that the disciplinary force of the market is 'likely to be limited to instances of gross managerial failure'.[42] It is certainly easy to see how the market would be too blunt an instrument to regulate the level of management remuneration, for example, since even the most extravagant sums currently paid amount to only a very small proportion of the cost of a successful bid.[43]

A second obstacle to the efficient operation of the market results from problems in the pricing of potential targets. For the market to be effective in transferring control to more efficient managements the company's share price must be an accurate reflection of its prospects under the existing board. If a company is over-priced desirable control transfers will be obstructed, while if it is under-priced control may be acquired by a management that will put the company's assets to a less profitable use. Although the stock market may be efficient in the sense that prices react quickly to new information, there are doubts about the completeness of the information available to the market and the ability of market participants to evaluate technical data and assess business uncertainties. Rather than being determined in accordance with estimations of fundamental value, share prices may thus result from a series of guesses about the likely behaviour of other market actors.[44] Moreover possible bidders also

---

39 See Franks and Harris, '*Shareholder Wealth Effects of UK Takeovers: Implications for Merger Policy*', in Fairburn and Kay, Mergers and Merger Policy (above, note 16), pp 154-5; Romano, '*A Guide to Takeovers: Theory, Evidence and Regulation*', in Hopt and Wymeersch (eds), European Takeovers: Law and Practice (London, 1992), pp 9-10.

40 See Peacock and Bannock, *Corporate Takeovers and the Public Interest* (above, note 15), p 13.

41 Typically 30 per cent of the pre-bid price, but often much more: ibid

42 Coffee, '*Regulating the Market for Corporate Control*' (above, note 38), p 1200.

43 As it has been said, 'excessive managerial remuneration ... is unlikely to be on such a scale as to prompt a hostile bid, but the fact that managers will not do unlimited damage to the company is not to say that they should not face accountability': Davis and Kay, '*Governance, Take-overs, and the Role of the Non-executive Director*', in Bishop and Kay, European Mergers and Merger Policy (above, note 7), p 207.

44 See Herman and Lowenstein, *Efficiency Effects of Hostile Takeovers*, in Coffee, Lowenstein, and Rose-Ackerman, *Knights, Raiders and Targets: The Impact of the Hostile Takeover* (New York, 1988), pp 214-5.

face difficulties in placing an accurate value on a target's assets, particularly in the case of conglomerates, where it may be impossible to divine from consolidated accounts the performance of individual operating units. These problems over information suggest that the scope for calculating the gap between performance and potential is seriously curtailed, adding an element of randomness to the operation of the market and reducing its disciplinary effect.[45]

From the fact that the market for control is imperfect and therefore does not exclude all divergent behaviour it does not follow that some alternative mode of governance would be more effective. It does not even follow that supplementing the market and the other existing governance mechanisms with additional controls would lead to a reduction in agency costs, since the controls themselves are liable to impose costs, such as the direct cost of monitoring and costs flowing from bureaucratic delay, which might exceed the benefits. The significance of the existence of imperfections in the market for control is rather that the question of the adequacy of current governance arrangements, given the separation of ownership and control, remains a live issue and governance reform an area that merits serious enquiry.

Yet even this view can be challenged. Thus, it is argued from the standpoint of the 'nexus of contracts' theory of the company that the position it adopts is methodologically unsound: the notion of a 'separation of ownership and control' implies a pathological condition, carrying with it a presumption, given the failure of markets to supply a complete solution to managerial inefficiency, of a need for some form of regulatory intervention. But the idea that there is a disciplinary gap in the modern public company because the shareholders fail to supervise management in an owner-like way depends on the initial categorisation of the members as owners. From the perspective of contract theory the members are not owners but simply one of several contracting parties supplying a factor of production, in their case capital, to the joint enterprise.[46] Since shareholders, now preponderantly sophisticated financial institutions, would not be willing to provide capital other than on terms that adequately safeguard their interests, it can be assumed that the contractual process will result in the adoption of appropriate governance provisions from which outside intervention can only detract.

---

45 There is evidence furthermore that the pre-bid share-price performance of target companies is not significantly worse than average: see Jenkinson and Mayer, *'The Assessment: Corporate Governance and Corporate Control'*, in Oxford Review of Economic Policy (above, note 36), p 3, but see also Romano, *'A Guide to Takeovers'* (above, note 39), at 9-10. If it is true that badly managed companies are no more at risk than efficient ones, the disciplinary effect of the market seems likely to be diminished, since '[i]f doing well is no protection, the incentive to avoid doing badly is weak': Buxbaum, *'Legitimacy, Economic Theory and Legal Doctrine'* (1984) 45 Ohio State LJ 56, at 531.

46 See Jensen and Meckling, *'Theory of the Firm'* (above, note 26); Fama, *'Agency Problems and the Theory of the Firm'* (above, note 37); Fischel, *'The Corporate Governance Movement'* (1982) 35 Vand L Rev 1259.

This is not the place for a detailed assessment of the nexus of contracts theory of the company, but it may be noted that the term 'contract' tends to be used in a special sense which, while a necessary concession to realism, substantially reduces the persuasiveness of the theory. 'Contract' is not intended to imply that governance provisions have been negotiated by the parties affected but rather means that they are priced and hence responsive to market forces. Managers who offer inadequate governance terms will suffer market penalties and hence they have an incentive to adopt controls that will be attractive to investors. Under the pressure of market forces efficient governance mechanisms will evolve.[47] A problem with this analysis, however, is that governance provisions are not separately priced. As Brudney explains, 'a purchase or sale [of shares] embodies a lump choice, one in which the many components of firm success – or expected success – are combined in the single bundle to be bought or sold. The choice to buy or sell thus represents a complex mixture of satisfactions and dissatisfactions with the components of the bundle'.[48] A firm that is profitable and hence attractive to investors can in other words carry sub-optimal governance provisions without there being serious consequences for share price. And because the constraining effect of markets is reduced by other market imperfections, such impact on share price as weak governance arrangements might produce may be insufficient to overcome the interest of managers in retaining relatively lax controls.[49] It is evident, therefore, that the thesis that governance reform is unnecessary, because effective mechanisms evolve without outside intervention, ultimately rests on an assumption about the efficiency of markets. But it is precisely because markets are imperfect that the possibility that excessive agency costs are tolerated under present arrangements arises in the first place. If markets are unable adequately to control divergent management behaviour they are also unlikely to be able to induce managers to adopt additional mechanisms to control that behaviour. This is again not to establish that there actually is a need for governance reform, but it is clear that if the separation of ownership and control is not a neutral starting point for enquiry, then neither is the nexus of contracts. Whether or not governance reform is necessary can be resolved only through an empirically-based assessment of the likely costs and benefits.

---

47 See Easterbrook and Fischel, *The Economic Structure of Corporate Law* (above, note 29), chapter 1.

48 Brudney, '*Corporate Governance, Agency Costs, and the Rhetoric of Contract*' (1985) 85 Colum L Rev 1403, at 1424. See also Eisenberg, '*The Structure of Corporation Law*' (1989) 89 Colum L Rev 1461, at 1502: 'There is strong evidence that many significant changes in a corporation's constitutive rules do not have a statistically significant effect on the price of the corporation's stock.' Cf Easterbrook and Fischel, *The Economic Structure of Corporate Law* (above, note 29), esp. p 20.

49 See Dallas, '*Two Models of Corporate Governance: Beyond Berle and Means*' (1988) 22 U Mich J L Ref 19, at 46-7.

3.3.2   Promoting social responsibility

Agency-costs literature generally treats the directors as agents exclusively for the shareholders,[50] on the assumption that the function of management is to maximise shareholder wealth.[51] It is not clear that managers are greatly disposed to sacrifice profits for 'socially responsible' purposes in any case,[52] but from this perspective such conduct would amount to an agency cost too, on a par with the expenditure of company funds for managers' personal benefit. The shareholders' favoured position in this scheme is attributed to their rights as owners, or alternatively, in terms of the contract analysis, to their contractual right to the firm's residual income. This concern with shareholder interests need not result only from a belief in the sanctity of private rights, however, but may also reflect a social purpose. Under conditions of perfect competition the maximisation of profit on the part of individual enterprises is conducive to the maximisation of the wealth of society as a whole, and so the role of governance in reducing agency costs becomes one of securing the efficient operation of the economy. It is the rejection of this view that an exclusive concern with profit is the best way of serving the public interest that underlies calls that governance mechanisms should perform a wider range of functions.

In the real world the maximisation of profit does not lead to the maximisation of social wealth because companies operate in imperfect markets. In markets containing monopolistic elements a profit-maximising firm will restrict output to below the socially optimal level. Allocative inefficiency will similarly result from the existence of externalities: because firms do not always bear the full cost of their activities or reap the full benefit they are likely to over – or under – engage in certain behaviour. The consequences include excessive levels of environmental damage, socially wasteful lay-offs and plant closures, and the provision of inadequate workforce training. An objection to profit maximisation therefore is that in reality it fails to meet the objective of social wealth maximisation on which it is premised.

A second objection questions whether wealth maximisation is in any event a goal that is worth pursuing. An analogy is sometimes drawn between the operation of markets and voting, with wealth maximisation seen as the aim of securing maximum compliance with the wishes of the consumer 'electorate'. The analogy is a misleading one, however, for two reasons. First, while

---

50 As a matter of strict law the directors are, of course, agents for the company rather than the members.

51 See further, Newton, *'Agents for the Truly Greedy'*, in Bowie and Freeman, Ethics and Agency Theory: an Introduction (New York, 1992), chapter 5.

52 See Parkinson, *Corporate Power and Responsibility* (above, note 23), pp 281-303.

individual preferences revealed in market transactions may constitute a rational response to the choices offered, because of the restricted nature of the choices available they do not necessarily reflect true preferences. To quote Hirsch's well-known example:

> '*purchase of books at discount stores eventually removes the local bookshop. Yet book buyers can never exercise a choice between cheaper books with no bookshop and dearer books with one. The choice they are offered is between books at cut price and books at full price: naturally, they take the former.*'[53]

The same phenomenon is repeated on a larger scale in relation to technological and organisational change. The introduction of new products and the demise of old ones, the use of novel production and marketing techniques, and changes in the location of economic activity have wide-ranging social consequences. It is not self-evident that the availability of new and better goods and services is always preferred to the preservation of employment patterns and community stability, but the market does not allow a desire for the latter to be communicated. Wealth maximisation is a measure of the satisfaction of individual wants only in so far as they can be expressed through market transactions.

Relatedly, the analogy also breaks down because of considerable inequalities in the distribution of wealth and income: some people simply have more votes than others. As a result of these inequalities the relationship between wealth maximisation and welfare is an even more limited one than just suggested.[54] A company policy which conduces to the maximisation of wealth may therefore nevertheless make a smaller contribution to overall utility than some alternative policy. A separate criticism furthermore is that even if wealth-maximising policies were also utility-maximising ones, the aggregate consequences of actions are not the only basis for moral evaluation. A policy premised on wealth maximisation might require an infringement of the moral or social rights of employees, for example, or neighbours, in a way that would be unacceptable from the perspective of a theory that demands respect for such rights.

To sum up, the argument that companies should be required to maximise their profits because in this way they best serve the public interest is open to

---

53 Hirsch, *Social Limits to Growth* (Cambridge, Mass, 1977), p 40.

54 See eg Veljanovski, '*The New Law-and-Economics: A Research Review*', in Ogus and Veljanovski (eds), Readings in the Economics of Law and Regulation (Oxford, 1984), p 22: 'if wealth is concentrated in the hands of a few rich landowners who buy Rolls Royces and caviar, then allocative efficiency will be consistent with the poor starving and the economy's productive capacity channelled into the manufacture of these luxury items. If wealth were distributed more equitably, less Rolls Royces and caviar and more necessities of life would be produced'. For a broader discussion of the ethical significance of wealth maximisation, see Dworkin, '*Is Wealth a Value?*' (1980) 9 J of Legal Studies 191, and the reply by Posner, *The Economics of Justice* (Cambridge, Mass, 1981), at 107-15.

objection because profit-maximising policies are not always wealth-maximising ones, and even where they are, wealth maximisation may not be the most desirable outcome. The traditional response to these objections is that they can be met, should that seem desirable, without interfering with business goals. Corporate and social interests can be realigned through a variety of regulatory techniques. Firms can, for example, be forced to limit harmful emissions through prohibitions, licensing or taxation. If we are dissatisfied with wealth and income inequalities then the solution lies in redistribution by the state. Similarly employment legislation and welfare and regional policy can cushion the impact of industrial restructuring. None of this requires managers to depart from the goal of profits, but merely to pursue profits subject to the framework of rules society lays down. That managers should do otherwise, as advocates of 'corporate social responsibility' sometimes contend, apart from being unnecessary, is also politically objectionable according to this view. Making decisions other than on the basis of profit involves policy choices that should be made by publicly accountable bodies and not private, unelected managers.[55]

There are obvious attractions to this approach and external regulation will no doubt remain of pre-eminent importance in modifying business conduct, if only because competitive pressure is hostile to profit-sacrificing behaviour that is less than mandatory. The question is whether other techniques can usefully play a supplementary role. The argument that they can points to the limits to what can be achieved through substantive rule-making. The problems, discussed in some detail by Stone, include the inevitable delay in the legal response to new sources of harm, lack of information in the standard-setting process, and difficulties in motivating a positive approach to social objectives through the use of negative sanctions.[56] These limitations suggest a function for law additional to providing the background framework of rules within which companies operate, namely, in Teubner's words, of bringing about an 'external mobilisation of internal self-control resources'.[57]

The role of 'external' forces in this programme also indicates a response to the political objection. An important strand in contemporary social

---

55 See eg Rostow, '*To Whom and for What Ends is Corporate Management Responsible?*', in Mason (ed), *The Corporation in Modern Society* (Cambridge, Mass, 1959), p 46; Friedman, '*The Social Responsibility of Business is to Increase its Profits*', New York Times Magazine 13 September 1970; Engel, '*An Approach to Corporate Social Responsibility*' (1979) 32 Stan L Rev 1. For a fuller catalogue of the objections to profit-sacrificing behaviour, see Davis, '*The Case for and Against Business Assumption of Social Responsibilities*' (1973) 16 Academy of Management Journal 312.

56 Stone, *Where the Law Ends* (above, note 24), chapter 11. See also Teubner, '*Corporate Fiduciary Duties and Their Beneficiaries: A Functional Approach to the Legal Institutionalisation of Corporate Responsibility*', in Hopt and Teubner, Corporate Governance and Directors' Liabilities (above, note 25), p 149.

57 ibid p 160.

responsibility literature adopts an approach which does not ascribe central importance to the moral preferences of managers, with the potential for arbitrary and idiosyncratic behaviour that that implies, but rather to the control of management decisions by increasing the sensitivity of the company to third-party interests.[58] Mechanisms to achieve this result might include disclosure (or otherwise facilitating access to company information), mandatory consultation and negotiation, and the internal representation of interests in decision-making. In addition to it being more likely that this approach, as distinct from a purely voluntaristic one, will actually produce a significant change in company behaviour, the outcome might claim a legitimacy based on interest-group participation that a merely 'moralised' version of management decisions might lack. It should be noted, however, that a change in managers' attitudes is usually also intended: the aim is not, having strengthened outside interests, that management should view the result simply as a revised set of costs. This would be to produce only a grudging, minimalist response, whereas the objective is a more ambitious one of creating the conditions for constructive dialogue. Furthermore, while the emphasis has been placed here on constraining company decisions by bringing outside influence to bear, the idea that managers, even in the absence of external stimulation, should suspend moral judgment as some versions of the political objection seem to imply is surely unattractive. If managers could be persuaded to inform themselves more fully about the consequences of company policies for affected groups, and to pay heed to public policy[59] and the social judgments implicit in the spirit as well as the letter of the law, it would be difficult to portray this as involving a usurpation of political power.

As just considered, the political objection places an emphasis on the role of an expanded discretion in securing socially responsible behaviour that, at least in relation to some conceptions of social responsibility, is inappropriate. It also seriously understates the extent to which managers exercise discretion in the existing situation in which they are required exclusively to pursue profits. The objection implies a bright-line distinction between a discretion-free economic realm, and the realm of politics, that simply does not exist. Given imperfect knowledge of present and future states of the world, selecting the profit-maximising option is largely a matter of speculation. Will the company's long-term profitability be better served by closing down a poorly performing plant or by re-equipping it? Such issues, which are capable

---

58   In addition to Teubner, ibid, see eg Steinmann, 'The Enterprise as a Political System', in Hopt and Teubner, Corporate Governance and Directors' Liabilities (above, note 25), 401; van Luijk, 'A Vision of Business in Europe', in Mahoney and Vallance, Business Ethics in a New Europe (Dordrecht, 1992), 15; Tolmie, 'Corporate Social Responsibility', (1992) 15 UNSW L J 268, esp. at 281.

59   On social responsibility as compliance with public policy, see Preston and Post, Private Management and Public Policy (above, note 22).

of producing massive social consequences, are not somehow automatically resolved by market forces but require the exercise of choice. The modern social responsibility agenda is concerned with creating structures to ensure that factors additional to profit are given due weight when such choices are made.

Necessarily, accepting that companies should be concerned not only with profit entails an expansion of the factors that managers may legitimately take into account in making decisions. For example, a firm committed to long-run profit maximisation ought to pay attention to the environmental consequences of its activities because of the need to comply with existing and future regulation and to avoid profit-threatening adverse publicity, but protecting the environment will have no weight in itself: expenditure will be controlled within a profit constraint. A firm that views environmental quality as an independent good, on the other hand, will make decisions not only about the measures that are required consistent with the profit-maximisation goal, but also whether and to what extent to trade-off compliance with that goal for environmental benefits. The range of decisional criteria is expanded, therefore, but for reasons suggested above, this need not entail an arrogation by management of political power. A separate question is whether when managers have competing responsibilities, the opportunities for shirking and the improper pursuit of self-interest increase. Easterbrook and Fischel put the point thus:

> 'a manager told to serve two masters (a little for the equity holders, a little for the community) has been freed of both and is answerable to neither. Faced with a demand from either group, the manager can appeal to the interests of the other. Agency costs rise and social wealth falls.'[60]

Whether managers do become accountable to no one when they are required to serve multiple objectives depends on the institutional structure within which they operate. We shall return to this issue shortly. As regards the improvement of companies' social performance, corporate governance has two kinds of role to play. First, governance mechanisms can be designed to bring consideration of third-party interests more fully into the company decision-making process. A great deal of work remains to be done in this area if a significant reorientation of management policies is to be achieved. Certainly, it seems premature to claim that business in Europe 'finds itself involved in a process of redefinition, in which it is being transformed into a constitutive element of a newly emerging participative society'.[61] As far as giving third parties a role internal to the company's decision-making structure is concerned, there is now substantial experience in Germany[62] with employee

---

60 Easterbrook and Fischel, *The Economic Structure of Corporate Law* (above, note 29), p 38.

61 van Luijk, '*A Vision of Business in Europe*' (above, note 58), p 23.

62 See further below.

participation at enterprise and workplace levels, but in relation to other groups there is an absence of proposals which are even satisfactory in theory. There is an obvious risk that because of conflicts of interest multi-constituency representation will simply be ineffectual, or alternatively, as Chirelstein has warned, it might produce arbitrary results, since it 'might scant important social interests because these were unrepresented or less well informed or because they lacked the bargaining strength to obtain concessions from the others'.[63] While there is plenty of scope for allowing employees to shape company policy through internal representation, therefore, it seems more likely that developments in relation to other groups will be confined to worthwhile but less than revolutionary efforts to improve the effectiveness of existing techniques of external control. Pressure from product and capital markets, social activists, public opinion, and regulatory bodies might, for example, be strengthened by increasing the transparency of corporate conduct.

The second way in which governance is connected with questions of responsiveness to social interests concerns the effect of the mechanisms designed to promote managerial efficiency on the ability of management to adopt a positive approach to such interests. If the objective is to enable managers to show a concern for the social impact of company activities, including in ways that might entail a sacrifice of profits, it is not desirable that they should be subject to a disciplinary regime that is premised on profit maximisation. Such an arrangement can only inhibit responsiveness to the interests of others and the process of constructive dialogue mentioned above. Acceptance that companies should sometimes depart from the goal of profit maximisation, however, does not imply that we should be any the less concerned about managerial incompetence, shirking, or pursuit of self-interested goals. The crucial question therefore becomes whether it is possible to have a system of governance that is able to discriminate between different types of non-profit-maximising behaviour, so that it is effective in minimising sources of inefficiency, but does not at the same time treat all deviations from the profit goal as agency costs. It is the design of governance arrangements that are tolerant of socially responsible profit-sacrificing conduct in this way, rather than the wider question of the design of arrangements to promote such conduct (accepting that in practice there is a degree of overlap), that will be the primary concern below.

This section has, therefore, identified two inter-connected standards by which governance mechanisms might be judged: how well they are able to secure the efficient operation of the enterprise, and whether in performing that function they are able to differentiate between improper self-serving behaviour on the one hand, and desirable (it has been assumed)

---

63 Chirelstein, 'Corporate Law Reform', in McKie (ed), Social Responsibility and the Business Predicament (Washington, 1974), p 71.

profit-sacrificing socially responsible behaviour on the other. In the next section the market for corporate control, as a disciplinary mechanism that relies on exit, will be assessed in accordance with these standards, and in 3.5 the system of corporate governance in Germany, exemplifying a system in which voice plays a central role, will be reviewed with the same issues in mind.

3.4   Exit: the market for corporate control

3.4.1   The market and corporate efficiency

That there are imperfections in the market for corporate control which limit the effectiveness of the threat of takeover in reducing agency costs has already been noted. This section will take up a separate point, which is that there are alleged to be certain side-effects associated with an active market in control which are damaging to the efficient operation of the economy. The criticisms include that takeovers lead to excessive market concentration[64] and unproductive defensive restructuring,[65] but the charge that will be explored here is that the crucial feature of the market for control as a disciplinary mechanism, that it gives management an incentive to maximise share price, has economically undesirable consequences. In particular, the market for control is said to cause, or exacerbate, an unhealthy preoccupation on the part of management with the company's short-term results.

Market mechanisms operate by reference to changes in price. In principle, a company will become a target if a bidder thinks that its share price has fallen low enough to enable the bidder to make a profit by replacing the company's management team. Existing managements as a result have a strong reason to be concerned with the price at which the company's shares trade. If the realities of the company's performance are accurately reflected in share price then this should work well. There are, however, doubts about the fidelity of the stock market's pricing mechanism, that is to say, it is argued that the factors that determine price differ from the 'fundamentals' of the company's performance. One consequence, already noted, is that inefficient control transfers may take place. The other is that management may respond to the factors that determine price rather than ensure that the company is efficient in a more authentic sense. An explanation of short-termism is that the stock market is systematically biased in favour of short-term rather than longer-term results.

---

64   See Peacock and Bannock, *Corporate Takeovers and the Public Interest* (above, note 15), pp 23-5.

65   eg the company may itself engage in a policy of acquisition to gain the protection associated with large size: see Cosh et al., *Takeovers and Short-termism in the UK* (London, 1990), p 10.

The consequences of an excessively short-term orientation may include under-investment in capital projects, research and development, and training. While limiting expenditure on these items may boost current profit figures, it means that future earnings are likely to be reduced and the performance of the economy as a whole will be weakened. That short-termism is a problem in this country seems fairly clear, at least judged by reference to comparative figures on research and development.[66]The extent to which takeovers contribute to it, however, remains controversial.[67] It may be that other factors, such as ill-designed performance-related pay schemes or divisionalised profit targets, or the mere perception on the part of management that investors are short-sighted, are at least as important.[68] According to orthodox corporate finance theory, giving managers a strong incentive to focus on share price provides no rational ground for them to adopt a short-termist attitude, because 'the share price of any company should reflect the present value of the company's stream of future cash flows'.[69] In other words, the current price of a company's shares should reflect expected future returns. Hence despite the fact that an investment will produce income only in the longer term it should have an immediate positive effect on share price. This being so, it ought to make no difference, even assuming it is true, that institutional investors, who now dominate the market, or more particularly, their investment managers, might themselves exhibit short-termist tendencies. Although fund managers may turn over their holdings frequently they can make a profit only by respectively buying and selling under – and over – priced shares and to be accurate these evaluations must take proper account of the company's long-term prospects.

The objection to this reasoning is that the stock market may not be efficient in the most relevant sense and that shares are mis-priced because the market excessively discounts future returns. While there is substantial evidence to support the thesis that the stock market reacts rapidly to new information, doubt has been cast on its ability accurately to reflect a company's expected future flow of earnings.[70] This has been attributed to difficulties in transferring highly technical and often confidential information

---

66 See Prentice, '*Some Aspects of the Corporate Governance Debate*', in Prentice and Holland, Contemporary Issues in Corporate Governance (above, note 13), p 31.

67 In the USA, the Massachusetts Institute of Technology Commission on Industrial Productivity was of the view that 'the wave of hostile takeovers and leveraged buyouts encourages or enforces an excessive and dangerous overvaluation of short-term profitability': Dertouzos, Lester, and Solow, *Made in America: Regaining the Productive Edge* (Cambridge, Mass, 1989), p 144.

68 See Marsh, *Short-Termism on Trial* (London, 1990), p 52-63.

69 ibid, p 9.

70 See Herman and Lowenstein, '*The Efficiency Effects of Hostile Takeovers*' (above, note 44), pp 214-5; Peacock and Bannock, *Corporate Takeovers and the Public Interest* (above, note 15), pp 45-9.

bearing on the company's future performance to the market,[71] but more fundamentally and less remediably, to the inability of the market to cope with uncertainty. Thus it has been suggested that what 'economists frequently characterise as quantifiable risks are in reality uncertainties of such large and incalculable proportions as to intimidate investors and send them scurrying to the seemingly safer ground of follow-the-leader'.[72] That is, market participants will react disproportionately to tangible indicators such as profit figures because they know that these, rather than more imponderable issues of fundamental value, motivate other participants and hence drive prices.

That the problem of short-termism seems to be confined to economies in which the stock market and the market for control play a dominant role provides some, inconclusive, support for this thesis.[73] It is easy enough to imagine in principle why a system of internal monitoring might be more conducive to investments with a long-term pay-back than is external supervision via the market. Internal monitors potentially have access to the facts about company performance and can have management policy explained to them unconstrained by the needs of confidentiality or for equal treatment of investors. And if a crucial element in short-termism is the inability of the stock market to cope with uncertainty, then internal monitoring would seem to have an important advantage. While the dynamics of the market may force managers to concentrate on tangible profit figures at the expense of investment, mechanisms that rely on voice can allow managers the freedom to take long-term positions even though the returns are not immediately quantifiable. That is, so long as those involved in monitoring have themselves a commitment to long-term growth.[74]

A second argument linking takeovers and short-termism should be mentioned. This is that changes in control disrupt long-term relationships. An active market in control is liable to create insecurity about continued employment and it has been suggested that this is likely to deter employees from engaging in firm-specific training and managers from investing in projects whose pay-back may come only after they have been removed from

71 There is evidence that share prices react favourably to announcements of investment projects: see McConnell and Muscarella, '*Corporate Capital Expenditure Decisions and the Market Value of the Firm*' (1985) 14 J Fin Econ 399 and the material in Marsh, *Short-Termism on Trial* (above, note 68), p 19, nn 18 and 19. This does not establish that the market responds to all developments that increase the present value of the firm, however, or that it responds proportionately.

72 Herman and Lowenstein, '*The Efficiency Effects of Hostile Takeovers*' (above, note 44), p 215.

73 See eg Coffee, '*Liquidity versus Control*' (above, note 14), p 1304, who notes that short-termism is not regarded as an issue in Germany.

74 Coffee, '*Liquidity Versus Control*' (above, note 14), at 1330-2, raises the possibility that institutional monitors, who might remain active traders of shares, would have the effect of making managers highly sensitive to the judgment of the market. In other words, short-termism might result even in the absence of hostile take-overs.

office.[75] It is important to remember here that the motives for takeover are not confined to the replacement of ineffective managements, but include also gaining entry to new markets, increasing market share, and diversification. In a system with few barriers to hostile takeover the threat of removal will not be restricted therefore to managers with a poor record of performance. A significantly greater level of insecurity might as a result be expected than in systems in which inefficient managers are removed by other means. The stultifying effect of instability may not be confined to managers and other employees, but changes in personnel and ownership may also prevent the creation of beneficial long-term relationships with customers and suppliers, because of their damaging effect on trust. The argument that an active takeover market produces conditions that are hostile to these relationships will be considered in a little more detail.

Recent literature has highlighted this variant on the short-termist argument. Mutually beneficial long-term relationships with suppliers and customers, reliant on 'relational' or 'implicit' contracts, are a conspicuous feature of the German, Japanese, and Swedish economies, among others, and have been identified as a major source of competitive advantage.[76] The attraction is that they offer a middle way between organising production internally within a firm on the one hand and on a purely arm's-length basis by way of 'classical' contracts on the other. It is widely accepted that it is rational to conduct an economic activity within an organisation when this can be done at lower cost than transacting in the market.[77] Internalisation gives more control over the way in which the activity is carried on. As Williamson has argued, it also protects the firm's transaction-specific investments from opportunistic behaviour on the part of suppliers or customers.[78] For instance, a motor manufacturer may prefer to make its own components because if its production becomes dependent on the input of a particular supplier that supplier obtains a position of strength which it might exploit to its own advantage. The supplier in turn may be reluctant to commit resources to an activity that is directed exclusively to one customer, for fear of similar opportunistic behaviour. But there comes a point at which further internalisation is no longer justified, and dealing in the market is again more

75   See Franks and Mayer, 'Capital Markets and Corporate Control: a Study of France, Germany and the UK' (1990) 10 Econ Policy 191, at 193-4; Jenkinson and Mayer, 'The Assessment' (above, note 45), p 8; Franks and Mayer, 'European Capital Markets and Corporate Control', in Bishop and Kay, European Mergers (above, note 7), pp 188-91.

76   See Kester, 'Industrial Groups as Systems of Contractual Governance', in Oxford Review of Economic Policy (above, note 36), p 24; Roe, 'Some Differences in Corporate Structure in Germany, Japan, and the United States' (1993) 102 Yale LJ 1927, at 1985-6; Gilson and Roe, 'Understanding the Keiretsu: Overlaps between Corporate Governance and Industrial Organisation' (1993) 102 Yale L J 871.

77   See Coase, 'The Nature of the Firm', (1937) 4 Economica (new series) 386.

78   See Williamson, The Economic Institutions of Capitalism: Firms, Markets, Relational Contracting (New York, 1985).

efficient. For example, as the distance of an activity from the product market increases, competitive pressure is reduced, and the larger and more complex the organisation becomes, the greater is the scope for bureaucratic delay and general loss of control. Changes in firm structure witness a continuous process of adjustment as the boundaries between market and hierarchy are shifted in an attempt to organise production at the lowest possible cost.

A position between integration and autonomy may, however, often prove to be a more satisfactory solution. In certain economies, of which Germany, and particularly Japan, are the most conspicuous examples, it is common for production to be organised within a loose grouping of companies. The groups are informal in the sense that one company does not own the other and hence have complete control over the relevant stage in the production process, but at the same time the participants work co-operatively, each partially internalising the interests of the other members. The parties deal on the basis of relational contracts. These are not contracts in the legal sense of definite, enforceable agreements, but often vague, open-ended, 'gentleman's agreements'. The virtue of relational contracting is that it allows the kind of flexibility that is otherwise associated only with ownership of an activity. If the relationship works well, a supplier will, for example, respond quickly to changes in the quantity of components required or in specification. There is no need for a lengthy process of renegotiation, or for each party to build detailed provisions into the agreement to protect its position. Further, as there is a mutual expectation that the relationship will be long-lasting and that the parties will deal with each other in good faith, there is an encouragement to make transaction-specific investments. In short some of the risks of arm's-length market contracting are removed, and there is therefore greater opportunity to reap the benefits of production in independent, relatively small-scale units. These include, as well as greater exposure to competition (assuming the firm operates in a competitive market), advantages associated with less hierarchical management. As Roe has pointed out, this is desirable in an age of modern, high-technology firms since a flatter authority structure increases speed of response to rapidly changing market conditions, facilitates information sharing, and seems likely to improve motivation by allowing more employees to participate in decision-making.[79]

An active market in control may produce conditions hostile to relational contracting because of the pressure it imposes to keep up profit figures and also the instability that it creates. A crucial point about the relationships discussed in the previous paragraph is that they are in the economic interests of the parties in the long term, but that in the near term they might require profits to be foregone, as where a supplier is required to change the specification of goods at short notice. Short-term sacrifices are made because

---

79 See Roe, *'Some Differences in Corporate Structure'* (above, note 76), at 1986.

the relationship itself brings long-run benefits and is accordingly worth preserving. If this willingness to bear costs in the short term cannot be relied on, however, or if it is anticipated that a party will exploit its position to make short-term gains, it is unlikely that relational contracts will be entered into in the first place. Pressure from the takeover market may create precisely this situation: it may undermine trust. The other point is that because relational contracts bring benefits over the longer term continuing relationships are essential. Ownership changes are likely to disrupt relationships, however, as where, for example, an acquirer integrates the business into its own operation. The high rate of executive turnover associated with hostile acquisitions may also make co-operative relations difficult to establish. As Kester explains, the success of relational contracts founded upon trust 'depends critically on preserving continuity in the identity of specific managers interacting at the trading interface'.[80]

The absence of an active takeover market in the economies in which relational contracting is commonplace is no doubt not the only reason for the viability of that practice. Cross-ownership of shares, for instance, seems of particular importance in stabilising relationships and deterring opportunism. As Roe points out, 'although stockholders without any other relationship to a firm will sometimes renege on an implicit agreement, stockholder-suppliers might honour the agreement because the gains they reap as reneging stockholders would be reduced by the losses they incur as affected suppliers'.[81] Since a number of factors are at work it follows that lowering the incidence of hostile takeovers in the UK would not necessarily bring about a new spirit of co-operativeness, permitting a re-casting of organisational structures on more efficient lines. It would, however, remove one of the obstacles. It should also be conceded that the types of relationship discussed above are not unknown in this country already, an example being that between Marks & Spencer and some of its suppliers. The measure of protection from takeover that its size and profitability give Marks and Spencer is presumably not without significance here.

This section has concentrated on the drawbacks of the market for corporate control in promoting efficiency, but it may also have strengths in comparison with mechanisms based on voice. A consideration of the positive features of the market will be postponed until a system of governance that relies on internal monitoring has been examined in 3.5.

---

80 Kester, *'Industrial Groups'* (above, note 76), p 32.
81 Roe, *'Some Differences in Corporate Structure'* (above, note 76), p 1986. See also Kester, *'Industrial Groups'* (above, note 76), pp 34-5.

3.4.2   The market and social responsibility

Profit-reducing social expenditure can be expected to provoke shareholder exit, driving down share price and rendering the company a potential target. If there were no imperfections in the market for control its operation would prevent managers from engaging in any social action that had a damaging effect on profits. As it is, the market is imperfect, with, as Manne suggests, the boundaries to management discretion being set by the costs that would have to be incurred by a non-altruistic bidder in order to remove the board.[82] This means that in practice managers have some freedom to sacrifice profits in the interests of non-shareholder groups, but they are nevertheless discouraged from so doing by the antagonistic market setting in which they operate.

That the market for control will curtail social expenditure assumes that shareholders' decisions to buy and sell shares are influenced purely by the expected financial return. The behaviour of some shareholders, especially ethical investment bodies, however, may be affected by other factors. Investors who disapprove of the arms trade may refuse to buy shares in companies with military involvements no matter how profitable, or shareholders who are opposed to the company's policy on, say, the promotion of tobacco products in the third world, may dispose of their holdings even though this may be contrary to their financial interests. The market price of a company's shares can therefore be affected by its social record and the market for control might have the effect of bringing management conduct into line with investors' social aspirations, or at least, might provide managers with some latitude to respect ethical considerations. It does not seem likely that these effects will be very significant in practice, however. Ethical investors are only a small proportion of the market;[83] it seems fair to assume that the majority of shareholders are motivated more or less exclusively by financial concerns,[84] in the case of the institutions, this being generally an obligation owed by them to their beneficiaries. The decisions of ethical investors to sell may accordingly be counter-balanced by the decisions of others to buy shares that may now be perceived as cheap.[85] Similarly where ethical bodies retain or acquire shares in a company that announces an ethically attractive but profit-reducing policy, the result is likely to be outweighed by decisions on the part of other shareholders to sell. Notwithstanding the presence of ethical investors the direction of market pressure will accordingly be against the adoption of the policy. The reality is that the market for control is a

---

82   See Manne and Wallich, *The Modern Corporation and Social Responsibility* (Washington, 1972), pp 15-20.

83   See Cooper and Schlegelmilch, *'Key Issues in Ethical Investment'* (1993) 2 Business Ethics: A European Review 213, at 214-5.

84   See eg *'The Case for a Social Audit'* (1973) 1 Social Audit, 4, at 9.

85   See Herman, *Corporate Control, Corporate Power* (above, note 29), p 269.

mechanism that aligns management conduct with shareholder preferences and in the absence of an implausible, widespread transformation in shareholder attitudes its effect will be to suppress social initiatives that do not promise to have at least a neutral impact on profits.

It is not only profit-sacrificing social responsibility that might be inhibited by the market for control, however. If it is true that the market encourages short-termism then this might take the additional form of avoiding expenditure that enhances the company's social impact in a way that would also be beneficial to the company, but only in the long term. For example, a reputation as a caring employer or as a business that is concerned for the environment is likely to bring benefits to the company, yet may be expensive in the short run. Respect for the law even may be eroded under the pressure to boost short-term results. The company might, for instance, engage in bribery to attract business or economise on safety precautions, endangering the well-being of employees, customers, or neighbours. The possible costs resulting from prosecution or reputational damage may be dismissed as problems for another day.

It may be concluded that the market for control creates an inhospitable environment for the expression of corporate social concern where this is likely to have an adverse impact on profits. It is possible, furthermore, that the market may have the effect of suppressing socially beneficial behaviour that is also in the long-term interests of the company. It should be noted finally that in addition to the influence of the threat of takeover on management behaviour, a full evaluation of the social consequences of the market for control would require an examination of the social effects of consummated bids, for example, the employment effects, which remain controversial.[86] This will not be undertaken here.

3.5   Voice: the German example

This section will examine certain features of corporate governance in Germany, the reliance on internal monitoring rather than the market for control being a distinctive characteristic of the German system. Germany has been chosen to illustrate the role of voice in governance because institutional arrangements to facilitate internal monitoring are better developed there than in other European countries or in Japan,[87] the other major economy in which a market in control is conspicuously absent, and because of the influence of German company law on the EC harmonisation programme. Corporate governance in Germany depends not only on its institutions, but also on shareholding practices which differ markedly from those found in this country.

---

86 See Peacock and Bannock, *Corporate Takeovers and the Public Interest* (above, note 15), pp 68-70.

87 For a discussion of governance in Japan (and other G7 countries) see Oxford Analytica, *Board Directors and Corporate Governance* (above, note 4).

Both these aspects need to be discussed in order to gain an adequate impression of the German system of corporate control and the extent to which it is exportable.

3.5.1   The governance system

In Germany the stock market is a much less important source of corporate finance than in the UK. There are fewer than 700 quoted companies, compared with almost 3,000 in Britain,[88] and market capitalisation is just over a third of that in this country.[89] The dependence on debt is correspondingly higher, with one estimate indicating that credit from German banks made up 32 per cent of the balance sheet total of German firms in 1987.[90] As far as equity capital is concerned the banks hold on their own behalf around 5 per cent of the shares of public companies, but their voting power is much greater than this by reason of the bearer shares held by them on deposit for clients. They are required to seek instructions from the beneficial owners of these shares on how they should vote, but this right is rarely exercised. Taking deposited shares into account, all the banks together exercise around 34 per cent of the votes in the largest 100 German companies. In the largest 10 companies they have over 50 per cent of the votes.[91] As between the banks, voting rights are very much concentrated in the hands of the three largest, which hold on average around 45 per cent of the votes in the 32 of the 100 largest companies in Germany, 50 per cent of whose shares are either widely held or controlled by banks. In 15 of these they have a majority.[92]

In addition to the large numbers of shares under bank control, it should also be stressed that companies are major shareholders in each other, the corporate sector holding 42 per cent of all shares in Germany.[93] A feature of these shareholdings and also of the banks' which distinguishes them from those in Britain is that they involve concentrated stakes. Thus of the 200 largest companies in Germany, nearly 90 per cent have at least one member with a holding of in excess of 25 per cent of the equity. In the UK in contrast in two-thirds of the 200 largest companies there is no shareholder with a stake greater than 10 per cent.[94] In this country it is the policy of the institutions,

88   ibid, p 80.

89   Schneider-Lenné, 'Corporate Control in Germany', in Oxford Review of Economic Policy (above, note 36), p 12.

90   See Baums, 'Corporate Governance in Germany: The Role of the Banks', (1992) 40 Am J Comp L 503, at 518 n 59. See also DTI, Barriers to Takeovers in the European Community: A Study by Coopers & Lybrand for the DTI (London, 1989), vol 1, pp 14-5.

91   Cable, 'Capital Market Information and Industrial Performance: The Role of West German Banks', (1985) 95 Econ J 118, at 120.

92   Baums, 'Corporate Governance in Germany' (above, note 90), pp 507-8.

93   Schneider-Lenné, 'Corporate Control in Germany' (above, note 89), p 14.

94   Jenkinson and Mayer, 'The Assessment' (above, note 45), p 6.

which now own something like 70 per cent of the equities of British companies, to spread risk through diversification and as a result they rarely hold as much as 5 per cent of a single company's shares.

German corporate holdings, which are often reciprocal, are not purely investments but also have a strategic purpose. This may be to reinforce a trading relationship and connectedly, to protect the company against takeover. Corporate shareholders differ from typical institutional investors in two important ways. First, because of the large size of their holdings and their long-term character, corporate members are disposed to participate in governance. Their position more nearly approximates to that of a conventional owner and they accordingly behave in a more owner-like way. Secondly, because of the strategic nature of their stakes corporate shareholders are less interested in increased dividends and more in the stability and growth of the companies in which they invest. This is reflected in dividend policy, with many companies having scarcely raised payments in line with earnings.[95]

The banks are active in governance too, taking a major role in providing and servicing members of companies' supervisory boards and in voting in general meetings. Participation in governance is expensive and it is important to know why the banks are prepared to devote considerable resources to it when institutional investors in other countries by and large are not. The banks' main incentive appears to be that participation enables them to protect their interests as major creditors, for example against management's engaging in too risky projects or making excessive distributions to shareholders. While their own beneficial shareholdings might in many cases be too small to provide an adequate incentive, what is important is the combination of the banks' equity and debt claims. The enhancement of their voting power through the shares they hold on deposit then gives them the leverage necessary to exercise real influence.[96]

The German banks, or at least many of them, are not themselves subject to the same governance pressures that they impose on the corporate sector, since in many cases their shares are widely dispersed. The question arises, therefore, whether in the German system the agency problem, rather than being solved, is merely displaced from companies to the banks that monitor them. It has been suggested in reply that the banks in fact do not suffer from organisational slack or other symptoms of poor discipline and that the explanation lies in their high gearing. The banks cannot afford to make mistakes because any indication of instability in the banking system would provoke a rapid regulatory response, threatening bank autonomy.[97]

---

95 See Oxford Analytica, *Board Directors and Corporate Governance* (above, note 4), p 80.

96 See Baums, '*Corporate Governance in Germany*' (above, note 90), pp 516-8. Another possible incentive is to attract or retain companies' financial business. There is, however, evidence to suggest that the bargaining power of large companies prevents exploitation of position by shareholding banks: see Oxford Analytica, *Board Directors and Corporate Governance* (above, note 4), p 86.

97 See Roe, '*Some Differences in Corporate Structure*' (above, note 76), p 1983-4.

The supervisory board is the principal forum for shareholder voice in the German system. Formally the powers of the supervisory and management boards are rigidly separated, the former having no right to interfere in the management process, though the company's constitution may require supervisory board consent to certain fundamental changes. The supervisory board appoints the members of the management board, and has the exclusive right to dismiss them, though only for cause within their contractual period of office (not exceeding 5 years). Management is obliged to make regular reports to the supervisory board on the state of the business, and the latter has the right to any additional information it requires. In companies with more than 2,000 employees, in addition to the shareholder representatives, half the supervisory board members are appointed by the workforce. The board is chaired by a nominee of the shareholders, however, who has a casting vote, thus ensuring that the shareholders will prevail should the two sides fail to agree. The supervisory boards of 75 of Germany's 84 largest companies contain a bank representative, who in many cases is the chairman of the board.[98] The numerical strength of bank nominees should not be exaggerated, however. In 1988 out of a total of 1,496 supervisory board places in the 100 largest companies, banks held 104 to the 385 controlled by other companies. Trade union representatives occupied 187 seats and other employees 542.[99]

The shareholder-elected supervisory board members differ from British non-executive directors in two important ways. First, they do not owe their positions to management, a situation which is surely a pre-condition for effective monitoring. Secondly, not only are the supervisory directors independent of management, but also they are usually representatives of powerful shareholders. The shareholders' role is important here in that they are prepared to assume the function of selecting and supplying a pool of suitably qualified candidates to serve as directors. The close connection between supervisory directors and shareholders ensures as well that the directors have access to valuable support services. Bank nominees, for example, are assisted by the banks' industrial departments which monitor the affairs of major companies. Briefings supplied by the banks arm directors with probing questions, making it more difficult for management to present a selective account of the company's record or prospects. Information available to supervisory directors in turn supplements that obtained by the banks in their capacity as lenders, further facilitating their ability to monitor performance. Since German banks and corporate shareholders generally hold shares on a long-term basis rather than for trading purposes they are not inhibited in gathering information by the fear of insider dealing, which might be a problem for British institutional investors were they to become more actively involved in the affairs of portfolio companies. Finally the inter-relationship

---

98   ibid p 83.
99   Schneider-Lenné, *'Corporate Control in Germany'* (above, note 89), p 19.

between supervisory directors and banks or corporate shareholders promotes continuity in monitoring. Even though personnel may change a new director does not face a lengthy learning process before being able to make an effective contribution.[100]

The connection in Germany between supervisory directors and those who appoint them is worth emphasising. It suggests that there is more to creating an effective system of internal high-level monitoring than merely legislating for a split in management and supervisory functions, as is required, for example, by the draft Fifth Directive.[101] The selection of candidates would need to be taken out of the hands of management altogether and serious consideration would have to be given to how the back-up that is provided to supervisory directors in Germany by their appointers could be emulated in a different shareholding culture. Something more will be said about these issues in the final section.

3.5.2 Governance and corporate efficiency

The facilities for voice may be better developed in Germany than in this country, but how effective is voice compared with exit as a means of limiting agency costs and promoting efficiency more generally? There is no conclusive answer to this question, though inferences can be drawn from the more obvious advantages and disadvantages of the two systems. It seems clear that a supervisory board is capable of having earlier access to more complete information about management performance and future plans than the market. Information can be made available to monitoring directors, as insiders, free of the constraints of commercial confidentiality. Supervisory directors are, furthermore, in a position actively to seek out information rather than being merely passive recipients of data that companies are obliged by regulatory rules to disclose or which managers choose to reveal. At least in theory, therefore, internal monitoring ought to be able to respond more quickly to managerial failure, and be better able to recognise it, than the market. The second factor in favour of internal monitoring is that the removal of unsatisfactory managements by a supervisory board is very substantially cheaper than removal through the takeover mechanism, and thus, other things being equal, ought to be more likely to occur. Indeed it has been suggested

---

100 The fact that German companies are typically faced with a plurality of monitors who are independent not only of management but also of each other seems likely also to have beneficial effects. As Roe explains, the presence of several large shareholders with the incentive to monitor deters shareholder opportunism (eg in relation to obtaining the company's banking business), and leads to power sharing, rather than the exercise of domination over management: 'Some Differences in Corporate Structure' (above, note 76), pp 1980-1.

101 For the latest proposals, see DTI, Amended Proposal for a Fifth Directive on the Harmonisation of Company Law in the European Community: A Consultative Document (London, 1990).

that 'a truly independent board would not tolerate sub-optimal performance by management resulting in a share discount large enough to elicit a takeover at any historically prevailing premium level'.[102]

A possible disadvantage of internal monitoring is that there might be a reluctance to remove management, something that is achieved ruthlessly by the takeover market. Collegiality may make supervisory directors too tolerant of poor performance, or (in the German case) companies with reciprocal shareholdings might engage in mutual protection of management. The theoretical advantages identified above may not, in other words, be realised in practice. The evidence shows that the dismissal of members of the management board in Germany during their contractual term of office is very rare, which seems to support this thesis. It has been established on the other hand that there is a significant level of non-renewal of contracts both of individual managers and entire management boards, and that this is not limited to cases of acute management failure but includes lesser instances of unsatisfactory performance.[103] Supervisory boards do, then, appear actively to engage in attempts to construct effective management teams, though it does not follow that they necessarily make the right decisions, or that they always act quickly enough. An interesting line of argument in this regard draws a distinction between ex post and ex ante management failure. It accepts that internal monitoring has advantages in dealing with the former, but holds that the market for control is better able to correct ex ante failure. Ex post failure exists where in absolute terms or relative to other firms corporate performance has been weak. In the case of ex ante failure the company may have performed acceptably by these standards, but there is a difference in expectations between investors and managers about how the company's assets can most profitably be used for the future.[104] In such a situation an enforced change in ownership, with control of the company shifting to those who anticipate the highest returns, may be the best way of ensuring that assets move to their most efficient use. A system of effecting management or policy changes that depends on internal monitoring may in contrast be less conducive to dynamic efficiency, since it seems likely that there will be a bias towards preserving the status quo in the absence of positive evidence of managerial weakness.

It may be the case therefore that internal monitoring and the market for control have respective advantages in correcting different forms of management failure. It does not necessarily follow, however, that the ideal arrangement involves a combination of the two systems. Thus, the price that has to be paid for the improved dynamic efficiency that arguably results from

102 Coffee, 'Regulating the Market for Corporate Control' (above, note 38), p 1203.
103 See Baums, 'Governance in Germany' (above, note 90), pp 515-6.
104 Franks and Mayer, 'European Capital Markets' (above, note 75), pp 184-91.

ownership changes may, as noted above, be the suppression of wealth-increasing co-operative relations between firms and the parties with whom they contract. More generally it has been suggested that the threat of takeover may be a crucial factor in management short-termism. In any overall assessment the relative significance of these countervailing effects would have to be evaluated. But as has been argued throughout this chapter efficiency is not the only possible standard of appraisal. In this connection American commentators have drawn attention to the fear of the 'community-threatening liquidity' that the market for control brings to investment as an explanation of judicial and legislative efforts to impede the takeover mechanism.[105] It has been suggested that there is a widely-shared belief that takeovers jeopardise 'non-economic values such as loyalty, community, and cultural continuity'. It is inevitable that the forces of competition and innovation that are inherent in market systems will put pressure on these values, but what is objectionable about the market for control is the 'unusual scope and rapidity of the change' that it engenders.[106] This change results not only from consummated takeovers, but also is a consequence of cost-cutting measures and other defensive action designed to reduce the risk of takeover. In short the market for control may promote dynamic efficiency, but as a society we may prefer less efficiency of that kind in order to obtain the benefits of greater social stability and the maintenance of community values.

3.5.3 Governance and social responsibility

From this last perspective there are, therefore, advantages in controlling agency costs through a system of internal monitoring even though, or rather, precisely because, this may result in a slower rate of industrial restructuring than that produced by the market for control. In relation to social issues more generally, governance mechanisms that rely on voice seem inherently capable of giving management room to depart from the exclusive pursuit of shareholder interests in a way that discipline from the takeover market cannot. As against the takeover mechanism, internal monitoring can more readily allow the interests of non-shareholder groups to be taken into account in governance, with the result that standards additional to and competing with profitability may be used to evaluate performance.

The German example offers some experience of interest-group participation in governance, with, for example, lenders, suppliers, and customers being involved (though they owe their position as members of the

---

105 Coffee, *'Liquidity Versus Control'* (above, note 12), at 1334, quoting Simon, *'Contract Versus Politics in Corporation Doctrine'*, in Kairys (ed), The Politics of Law (New York, 1990), p 397.

106 Gordon, *'Corporations, Markets, and Courts'* (1991) 91 Colum L Rev 1931, at 1972.

supervisory board to their status as shareholders). It was noted in 3.4 how this arrangement enables the company to resist demands for short-term profit maximisation and thus facilitates mutually beneficial accommodations of interest. It is less clear how well the interests of unrepresented groups are served, such as consumers, the local community, or society as a whole, for example in having an unpolluted environment. The formal position of management is that it is under a duty to promote the interests of 'the company as a whole', which is taken to include these groups,[107] and there is a general background duty to act in a socially responsible way.[108] The absence of short-termist pressures at least means that the company is less likely to disregard societal interests in favour of a quick return, though the extent to which, if at all, managements go beyond this and trade-off profits in favour of social-welfare considerations is not readily apparent.

The most conspicuous feature of the German system of governance from the social point of view is the presence of employee directors on the supervisory board. It should, however, be noted that board membership is but one facet of co-determination, the functioning of which cannot be understood in isolation from the works councils and the trade union structure.[109] It is widely agreed that co-determination has not subverted the central objectives of the capitalist economy, even in those industries in which there is parity employee representation.[110] Nevertheless it is argued that it has had an important effect in increasing job security by significantly reducing the ability of employers to shed labour.[111] The consequences of co-determination cannot be examined in any further detail here, but it is appropriate to notice that the location of co-determination within a system of governance that relies on internal monitoring rather than the market for control seems likely to have played an important part in its functioning. Streek observes that 'a co-determined manpower policy is costly since it may involve extended delivery terms in times of peak demand, stockbuilding during demand slumps, internalisation of training costs, and even the postponement or modification of investment plans to fit the constraints of the existing manpower structure'.[112] These short-term costs may be compensated in the long run by gains from increased employee co-operation, for example over the introduction of new technology. It is not implausible to suppose that in a market-based system there would be less willingness to incur the short-term costs that are liable to

---

107 See Schneider-Lenné, *'Corporate Control in Germany'* (above, note 89), pp 15-6.

108 See Wedderburn, *'Companies and Employees: Common Law or Social Dimension?'* (1993) 109 LQR 220, at 234.

109 See Streek, *Social Institutions and Economic Performance* (London, 1992), p 137.

110 See Biendenkopt Report: *Co-determination in the Company*, Report of the Committee of Experts trans. O'Neill (Belfast, 1970).

111 Streek, *Social Institutions and Economic Performance* (above, note 109), pp 159-67.

112 ibid at 165.

flow from empowering the workforce and hence that there would be greater friction in the operation of co-determination machinery. This might result not only in fewer benefits for employees, but also in a failure of the business to gain the advantages of a workforce willing to react constructively to the exigencies of rapid market and technological change. It should be noted however that the smooth operation of co-determination may have been assisted not simply by the existence of a system of internal monitoring, but also by the particular make-up of the monitoring board. Thus, it has been argued that the banks' debt holdings represent fixed claims which place them in a position similar to that of employees. At the same time the banks also hold equity, giving them capital-like incentives. The mixed nature of their claims, it has been suggested, makes the banks ideal mediators between shareholder and employee/community interests.[113] This feature is likely to be difficult to duplicate in other national contexts.

3.6   Increasing the role of voice

This final section will briefly consider how voice might be given an increased role in governance in this country. It may be noted that two possible policy objectives flow from the above discussion. One recognises that exit and voice have complementary strengths, and thus argues for the supplementation of exit with increased voice. The other notes that criticism of the exit option is not confined to questioning its effectiveness as a source of management discipline; it is argued in addition that an active market in control has side-effects that are damaging to economic efficiency and which produce other adverse social consequences. If this is so then it needs to be asked whether a substitute for the takeover mechanism, and not just a supplement, should be sought.

One obvious source of increased voice is more active monitoring of company affairs by institutional investors. The respective private costs and benefits, however, suggest that the institutions are unlikely to involve themselves in detailed, continuous monitoring of management,[114] as distinct from seeking to impose their wishes collectively in relation to structural questions[115] or intervening in the event of crisis. But even if shareholders had the necessary incentives, problems over access to management information would obstruct a close monitoring role. The institutions may be reluctant to obtain price-sensitive information lest their ability to trade in shares be inhibited through fear of insider dealing. Furthermore commercial confidentiality may mean that information cannot be made publicly available,

---

113 Oxford Analytica, *Board Directors and Corporate Governance* (above, note 4), p 86.

114 See note 20, above.

115 The NAPF and the ABI have, for example, drawn up guidelines on directors' share incentive schemes and disapplication of pre-emption rights.

while at the same time the need to treat shareholders equally forbids its selective release.

Board-level monitoring, either by independent directors on a single-tier board or by a separate supervisory board offers a more practicable alternative. The institutions, lacking the incentives enjoyed by the German banks flowing from their interests as creditors as well as shareholders, have not, however, shown themselves willing to seek the appointment of their own representatives to the board, and this seems unlikely to change. The present position is therefore that non-executive directors are selected by, and owe their tenure to the support of, management. Stipulations that non-executives be independent in the sense of having no business connection with the company[116] clearly do not go to the root of the problem.

An imaginative possibility is that suggested by Gilson and Kraakman, which recognises that while it may not be rational for institutions with widely dispersed holdings to scrutinise closely the affairs of individual companies, action to improve the operation of the corporate economy as a whole, by reforming the corporate governance system, may bring them net benefits.[117] The suggestion is that the institutions might form an agency to recruit and nominate monitoring directors to particular companies. Since appointments would be taken out of the hands of management, this would enable genuinely independent directors to hold office. A further advantage claimed by Gilson and Kraakman is that their proposal provides an 'analytically satisfying answer to the question of who will monitor the monitors'.[118] This task can be performed by the appointing agency on the institutions' behalf. It would seem to be desirable in practice to have a number of agencies in order to make this a more manageable task and to make it feasible for the agencies to provide support services to independent directors in the manner of the German banks. Of course, there is no reason why implementation of a proposal along these lines need be left to the institutions. In default of institutional action the state could take the initiative in setting up, but not necessarily operating the agencies; the appointment of independent directors could also be made mandatory. The Gilson and Kraakman scheme envisages furthermore the independent directors being in the minority on a unitary board, but they are likely to have a much more significant impact if they have the power to appoint and remove the executive directors. If only for reasons of functional clarity this role might be performed better by a separate supervisory board.[119]

---

116 See the Cadbury Report (above, note 17), para4.12.

117 Gilson and Kraakman, '*Reinventing the Outside Director: An Agenda for Institutional Investors*', (1991) 43 Stan L Rev 863.

118 ibid pp 873-4.

119 See also Davis and Kay, '*Corporate Governance, Take-overs, and the Role of the Non-executive Director*', in Bishop and Kay, European Mergers (above, note 7), pp 208-15, who suggest that independent directors should not be involved in management decisions, since by participating in policy-making they lose the ability to assess management performance objectively. This points to the need for a supervisory board.

These proposals contain the outline of what might be an effective system of internal monitoring, capable in principle of replacing and not merely supplementing the market in control. It is also possible that they could be adapted so that the monitoring function was concerned with social as well as economic performance. It might be part of the role-specification of independent directors that they monitor compliance with legal and regulatory requirements, and with such social policies going beyond these that the company might have developed, giving management some latitude to sacrifice profits in appropriate cases. There is no reason why it need be inevitable, as Easterbrook and Fischel suggest,[120] that departure from the single standard of profitability would render managers unaccountable and hence give them a wide discretion to run the business in their own interests. A broadening of performance criteria need not entail abandoning a concern with economic performance. The usual financial indicators would after all remain; what is needed is for monitors with an appropriate orientation to develop an articulate policy on the circumstances in which departure from the profit goal is permissible. This arrangement would not see the monitoring directors as the prime initiators of corporate responsibility; increasing management responsiveness would depend on the introduction of external stimulants of the kind mentioned earlier or internal participatory mechanisms, such as works councils.[121]

As to the 'appropriate orientation' of the monitoring directors it is not likely that directors elected exclusively by the shareholders would be tolerant of socially responsible behaviour going much beyond that which is consistent with long-term profitability. If it were thought desirable to give management greater scope to give effect to social policy it would seem to be necessary to broaden the electoral base to take in other groups. The employees and the local community, as represented by local government, are obvious possibilities. Directors nominated by Gilson and Kraakman's nominating agency could then be elected by different constituencies, or alternatively each constituency could have a right of veto. The purpose of this arrangement would not be that directors should represent the interests of the different groups, but simply to prevent an exclusively shareholder constituency from selecting out directors who were perceived not to be committed to serving shareholder interests alone. In this way companies might be equipped with a system of governance which is not premised solely on profits, and which is able to promote a better balance between economic and social performance.

---

120 See above.

121 See McCarthy, *The Future of Industrial Democracy*, Fabian Tract No 526 (London, 1988).

Chapter 4

Creditor Interests and Directors' Obligations

Vanessa Finch
London School of Economics and Political Science

A major aspect of the corporate governance debate is the quest for accountability to shareholders. It is important, however, to remember that the debate extends also to the wider responsibilities of companies. Thus it may be queried whether public companies should be concerned solely with the benefit of shareholders. Companies may owe wider duties to creditors, employees or even the community at large. Here my central concern is the position of the creditor.

In recent years the courts and legislatures have shown themselves to be increasingly willing to impose duties on directors in a manner that holds out the prospect of protection for corporate creditors[1] The judges have yet, however, to establish a clarity of approach that lends conviction to such new willingness.

This chapter explores the issue of creditor protection by reviewing the extent to which directors can be said to owe legal duties to creditors; by asking whether the imposition of legal duties upon directors can be expected in practice to offer effective protection for creditors; by noting ways of protecting creditors other than imposing legal duties; and, finally, by examining whether corporate creditors should, in any event, be offered statutory or common law protections against the failings of company directors.

4.1 Do directors owe duties to creditors?

4.1.1 The common law

It can now be said that at common law directors owe certain duties to creditors but the judges have yet to resolve a number of uncertainties – concerning most notably the nature of the duty; to whom it is owed; when it comes into effect and how it is to be enforced.

---

1   See Grantham, *'The Judicial Extension of Directors' Duties to Creditors'* (1991) JBL 1; Sappideen, *'Fiduciary Obligations to Corporate Creditors'* (1991) JBL 365; Finch, *'Directors' Duties Towards Creditors'* (1989) Co Law 23; Riley, *'Directors' Duties And The Interests of Creditors'* (1989) Co Law 87. For an outlook from the continent see Hopt, *'Directors' Duties to Shareholders, Employees and Other Creditors: A View From the Continent'* in *Commercial Aspects of Trusts and Fiduciary Obligations* McKendrick (ed), (Clarendon, 1992), pp 130-31.

4.1.1.1 The nature of the duty

The courts have taken divergent views on the nature of the duty owed by directors to creditors. Is it to be seen as an aspect of the traditional fiduciary duty of directors to act bona fide in the interests of the company,[2] or is it an independent, positive duty owed directly to creditors and founded either on ordinary principles of directors' duty of care or on tortious principles?

In favour of the idea that duties to creditors flow from the traditional fiduciary duty to act in the best interests of the company are a number of English court decisions that build on a series of Commonwealth cases. Notable among the latter is *Walker v Wimborne*[3] in which the Australian High Court spoke of 'directors of a company in discharging their duty to the company (having to) take account of the interest of its shareholders and its creditors' (Mason J). Similarly, in *Nicholson v Permakraft*[4] Cooke J, sitting in the New Zealand Court of Appeal, concluded obiter that directors' duties to the company 'may require them to consider *inter alia* the interests of creditors.'[5] During the 1980s the English courts echoed this approach. In *Lonrho v Shell Petroleum*[6] Diplock LJ indicated that 'best interests of the company' might not be exclusively those of its shareholders 'but may include those of its creditors'. Buckley LJ in *Re Horsley & Weight Ltd*[7] referred to the 'loose' terminology of 'directors owing an indirect duty to creditors not to permit any unlawful reduction of capital to occur' and stated that it was more accurate to say that directors 'owe a duty to the company in this respect'. In both the Court of Appeal and the House of Lords' decisions in *Brady v Brady*[8] it was indicated (by Nourse LJ and Lord Oliver) that directors needed to consider creditors' interests if they were to act in the interests of the company.

Contrasting with this approach are dicta suggesting that there is a direct and specific duty owed to creditors. Thus, in *Winkworth v Edward Baron Developments Co Ltd*[9] Lord Templeman denied the enforcement of a constructive trust in favour of a director on the grounds that it defeated creditors' claims, stating:

---

2   See *Re Smith & Fawcett* [1942] Ch 304.
3   (1976) 50 ALJR 446 at 449. Noted: Barret (1977) 40 MLR 226; Baxt, (1976) 50 ALJ 591.
4   (1985) 1 NZLR 242.
5   ibid at 249. Noted (1985) JBL 413. See also *Kinsela v Russell Kinsela Pty Ltd* (1986) 4 ACLC 215, noted Baxt (1986) 14 ABLR 320.
6   [1980] 1 WLR 627 at 634.
7   [1982] 3 All ER 1045 at 1055-6.
8   (1989) 3 BCC 535 (Court of Appeal); [1988] 2 All ER 617 (HL). See Riley, above, note 1.
9   [1987] 1 All ER 114.

'*A duty is owed by the directors to the company and to the creditors of the company to ensure that the affairs of the company are properly administered and that its property is not dissipated or exploited for the benefit of directors themselves to the prejudice of creditors.*'[10]

His Lordship's distinction between the company and the creditors here implied the notion of a specific duty to the latter. Again in *Hooker Investments Pty Ltd v Email Ltd*[11] Young J felt unable to deny categorically that creditors had no personal cause of action against directors for breach of duty. If such a specific duty is seen as an extension of the director's traditional duty of care, creditors will be offered protection along the lines of that offered to shareholders. In the past such protection might have proved insubstantial but there are now indications of a judicial willingness to reformulate the common law duty along the lines suggested by the wrongful trading provisions of the Insolvency Act 1986[12] so as to apply more objective testing of directorial behaviour. Creditors, accordingly, may look to higher levels of protection than were formerly available.

Conversely, a direct duty to creditors may ground in tort and this was suggested by Cooke J in *Nicholson*[13] in speaking of the 'possibility of an action by a particular creditor against the directors of the company for breach of a particular duty of care arising on ordinary negligence principles'. Against a tortious view, it can be pointed out that a duty to take care, if seen in tortious terms, is at tension with the director's role as risk-taker. The tortious approach does not accord with the judges' traditional view of directors' duties and to expand tortious duties on this new front would sit uneasily with their reluctance to expand the scope of negligence as a tort in other areas – as exemplified in decisions on auditors (*Caparo*[14] and *El Saudi Banque*[15]) and in Lord Templeman's dicta in *China and South Sea Bank v Tan*.[16]

Which of the above approaches should be preferred? A duty owed directly, whether viewed in duty of care or tortious terms, might, on its face, appear attractive to creditors but there are, as discussed below, material conflicts of interests between different types of creditor. Were such duties enforceable by individual creditors there would be a conflict with *pari passu* principles and the collectivist basis of insolvency law. In practice, individualism might lead

---

10   ibid at 1518.

11   (1986) 10 ACLR 443.

12   See Finch, '*Company Directors: Who Cares About Skill And Care?*' (1992) 55 MLR 179, 202-204; '*Directors' Duties: Insolvency And The Unsecured Creditor*' in Clarke (ed), *Current Issues in Insolvency Law* (Stevens 1991) at 96-7. See also *Norman v Theodore Goddard* (1992) BCC 14, 15; *Re D'Jan of London Ltd* (1993) BCC 646, 648. See Insolvency Act 1986 s 214.

13   op cit, note 4, at 250.

14   *Caparo Industries plc v Dickman* (1990) 2 AC 605. See Huxley (1990) 53 MLR 369.

15   (1989) 5 BCC 822; see Huxley, op cit.

16   [1989] 3 All ER 839 at 841.

to a multiplicity of suits, excessive incentives to litigate early and improper pressures being brought on directors to settle particular claims. The alternative is to allow creditors to enforce such duties as a class.[17] Again, there are problems of conflict of interest within such a class. In practice, however, only unsecured creditors[18] would have to rely principally on such an action (secured creditors would be able to rely on their security) and there could, accordingly, be a case for allowing enforcement only by the class of unsecured creditor (see below).

To view duties to creditors as part of the traditional duty to act bona fide in the company's interests may avoid problems of individualism but other difficulties may be encountered. For example: are creditors' interests to be considered independently or merely in so far as they are relevant to the company's interest?[19] Are creditors' interests to be part of a package of claims (ie including those of shareholders and employees[20]), in which case how will directors proceed if these constituent company interests conflict?[21] Is, moreover, directorial consideration of creditors' interests to be assessed subjectively or objectively? The former may be consistent with principle[22] but would pose problems of accountability[23] and the latter could draw the judges into assessments of directors' business decisions.[24] The judges have yet to resolve these questions (see below p 120) but judicial opinion does currently favour viewing the duty as part of the 'interests of the company'. Thus the Federal Court of Australia has recently re-emphasised that the duty to creditors is to be seen as an aspect of the director's duty to the company as a whole.[25]

---

17 See further Finch, *'Directors' Duties: Insolvency And The Unsecured Creditor'* above, note 12, pp 104-105, 109-111.

18 Of course secured creditors may become unsecured creditors to the extent that their security fails on realisation to satisfy their debt.

19 See Finn, *Equity and Commercial Relations* (1987) chapter 5, where Heydon argues that conduct which injures a creditor may also injure the company in that it may force a receiver's appointment, damaging the reputation and life of an otherwise successful company.

20 See s 309(1), Companies Act 1985.

21 See Finch, *'Directors' Duties Towards Creditors'* above, note 1; Riley, above, note 1. For example, if the company is unstable financially it may be in the creditors' interests to wind up (triggering collective enforcement via the liquidator) while the shareholders and directors may prefer to struggle on.

22 See *Re Smith & Fawcett*, above, note 2: the duty is to act bona fide in what the director considers, and not what the court considers, is in the company's interests (per Lord Greene).

23 How could creditors ever be secure in the knowledge that consideration of their interests was ever more than lip service? See Sealy, *'Directors' "Wider Responsibilities" – Problems Conceptual, Practical and Procedural'* (1987) 13 Mon LR 164.

24 See *Carlen v Drury* (1812) 1 Ves & B 154. But see dicta of Temple LJ in *Re Horsley & Weight Ltd*, above, note 7, – 'the directors ought to have known the facts' at 1056; Cooke J in *Nicholson* (above, note 4) at 250, also favouring an objective approach.

25 *Re New World Alliance Pty Ltd* FED No. 332/94, 26 May 1994. See also *Kuwait Asia Bank EU v National Mutual Life Nominees Ltd* [1991] 1 AC 187 for emphasis (by the Privy Council) that prior to insolvency directors owe no direct duties to creditors.

4.1.1.2 To whom is the duty owed?

Judges have tended to speak of creditors as an homogenous group and have failed to state clearly whether directors owe a duty to creditors generally, to individual creditors, or to a class of creditors. Attempts have been made to distinguish the interests of existing creditors from those of future creditors but, even in this endeavour, inconsistent approaches are to be encountered. Thus, in *Nicholson v Permakraft*[26] Cooke J indicated that future creditors might normally be expected to 'take the company as it is' and guard their own interests, whereas in *Winkworth and Edward Baron*[27] Lord Templeman urged that 'duties were owed to creditors present and future to keep its property inviolate and available for the repayment of debts.'

As for existing creditors, these may possess highly conflicting interests: the unsecured trade creditor is in a quite different position from the bank with a floating charge over the company's property.[28] The courts have yet to offer clear guidance to the director who has to choose between such competing interests[29] and an undifferentiated approach may reduce the force of such a duty quite considerably:

> '*Where duties are owed to persons with potentially opposed interests, the duty bifurcates and fragments so that it amounts ultimately to no more than a vague obligation to be fair ... If the law does this it abandons all effective control over the decisionmaker.*'[30]

Distinguishing between classes of creditor seems necessary, if nothing else, for the purposes of rendering duties potentially effective. If unsecured creditors are to be protected, the judges would have to construe the duty as owed to them either individually or as a specific class and the latter approach would be more consistent with the notion of bankruptcy as a collective procedure concerned with *pari passu* distribution according to pre-bankruptcy entitlements.[31] To give unsecured creditors a class action would guide directors rather than leaving them to attempt to be fair 'to all creditors' and

---

26 See above, note 4.

27 See above, note 9. See also *Kinsela*, (above, note 5) (future creditors) at 221; *Jeffree v National Companies & Securities Commission* (1989) 7 ACL 556 (contingent creditors) at 561.

28 See Riley, above, note 1.

29 eg directors may have to choose between using remaining assets to pay off preferential creditors or to continue trading hoping to benefit unsecured creditors. (Of course choosing to trade on for the benefit of unsecured creditors rather than immediately paying preferential debts is not necessarily improper – see *Re C U Fittings Ltd* (1989) 5 BCC 210 (a disqualification case) noted Finch (1990) 53 MLR 385.

30 Sealy (above, note 23) at 175.

31 See Jackson, *Logics and Limits of Bankruptcy Law* (1986); '*Bankruptcy, Non-bankruptcy Entitlements And The Creditors' Bargain*' (1982) 91 Yale LJ 857.

would not seem prejudicial to secured creditors who would be able to realise their security or appoint a receiver to act on their behalf.[32]

A further issue the courts have yet to resolve concerns the exclusivity of the attention that directors should give to creditor interests when those interests fall to be considered.[33] Some authorities come close to making creditor interests an exclusive focus. Thus, in *Brady v Brady*[34] Nourse LJ, in the Court of Appeal, indicated that post-insolvency (or doubtful insolvency) the interests of the company 'are in reality the interest of existing creditors alone'.[35] This implies that the directors have a duty to pursue the advantage of creditors – an approach consistent with the comments of Street CJ in *Kinsela*[36] to the effect that in an insolvent company it is the creditors' and not the shareholders' assets that are under the management of the directors.[37]

A contrasting approach allows directors to act post-insolvency in the interests of the company as a whole, provided that actions do not prejudice creditors. Thus, in *Nicholson*,[38] Cooke J stated: 'given good faith and a decision which could reasonably be regarded as in the interests of the company as a whole and not likely to cause loss to creditors, the matter was one for the directors, not the court.'[39] This view was echoed in Lord Templeman's judgment in *Winkworth*[40] Other judges, moreover, have made it clear that, even post-insolvency, creditors interests may not have primacy. Thus, in *Re Welfab Engineers Ltd*,[41] Hoffmann J considered the position where a company was insolvent but had not been placed in the hands of a receiver. He stated that although the directors were not, at such a stage, entitled to act in a manner leaving the creditors in a worse position than on a liquidation, they had not failed in their duty to the company when they had borne in mind the effect on employees of different courses of action. As has been pointed out: 'the importance of *Welfab* lies in Hoffmann J's affirmation that, while they should not be exploited, so long as creditors leave the company in the directors' hands, the company will not be run primarily for their benefit'[42]

A way to resolve tensions in the above caselaw is to read dicta in *Brady* and *Kinsela* as being concerned with the reorientation of focus from

---

32   See further Finch, above, note 17, p 105.

33   See generally Grantham, *'Directors' Duties And Insolvent Companies'* (1991) 54 MLR 576.

34   (1989) 3 BCC 535.

35   ibid, p 552. This point appears unaffected by the House of Lords decision in *Brady* and indeed in impliedly accepted by Lord Oliver – see [1988] 2 All ER 617, 632.

36   See above, note 5.

37   ibid at 730.

38   See above, note 4.

39   ibid at 253.

40   See above, note 9, at 118.

41   (1990) BCC 600.

42   See Grantham, above, note 33, p 578.

shareholder to creditor interests that occurs around the point of insolvency rather than being concerned to address the issue of exclusivity of interest. A way forward would be for the judges to endorse *Welfab*, stressing that creditor interests fall to be considered on insolvency (or doubtful insolvency) but that such interests do not have to be the exclusive concerns of directors. Just as directors are entitled to look beyond shareholder interests before insolvency[43] they should be given a degree of flexibility in relation to the interests of the creditors, who on insolvency, have stepped into the shoes of the shareholders.

4.1.1.3 When does the duty arise?

Even if it is accepted that the duty to creditors flows from the traditional duty to act in the company's interests, the courts have been tentative in stating when creditors' interests fall to be considered by directors as part of those company interests. Three positions on the issue can be distinguished:

(i) When a company becomes insolvent the interests of creditors are company interests.

(ii) Creditors' interests transform into company interests as the company approaches insolvency or when insolvency is threatened.

(iii) The interests of the company include those of creditors and directors should bear in mind creditor interests at all times.

The judges have hovered, sometimes uneasily, between these three positions. In support of position (i) is the *West Mercia*[44] decision of the Court of Appeal in which a director effected a fraudulent preference and was found to be guilty of a breach of duty (the director had, for his own purposes, made a transfer between accounts in disregard of the interests of the general creditors of the insolvent company). *West Mercia* indicated that where a company is insolvent, a director's duty to act in the best interests of the company includes a duty to protect the interests of the company's creditors. Dillon LJ noted with approval Street CJ's statement in the Australian case of *Kinsela v Russell Kinsela Property Ltd*:[45]

> '*In a solvent company the proprietary interests of the shareholders entitle them as a general body to be regarded as the company when questions of the duty of directors arise ... But where a company is insolvent the interests of creditors intrude. They become prospectively entitled, through the mechanism of liquidation, to displace the power of the shareholders and directors to deal with the company's assets ...*'

---

43   See Sealy, (above, note 23); s 309 Companies Act 1985.
44   *West Mercia Safetywear Ltd v Dodd* (1988) 4 BCC 30.
45   See above, note 5, at 401.

Whether insolvency is a precondition of creditor interests being subsumed within company interests is, however, a matter not beyond doubt. A number of cases extend the principle to incipient insolvency or even threatened insolvency. Thus the Court of Appeal in *Re Horsley & Weight Ltd*[46] stated that insolvency, or near insolvency, was a precondition and a similar stance appeared to be taken by the New Zealand Court of Appeal in *Nicholson v Permakraft*.[47] In Nicholson the company was solvent at the relevant time but Cooke J considered situations in which directors should consider creditors' interests. These included circumstances of insolvency or near insolvency or doubtful insolvency or if the 'contemplated payment or other course of action could jeopardise its solvency'. Such reasoning may accord to some extent with position (ii) and the idea that creditor interests fall to be considered in so far as insolvency looms. This is echoed in, for example, Nourse LJ's dicta in *Brady* and *Brady*[48] where His Lordship considered the meaning of 'given in good faith in the interest of the company' in s 153 Companies Act 1985[49] and stated that where the company is insolvent or even doubtfully solvent, the interests of the company were in reality the interests of the existing creditors alone.

Certain cases go further and adopt a stance close to position (iii) by suggesting that insolvency *per se* is no precondition to consideration of creditors' interests. In the High Court of Australia in *Walker v Wimborne*[50] Mason J indicated that creditors' interests should be considered even before insolvency because 'those interests may be prejudiced by the movement of funds between companies in the event that the companies become insolvent'. Thus, creditors' interests could always be relevant given the theoretical possibility of future insolvency.[51] *Nicholson v Permakraft*[52] is not far short of this position in referring to circumstances in which a contemplated payment or other course of action might jeopardise solvency. There are dicta, moreover, in two House of Lords decisions in which the issue of insolvency is not even referred to. In the *Lonrho* case[53] Lord Diplock, when speaking of the best interests of the company not necessarily being those of shareholders alone but

---

46   See above, note 7.

47   See above, note 4. See also *Grove v Flavel* (1986) 4 ACLC 654 where the court rejected the argument that there was a general duty owed by directors to protect creditors' interests irrespective of the company's financial position.

48   See above, note 8, at 552.

49   Nourse LJ assumed that the words in s 153(1)(b) Companies Act 1985 had the same meaning in that context as when considering directors' fiduciary duties.

50   See above, note 3.

51   See Barrett (1977) 40 MLR 229.

52   See above, note 4.

53   See above, note 6.

possibly including those of creditors, made no mention of solvency or insolvency. Neither did Lord Templeman in *Winkworth v Edward Baron*[54] when he was speaking of the duty apparently directly owed to creditors.

The courts have thus adopted a variety of positions on directors' duties to creditors and, although *West Mercia*[55] seeks to clarify the common law in pointing to an intrusion of creditors' interests on insolvency or prospective insolvency, a good deal of further clarification is required. *West Mercia* did not explain in a satisfactory manner how to identify the point at which a prospective insolvency becomes real enough to call for the reorientation of directors' attitudes towards creditors. *West Mercia*, moreover, does not address the issue of how the director's state of appreciation of the company's solvency is to be judged. Is it to be ascertained objectively or subjectively?

On the 'prospect of insolvency' issue, the Cork Committee[56] acknowledged that although insolvency arises at the moment when debts have not been met as they fall due, 'the moment is often difficult to pinpoint precisely.' The English courts, nevertheless, would not be without guidance in seeking to devise a test. Cooke J in *Nicholson* suggested that, although balance sheet solvency and the ability to pay capital dividends were important in assessing any actions taken, nevertheless:

> '*as a matter of business ethics it is proper for directors to consider also whether what they will do will prejudice the company's practical ability to discharge promptly debts owed to current and likely continuing trade creditors ... because if the company's financial position is precarious the futures of such suppliers may be so linked with those of the company as to bring them within the reasonable scope of the director's duty.*'[57]

An alternative approach to definition might be derived from the statutory criteria of the Insolvency Act 1986 – for example the definition of inability to pay debts found in s 123(2) which, *inter alia*, adopts the liabilities test and the strict balance sheet approach of total assets exceeding total liabilities 'taking into account contingent and prospective liabilities'. Section 123(1)(e), on the other hand, provides a cash flow test by which a company is deemed unable to pay its debts 'if it is proved to the satisfaction of the court that the company is unable to pay its debts as they fall due'.[58]

---

54 See above, note 9.
55 See above, note 44.
56 *The Report of the Review Committee on Insolvency Law and Practice* (Cmnd 8558) (1982) (hereafter Cork).
57 See above, note 4, at 249.
58 See further Goode, *Principles of Corporate Insolvency Law* (1990) chapter III.

As for the test to be applied regarding the director's state of appreciation of the company's solvency, different approaches, again, might be taken. Templeman LJ suggested in *Horsley & Weight* an objective test in stating that if expenditure threatens the existence of the company 'the directors ought to have known the facts'.[59] In contrast, it can be argued that the subjective approach is appropriate in all cases involving the general fiduciary duty of directors to act in good faith in the interest of the company. Thus Nourse LJ said in *Brady* that the duty to act in good faith is what the director considers, and not what the court considers, is in the company's interest. This approach is supported in so far as *West Mercia* treats consideration of creditors' interests as just another aspect of the interests of the company test.

One reason for moving to greater objectivity is the argument that creditors' interests warrant greater protection than can be offered by a subjective test. After all, it can be contended, if creditors' interests only enter the scene when solvency is at issue and if creditors are disadvantaged *vis-à-vis* shareholders in so far as they are likely to have less information as to the company's solvency, then a director's appreciation of whether a transaction will prejudice the creditors further should be measured against an objective benchmark. Such reasoning favours approach adopted in the wrongful trading provisions of s 214 of the Insolvency Act 1986.[60] According to this approach directors should be expected to exhibit the same degree of appreciation of their company's viability as would reasonably be expected of a diligent person exercising their functions in the company. A standard of performance is demanded, accordingly, which is consistent with the idea of a level of minimum competence.[61] Directors, on this view, would be bound to consider creditors' interests the moment they know or ought to have concluded that the company's solvency is at the very least doubtful.

To summarise, then, the judges have failed to state clearly when the duty arises or what state of mind or knowledge renders the director potentially liable. Directors seeking guidance on the former issue have to rely on a confusion of *dicta* and statutory tests. Judges may inevitably have to exercise discretion in assessing the point of doubtful solvency in particular contexts but more coherent structuring of that discretion is necessary if directors and creditors are to know where they stand. On the second issue – the director's appreciation of corporate viability – a clear choice should be made in favour of objective assessments.

---

59 See above, note 7, at 1056.

60 See s 214(4)(a).

61 This might be employed in relation to the general duty of skill and care – see Finch; *'Company Directors: Who Cares About Skill And Care?'* above, note 12.

4.1.1.4 How is the duty to be enforced?

The judges have tended to see directors' duties to creditors in exhortatory terms and so have failed to grasp the enforcement nettle. If creditor interests derive from general duties owed to the company then breaches should properly be dealt with by the company as contemplated in *Nicholson*[62] and *Walker v Wimborne*[63] The problem, however, is that enforcement of the duty is likely to be difficult before the company goes into administration, receivership or liquidation since creditors cannot rely on the existing board or the shareholders to complain about the ill treatment of creditor interests. On liquidation, the possibility arises of a misfeasance action under s 212 of the Insolvency Act 1986, which allows proceedings where a director has been guilty of 'any misfeasance or breach of any fiduciary or other duty in relation to the company'. Duties to creditors may thus arise at the stage of doubtful solvency but creditors per se are given a right of action only on winding up.

Such enforcement may, of course, assist unsecured creditors little since funds will go to company assets and fall within the scope of any floating charge.[64] (Such a creditor might, however, buy the liquidator's right of action, which is assignable, and thus would keep the proceeds of a successful action.) As for secured creditors, the receiver, as the company's agent,[65] might assist by bringing an action against a director for a breach. Some solace for creditors can be derived from case law which now indicates that shareholders cannot extinguish the duty to creditors by ratifying directorial breaches of it.[66] Whether reforms might be introduced to facilitate creditor enforcement of directorial duties is an issue to be returned to below in 4.2.

4.1.2   Statute law

English insolvency legislation offers a number of protections for creditors. It should be noted at the outset, however, that protection is not given in form of duties directly owed to creditors by directors – rather the courts may be called upon by parties other than creditors, for example liquidators, to make assessments of the impact on creditors of directorial conduct. Such conduct is

---

62   See above, note 4, at 250.

63   See above, note 3, at 449.

64   See *Anglo-Austrian Printing & Publishing Union* (1985) 2 Ch 891 (damages received from directors for misfeasance are available to the chargeholder).

65   See *Gomba Holdings Ltd v Homan* (1986) 1 WLR 1301; s 44(1)(a) Insolvency Act 1986.

66   See *Kinsela* above, note 5, at 223; *Re Horsley & Weight Ltd* above, note 7, judgments of Cumming-Bruce and Templeman LJJ; *Nicholson v Permakraft*, above, note 4, at 460; *Re New World Alliance Pty Ltd*, above, note 25, at 65 (Gummow J).

generally judged in the context of liquidation once the company's insolvency has been determined.[67]

The Cork Committee proposed that directors be made liable for the debts of a company where the company incurs liabilities with no reasonable prospect of meeting them.[68] The objective of this proposal was to encourage directors to take immediate steps on viewing their company as insolvent to place it in receivership, administration or liquidation.[69] Section 214 of the 1986 Insolvency Act (the 'wrongful trading' provision) seeks to give effect to the proposal. This section imposes a duty on directors of companies which are subsequently wound up to take every step (s 214(3)) with a view to minimising the potential loss to company creditors once they know, or ought to know, that there is no reasonable prospect of the company avoiding insolvent liquidation (defined in s 214(6) in balance sheet terms). Thus there is a movement away from the purely subjective test of skill and care applied to directors in the common law cases such as *Re City Equitable Fire Insurance Co*.[70] Under s 214 a director is judged not only by the knowledge, skill and experience which he actually has (s 214(4)(b)) but also by 'the general knowledge, skill and experience that may reasonably be expected of a person carrying out the same functions ...' (s 214(4)(a)). A director can therefore, under this limb, be judged by the standards of reasonableness even though he may be well below those standards himself.[71]

The court may, under s 214(1), order anyone liable to make such contribution to the company's assets as it thinks proper. In exercising its jurisdiction the court will determine the extent to which the director's conduct has caused loss to the creditors. In *Re Produce Marketing*[72] the court held that its jurisdiction under s 214 was 'primarily compensatory' and Knox J considered the following factors to be relevant in determining directorial contributions:[73] the ignoring by directors of auditors' warnings concerning the dangers of continuing to trade; the fact that any contribution would go, in the first place, to meeting the bank's secured claims and so would reduce the liability of the director on his guarantee to the bank; and the need to act in a way that would benefit unsecured creditors, bearing in mind that the bank, as a secured creditor, would be the first to benefit from the contribution.

---

67   See Prentice, 'Effect of Insolvency on Pre-Liquidation Transactions' in Pettet (ed) *Company Law in Change* (1987).

68   Cork, above, note 56, para 1783.

69   ibid, para 1786.

70   (1925) Ch 407.

71   Regard can be had to the particular company and its business – see *Re Produce Marketing Consortium* (1989) BCLC 520. See Prentice, 'Creditors' Interests and Directors' Duties' (10) OJLS 215.

72   ibid.

73   ibid at 554.

In s 214 we can see that the primary duty of directors of ailing companies is to cut the potential loss to their creditors. This will not, however, always be achieved by directors putting their company into voluntary liquidation or administration. If directors reasonably believe that creditors may fare worse in a premature sale of assets, the directors' duty under s 214 may well include a duty to attempt a company rescue or stay at the helm.

Section 213 of the 1986 Insolvency Act also bears on directors' duties to creditors. This provision, relating to fraudulent trading, is aimed at preventing directors from carrying on a business with an intend to defraud creditors or for any fraudulent purpose. It is recognised[74] now, however, that the aim of the fraudulent trading provisions (to discourage directors from carrying on business at the expense of creditors) is severely restricted by the requirement of dishonest intent[75] and the courts' insistence on strict standards of pleading and proof.

Other provisions of the 1986 Insolvency Act are also aimed at preventing directors from diminishing the company's assets in ways that prejudice the company's general creditors. These 'avoidance provisions' attempt to preserve the corporate pool of assets and can be seen as a positive side of the *pari passu* principle from the unsecured creditors' point of view.[76] Thus there are the new provisions dealing with the setting aside of preferences and transactions at undervalue.

A 'preference' under s 239 Insolvency Act 1986 occurs when a company does anything which puts a creditor in a better position than he would have occupied on the insolvent liquidation of the company and the company in carrying out the act was 'influenced by a desire' to put the creditor in a more favourable position. Unless the transaction involved a 'connected person'[77] it can only be challenged by an administrator or liquidator if it is within 6 months of 'the onset of insolvency'. Accepting that 'the company' in practice means the directors,[78] unsecured creditors can interpret s 239 as a means of ensuring equal treatment by directors.

Transactions at undervalue per s 238 Insolvency Act 1986 can also be seen as being concerned with protecting creditors against directorial misbehaviour and, indeed, many transactions falling within s 238 will also be vulnerable as

---

74 See Cork (above, note 56) Ch 44, p 398.
75 Eg 'actual dishonesty ... real moral blame' per Maugham J in *Patrick v Legon Ltd* (1933) Ch 787. See also *Re William Leitch Bros Ltd* (1932) 2 Ch 71; *Re L Todd (Swanscombe) Ltd* (1990) BCC 125.
76 See Jackson, *'Avoiding Powers in Bankruptcy'* (1984) 36 Stan L Rev 725; Goode, (above, note 58) p 61.
77 Insolvency Act 1986, s 239(6); s 240(1)(a) Insolvency Act 1986 – two years.
78 See Art 70, Table A (Companies Tables A-F) Regulations 1985, s 1.805. See *Breckland Group Holdings Ltd v London & Suffolk Properties Ltd* (1988) 4 BCC 542, noted Wedderburn, (1989) 52 MLR 401.

preferences under s 239. The transactions at undervalue section protects creditors by precluding third parties from benefiting at their expense by receiving, in a two-year period prior to the company's insolvency, the company's assets for no or an inadequate consideration. For the transaction to be saved, the court will have to be convinced that the transaction was a genuine one entered into in good faith for the purposes of the company's business and that, at the time, there were reasonable grounds to believe that the transaction would benefit the company (s 238(5)).[79] From the creditors point of view, the advantage of this new power is that now the question of balancing the interests of unpaid creditors against those who have received gratuitous dispositions from the company is considered directly rather than indirectly as formerly under the ultra vires doctrine or breach of directors' fiduciary duty.[80]

An alternative provision, focusing on the same definition of transactions at undervalue, could provide direct assistance for creditors. That is the revised s 423 of the 1986 Insolvency Act relating to undervalue transactions entered into by the company (directors) for the purpose of putting the assets beyond the reach of a claimant or otherwise prejudicing a claimant (s 423(3)). This section is of potential interest to individual creditors in that there is no time limit applicable, no prerequisite of winding up or administration and the courts have the power under s 423(2) to order reimbursement to the particular party prejudiced.

The avoidance provisions in the 1986 Act are not the only statutory means of ensuring certain directorial standards towards creditors. Both the Cork Report[81] and the Government's subsequent White Paper[82] suggested that creditors, particularly unsecured creditors, might be protected more effectively by extending and tightening up not merely provisions on directors' personal liability[83] but also on their disqualification. Now there are wider grounds of disqualifying delinquent directors under the Company Directors Disqualification Act 1986. For example, directors' duties to file returns and accounts and give notices under the companies legislation have been backed

---

79   See further (re statutory defence of s 238(5)) Goode, (above, note 58). For the view that the 'benefit of the company' in s 238(5) Insolvency Act 1986 means effectively the 'company's existing creditors', see Berg (1988) JBL 65.

80   Since 1603 (1 Jac 1 C 15, 55) trustees in bankruptcy have been able to recover gratuitous dispositions whereas liquidators had to use company law doctrines with unpredictable results. Cork recommended with some hesitancy liquidators being given the power to challenge transactions at undervalue. Of course the capital maintenance doctrine in company law is designed for creditor protection – see Jessell MR in *Re Exchange Banking Co., Flitcroft's Case* (1882) 21 Ch D 519, pp 533-534. Note also the policy of capital integrity proclaimed in preamble to EEC Second Directive.

81   See above, note 56, para 1743.

82   *A Revised Framework for Insolvency Law* (Cmnd 9175).

83   See eg s 214 Insolvency Act 1986 and previous discussion.

up with discretionary disqualification for persistent failure[84] and s 6 of the Company Directors Disqualification Act 1986 *requires* disqualification on the application of the Secretary of State in the case of a director whose company has become insolvent and whose conduct makes him unfit to manage. In deciding whether a director is unfit, the court is referred to a wide range of matters for consideration in Schedule 1, Parts 1 and 2. These include, where the company has become insolvent: the director's part in the causes of the insolvency; and his role in the company's failure to supply goods and services which have been paid for in whole or in part.[85] Reference to the latter role reflects the Cork Committee's concern for the consumer unsecured creditor. Such a creditor now knows the courts can use disqualification to deter directors from using consumer prepayments to bolster a company's failing cash flow. The Schedule 1 guidelines, moreover, are not exhaustive of directors' obligations. The court has power to condemn any conduct as evidencing unfitness – potential surely for incompetent directors to be taken to task and for taking into account such relevant considerations as the under capitalisation of a company or the director's possession of sufficient financial information and feasibility studies to enable effective policy or decision-making.[86]

Section 6 provides the legislative basis upon which a willing judiciary might secure an upgrading of directorial duties particularly to the unsecured creditor. Any expectations that s 6 would lead to an upgrading of the duties of skill and care still remain to be satisfied, however, as the judges have, at least to date, seemed unwilling to disqualify directors for anything short of 'gross' or 'total' incompetence[87] or negligence 'in a very marked degree.'[88]

4.2   Do directors' duties protect creditors?

In questioning whether directors' duties offer effective protections for creditors it is necessary to bear in mind once more the danger of seeing creditors as an homogenous group and to note the variety of conflicting interests that is to be found in the body of existing creditors as well as between present and future creditors. Directors, it should be emphasised, often have to make difficult decisions as to which pattern of interests is to be favoured by a contemplated course of action – whether, for instance, to use remaining assets

---

84   Company Directors Disqualification Act 1986, s 3(1).

85   Paras 6 and 7, Part II, Sched 1, Insolvency Act 1986.

86   See DTI *Guidance Notes to Office Holders*, March 1986.

87   Eg see *Re Lo-Line Electric* (1988) BCCL 698; *Re Churchill Hotel (Plymouth) Ltd* (1988) BCCL 34). See Finch, (above, note 29) and *'Disqualifying Directors: Issues of Rights, Privileges and Employment'* (1933) ILJ 35; Drake, (1989) JBL 474.

88   See *Re Sevenoaks Stationers (Retail) Ltd* (1990) BCC 765.

to pay off preferential creditors or to prejudice these by continuing to trade in the hope of benefiting unsecured creditors. Duties that are effective in the hands of one set of creditors may, accordingly, operate to the detriment of other creditor classes.

It is also necessary to be clear concerning the nature of effective creditor protection. Here I argue on the basis that effective protection has compensatory and preventative aspects – it should allow creditors not merely to obtain compensation when they suffer as a result of unacceptable actions by directors but also should enable them to take reasonable steps to prevent directors from taking such actions.

Directors' duties might protect creditors if they could be enforced and if they produced results. Are creditors, however, in a good position to enforce duties against directors? As has been argued elsewhere[89] effective enforcement demands: an ability to acquire and use information; expertise or understanding of the relevant activity; a commitment to act; and an ability to bring pressure or sanctions to bear on the party to be controlled.

On the first issue, creditors may have not inconsiderable access to information. The disclosure rules operating throughout company legislation generally reflect the principle that these operate for creditors' as well as shareholders' benefit. Creditors, like shareholders, can obtain information on the financial state of the company at the Company Registry in the form of copies of certain classes of resolution, annual accounts and directors' and auditors' reports. Copies of these documents have, moreover, to be sent to 'all debenture holders'. When a company enters or nears insolvency further sources of information arise. Receivers appointed by debenture holders must be furnished with a statement of affairs from the company's officers and must report in turn to all creditors and creditors meetings.[90] Where voluntary arrangements are made in order to conclude an agreement with creditors, the directors' proposal and statement of the company's affairs will become available to creditors[91] and when administrators or liquidators act they will provide creditors meetings with a body of information.

Data concerning directorial behaviour may also flow from the creation of contractual rights to information. The terms of debentures may provide for the supply of information, for example, financial data and detailed figures may be requested on a periodic basis by financial creditors.

The value of information deriving from insolvency-related regimes may, however, be questioned. Creditors may well gain much information only at a

---

89 Finch, *'Company Directors: Who Cares About Skill And Care?'* (above, note 12).
90 Insolvency Act 1986 ss 47(1), 48(1) and (2).
91 Insolvency Act 1986 s 2(1), (2) and (3); Insolvency Rules 1986 rr 1(3)(1) and (2); Insolvency Rules 1986 rr 1(5)(1) (2), 1(12)(3); Insolvency Act 1986 s 3(2) and (2); Insolvency Rules 1986, r 1(13)(8).

very late stage in corporate troubles and this will often rule out actions designed to forestall directorial failures or negligence. As with shareholders, however, informal sources of information may assist creditors and major financial creditors will often use their influence to obtain a steady flow of information from senior managers. Major creditors may also obtain representation on the company's board and subsequently will gain access to new sources of information. Trade creditors will be less likely to use such sources but if a continuing trading relationship has been formed, they may acquire information informally.

The expertise of creditors and their ability to use information also varies. Financial creditors might be expected to be expert in assessing risks and managerial performance but, in contrast, trade creditors may possess expertise in a particular business sector only and may be less able to evaluate directorial performance beyond those areas.

Will creditors be committed to enforcing directorial duties? They may be where they foresee a threat to prospects of repayment but, in general, creditors are not disposed to review the actions of managers. Factors that might, nevertheless, affect the propensity to enforce might be the size of the investment, the nature of any security, the type of business and the levels of directorial discretion usual in the sector. For small trade creditors such factors may well not come into play unless the debtor is a major purchaser of the creditor's product. Such creditors will tend to look for supply elsewhere rather than to continue a relationship in the hope of recovering from directors on the basis of breach of duty.

What incentive, indeed, is there for creditors to seek to recover from directors? Secured creditors will focus on realising their security by appointing a receiver. Only if such realisation fails to meet the sum outstanding, will such creditors have anything to gain from the contributions of directors. In the case of creditors secured with floating charges, incentives may similarly operate only to cover shortfalls (directorial contributions will form part of the company's assets). Ordinary unsecured trade creditors will possess questionable incentives to pursue errant directors since they will be paid after floating charge holders.

After a liquidation has been initiated by qualifying creditors, actions may be brought by creditors against directors under a number of heads. For example, misfeasance actions for breaches of fiduciary or other duties in relation to the company.[92] Such duties, however, are, as noted already, owed to the company and contributions obtained from directors as a result will go to the company assets for the benefit of all creditors. Individual creditors may be discouraged from bringing such actions, moreover, because the liquidator may proceed similarly on behalf of all creditors and will have investigative powers

---

92 See further Finch, (above, note 12) p 193.

that individual creditors do not possess.[93] As for liquidators' actions, creditors may have to indemnify costs where it is anticipated that there may be insufficient assets to support litigation and, in the case of preferences and transactions at undervalue it has been held in *Re M C Bacon (No 2)*[94] that the expenses of actions cannot be deemed expenses of winding-up. Liquidators, accordingly, may feel obliged to seek indemnification from creditors before proceeding with such claims.[95]

Questions can also be asked about the scope of protection offered by s 214 – the wrongful trading section – that Cork placed great faith in as a shield for creditors. Section 214 looks to directorial deficiencies in taking steps to protect creditors beyond the point when corporate failure seems inevitable[96] – it is not concerned with the incompetence or mismanagement that may have brought the company to the verge of insolvency. A liquidator might attack the actions of directors prior to insolvency under the Company Directors Disqualification Act s 6 by making a report to the DTI presenting evidence of directors being 'unfit to be concerned with the management of a company'. Since, however, the liquidator has little to gain financially from this course, and may incur costs, there may be little incentive so to act.[97]

Creditors' claims might, alternatively, be based not on statutory breaches but on allegations of breach of the director's duty to act in the company's best interests. This obligation would, as stated, come within the ambit of s 212 Insolvency Act 1986 – the misfeasance provisions – and is capable of enforcement against directors by the liquidator or by 'any creditor' (s 212(3)). Thus, unusually in the insolvency context, creditors per se are given a right of action. Moreover, although the enforcement arises *ex post facto*, on the company's winding up, the duty can arise well before this in cases of threatened or incipient insolvency.[98] It should be repeated, however, that incentives to proceed by this route may be limited. Compensation will go to the company's assets (falling within the ambit of a floating charge)[99] and liquidators might thus doubt the return to creditors. For their part, individual creditors might anticipate bearing the expenses of their action without the prospect of personally reaping the rewards.

---

93 Insolvency Act 1986 ss 131-134, 235.

94 (1990) BCC 430. Similarly expenses of s 214 Insolvency Act 1986 actions.

95 See Hunt, '*Avoidance of Antecedent Transactions – Who Foots The Bill?*' (1992) 6 Ins Law & Practice 184; Middleton, '*Wrongful Trading And Voidable Preference*' (1992) NLJ 1582.

96 Insolvency Act 1986, s 214(2)(b).

97 See Wheeler, '*Disqualification of Directors*' in Rajak (ed) *Insolvency Law: Theory and Practice* (1993, Sweet & Maxwell).

98 See Cooke J in *Nicholson* (above, note 4) at 249.

99 See *Anglo-Austrian Printing & Publishing Union* (above, note 64).

For unsecured creditors, in particular, a number of problems afflict enforcement of common law or statutory directorial duties. First, the statutory duties (apart from s 423 which protects particular prejudiced creditors rather than creditors as a whole against transactions at undervalue) are only capable of enforcement by office holders. This is consistent with the collective nature of insolvency proceedings but unsecured creditors may feel frustrated by their dependence on the liquidator's application.[100] The second problem for unsecured creditors is the destination of sums recovered for breaches of duty. Do these form part of the company's assets – thus being liable to be swallowed up by a floating charge – or do they accrue to the estate for distribution to the general body of creditors? Will charges over assets catch sums recovered by the liquidator under ss 238-239, 213 and 214 of the 1986 Insolvency Act? Section 239, it appears, impresses proceeds recovered as a result of a preference with a trust in favour of unsecured creditors[101] but the same cannot be said in relation to s 238 transactions at undervalue or in relation to instances of fraudulent and wrongful trading. The post-1986 position appears to be that contributions go to 'the company's assets' and fall within the scope of a charge over after-acquired property.[102] The wrongful trading legislation, far from offering a directorial duty potent in the hands of the unsecured creditor, may turn out to be a duty without real substance.

Turning to the common law duty, this again offers little to the unsecured creditor since it is owed to the general body of creditors rather than unsecured creditors individually or as a class. A duty owed directly to individual creditors would, as already noted, conflict with insolvency's collectivist principles, might lead to a multiplicity of suits and could lead individual creditors to place improper pressure on directors to settle their particular claim.[103]

If a direct duty to individual creditors cannot be argued for with conviction, a stronger case can be made for placing directors under a duty to unsecured creditors as a class. It is, after all, only the unsecured creditors who are in practice bound by collective principles – secured creditors have their own contractual remedies and may appoint receivers to act for them. A direct class approach would normally have to await liquidation for enforcement to

---

100 On court supervision of the liquidator's decision, see Insolvency Act 1986, ss 112, 167.

101 See *Re Yagerphone Ltd* (1935) Ch 392, approved on this point by Millet J in *Re M C Bacon (No 2)* (above, note 94) at 434.

102 See Knox J in *Re Produce Marketing Consortium* (above, note 71); *Re Anglo-Austrian Printing & Publishing Union* (above, note 64); Wheeler, *'Swelling the Assets for Distribution in Corporate Insolvency'* (1993) JBL 256. Of course, in relation to transactions at undervalue (see s 283(3), Insolvency Act 1986) to give proceeds to the general creditors may not be appropriate, for if the transaction had not occurred a chargee might have attained/retained a security interest over the asset transferred.

103 See further Grantham (above, note 1), at 12-13; Prentice, in McKendrick (ed), *Commercial Aspects of Trusts and Fiduciary Obligations* (Clarendon, 1992) pp 74-5.

occur (or else the wrongful trading provisions of s 214 could be undermined) but would be advantageous to unsecured creditors in allowing them to secure damages without losing out to the holders of floating charges. It could exceptionally, however, allow them to bring injunctions where necessary to prevent directors from acting in a manner jeopardising the company's solvency or to ensure the consideration of unsecured creditors interests in circumstances of marginal solvency. For their part, directors might have few grounds to fear that unsecured creditors would interfere in the workings of the company. Such creditors would have to demonstrate to a court reasonable cause to anticipate that insolvency would result from the action in question. This would be a onerous burden to discharge.

The position of creditors generally might be strengthened by another reform – one to allow creditors to take action in the company's name in enforcement of directorial duties. A case for a new statutory derivative action for shareholders has been considered elsewhere[104] but are there good reasons for a creditors' counterpart?[105] The Australian Companies and Securities Law Review Committee (CSLRC)[106] recommended that creditors be included in the potential class of applicants for a derivative action (as well as shareholders, directors and officers and creditors of related companies). The main reason for including creditors was that, in some circumstances, creditors might be in receipt of better relevant information than was available to 'other outsiders'.[107] The opportunity of using creditors as monitors of corporate management is, however, a less convincing reason for introducing such an action than is the need to protect creditor interests. If, as was indicated in *Horsley & Weight, Nicholson* and *Brady v Brady*, creditor interests become company interests not merely post-insolvency but also when insolvency threatens, it would be appropriate to allow creditors to act before the liquidator comes onto the scene so as to protect their interests by injuncting any directorial actions that are likely to prejudice solvency.[108]

Against the introduction of such an action, it might be contended that creditors face four main problems: the payment of excessive dividends; the incurring of debts with similar or higher priorities; the substitute of non saleable assets for saleable assets; and excessive risk taking. These problems

---

104 See Finch, *'Company Directors: Who Cares About Skill And Care?'* (above, note 12) pp 204-206.

105 See generally Ramsay, *'Corporate Governance, Shareholder Litigation and The Prospects For a Statutory Derivative Action'* (1992) 15 UNSW LJ 149, pp 165-166; Kluwer, *'Derivative Actions and The Rule in Foss v Harbottle: Do We Need a Statutory Remedy?'* (1993) CSLJ 7.

106 Companies and Securities Law Review Committee, *Enforcement of the Duties of Directors and Officers of a Company by Means of a Statutory Derivative Action (Report No 12, 1990)* (hereafter CSLRC). See also *Report of House of Representatives Standing Committee on Legal and Constitutional Affairs, Corporate Practices and the Rights of Shareholders* 1991.

107 CSLRC, p 50.

108 See eg s 1234 Corporations Law 1991 (Australia) enabling courts to grant injunctive relief to 'any person' affected by contraventions of the Corporations Law.

might be expected to be dealt with by means of contractual provisions. In reply, the limitations of contractual protections could be pointed to (these are discussed below in 4.3.1). A second objection is that the interests of creditors and the company may diverge and creditors might abuse such an action. The fear is that creditors might bring what in North America have been called 'strike suits' – actions designed to destabilise management in order to further the interests of third parties – for example potential takeover offerors who would be grateful for the drop in share price that might flow from such an action. Such potential abuses may, however, be countered - the CSLRC was confident that a requirement that leave be sought for such actions would allow courts to 'filter out valueless claims or improper attempts to harass management'.[109] Creditors, furthermore, who abused the procedure would risk bearing their own and respondents' costs.

As for the point that creditor and company interests diverge, this can be addressed by making it clear in the rules giving standing for such a derivative action that creditors will be given standing only where the contested action places creditor interests at issue – that is where the action is liable to involve a serious risk of corporate insolvency. The purpose of such a derivative action would not be to give creditors an increased role in monitoring the management of solvent companies[110] – it would be to allow creditors to act in the company's name in situations bringing their and the company's interests together, in the *Nicholson* sense (ie situations of insolvency or threatened insolvency).

It might be objected that a creditor derivative action would 'result in creditors endeavouring to use the courts as a forum to argue for protection by means of an expanded definition of directors duties'.[111] But, again, a leave requirement would reduce this danger and the fear of such an expansion is a weak reason for refusing creditors a means of protecting interests already acknowledged to ride on the bow wave of insolvency.

In summary, then, there is a case for such an action provided that standing is limited as described.[112] Whether directors' duties to creditors should be expanded turns on whether creditors are thought to be in need of more extensive or more effective legal protections against managerial failings. This is a matter to be discussed in 4.4.

---

109 CSLRC (above, note 106) p 65.

110 Justifications for such an action that are based on its encouraging honesty in management are, accordingly, not directly in point here: for such justifications see, Note: *'Creditors' Derivative Suits on Behalf of Solvent Companies'* (1979) 88 Yale LJ 1299.

111 See Ramsay (above, note 105) at 165.

112 In Australia the CSLRC's proposal was not implemented but the availability of alternative remedies per s 1234 Corporations Law 1991 (see above, note 108) constituted an objection not replicated in England. A number of objections related to the CSLRC's notion of an action able to be used during periods of solvency - objections met by the restrictions on standing indicated in the text. On the use of a creditors' derivative action during solvency see Note: (1979) 88 Yale LJ 1279 (above, note 110).

In assessing directors duties as protections for creditors the relevance of directors' and officers' ('D & O') insurance should be noted. Such insurance can, as a result of s 137(1) of the 1989 Companies Act, be purchased for directors by companies.[113] In a recent survey, 62 per cent of companies had purchased such insurance.[114] Many directors who fail in their obligations accordingly present gateways to the deeper pockets of their insurers. The economic incentives for creditors to pursue errant directors are, as a result, far greater than they were before the 1989 Companies Act amendment and it can accordingly be said that protections for creditors have to some extent been enhanced.

Can it be concluded that the imposition of legal obligations on directors offers an effective scheme of protection for creditors? The common law has been developed in a manner apparently sympathetic to creditors and new statutory rules on, for example, wrongful trading were introduced for protective reasons. As seen in 4.1, however, a number of uncertainties affect any assessment of the common law duties owed by directors to creditors – concerning in particular the nature of the duty, to whom it is owed, when it comes into effect, and how it is to be enforced. The protection offered by statutory provisions is, in turn, limited by the indirect nature of the duties imposed and the uncertain returns that are available to some creditors.

In 4.1 the divergent interests of creditors were noted and this in itself was said to weaken the force of duties owed generally to creditors. Informationally, a significant problem for creditors is a tendency to acquire information at the eleventh hour in the company's decline and trade creditors may be particularly short of such information as allows them to hold directors to account or to protect their interests by acting to forestall disaster. Small trade creditors may, furthermore, possess low levels of expertise and commitment to enforce. As for incentives to make duties bite, secured creditors will tend to rely on contractually-established protections and unsecured creditors will rank so low in the scheme of priorities that they may feel very weak incentives to proceed. In any event, the levels of misconduct that have to be proven may be dauntingly high (in the case of common law duties) and unsecured creditors may be frustrated at having to rely on other parties to bring actions based on statutory breaches. The absence of a direct class action for unsecured creditors seems a conspicuous weakness in the protective system.

---

113 See Finch, *'Personal Accountability and Corporate Control: The Role of Directors' and Officers' Liability Insurance'* (1994) 57 MLR 880.

114 ibid at 900.

4.3   Alternative means of protection

If creditors' interests are to be protected – in both the compensatory and preventative senses – then doing so by imposing legal obligations upon directors is only advisable if such a strategy is likely to be more effective than other available techniques. Thus far it appears that the imposition of duties provides highly imperfect protections.

The major alternatives to be considered involve reliance upon:

- contractual protections;
- the corporate governance system;
- the professionalisation and training of directors; and
- external controls on directors.

4.3.1   Contractual protections

If creditors are viewed as contractual claimants – in contrast to shareholders who may be seen as owners of the company[115] – it might be argued that creditors should not be owed duties by directors but should protect themselves against shareholder claims by express contract.[116] On this view, creditors, after all, are only entitled to what has been agreed to under the relevant debt agreement.

There are, however, a number of reasons why contractual stipulations can offer only limited protections for creditors. First, normal trade or service agreements involve sums of money that are too small and timescales that are too short to justify extensive contractual stipulations. In any event, contracts to anticipate all contingencies and modes of directorial failure are beyond all drafting capacity. Secondly, even in the face of debt contracts there may be high costs and difficulties in documenting such contracts, in monitoring them, detecting breaches and bringing enforcement actions. Third, although the interest charged by creditors could be said to offer built-in compensation for the risks of managerial failure, managers may take actions that circumvent the protections provided for in contracts. Thus, where a given rate of return is agreed in anticipation of a loan offered at a given risk, the directors may change the gearing of the company so that old agreements on interests rates do not adequately reflect risks and there is creditor claim dilution. Countering

---

115 But on the contractarian view of the company see eg Jensen & Meckling, 'Theory of The Firm: Managerial Behaviour, Agency Costs and Ownership Structure' (1976) 3 J of Fin Econ 305; Symposium, 'Contractual Freedoms in Corporate Law' (1988) 89 Col L Rev 1385; Easterbrook & Fischel, 'Corporate Control Transactions' (1982) 91 Yale LJ 697; Riley, 'Contracting Out of Company Law' (1992) 55 MLR 82.

116 See Sappideen (above, note 1) at 366; Macey and Miller, 'Corporate Stakeholders: A Contractual Perspective' (1993) U I Toronto LJ 401. On protection by 'bilateral safeguards', see Williamson, The Economic Institutions of Capitalism (New York, 1985), pp 311-12.

such behaviour by express contractual stipulation, followed by the policing of management, may impose unreasonable costs on creditors. Fourth, there is doubt whether the market for credit is sufficiently informed and rigorous to police directors effectively[117] and the market for corporate control is unlikely to remedy this weakness of control. Finally, directors will resist contracts that impose high costs of compliance (or costs of circumvention) upon themselves. They will, in particular, not agree to stipulations that constrain their abilities to take wealth-increasing actions.[118]

The problems of contracting for protection may in some eyes[119] constitute arguments for treating creditor interests as company interests long before insolvency. Whether such arguments have force will be discussed in 4.4. What can be said at this stage is that contractual protections are too flawed to substitute completely for other modes of creditor protection.

4.3.2   The corporate governance system

A number of proposals to reform the structure of the corporate governance system might be thought potentially to enhance the position of the creditor. It should not be assumed, however, that reforms aimed at increasing the shareholder voice in the company[120] would necessarily protect creditors. A strong shareholder voice could be useful to creditors in encouraging non-negligent management[121] but creditors and shareholders have divergent interests and a strong shareholder voice might press directors to act in ways inconsistent with creditor concerns. Thus, creditors may fear that directors will dilute their claims or asset-substitute and use loans for risker ventures than the creditors anticipated – shareholders, in contrast, may be quite happy that higher gearing is being operated or higher risks are being taken in pursuit of higher returns.

Of assistance to creditors may be improvements in the supply of information. Creditor representation on boards might be increased but even the institutional lenders have not the resources to put representatives on large numbers of boards. It has been argued, moreover, that when banks put

---

117 Sappideen, op cit pp 373-4.

118 See McDaniel, *'Bondholders and Corporate Governance'* (1986) 41 Bus Lawyer 413; *'Bondholders and Stock-holders'* (1988) J of Corporations Law 205, 236-7.

119 Eg Sappideen (above, note 1).

120 See chapters 2 and 3.

121 See Finch, *'Company Directors: Who Cares About Skill And Care?'* (above, note 12) pp 206-208.

representatives on boards they tend to do so in order to cement a business relationship rather than for any serious informational reasons.[122] More rigorous rules on disclosure to creditors might be developed but these, though offering protection against gradual decline in a company fortunes, may not assist creditors when there is a sudden, unexpected, announcement of a course of action prejudicial to creditor interests.

Will such reforms as a strengthened independent element on the board – with increased use of non-executive directors or greater reliance on audit committees – assist creditors? Again, such proposals may help to some extent in controlling managerial negligence and reckless disregard of creditor interests may be unearthed but it cannot be assumed, by any means, that, where shareholder and creditor interests diverge in the normal course of events, directors will do anything other than pursue shareholder interests.

4.3.3 Professionalisation and training

The full-scale professionalisation of directors is not on the current political agenda but new avenues for training directors are constantly being developed.[123] In 1990 less than 10 per cent of directors had received any training and less than one-quarter possessed any professional or managerial qualifications.[124] Now, however, courses and workshops on company direction are to be found across the country and these figures might be expected to have grown. Increased training may impact to some extent on levels of directorial incompetence and negligence, but prejudice to creditors' interests may stem, as noted, from competent direction and, in any event, the role of training in eradicating incompetence should not be exaggerated. Training is voluntary and its principal effect may be to improve the brightest and the best rather than to remove poor performers.

4.3.4 External controls

It is difficult to see how more extensive state regulation of companies might materially improve protections available for creditors. The DTI could not, for resource reasons, be expected to monitor directors to see if creditor interests were being looked to in the course of company operations. Similarly, resource constraints would limit the role of any complaints referee or ombudsman.

---

122 See Herman, *Corporate Control, Corporate Power* (CUP, 1981) p 134.

123 See Finch, *'Company Directors: Who Cares About Skill And Care?'* (above, note 12) p 210.

124 See *Professional Development of and for the Board IOD*, January 1990.

Might, however, those insurance companies that offer 'D and O' insurance be seen as monitors of directors and potential protectors of creditors?[125] The indications are that insurers meet their larger 'D and O' clients on a regular basis and they will conduct 'paper' scrutinies of clients (reviewing annual reports etc). UK insurers have not to-date, however, developed monitoring systems of any rigour or sophistication. Were UK insurers to engage in more intensive monitoring, they might, nevertheless, encourage directors to give creditor interests higher priority because creditors constitute a class of potential claimants against the insurance fund. 'D and O' insurance, moreover, encourages directors and shareholders to pay greater attention to the performance of the individual director yet it offers, at the end of the day, incomplete protection for the director. The end result may be modes of direction that are low risk or defensive (in so far as directors fear falling through the insurance net). Directors, instead of taking all commercially justifiable risks, may play safe. Such playing safe may not be in the interests of shareholders who seek large dividends but may be welcomed by creditors who are concerned that their prospects of repayment are not subjected to higher than necessary levels of risk. To seek to protect creditors by creating 'D and O' insurance schemes that would discourage risk taking (and would accordingly hinder wealth creation) might, however, be to opt for protection at too high a price.

To summarise this section, the major alternatives to legal duties offer no ready blueprints for the more effective protection of creditors. Contractual protections are necessarily incomplete, expensive to apply and liable to circumvention as well as directorial resistance. Corporate governance reforms might increase the information available to creditors, but this in itself may not conduce to the effective prevention of prejudicial actions by directors. Professionalisation and training is not likely to assist creditors largely because it does not reorientate directors away from the pursuit of shareholder interests. Only in the case of external controls by insurers is there a glimmer of greater priority being given to creditor concerns. This glimmer, however, remains just that.

If, accordingly, creditor interests do merit protection then a conclusion being forced is that a considerable role will have to be played by legally-imposed duties on directors. How extensive these duties should be and how much protection creditors should be given are matters to which we now turn.

---

125 See Finch, *'Personal Accountability and Corporate Control: The Role of Directors' and Officers' Liability Insurance'* (above, note 113), p 908.

4.4 Should creditors be protected?

Why should creditors be empowered, in some circumstances, to prevent directors from prejudicing their prospects of repayment? Why should creditors be able to secure compensation from directors who fail to pay proper regard to creditor interests?

I will answer these questions by reviewing the case for protecting creditor interests long before insolvency and then arguing for recognition of creditor interests only after insolvency is threatened. The statement of the former case I will focus on is that offered by Razeen Sappideen[126] who emphasises, *inter alia*, the following points:

- Creditors cannot self-protect effectively by contractual means because contracts cannot be comprehensive; monitoring and detection costs are high; enforcement is often impracticable; and directors may resist or circumvent contractual stipulations.

- Creditors require protection from various types of managerial actions eg shirking, under-investment, asset substitution, diluting creditors claims, excessive dividend payouts and failures to exploit the full opportunities for which the loan was advanced.

- The market will not protect creditors by punishing directors who hurt creditors.

- 'The major protection afforded to the debenture holder is the continuing profitability of the investee company.'[127]

- From an economic perspective, fiduciary principles offer low cost deterrence as a substitute for costly direct supervision of agents. Such principles operate as 'standard form penalty clauses' in contracts – they guide courts and lower the costs of debt.

- The conventional classification of shareholders as owners of the company and creditors as mere lenders of money for fixed returns, is no longer appropriate in a large modern enterprise. In economic terms, shareholders and creditors are similar: 'both are making a capital investment and both expect to get their money back plus a return on their investment'.[128]

- 'At least seven theories seek to justify and explain the imposition of fiduciary obligations. These are, (1) unjust enrichment; (2) commercial utility; (3) reliance; (4) unequal relationship; (5) property; (6) undertaking or contractual; and (7) power and discretion theories. The imposition of fiduciary obligations on directors with respect to the corporation,

---

126 Sappideen, (see above, note 1).
127 ibid, p 376.
128 ibid, p 382.

shareholders and creditors can be justified under each of the above theories'.[129]

- The view that duties to creditors should depend on insolvency is 'well under siege' in the courts as exemplified in such cases as *Walker v Wimborne*,[130] *Lonrho*,[131] *Winkworth*[132] and *Jeffree*.[133] In Winkworth Lord Templeman, furthermore, indicated that directors owed fiduciary duties to creditors rather than owed a duty to the company to consider creditors interests. This approach was followed in *Jeffree*.

- 'A duty to maximise shareholder wealth invites managers to maximise shareholder wealth at debt holders' expense. Such a duty is inconsistent with fiduciary debts to debenture holders. Directors should be required to maximise the value of the firm ... not make an investor's slice larger at the expense of another investor'.[134]

- The best way to achieve creditor protection is through a general statutory provision requiring directors to be even-handed to both shareholders and creditor interests.

A first response to Sappideen is to contest the notion that creditors and shareholders are really involved in the same (contractual) game and should be treated in similar fashion. Some forms of security may resemble some modes of shareholding but creditors and shareholders are engaged in activities that effect quite different trade-offs between risks borne and compensating rewards and rights. Creditors contract for small rewards and have little control over company operations but, balancing this, they are able to reduce risks by taking security, charging interest and they enjoy priority of interest as against shareholders on insolvency. Shareholders, in contrast, stand to reap substantial rewards for corporate success, they enjoy a good deal of control over management but they bear considerable risks in so far as their claims are subordinate to those of creditors in a corporate failure. To argue that creditors should, like shareholders, be owed fiduciary duties by directors is to allow creditors to have their cake and eat it.

Secondly, the practicability of fiduciary duties owed to creditors is highly questionable. As has been noted already, duties owed to groups containing divergent interests tend to fragment into vague exhortations. Were directors to owe duties to treat shareholder and creditor interests evenly, a catalogue of divergent interests would be involved and neither courts nor directors could

---

129 ibid, p 383.
130 See note 3.
131 See note 6, at 634.
132 See 12 note 9.
133 *Jeffree v National Companies and Securities Commission* (above, note 27).
134 See Sappideen, (above, note 1) p 393.

proceed with any confidence. Would, furthermore, an objective or subjective test be applied to the (almost inevitably confused) director?

Thirdly, the efficiency of fiduciary duties cannot be taken for granted. Just as contractual stipulations cannot be complete, so the particular import of a fiduciary duty in a given context would have to be fleshed-out incrementally by the courts. Uncertainties would abound and, for creditors, this would by no means be a cost free exercise. Directors would not be effectively deterred from prejudicing creditors – they might well spend large sums of money seeking advice from lawyers on how to proceed on a commercial basis while avoiding being found to have breached a fiduciary duty to creditors. The unavoidable uncertainties of the legal rules involved would, to some extent, put a blight upon effective entrepreneurial activity.

The present system, offering no fiduciary duties to creditors prior to the prospect of insolvency, but allowing a variety of securities to be taken, makes creditors, in effect, their own insurers of directorial wrongdoing *vis-à-vis* their interests. Since creditors often issue loans to a wide variety of parties, they can accordingly risk-spread efficiently by adjusting their interest rates. This is likely to be a more efficient use of resources than attempting to establish the liability of directors. The latter endeavour will prove costly when lawyers and courts are involved and, if creditors are successful, the result may in any event be risk-spreading by 'D and O' insurers through the medium of higher insurance premiums. At the end of the day, the company will, within each system, pay for directorial failings in the form of either rises in interests rates or in premiums but the route through insurance is likely to prove considerably more costly for the company.

To say that creditors should not be owed fiduciary duties by directors while the company is solvent does not, however, mean that they do not have interests worthy of protection when insolvency occurs or is threatened.[135] As was indicated in *Kinsela* and *West Mercia*, the interests of creditors intrude and become company interests on insolvency. The basis for this intrusion is that the directors have, in reality, become agents for the creditors – those whose interests are now at risk.[136] There is logic, furthermore, in the line of Cooke J in *Nicholson v Permakraft*, for, if creditors' interests should be considered on insolvency, it is difficult to deny the relevance of such interests when decisions are at issue in circumstances of dubious solvency or where the contemplated action might jeopardise solvency. Similarly, a means to reconcile the dicta of Templeman LJ in *Winkworth & Edward Baron* with the

---

135 See eg *New Zealand Law Commission Discussion Paper No 5 on Company Law* (1987) para 211: '... as a matter of general law directors of solvent companies ought not to owe duties of care or good faith to creditors. It can be said that the general insolvency law should be exhaustive of the circumstances in which liability should be imposed.'

136 See *Brady v Brady* (above, note 8) at 522.

notion of dubious solvency[137] is to note Templeman LJ's reference to directors acting 'to the prejudice of creditors' in outlining the duty owed. It is arguable that directors only prejudice creditors when they bring solvency into doubt or jeopardise it.

Creditors should be empowered to prevent directors from prejudicing their prospects of repayment, but should be able to do so only when solvency is at issue.

4.5   Conclusion

A review of common law and statutory provisions reveals that the law promises a series of protections to creditors with regard to directors' actions but the law fails to deliver in a number of respects. The common law provisions leave serious doubts concerning the nature of the duty, to whom it is owed, when it is effective and how it is to be enforced. The judges have failed to guide directors on how different kinds of creditor interests are to be balanced and, although duties to consider creditors interests have been said to arise at the stage of doubtful solvency, creditors cannot prevent prejudice to their interests and are only given a right of action post a winding up. The relevant statute law leaves unsecured creditors in a particularly weak position and the wrongful trading provisions have little force in the period leading up to, rather than following, the verge of insolvency.

Reforms could be instituted to move the law beyond exhortation and render it enforceable in practice – for instance to allow creditors to take injunctive action to forestall prejudice and two potential routes suggested have been the introduction of a duty owed to unsecured creditors as a class and the creation of a statutory derivative action for creditors. The latter, it has been stressed, should only be made available to creditors for the purposes of protecting creditor interests in insolvency or on threatened insolvency.

As for protections other than the imposition of legal duties, it seems that these are limited: contractual protections, corporate governance reforms, professionalisation and training, and external controls offer no easy answers. In the case of 'D and O' insurance creditors' interests could benefit were 'D and O' to be operated in a manner conducive to low-risk directorial decisionmaking, but the price to be paid for this gain might be considerable.

Creditors' interests do merit protection, not because creditors and shareholders have the same relationship to the company, but because, as insolvency approaches, creditors supplant shareholders as the parties most liable to be affected and prejudiced by directorial failings. It is only,

---

137 The idea of a duty owed directly to creditors contained in Lord Templeman's judgment is less easily reconciled with the body of cases.

accordingly, in relation to the threat of insolvency and the prejudice to creditor interest that flows from insolvency that creditors should be empowered to enforce duties against directors. Creditor protection does depend very much on the set of legal duties owed by directors and, accordingly, the reforms discussed above merit further attention. Corporate governance reforms, statutory or otherwise, should consider the position of all interested parties. It is time for creditor concerns to be brought in from the wings of the corporate governance debate.

Chapter 5

Corporate Governance – Great Expectations

Sir Owen Green
Former Chairman of BTR

5.1   Introduction

The concept of corporate governance has been enlarging for more than a century. It has now attained the status of a regime and the busy-ness of an industry. Its growth can be associated with the failure of our law-making system to cope with the pace of corporate development. That development, in size, complexity and in economic influence, continues as the boundaries of our trading world vanish, the opportunities for investment increase and the aggregation of funds accelerates.

Corporate growth, particularly in size and complexity, demanded greater expertise in management than that provided by a lifetime dedication of a founding father. His commitment was superseded by the career interest of the professional manager. Thus the distinction between ownership and managerial control became inevitable.[1] With a similar result, but for different reasons, the pattern of share ownership also changed from that by individuals to that by institutions.[2] Thus developed a further distinction, that of the professional fund manager, the institution – and his client, the ultimate investor, who might be an individual, a pensioner, an insurance holder etc.

The growth of corporate governance as an 'ism' spurred the identification of other interested parties in addition to shareholders. 'Stakeholders' as they are sometimes called, include employees, bankers, lenders, suppliers, customers. Such a variety of interests inevitably entails a broad diversity of particular aims, objectives and expectations.[3]

---

1   For a consideration of the apparent separation between ownership and control, see Berle & Means, *The Modern Corporation and Private Property* (1933).

2   See in particular Florence, *The Logic of British Industry and American Society* (1953); Florence, *Ownership, Control and Success of Large Companies* (1961); Scott, *Capitalist Property and Financial Power* (1986); and Nyman & Silbertson, *'The Ownership and Control of Industry'* (1976) 30, Oxford Economic Papers, 75.

3   Corporate managers have been perceived as 'trustees' for the various shareholders. For a debate on the 'trusteeship' principle see Wedderburn, *'The Social Responsibilities of Companies'* (1985) 15 Melbourne University Law Review 1; and his *'The Legal Development of Corporate Responsibility: For Whom Will Corporate Managers Be Trustees?'* in Teubner (ed) Corporate Governance and Directors' Liabilities; Berle, *'Corporate Powers in Trust'* (1931) 44 Harv Law Rev 1145; Dodd, *'For Whom Are Corporate Managers Trustees?'* (1932) 45 Harv Law Rev 1145; and his *'Is Effective Enforcement of Fiduciary Duties of Corporate Management Practicable?'* (1935) 2 University of Chicago Law Review 194.

Small shareholders may require security, regular dividends and some growth. Fund managers may require anything from short term high performance recovery stocks to long term capital growth performance. The employee will seek security of employment and the opportunity for improvement. The banker prefers a client who 'works' his account. The supplier seeks a stable relationship with a paying customer and the community seeks a good contributor to its well-being.[4]

A design capable of governing the attainment of each of these separate objectives might have taxed the Athenians, even a B School professor. The experienced and pragmatic corporate practitioner realises that the ultimate requirement from any such design is that it does not impede the pursuit of profitability, without which any and all the other interests become substantially irrelevant.

It follows that any system of corporate governance must have as its basis a recognition of that imperative corporate aim – profitability.[5]

5.2   The corporate environment

The Austrian economist Joseph Schumpeter provided what I believe to be the best description of a world of advancing living standards. He described it as being dependant on genuine market economies – a specification now accepted by all major economic groups, even including, to a growing extent, that most cautious of advancing nations – China. Schumpeter viewed our world as an open economy forever growing under a process of structural change rather than in static equilibrium.[6] That process of structural change is brought about by creative destruction which through innovation obsolesces existing equipment and processes and their cost. That is to be contrasted with the static circular-flow characteristics of the old command economies.

The introduction of the concept of limited liability was perhaps the greatest single contribution made to the health of that process. That concept enabled, even encouraged, the recruitment of funds on the scale necessary to meet those requirements of a dynamic, thrusting, albeit risk-strewn world. But it

---

4   See further *Parkinson, Corporate Power and Responsibility*, (1993) chapter 1.

5   The concept of 'profit maximisation' is also advocated by Friedman in *'The Social Responsibility of Business is to Increase Its Profits'*, in Steiner & Steiner (eds) Issues in Business and Society (1977); and also his *An Economist's Protest* (1972); and *Capitalist and Freedom*. See too Hayek *'The Corporation in a Democratic Society: In Whose Interests Ought It And Will It Be Run?'* in Anshen & Bach (eds) Management and Corporations in 1985 (1985).

6   Schumpeter, *The Theory of Economic Development* (1934); and his *Capitalism, Socialism and Democracy*, (1942).

protected the investor from the unlimited risks of partnership or of sole trading.[7]

The new funds collected in the process were used for specific purposes to be pursued by entrepreneurs or by professional managers. A distinction between their roles as the drivers of the enterprise and their responsibility for governance does not seem to have been too important in earlier times. The use of non-executive directors was more related to their money-drawing power and their PR potential.

As and when shortcomings appeared in the system additional legislation was framed. Nevertheless, law breaking was not unknown and corporate scandals occurred, perhaps more often than in recent years!

5.3 The problem

Corporate failures are due to market conditions, incompetence, lack of integrity or misconduct. Market conditions are usually beyond the influence of individual corporations. Incompetence and lack of integrity may flourish in conditions of looseness in accounting practices and surveillance. Misconduct is an intolerable cause for which the law must provide the sanction and the punishment.[8] Although the frequency of corporate failure through misconduct may not have grown over the years, its consequences have spread more widely and affected more investors than in earlier times for a variety of reasons.

A main reason relates to growth in all forms of personal savings, particularly in the form of pensions, house ownership and wider share participation, which have been fuelled by successive governments in the UK for political or budgetary reasons. Substantial tax reliefs have been provided to encourage those savings and much advantage has been taken of them. A large part of those funds has been placed through stockmarkets into corporate enterprises and the number and spread of investors, direct and indirect, has greatly increased.

There has been an explosion of mega-force proportions in the size of the world of finance. The money illusion has ballooned and there are now more illusionists, to match the ever-growing supply of the gullible. The old idea that 2 + 2 could only equal 4 has long been obsolesced, synergy is the name of the game and fortunes are made, sometimes lost, on paper-structured innovations.

---

7   On the concept of 'limited liability' and its legal consequences, see *Gower, Principles of Modern Company Law*, (1992) chapters 5 and 6, pp 80-134; and Farrer's *Company Law*, (1991) chapter 7 pp 70-83.

8   See in particular the Company Directors Disqualification Act 1986; s 212 Insolvency Act 1986 (misfeasance); s 213 Insolvency Act 1986 (fraudulent trading); and s 214 Insolvency Act 1986 (wrongful trading). On the duties of directors towards creditors especially, see chapter 4.

On economic grounds and for other sound reasons, the need to dismantle the corporate state required a shift in society's attitudes. The return to self-dependence and the 'feel-good' factor of personal wealth, through geared home-ownership, and the pursuit of material values involved other changes, some of them unintentional. There is little doubt for example that moral standards were affected and the corporate world has not been immune from those changes.

Accounting problems have spread like a plague. Amongst them the desire to produce a universal definition of profit, the determination of values and the monetising of assets, fixed or floating – sometimes twice over – have done little to ease the tasks or aid the standing of the auditing profession.[9]

To the extent that these problems have a legal or technical base they should be dealt with by legal or technical attention. There is much work being undertaken in the field of accounting in the development of standards and for the requirement for explanatory notes in published material, but one wonders whether this campaign for knowledge and statistical 'corrections' is not too important to leave to the generals.

The lack of success in law enforcement is a matter of general concern which is said now to be receiving government attention. Any inadequacy of law itself should be remedied by law. In the environment of the 1990s the current resort to the production of codes may have attractions but like any quick-paste job they are unlikely to stand the test of time.[10]

How much better would it be if our efforts were to be directed towards identifying the criminal, as they do in the USA, rather than to the rolling out of more coded regulations which burden the innocent and do little to turn the intent of the wrongdoer.

5.4   The parties

I have referred to several parties involved in corporate sector activity which claim, and in some instances need safeguards. What are their expectations from corporate governance and how reasonable are they?

The generic expression for some of these parties is 'stakeholders'. That word takes us beyond current legal definition – rather like the use of the word 'owner' to describe a shareholder.

---

9   On the concept of 'profit', see chapter 1.
10 For further reference to Codes of Conduct, see chapters 12 and 18.

5.4.1 Employees

However, 'stakeholders' does seem to be an appropriate description for employees for their very livelihood depends on their employment with the enterprise. Indeed it is argued that employees by virtue of their length of service and by the relative inflexibility of their connection, ie their job, may have made a greater investment than that of the shareholders, in the business. They may also be regarded as having a greater interest in the future of the business for those same reasons.[11]

The German system of governance, the two-tier board, gives some recognition to the employee's status, and has developed from their post-World War II consensus approach to all forms of government.[12] No other major country appears to provide, statutorily, for employee participation in corporate governance. It is to be noted, however, that in the UK, it is not uncommon for employees to have representation on the boards of company pension funds. The importance and sensitivity of pensions schemes and the contributory nature of their funding from employees should indeed entitle them to representation on the relevant Board. Additionally, I believe the benefit of this particular window of representation is much underrated in the area of communication.

Pension matters apart, one detects little support from management or labour for the notion of separate employee representation on governing boards. Since his role is wholly executive – doing things – the employee's contribution to and participation in governance should be embraced in and through the executive route. Rather than underplaying the importance of the workforce, that view further emphasises another aspect of the vital role of management executives as members of the board.

5.4.2 Bankers

Bankers and lenders are quite well provided for in law and through the terms and conditions of their relationships. They write their own rules governing their relations with the client. Any failure in this regard must be largely of their own making.

---

11 Company law requires directors to take account of employees' interest in matters affecting the company. However, under s 309 of the Companies Act 1985, directors are also required to consider the interests of shareholders. It would appear that in balancing the interests of employees and shareholders, the interests of shareholders would prevail. There is no enforcement mechanism for employees where directors fail to take account of their employees' interests. See too s 719 Companies Act 1985 and s 187 Insolvency Act 1986.

12 See also chapter 2.

5.4.3 Related traders

Customers, clients and suppliers normally have contractual relationships which, for customers at least, usually insure against loss through the inadequate conduct of their suppliers. One is aware, however, of recurring complaints such as late settlement of debts and the misuse of monopoly purchasing power particularly as these affect small suppliers. Although such complaints are often specious, there may be something further to consider in the light of reasonable expectations in these matters. It is to be noted that the government have once more agreed to examine this question.

5.4.4 The community

The reasonable requirements of the community are mainly satisfied through legislation embracing acceptable levels of adequacy of behaviour. Basic manufacturing standards relating to health, hygiene, environment (noise, smell, effluent) do require regulations. Such considerations apart, the community should have no greater position in relation to the governance of corporations than it has in the conduct of an individual. Arguably less, for the individual is nationally and locally enfranchised. The corporation has no similar franchise despite its proportionately larger contribution at state and local level to the coffers of the community. Why should 'no taxation without representation' fail to apply to the artificial legal person – the company.

Clearly, each of these parties or stakeholders, to some degree, affects and is affected by corporate behaviour. But the view that this is great enough to require specific recognition by the corporation, much less to be a required inclusion in aims and objective statements is arguable.

In Milton Friedman's words, 'broadening the scope of management concerns is a fundamentally subversive doctrine that could thoroughly undermine the very foundations of our free society'.[13]

Another US view – a legal one – is that a business should have as its objective the conduct of business activity with a view to enhancing corporate profit and shareholder gain. An expansion of these objectives, however sociologically appealing, will inevitably reduce the concentration of management from its primary purpose.

As Martin Lipton puts it, 'management is ill-equipped to deal with questions of a general public interest which would blur the efficient conduct of a focused operation'. And so say many of us.[14]

---

13   Friedman, op cit., note 5.

14   Some innovative suggestions are made for reform of the corporate governance system by Lipton & Rosenblum, '*A New System of Corporate Governance: the Quinquennial Election of Directors*' (1991) 58 The University of Chicago Law Review, 187.

5.4.5 The shareholder

The most important of these stakeholders, in law, in life and in fact, is the shareholder. Jonathan Charkham, a member of the Cadbury Committee, agrees that under UK legislation the shareholders are technically supreme. The Board which they alone elect is accountable to them. That relationship has clarity and simplicity.[15]

What then are the expectations of the shareholder clothed in his technical supremacy. He is commonly regarded as the owner of the company.[16] Since that view is the one on which Cadbury relies for the implementation of its 'market-based regulation' to turn its proposals into action, the concept merits some discussion.

Charles Handy suggests that we should look at our shareholders more as other countries do, as financiers rather than owners. To satisfy them then becomes a requirement, not a purpose. To reverse this view, he says, runs the risk of confusing means with ends. Shareholders do not have the balancing responsibilities of ownership. He suggests that investing institutions must become guardians, neither owners nor traders. The last exclusion – as traders – I do not share. Nor do the institutions.

Martin Lipton maintains that the modern public corporation is not private property like other private property. Rather it is the central productive (I prefer wealth-creating) element of the economies of the USA and the UK at least. He argues that the rules of corporate ownership and governance must take account of many more interests than do the rules governing less complex property. I agree with his distinction but not his reasons.[17]

To the question – 'Where then does ownership of the enterprise reside?' – my suggestion is that it is indeed with the equity shareholders but only as an indivisible collective group. Their ownership is analogous to that of a freeholder landlord whose lease is held by the board and whose rent is determined in the form of dividends. Separately the investor may also profit from changes in the market value of his investment as determined by market forces.

A further example of recognition of the collective and indivisible nature of shareholders' relationship with the company is provided in the House of Lords ruling in the *Caparo* case and as set out in the Cadbury report. In that case it

---

15 Charkham, *Keeping Good Company* (1994).

16 For USA perspective on the role of shareholders, see Livingston, *The American Shareholder*, (1958); and Rubner, *The Ensnared Shareholder* (1965).

17 Lipton & Rosenblum, op cit., note 14.

was found that the auditors' duty of care is owed to the body of shareholders as a whole but not to shareholders as individuals.[18]

Notwithstanding these issues of ownership, what are the shareholder's expectations? His individual requirements will relate to the nature of the investment but his underlying universal expectation will be of a company governed with integrity and competence – the twin towers of an enduring business structure.

To the extent that stakeholders can be protected by law, then society's obligation lies in that direction. Equity investment holds its own risks and these are well publicised in the 'health warnings' liberally displayed in promotional literature. Codes of conduct may save parliamentary time but they have neither the craftsmanship of parliamentary lawyers nor the authority which is created through the scrutiny of experienced legislators.

But the law must be enforced. Were Maxwell, BCCI, Polly Peck, Queens Moat *et al.* to have been regarded as operating within the relevant regulations until their last moments? There is a widely held impression that the judiciary regard fraud and other financial offences as having an abstract quality as expressed by the view of insider trading as a victimless crime. A legion of disadvantaged shareholders, pensioners and creditors think otherwise. Perhaps a touch of the Judge Jeffries or, and more relevantly, a Lord Shawcross might restore balance.

5.5   International comparisons of governance

What can our system of corporate governance learn from those adopted by other major world economies? There appear to be some marked differences and little likelihood of early convergence (with the ominous exception of the European Union) due to the differing local requirements of the law, of politics and of custom and practice.

---

18   *Caparo Industries plc v Dickman* [1990] 2 AC 605; and *The Cadbury Committee on the Financial Aspects of Corporate Governance* (December 1992) appendix 6 pp 80-5. On the auditors' duty towards shareholders see too *Morgan Crucible & Co v Hill Samuel & Co.* [1991] Ch 295; *McNaughton Ltd v Hicks Anderson & Co* [1991] 2 QB 113; *JEB Fasteners Ltd v Marks Bloom & Co* [1981] 3 All ER 289; *Al Nakib Investments Ltd v Longcroft* [1990] 1 WLR 1390. In *Re Kingston Cotton Mills [No.2]* [1896] Ch 279 at 288-9, Lopez LJ stated that an auditor is: 'a watchdog not a bloodhound. He is justified in believing tried servants of the company in whom confidence is placed by the company. He is entitled to assume that they are honest and to rely on their representations provided that he takes reasonable care. [But if] there is anything calculated to excite suspicion he should probe it to the bottom.' See too *Ownership and Control of Firms of Auditors Under the Companies Act 1989*, a consultative paper published by the DTI in December 1989.

5.5.1   Europe

The German model of a two-tier board is, one suspects, the guiding light of those responsible for UK regulatory development. For that reason the concept of a supervisory board and a second tier executive board is worth further examination. The model was proposed for the UK by the Bullock Committee years ago, and rejected.[19]

Historically, German industry was financed mainly by the banking system. Unusually, when compared with US and UK custom, this finance was provided initially as equity. Without the availability of a charge on assets which a lending bank would normally seek, the German banks sought some direct control over the funds resulting from their equity subscription. That desire was reinforced by the bank proxy custom under which the banks require or shareholders offer their proxies for shareholdings held by banks as nominees.

The banks recognised that they could not manage the businesses underlying their investments and membership of the supervisory tier board afforded an ideal solution. A solution, I would add, that is often more of form than of substance. In passing, the conflicts of interest which would arise in US or UK banks, if this model was mirrored, would be huge.

The emergent supervisory board, typically with significant bank representation but including worker members, and the executive board composed equally of management and labour, also reflected the understandable post-war German commitment to co-determination.

Sir Adrian Cadbury is reported recently to envisage an ultimate convergence between the European and the Anglo Saxon models of governance. Based on the history of the European Community legislation, the power of the Franco-German axis and the whole thrust of Cadbury it is not difficult to envisage who will be expected to do the converging.

Other European board structures – French and Italian – reflect the importance of family or state holdings, leaving little scope for protection of other shareholder interest. There is movement, however, in State owned industries in France towards co-determination on German lines. It will be interesting to study the development of French corporate governance as their programme of privatisation proceeds.

---

19   Bullock Committee, *Report of The Committee of Inquiry on Industrial Democracy* (1977) Cmnd 6706, HMSO, London.

5.5.2　USA

The USA appears to have been the most concerned with the development of governance, and may continue to be so.[20] That is hardly surprising, bearing in mind that it is the most imaginative and litigious of communities on the one hand, and it holds the fiercest concern for so-called democratic principles on the other. It claims to hold world leadership of the unitary board concept – but in practice its use of a two-tier type structure is evident in many large corporations. It is difficult to believe that the executive committee of management in US corporations do not determine most significant issues including those of Governance for formal endorsement by the board where necessary.[21] This *modus operandi* is also not uncommon to larger companies in the UK and Germany. Indeed the articles of association of many of the largest UK companies permit management board authority involving the widest of discretion.

5.5.3　Japan

The typical Japanese board is very difficult and perhaps least likely to change. The few outside directors probably come from the web of interconnected associated companies – Keiretsu. The Japanese system believes in the concentration of power in the president/chief executive and his operating committee. This reflects their regard for executive strength, for continuity, for long-termism and for the cult of seniority-based experience. This is the nation which alone continues the distinguished tradition under which the most senior officer accepts responsibility for failure. One recalls the head of Japan Airlines visiting and apologising to each family bereaved as a result of an airliner disaster, then giving his resignation. We can no longer expect that behaviour of our political leaders, nor do our industrialists appear to regard this as other than a quaint but obsolete recognition of the honourable dimension in responsibility.

It will be seen that there is not too much international coincidence of view as to the structure of board governance.

5.6　The UK revisionists

The most recent developments in UK corporate governance have been codified in the Cadbury Report of December 1992.[22]

20　See also chapter 1.

21　Mace, *Directors: Myth and Reality* (1971); and his *'Directors: Myth and Reality – Ten Years Later'* (1979), vol 32 Rutgers Law Review 293.

22　*The Cadbury Committee on the Financial Aspects of Corporate Governance* (December 1992). On the implications of the Cadbury Committee's recommendations see chapters 17 and 18.

5.6.1   Some legal considerations

There was an attempt in 1988 to pass a Bill dealing with audit committees through Parliament. That Bill sought to define the term 'independent' directors. The Bill passed through all of its Commons stage in one sitting but it was subsequently rejected in the Upper House. Perhaps it was with that precedent in mind that other avenues were sought to provide that which was thought to be too difficult for conventional legislation.

Alterations to or extension of the structure of limited liability companies and the responsibilities of its directors and officers should require to be made through legislation properly drawn up and debated in Parliament before enforcement.[23]

It is important to recognise that Cadbury does not have the force of law but it will have legal consequences. Our company law concepts and our bases of liability stem from the fundamental premise of a unitary board. The consequence of an endeavour to obtain a 'half way house' between unitary and two tier boards must create legal confusion. In the event that the courts are involved in any issues of governance they will take the code as representing the reasonable requirements of directors. One questions whether non-executive directors appreciate that their personal liability may have been substantially increased. Their basic duty of care and skill would formerly have been governed by the concept of subjective reasonableness as determined by their personal background and experience. Executive directors owe a more onerous duty to be judged by objective reasonableness, irrespective of their personal abilities. The strength of this distinction may have been diluted, perhaps extinguished, in the case of members of audit, remuneration and nomination committees whose personal liability may have been increased.

With that potentially enlarged exposure in mind, the increased minimum requirement for non-executive directors will only be met with difficulty. This may be so, particularly in the case of less well-regarded companies where there is of course the greatest need. The plight of small company boards over the proportional requirement in numbers has already yielded the possibility of some modification.

---

23   On the argument for a clarification of directors' duties, see Finch, '*Company Directors: Who Cares About Skill And Care?*' (1992) 55 MLR 179.

5.6.2   The board's responsibilities

Corporate governance has been defined by Cadbury as the system by which companies are directed and controlled.[24]

Within this system, the shareholder's role is to appoint (I think they mean 'elect') the directors, appoint the auditors and satisfy themselves that an appropriate governance structure is in place.

Cadbury believes that the board's responsibilities include:

5.6.2.1 Setting the company's strategic aims

I wonder how many senior executives of successful growth-achieving companies, even the largest, would honestly subscribe to that view. Who better to assess short, middle and long term market requirements and asset deployment of the business than those executives steeped in the knowledge of the products and their markets. Board review and endorsement of strategy – yes, but the idea of non-executives making significant contributions to strategy is not very realistic. As an analogy one recalls the eminent contributions to the strategies of war made by von Clauswitz, Liddle Hart, De Gaulle and Guderian, all men steeped in the technology of their subject. In contrast the contributions to strategy by Churchill and his cabinets and Hitler and his political posse have not been well-regarded by historians.

5.6.2.2 Providing the leadership to put them into effect

The selection of the chief executive and a review of the appointment of his lieutenants is a reasonable expectation of the board. To extend this requirement further may well interfere with the chemistry of the reaction of the chief executive with his men, a process in which the board would be an inappropriate catalyst.

5.6.2.3 Supervising the management of the business

This takes the board close to participation in executive affairs, weakening its ability to preserve the important distinction of management accountability.

5.6.2.4 Reporting to shareholders on their stewardship

On this subject, Cadbury is to be supported in its recommendations on shareholder communication, particularly with regard to the AGM.[25] While

---

24   Cadbury Committee, op cit., note 18, paras 2.5-2.8, p 15.
25   On reforming the AGM, see chapter 11.

institutions may feel that not to be an ideal forum for their participation by their attendance, it is often the only opportunity for smaller shareholders publicly to air their views. More should be made of that forum and it is to the credit of some companies with large share registers that they arrange annual opportunities for shareholder questions at venues geographically accessible to their members.

5.6.3 The chairman

While describing the chairman's role as 'crucial', Cadbury wavered on its separation from that of the chief executive. That was a mistake, although it is encouraging to note that, in larger companies at least, the two roles are increasingly recognised as separate and distinct yet compatible.[26]

The general expectation of a chairman's role is of one who holds the ring, ensures the orderly conduct of a meeting, assisted by the secretary (an under-emphasised functionary) who takes account of and summarises views and, where necessary, declaring the result of votes.

It is difficult to imagine this being done impartially by the chief executive officer and it is also an unnecessary requirement of him. It would be preferable that there is a mandatory separation of roles in any company having outside shareholding interests.

In smaller companies a local lawyer should prove a good chairman and he would have the added advantage of familiarity with the general requirements of corporate law and of formal meetings. Those who decry this proposition may have an excessively broad view of the executive functions of the board, a view shared by some academics and non-practitioners and from which Cadbury is not totally exempt.

5.6.4 Remuneration

The Cadbury recommendations on board remuneration recognise a problem which has, in the eyes of the general public, grown rapidly in recent years. It is in this aspect of governance that companies are providing the less attractive features of free markets in which liberty is not licence – a self-discipline of which we need to be constantly reminded.

It is, unfortunately, not rare for there to be at least three elements of compensation. The basic salary recognises the task as described being properly executed. The bonus or performance related pay is an additional

---

26 See too chapters 10 and 18.

reward for doing the same thing but surpassing the requirement. The third element, the share option, will usually represent the reward for the value of the corporate effort over the longer term. That value is normally related to the increase in the share price and the individual's share is usually related to his salary level.

My belief is that the bonus is a hangover from pre-share option days. But the combination of the two represents a double-dip into the barrel of available incentive monies. It must be divisive, inflationary and, for as long as it is available, greed promoting. There is little proof of its effectiveness in relation to management performance.

But these items do not amount to the sum of the packages. Frequently these include the pension adjustment – met by the company; termination provisions – often discriminate as to entitlement, and signing-on fees reducing the status of top executives to that of professional footballers.

As a first measure for moderation a requirement for total disclosure of all benefits of the highest paid group of executives on the lines of the US SEC compensation tables would identify the true size of these packages.

The Cadbury suggestion of remuneration committees of non-executive directors is demonstrably not a solution, nor is the likelihood of concern or intervention by institutional shareholders who are often and perhaps properly more concerned with the resultant bottom line. Passing the problem to the AGM seems impracticable, nor does moderation appear to be achievable by legislation or through taxation.

But there remain several bodies of influence who might be shamed into disapproving the practice and the persons involved in excessive remuneration packages. That disapproval could be shown, each in its own way, by government departments, the Honours Committee, the IoD and the CBI in their councils, by the media and by society itself in a demonstrable lack of regard for that over-indulgence.[27]

5.6.5   The auditor

The report states that the auditor's role is to provide the shareholders with an external and objective check on the directors' financial statements which form the basis of the reporting system.[28] This area is clearly regarded by Cadbury as complex, controversial and requiring much consideration. The evidence is in the devotion of 20 out of the 72 pages of the report proper to these matters.

---

27   The CBI has established a new group to report on directors' excessive remuneration. See chapter 18; and Institute of Directors, *The Remuneration of Directors: A Framework For Remuneration Committees* (January 1995).

28   Cadbury Committee, op cit, note 18, para 2.7, p 15.

Cadbury further defines the role of auditors as that of providing the shareholders with an external and objective check on the directors' financial statements. It then adds that the framework in which auditors operate is not well designed to provide objectivity because:

- Accounting standards, currently, allow too much scope for presentation and auditors cannot stand firm against their clients choice of accounting treatment if that is within permitted standards.

  Why, in that event, might auditors wish to 'stand firm'? If their objection is strong enough why would they not seek to add a rider to their report? Why are there so many bodies currently engaged in producing new standards, often additional and usually controversial? Who are seeking these innovations? Is it the shareholders in whose interests, mainly if not exclusively, these standards exist? Cadbury observes that the shareholders (and others) need a coherent narrative, supported by figures, of the company's performance and prospects. We can all subscribe to that. But have we not arrived at a point at which the average investor – even the average analyst – is bemused by a growing complex of figures accompanied by ever lengthening notes couched in professional language, supported by a chairman's report, a chief executive's report, a finance director's statement, an environmental report and now a corporate governance statement?

- 'Auditors have to work closely with management and will wish to have a constructive relationship with their clients'.

  It is indeed sad to read words the barely concealed meaning of which infer that auditors are hired by managements whose wishes are to be taken as instructions, provided they do not breach the broad and versatile accounting standards.

Another feature of the poor framework for objectivity expressed by Cadbury reads 'to the extent however that audit firms compete on price and on meeting the needs of their clients' (this must mean the management) 'this may be at the expense of meeting the needs of the shareholders'.

These reflections offered by twelve good men and true indicate the level of general regard to which the auditing profession has fallen. Detracting not at all from the problem of the 'expectations gap', albeit a shrinking gap – between what audits do achieve and what they are thought to or should achieve – it is surely unacceptable that the reputation of a profession of the first rank only 30 years ago should have become so controversial. The recently retired senior partner of KPMG Peat Marwick was reported in the Financial Times as believing that, in the past, clients treated the auditor with more respect as a feared and independent character, invariably calling him 'Mr'. I can recall a few other names but they all conveyed that feeling of awe.

Shareholders should expect their company's auditors (not the management's auditors) to challenge the management views where the auditors' principles are involved and to reject those views where they encourage or condone management bias against shareholder interests. It is difficult to excuse any reluctance on the part of auditors to stand for those principles on which their right to professional respect is based. Their clients are the companies, not the managers. Their re-appointment is not within the gift of the managers but of the shareholders acting as a body, in Annual General Meeting. What additional protection do they need to ensure their status and their independence of management? Whatever it is, let them have it.

An in-depth review of the auditing profession is well overdue. The risk of confusion of the role of auditor with those of management consultants et al. must be eliminated. Secure the auditor's independence by requiring any change to be made by a special or extraordinary resolution of the company. Consider limitation of his liability in certain circumstances. Restore his role as professional watchdog (but not bloodhound), releasing non-executive directors to more constructive purposes.

5.6.6   Corporate governance or over-governance

My first impression of the draft Cadbury report was that it was long on accountability but short on drive and efficiency. The final version altered that view a little. It is fair to say that the committee's purpose was to review those aspects of corporate governance specifically related to financial reporting and accountability.[29] In doing so it has raised the hopes of those who suffered from or were otherwise interested in, and I quote from the preface, 'BCCI, Maxwell and the controversy over directors pay'.

Many people might take the view that the spectacular corporate failures of recent years, rare as they have been, were more due to the neglect of requirements of commercial, corporate or common law or inadequacy of due diligence. The Cadbury recommendations will not eliminate those hazards or shortcomings. Indeed, 1993 witnessed more dramatic setbacks or failures and an increase in the controversy on directors' pay.

Against these views it should be recognised that the talent which can identify, achieve, or introduce wealth-creating innovation is rare. It is what most of us would regard as enterprising. It is that same spirit which sees the glass as half full, never half empty. The measure is identical but the interpretation is crucially different. Our establishments often seem too easily to develop the 'half empty' syndrome. Fear of failure, which has often been a strong and successful motivator, can also lead to reactionary behaviour which

---

29   See Postscript.

fosters regulatory inhibitions which are then presented as safeguards. There is danger in an over-emphasis on monitoring; on non-executive directors' independence from the business of the corporation; on controls over decision making activities of companies. When coupled with the clearly reduced status of executives on the governing boards, such requirements must blunt the competitive edge and deflect the entrepreneurial drive which characterises participation, let alone success, in a free market.

The current thrust of the regulations on corporate governance is towards the distinction of the roles of executive and non-executive or 'independent' director. It will lead to a distinction of purpose and, sooner or later, of behaviour.

The emphasis on the special role of the non-executive director has by definition to be on non-executive matters. In stressing his independent judgment, his appointment for a specific term, his requirement to review the performance of the board and the executive, Cadbury casts his role as chiefly that of a watchdog.[30] One only has to read the media reaction to corporate failures of recent years and months to accept that the general expectation of these appointments is as watchdogs and it will be the most human of consequences that the watchdog role will be predominant.

That there should be at least three 'watchdogs' on each board renders more and more remote the idea of a thrusting, innovative, creative group of people ensuring that their organisation is equipped to meet the challenge of Schumpeter's open economy.

Cadbury (I) indicates issues to be considered by 'Son of Cadbury', its successor body. Some of these issues, for example the disclosure of directors' remuneration, may not be regarded as contentious. Much effort might be saved if the US proposals in this and other regards were adopted. But the fading reality of a unitary board will be further diluted by continuing emphasis on the distinctive roles of non-executives in governance. In that event the introduction, de facto, of the upper tier Teutonic shield of the great and the good will not be long delayed. What an irony it would be if the behaviour of non-executive directors under the influence of some of the Cadbury proposals succeeds in persuading executives of the advantage of such a change.

5.7 Conclusion

In this submission I have described the corporate environment in terms of ceaseless change. Its universe contains a galaxy of investment opportunities – some as transitory as a comet, others as permanent as Mother Earth.

---

30 Cadbury Committee, op cit, note 18, para 4.10-4.17, pp 22-4.

The problems presented by this dynamic state reflect the differing requirements of the parties involved. The natural diversity of these requirements are such that the lightest of regulation must affect the expectations of one as it protects the expectations of another. codes of conduct aimed to prevent the worst performance are likely to exclude the best performance.

International comparisons of governance systems reflect local differences in laws, politics, customs and practice. They are manifestly no more effective than the old UK model.

The potential legal liabilities of non-executive directors have increased and they are not well understood.

The distinctive role of auditor should be re-established, thus releasing the non-executive director from the Cadburian collegiate watchdog to more constructive ends.

As a pre-Cadbury practitioner, I have yet to learn of any system of control of a corporation which will be an improvement on the old unitary concept, its administrative simplicity, its structural homogeneity and its legal convenience.

Long may it endure.

Chapter 6

Ownership and Accountability in Corporate Governance

Stanley Wright
Author of Two Cheers for the Institutions
(Social Market Foundation, April 1994)

This chapter briefly indicates the function of market-oriented companies. It identifies the essential problem of 'corporate governance' and shows why it has become a matter of increasing concern. It points to the potentially damaging effects of undue managerial autonomy and to the limited efficacy and appropriateness of codes. Finally a set of proposals is made for legislative change to redress the balance of power in favour of owners (ie shareholders) and by the same token, of the 'common weal'.

6.1 Companies, shareholders and the economy

The origin and purpose of limited liability companies is and was to make profits for their shareholders. Limited liability has made practicable enterprises too large and/or too risky to be financed by a small number of partners. Moreover, with growing wealth and a wider spread of savings, limited liability companies have enabled the savings of individuals (whether directly or as insurance policy holders, pension contributors or unit holders, etc) to be channelled into productive activity. Such companies have thus become an essential part of the market economy which, imperfect though it may be, has historically been essential to sustained economic growth (and a necessary though not sufficient condition of liberty).

Indeed it is difficult to understand how, in the face of the failure of the centrally planned economies of the communist world and the record of 'government failure' in the industrial and commercial sphere in the UK and elsewhere, it can still be believed that the identification of needs and the production of goods and services to satisfy them is generally best undertaken under government auspices or control. Clearly there is room for differences of view about income distribution and about which activities should be part of the 'agenda' of government. However, to make industry and commerce generally accountable to government would be to reject consumer interests in favour of producer interests and to put economic decisions into the political market-place of pressure groups and votes, with the prizes going to the persuasive rather than to the productive.

Prices and profits are the signalling system for resource allocation in a market economy. Provided that the signals are not unduly distorted by government action or by failure to deal with monopoly and otherwise provide a competitive environment, efficient corporate response to market signals is an engine for economic growth. Shareholders may often be ill-informed, but they have an unambiguous interest in seeing their companies respond to the signals, so that profits can be made and dividends paid. Shareholder interests as owners are thus aligned to those of the wider public interest.

This (rather than, as some seem to imply, the prevention of fraud) should be the main starting point for addressing the problems of corporate accountability.

6.2   Corporate governance and 'management choice theory'

The problem of management accountability is quite simply that managers are like the rest of us. It is therefore a reasonable working hypothesis that other things being equal they will normally pursue their own interests (disciples of Adam Smith and believers in the doctrine of original sin will surely both concur in this). The interests of managers are not the same as those of shareholders. There may well therefore be scope for a branch of economics which I would call 'management choice theory' (analogously to public choice theory).

Let me offer some basic precepts. The natural (conscious and/or unconscious) predilection of managers must be for high and rising remuneration, security of tenure and/or large compensation for departure in circumstances of failure or takeover, together with ever-growing 'empires'. Not all, moreover, can resist the temptation to surround themselves with the costly trappings of power: prestigious motor cars, large offices, excessive secretarial backing and flattering PR persons and consultants. There is the further temptation, aggravated by a government often unable to distinguish between businessmen and business executives and unduly impressed by both, to neglect shareholders' interests in order to please government and pursue honours.

From this perspective accountability to financial markets and to shareholders is seen as a nuisance: perhaps, if the company is big enough, to be dealt with by a department of 'shareholder relations'. While there are good examples of a genuine concern to look to shareholders' interests, improved arrangements for accountability are needed to ensure this.

6.3   The present preoccupation with accountability

Adam Smith warned:

> '*the directors of joint stock companies being the managers rather of other people's money than of their own, it cannot well be expected that they should watch over it with the same anxious vigilance with which the partners in a private copartnery frequently watch over their own.*'

In an increasingly managerial society with widespread share-ownership the problem is aggravated, for the temptations described in 6.2 are not constrained by owner-directors.

However, as Jonathan Charkham has pointed out,[1] the term 'corporate governance' is of very recent origin. This points to an increasing preoccupation with a long-standing problem.

Indeed, in his preface to the report which bears his name, Cadbury says 'it is however the continuing concern about standards of financial reporting and accountability, heightened by BCCI, Maxwell and the controversy over directors' pay, which has kept corporate governance in the public eye'.

This may well describe accurately the proximate cause of the appointment of the Cadbury Committee. However, as the committee recognised 'no system of control can eliminate the risks of fraud without so shackling companies as to impede their ability to compete in the market place'. Safeguards against fraud are important but are an area in which government and other regulators and perhaps auditors (with reduced financial liability) should play a major part. Fraud is not, however, the main accountability issue.

Directors' pay, to which Cadbury's preface also refers, is another matter. It is one of the more blatant symptoms of the contempt in which managers have come to hold their owners (the shareholders) and indeed their fellow countrymen at large.

The problem of which this is a symptom has become significantly worse in the post war period. Companies have got much bigger which generally means less concentrated shareholding with consequent greater power to management. Non-executive directors, who traditionally tended to be major shareholders, are increasingly drawn from among professional managers or ex-managers elsewhere, who broadly have the same interests and approach as a company's executive directors.

Tax policy moreover has tended to enhance the power of, and encourage lack of accountability among, top executives. The classical corporation tax introduced by the Labour government in 1965 aimed to tax dividends much more heavily than retained profits. The purpose was to encourage retentions

---

1   Jonathan Charkham, *Keeping Good Company* (1994) OUP.

on the assumption that this would encourage investment. Moreover, the 'classical' system under which all profits were taxed at the same corporation tax rate and then dividends were separately taxed in the hands of the shareholder was coupled with high and rising marginal rates of income tax. Thus, individual shareholders had to look for their return essentially to capital gains, which were subject to a much lower rate of tax. This had serious and curiously long-lasting effects on the attitudes of managers and intermediaries. They could rationalise high retentions and high dividend cover both on 'growth' grounds and on tax grounds. This encouraged the implicit view among managements that the profits were 'theirs'. Indeed they often speak of 'the company' or the business as though it had purposes and interests different from those of the body of shareholders; in fact these terms are normally a mask, conscious or unconscious, for managerial preferences and interests.

These attitudes have outlived the replacement of the classical corporation tax by the imputation system in the early 1970s. There is a wealth of anecdotal evidence that top managements often still see companies as 'their' companies.

The imputation system, introduced by the Heath government, was intended to encourage dividend distribution and the allocation of capital through the market. It failed to do so because it was followed almost immediately by a policy of dividend restraint, and subsequently by a period of so-called tax exhaustion caused by the interaction of generous capital allowances and low profits which together had the effect that many companies (even banks and other financial companies who 'sold' their capital allowances via leasing) were paying no mainstream corporation tax. Consequently, and contrary to the intention, dividends gave rise to tax in the form of advance corporation tax, while retained profits gave rise to none. Thus the addiction to low pay-out ratios, and to the control by managements rather than shareholders over what happened to profits was perpetuated.

Not until Lawson introduced the corporation tax changes of 1984 was this situation reversed. The favourable capital allowances for investment were removed, the top rate of income tax was reduced (eventually to 40 per cent) and, subsequently, the marginal rates for individual income tax and capital gains tax were equated. The corporation tax changes, together with high and rising profits, led to the rapid disappearance of accumulated tax losses. After some time-lag this led to higher dividends and to some, if inadequate, reassertion of the primacy of shareholder interests.

There have been recent indications that in some government circles there is a hankering to return to the 'survival of the fattest' (as Heath characterised the classical corporation tax system) by constraining or discouraging dividends. This is based on the false premise that investment and dividends are alternatives. This could be true for an occasional company in the short run; it may also be true that companies are slow to react to changing circumstances and therefore to adjust their dividends (but dividends are not the only area where slow reaction can be observed). However it is clear that with increasingly widespread savings (albeit often via institutions) and an ageing population, the purchase of equities and therefore industrial and commercial investment will be inhibited rather than encouraged by reduced dividends. On the other hand the tendency of managers to sit comfortably on cash balances (and there are well-known examples of this) or to undertake inadequately regarding investments will be aggravated. (At the time of writing the Prime Minister has recently denied any intention to 'control' dividends - it remains to be seen whether this applies equally to fiscal measures.)

6.4   Examples of managerial choice

Having outlined the proximate causes of recent preoccupation with 'corporate governance' and the roots of some current managerial attitudes, let us turn to some of the consequences of these attitudes.

Cadbury recognises that the 'controversy over directors' pay' has contributed to keeping corporate governance in the public eye. Despite new machinery, better information and mounting public concern, top management remuneration continues to spiral upwards, and what is worse, very substantial compensation is paid to those who fail and/or resign.

It is worth considering why an increasing preoccupation with accountability has failed to make a perceptible impact in this area.

There is little doubt that, as noted above, the cultural climate including government attitudes has in recent years been extremely flattering to the egos of top businessmen. The mantle of the mandarins has been assumed by some top business executives, who have come to regard themselves as 'not as other men are'. They are therefore resentful of, rather than responsive to, criticism of their high and rising remuneration. Against this background, non-executive directors, often themselves managers elsewhere, with a vested interest in a climate of high remuneration, are not likely to impose much restraint.

A second and very important factor is that there is no real market in top executive remuneration. The 'purchasers' are the shareholders, but there is little provision for them to have a say in the remuneration of 'their' executives. As suggested above, non-executive directors are at best indifferent surrogates.

The inadequacy of the market is compounded by intermediaries and other interested parties, who propagate or encourage a number of fallacies, in particular they contend that there is an international market in top executives and that there is a great shortage of suitable people.

In fact it seems unlikely that more than a very limited number of top managers (other than technical specialists and those with some special skills in the financial sector) would be willing and capable to run major enterprises in other countries and under foreign ownership.

Age limits, upper and lower, help to restrict the effective supply of good managers, as indeed does the tendency of head-hunters to limit their choice of candidates to those doing the 'next job down' elsewhere.

The intermediaries in the 'human resource' industry moreover are the source of surveys, with the emphatic message that the remuneration trend is strongly upwards and that every class of benefit is becoming normal. This is scarcely surprising given that the intermediaries' interest as fee earners is in ever higher executive remuneration and ever faster turnover, just as estate agents and stockbrokers benefit from high prices and turnover in property and equity.

The highly geared structure of the tax relieved forms of remuneration has the effect of encouraging upward pressure on total remuneration and benefits. To give an executive more pension or life insurance cover or more options you also have to make a salary increase; conversely if salary is increased then, other things being equal, pension (since 1989 there has been a 'cap' on pensions for new entrants to schemes) and related rights will increase and more options will be expected. All this has tended to become regarded as 'normal'.

Surveys usually identify 'median' and 'average' remuneration for various categories of executive job; and only too often those determining pay will be afraid 'of getting behind' and in particular of paying 'their' people below the average or the median. Universalisation of this attitude will of course cause an indefinite and rapid upward spiral (this reality is difficult to get across to a remuneration committee). Management power in respect of its own remuneration is thus minimally constrained; and the problem is compounded by long-term contracts under which substantial compensation is available. (Even under the Cadbury proposals, tenure can be three years rolling.)

The takeover cult is another manifestation of inadequately constrained executive power and lack of accountability. There is less constraint on issuing shares as consideration for a takeover than on issuing them for cash. Takeovers are very rarely beneficial to the shareholder of the 'bidder' companies. The beneficiaries are usually the shareholders in the 'biddee' companies and almost invariably the top management of the bidding company, who overnight become more powerful and have, by the standards which commonly obtain, a better case for bigger remuneration. Intermediaries in search of fees and some specialist journalists in search of copy encourage and flatter those who wish to engage in takeovers. This is why managements often prefer takeovers of other listed companies, despite the premium which the financial markets demand, to the purchase of private companies, which can only be bought from a willing seller and can readily be the subject of thorough 'due diligence'. It is also why top managements in big companies tend to prefer takeovers to organic growth.

In short, we all tend to favour free trade in the goods we buy, but not usually in the goods we sell. Similarly top management, regardless of the interests of shareholders, wants freedom to bid but protection to being bid for (eg by foreign 'predators'). Because of the problems of management motivation and the relatively high price paid to acquire quoted companies, greater accountability is needed in this area.

It is perhaps worth noting that managements from time to time, and sometimes abetted by advisers, press for greater freedom to raise cash by the issue of equity or quasi-equity (eg convertibles) than the institutions are prepared to sanction. This is essentially another manifestation of the desire to avoid accountability: ie to be in a position to dispose of shareholders' 'property' (and 'dilute' their ownership rights) without their consent. Institutional shareholder power is an essential protection against this.

6.5   The Cadbury Report

The Cadbury Committee's purpose was 'to review those aspects of corporate governance specifically related to financial reporting and accountability'. Any assessment of it should take account of this limited mandate. It contains a great deal of valuable information and comment about matters such as the actual and potential role of auditors and of directors, together with some proposals for making these clearer.

Otherwise, it is essentially concerned with 'process' and with the dissemination of information, together with (perhaps unconsciously) imposing implied new duties on non-executive directors, without significantly increasing their powers to undertake them. Sometimes, moreover, the committee appears to be arrogating to itself the powers of the legislature, eg 'Non-executive directors should be appointed for specific terms and reappointment should not be "automatic".' In fact under law and company instruments, directors are elected by shareholders (having perhaps been co-opted beforehand) for specific terms. No-one would reasonably differ from the view that re-election (not re-appointment) should not be automatic, but the implication that non-executive directors should in effect have contracts (see para 4.16 of the report) with the board is disturbing. There may well, moreover, be a case for making a clear distinction in law between executive and non-executive directors, but it is surely improper that different duties should be prescribed by a code written by or for a committee, particularly given that with our system of law the code may well be cited in courts.

Moreover, as Sir Owen Green has said 'codes of conduct aimed to prevent the worst performance are likely to exclude the best performance'. In fact, the emphasis on process in the Cadbury report seems in many respects to be counter-productive. The very thoroughness of the specification of duties, of information requirements and of processes, is sure to give credence among directors to the view that it does not matter what we do as long as we put it through the right committee and reveal it in the fine print of the annual report.

For example, the committee having recognised the scandal (my word not theirs) of executive pay, seems to show a touching faith in the remedial efficacy of remuneration committees manned by non-executives. To date, no casual reader of the financial press can do other than conclude that remuneration committees have been ineffective. As indicated above, non-executive directors only too often are or have recently been executive directors elsewhere and cannot be regarded as 'independent' in this matter. Moreover, the cultural pressures and available information are inimical to attempts to constrain executive remuneration. Indeed the spread of remuneration committees has almost certainly led to 'levelling up' and perhaps on grounds of comparability to even bigger increases where remuneration was already high. Such committees seem to be providing a fig-leaf rather than a constraint. There are few if any incentives for a non-executive to be a hard-liner on pay. Reasonable constraint in this area can only result from an effective shareholder voice.

Cadbury exhorts shareholders to assert more influence over corporate policy and top personnel while offering no suggestion as to how they might be motivated to do so.

Given the report's immediate context of fraud it is inevitable that there is an implied preoccupation with this subject (which, important though it is, should be first and foremost for the legally prescribed 'watch dog' institutions and the regulatory professions).

Partly because of this background the Cadbury report often comes across as a hole-plugging exercise in over-prescription. Corporate governance should rest on basic economic and behavioural principles, backed by law, not on *ad hoc* codes.

6.6   Some suggestions

The shareholders are the legal owners of a company. They have a general right to anything of value that a company distributes. They elect the directors and have ultimate control of the company. Nevertheless the exercise of shareholder power over executives, eg by changing the management or preventing them from embarking on undesirable takeover bids, is despite current concerns still very much the exception. Shareholders normally behave as passive investors and 'vote with their feet', ie by selling their shares if dissatisfied.

Accountability in anything other than a formal sense calls for the regular exercise of shareholder sovereignty. This will not and cannot happen without information, motive and opportunity.

Information is increasing and sometimes improving. The recommendations of the Cadbury committee should give a considerable impetus to this process, particularly in the area of remuneration but published information has little point unless somebody is prepared to act on it.

The biggest problem here is that of motives. Small shareholders are powerless to do much to enforce accountability, for however vociferous individuals might be at company meetings, the costs for small shareholders to combine for sustained action are prohibitive. There has recently been an encouraging increase in the number of cases in which institutional shareholders have individually or collectively made their voices heard. They do have the power; the need is to give them greater motive to act, rather than to vote with their feet and to allow themselves to be unduly influenced by the free-rider problem (ie incurring the costs of action when the benefits are spread among all shareholders).

While nothing can ensure accountability, there is scope for effective reform by creating more specific and readily enforceable powers for shareholders with greater incentives for them to be exercised, particularly by institutional shareholders.

Such powers need to be the subject of legislation. The following is suggested:

- Every director should be subject to re-election by the shareholders in general meeting, every two years, with proposed board fees disclosed in the case of non-executives, as well as full remuneration for executives.
- The maximum legally permissible length of unexpired contract for executive directors, without shareholder consent, should be reduced from five years to one (Cadbury's three-year proposal merely codifies what has become normal practice).
- The remuneration of directors for the current year should be approved by shareholders in general meeting, on the basis of recommendation and/or comment by the non-executive directors.
- Any proposal to take over another listed company should be subject to shareholder approval.
- No resolution in general meeting should be valid unless 75 per cent of the shares entitled to be voted have been voted by presence or by proxy, and the percentage majority appropriate to the nature of the resolution has been obtained.
- The dividend resolution should not be valid unless 75 per cent of shares have been voted, not only on it, but also on all other resolutions before the same meeting.

Such provisions would highlight the fact that shareholders have duties as well as rights. Institutional and individual shareholders alike would feel greater compulsion to give proper consideration to the issues on which they vote. Moreover, the fact that the dividend resolution would require 75 per cent of shares to be voted on all resolutions would be a powerful incentive to shareholders to fill in a proxy card. Indeed legislation on the above lines would provide both the opportunity and motive for the exercise of shareholder sovereignty (the opposite side of the coin to accountability).

There is, as indicated above, a great deal of published information on companies and there is to be more. Do shareholders need more interpretation, other than by analysts, of what they can read?

Non-executive directors continue to be cast by conventional expectations (eg in the Cadbury report) in the roles of shareholders' policemen and 'signallers' between executive management and shareholders. Expectations about what they can reasonably be expected to do are growing and are excessive in relation to their powers. (In the last resort a non-executive director can only resign once and credibly threaten to do so perhaps once or twice.) Moreover non-executive directors do not exist in law.

Sir Owen Green[2] believes that 'the fading reality of a unitary board will be further diluted by continuing emphasis on the distinctive role of non-executives in governance. In that event the introduction, *de facto*, of the upper tier Teutonic shield of the Great and the Good will not be long delayed.' Whether the German economy has thrived because of or despite this system is arguable. However, given the way corporatism has worked in this country, that structure would simply be a recipe for heavily increased overheads and uncertainty of purpose.

It is, however, hardly practicable to go into reverse. The answer must be to legislate now to produce a clear definition of non-executive directors and their role (law not 'codes' devised by the great and good are surely the hallmark of a liberal and democratic society) and to give them powers at once commensurate with the expectations of them and designed to contribute to shareholder sovereignty.

Here are some suggestions for appropriate legislative provision (perhaps restricted to PLCs for many exemptions would be required for private companies):

* Non-executive directors should be defined as 'independent persons elected for longer but not having 'tenure' with the company of more than 12 months' and 'independent' should be defined to exclude: directors or employees of customers, suppliers and advisors; holders of more than three other directorships of listed companies; and ex-employees including ex-executive directors.

2   Pall Mall lecture, 24 February 1994.

- Non-executive directors' remuneration should be limited to board fees (plus one-off fees for exceptional time commitment on specific tasks); they should not include benefits such as pension rights, cars, etc.
- Company chairmen should be non-executive, with the implication that companies should have separate chief executives (provision for exceptions in unusual circumstances might be made).
- PLCs should be required to have not less than two and not more than, say, five non-executive directors (more must be dilative of effectiveness and influence).
- Non-executive directors should have a specific legal right to circulate their views to shareholders at company expense.
- Non-executive directors should not only be subject to re-election by shareholders at two-yearly intervals but also their past and proposed fees and associations should be tabled on these occasions, the past for information and the proposed for approval.
- Non-executive directors should be required to endorse or otherwise comment on annual proposals to shareholders (see above) about executive director remuneration.
- Regulatory bodies such as the DTI, the SIB and its offshoots, the Stock Exchange and indeed the Bank of England should be required to bring directly to the attention of non-executive directors any *prima facie* evidence they have of improprieties or misconduct in PLCs.

Any legislation might describe non-executive directors as 'non-employee' directors; such directors would be clearly recognisable as being 'officers' of the company only, while executive directors would be both officers and 'contracted' employees. As regards h. above, this might well do more to counteract fraud than any of the Cadbury proposals.

Overall, however, the thrust of these proposals is: to define and delineate the special responsibilities of non-executive directors, without detracting from the responsibilities which they share with non-executive directors; and to reinforce the powers of shareholders.

6.7   Final comment

Provided the legislative environment is right (in respect of competition and absence of subsidy as well as of 'powers') the interests of shareholders will, albeit imperfectly, serve the common weal. No other system of governance or accountability is likely to do it as well. It follows that the problem of accountability is in motivating shareholders to pressurise management into pursuing shareholders' interests rather than the purposes suggested by what I have called 'management choice theory'.

Chapter 7

The Governance of Co-operative Societies

Professor Brian Harvey[1]
The Co-operative Bank Professor of Corporate Responsibility,
Manchester Business School, University of Manchester

7.1   Introduction

The consumer co-operative movement in the UK, as represented by the national federation – the Co-operative Union – constitutes a significant sector of the economy, with 4,000 shops, 75,000 full-time equivalent employees and a turnover of more than seven billion pounds.

The good governance of this sector matters – not least to its member-societies, for over the last 30 years both food and non-food market share has more than halved; poor financial performance has resulted in 800 independent societies being subsumed; and the continued ability and willingness of the remaining 50 or so societies to absorb failed societies is uncertain.

This article describes the governance issues facing the consumer co-operative movement in the UK, and proposed measures to deal with them. These proposals were the outcome of a Working Group on governance established by the Co-operative Union, chaired by the author, and whose terms of reference were based on the Cadbury Code.

In December 1992, the Cadbury Committee, sponsored by the London Stock Exchange, the Financial Reporting Council and the accountancy profession, published its report on 'The Financial Aspects of Corporate Governance'. The report attracted far more attention that its chairman anticipated, due to 'continuing concern about standards of financial reporting and accountability, heightened by BCCI, Maxwell and the controversy over directors' pay'.[2]

Its Code of Best Practice provided a valuable summary of the practical issues which determine the quality of corporate governance – the selection

---

1   Professor Harvey was Chairman of the Working Group on Co-operative Governance. This contribution was originally commissioned by the Plunkett Foundation for 'The World of Co-operative Enterprise 1995.'

2   Cadbury Report, p 9.

and conditions of service of executive and non-executive directors, the functioning of the Board, and its systems of reporting and control.

The appearance of Cadbury's summary of best practice, at a time of widespread concern about standards of governance in registered companies, provided a good opportunity for other forms of enterprise at least to review and tidy their arrangements. The Building Societies Commission, for example, issued 'a consultation draft prudential note', and the Friendly Societies Commission, in a consultation document, said that 'it is not possible to ensure that a society pays proper attention to the interests of its members unless an adequate system of checks and balances is in place to ensure that the governance of the society is not tilted towards the interests of management and/or other categories of people rather than those of members, nor tilted towards one class or generation of members rather than others ...'[3]

A Corporate Governance Working Group was established by the Co-operative Union in the UK in the autumn of 1993 to report on the direction and control of co-operative societies to its annual congress in the following year, and 'make recommendations on good practice to achieve the necessary high standards of reporting and accountability'.

The Co-operative Union is the national federation of, largely, retail (consumer) co-operative societies, and the Union's Governance Working Group focused its attention on this sector, which has over 4,000 co-operative shops, 75,000 full-time equivalent staff, and a turnover in excess of £7 billion.

The good governance of this significant sector of the UK economy matters. The role of the Governance Working Group was not simply that of 'good housekeeper', tidily furnishing the co-operative retail sector with its own, 'me too', version of the Cadbury Report. Over the last 30 years, both food and non-food market share has more than halved; poor financial performance has resulted in eight hundred independent societies being subsumed; and the continued ability and willingness of the remaining fifty or so societies to absorb failed societies is uncertain.

These trends heap continuing doubt on belief in the existence of a co-operative 'difference'. If that difference is better expressed primarily in terms of the 'process' of democratic participation and control, rather than in the delivery of a distinctive retail service 'product', then attention is focused sharply on the substantive meaning of co-operative 'membership' for a nominal eight million people. How are members' interests articulated?; how effectively are these interests represented by the elected (non-executive) directors of which society boards are entirely composed?; and how successful are those boards in governing the performance of the chief executive and professional team to whom they delegate operational management?

---

3   Commission Practice Note 1994/1.

The Co-operative Union offers an advisory and information role to its member societies. Within the co-operative retail sector there is a long and continuing history of effort to stimulate effective membership and, more recently, to train directors. However, at this point in the evolution (or decline) of the consumer co-operative sector, the establishment of a working group on corporate governance should not be regarded as a routine continuation of long-standing revitalising efforts. The selection, conditions of service and responsibilities of executives and directors, the functioning of the board, and its systems of reporting and control – the elements of corporate governance – have a vitally important function. They are central, both to the commercial success and effective member-control of co-operatives – and therefore to the survival of the co-operative form of retail enterprise.

Retail co-operative societies are not subject to Companies Acts, or Stock Exchange Listing Rules, they are subject to Industrial and Provident Society legislation. However, this combination of lack of conventional pressure in one area, and special constraint in another, need not inhibit action. Without legislative change, but through rule changes, societies have the ability to subject themselves to accounting rules and disclosure requirements similar to those of companies. Also, in the same way, many of the duties and obligations imposed on company directors may be applied to senior executives of co-operative societies.

The terms of reference given to the working group were:

- The responsibilities of directors for reviewing and reporting on performance to members and other interested parties; and the frequency, clarity and form in which information should be provided.
- The merits of establishing sub-committees of the board and their composition and role.
- The relationship between members, boards, senior executives and auditors.
- The establishment of a code of ethics; statement of business practice for internal and external use.
- The question of new legislation to back up any recommendations.
- Any other relevant matters.

In its response to these terms of reference and the evidence submitted to it, the working group was guided by the conviction that priority should be given in its recommendations to the requirement for transparency and accountability in the governance of retail co-operative societies. There is no reason why such societies should choose to be less financially accountable than the best companies of similar size, or, as member organisations, why they should not subject themselves to the highest standards of transparency.

The working group saw its commission – to produce a report on the requirements for the good governance of retail co-operative societies – as making an important contribution to:

- improving the quality of direction and management in pursuit of improved business performance;
- achieving the highest standards in management's accountability to the Board;
- promoting openness and transparency in relations between directors and members;
- re-invigorating membership recruitment and involvement.

7.2 Quality of direction

One of the key distinguishing features of co-operative societies is that the board of directors is made up entirely of 'lay', or non-executive directors. These are elected from the membership of the society, they do not necessarily (or usually) have relevant professional or managerial experience. They rely upon their appointed chief executive to run what have in many cases become multi-million pound retail businesses. Several of the recommendations of the governance report aimed to ensure high quality in the direction of societies, by:

- emphasising the collective responsibility of the board, whatever the quality of the advice they receive from the managers, and the need for a formal schedule of matters specifically reserved for board decision;
- proposing that the level of directors' fees should reflect the serious responsibilities of the office;
- stressing the requirement for systematic director training and development;
- encouraging directors to take independent professional advice as required, even by a minority of the board, and also to consider appointing an appropriate outside director to the board, having made its own assessment of the skills, training and experience of its elected members.

7.3 Management accountability

The accountability of professional management to the elected board is a central issue in the quality of governance, and of commercial management, in co-operative societies. The chief executive is the inevitable focus of great power and influence. He or she supplies information and advice to the board, and is the filter for communications between the board and the management team. However, this power, even where it is not abused, is not necessarily matched by an equivalent sense of responsibility. In the case of co-operatives, unlike the company sector, the chief executive is not a director. It is quite possible for the holders of that office to believe and/or claim that as mere employees they are not truly responsible for their society's policy, strategy and overall performance. One of the major recommendations of the working group was that chief executives and financial controllers should be appointed to the board.

Other recommendations aimed at strengthening the accountability of management to the boards of societies included:

* requiring the whole board to make the final selection and determine the terms of appointment of the chief executive;

* imposing a maximum three-year limit on the service contracts of senior executives

* establishing a remuneration committee to advise the board on senior executive pay;

* including details of senior management remuneration in reports to the Co-operative Union and in society reports;

* reviewing the conventional linking of executive pay to business turnover;

* excluding the chief executive from also holding the office of society president or chairman, or serving on board committees dealing with executive remuneration, or with the audit process;

* emphasising the responsibility of the main society board for any subsidiary companies, and the requirement for some non-executive members of the main board to serve on the boards of such subsidiaries.

7.4   Openness and transparency

As member-based organisations guided by co-operative principles, co-operative societies should be characterised by openness and transparency in their relations with members. This requirement translates specifically into an obligation upon a society's elected directors. Several of the working group's recommendations aimed to highlight these obligations:

* to reduce the risk of conflicts of interest which might threaten the primacy of members' interests in the conduct of society affairs, limits were recommended on the combined board voting strength of directors who are suppliers, employees, ex-employees of the society or the spouses of any of these, and such directors should not be eligible for the office of president or chairman of the society;

* to reduce the risk of 'permanent' occupation of the office of chairman, it was recommended that rules require no one could serve for a period of more than five years without a break of at least one year between successive periods of office;

* emphasis was given to the duty of the board to give a balanced, fair and understandable annual report to members, and to introduce the practice of half-yearly reporting of financial information;

- financial reporting by societies should conform strictly to the standards set by the Co-operative Accounting Standards Committee;
- all transactions involving 25 per cent or more of net assets should be reported to members at a general meeting, and Societies may wish to go further and invite members' approval of such decisions;
- in the event of a transfer of engagements, when a society's assets and liabilities are transferred to another society within the co-operative movement, the directors have a special obligation to provide information and safeguard their members' interests.

7.5 Effective membership

In a member-based organisation such as a co-operative society, the ultimate guarantee of effective governance is an active and informed body of members. The need for a working group on co-operative governance is evidence in itself, therefore, that all is not well with co-operative membership. Most of the recommendations of the working group were aimed at putting an effective mechanism of governance in place in the absence of an adequate level of membership participation and vigilance. However, with the longer term future of the co-operative movement in mind, the working group also made the recommendation that:

'the directors of societies should undertake a comprehensive review of all aspects of their membership activity policies and practices – taking note of the numbers joining, attending meetings and participating in society elections.'

7.6 A co-operative code of business ethics

The Cadbury Report recognised the need for acceptable employee behaviour and recommended that: 'It is important that all employees should know what standards of conduct are expected of them. We regard it as good practice for Boards of directors to draw up codes of ethics or statements of business practice and to publish them both internally and externally.'

By their nature and constitution, co-operative societies are expected to operate to the highest ethical standards and any that do not do so cast doubts on the other constituent parts of the movement. Recent failures of judgment in both the private and co-operative sectors have led to a loss of public confidence. Changes are required if the behaviour of business is to match its good intentions. Co-operative societies should also recognise that there are many positive aspects to co-operation that co-operators recognise themselves but fail to communicate effectively to their customers or the wider community. The values which guided the movement in its formative and highly successful years still have a relevance in today's highly competitive retail environment. To promote the co-operative form of business to a wider audience, these co-operative values should be articulated in a code of business ethics.

Research both in the UK and the USA has indicated the benefits which accrue to an organisation which has a comprehensive and enforced code. Corporate codes of conduct are in fact business guidelines that, at a minimum, organisations utilise to monitor the conduct of the firm and its employees in their business activities. They can also be another important system of checks and balances that govern the way an organisation interacts with those directly and indirectly involved in its business.

Benefits perceived by having codes include:

- providing guidance to managers and employees on the values and objectives of an organisation;
- sharpening and defining an organisation's policies and establishing a common language, attitude and consensus regarding ethics, proper conduct and honesty;
- contributing to overall strategic direction;
- signalling expectations of proper conduct to suppliers and customers;
- offering a self-regulatory alternative to legislation;
- communicating to consumers and the public that an organisation stands for ethical principles;
- enhancing employees' self images and recruiting staff who share such values;
- responding to shareholders' concerns about proper conduct;
- enhancing an organisation's public image and confidence;
- nurturing a business environment of open communication.

It is essential that each co-operative society develops its own code. The main reason is not that individual society's scales of operation, trading profile, locality and culture vary, although they do. Neither is it that there is a lack of commonality in the broad categories of those who have a stake in the co-operative enterprise, who can contribute to its success, and/or are affected by its operations. The code of business ethics of any co-operative society is likely to include the obligations its board accepts, and the standards it sets, in its relations with members, depositors, customers, employees, suppliers, other co-operative organisations, and the wider community. However, it is vital that each society must 'own' and be committed to the implementation of its code. Widespread participation by directors, senior managers and employees in the process of developing a code for their society is essential – not only if the content and the priorities of the code are to be relevant to the particular circumstances of that society, but also to ensure that it is effectively implemented.

It was not appropriate, therefore, for the working group to offer an 'off the peg' code of business ethics for 'Anytown Co-operative Society'. However, any code is likely to be based on an initial 'credo' statement setting out the society's overall commitment to certain values (such as democracy and mutuality), business objectives and stakeholder groups. The consequent obligations and standards in the society's relations with particular stakeholders would then be expressed in directive statements which gave guidance on, or prohibited, specific conduct.

Senior management, with initial guidance from the board, would be required to design an effective system of implementation. This might include:

- staff induction and training, not only on the content of the code, but also on the ability to recognise additional issues as they arise, and also on relevant procedures;
- the role of line management, the secretary's department, or other internal units in the management of compliance;
- annual reports to the board on the level of employee knowledge of the code, and experience of its application;
- an annual, participative review of the content and application of the code.

7.7   Conclusion

I have approached the task of writing a short essay on effective governance in co-operatives by focusing on the context and main recommendations of the Co-operative Union's Working Group which reported in 1994 to the Co-operative Congress in the UK. In a sense, therefore, I have told only half of the story. The working group recognised obstacles to the implementation of its recommendations. It is for the board of each independent society to accept and act upon the recommendations. The report suggests how the Co-operative Union might play a role, while recognising the limits to the authority of a trade association over its member organisations, and also proposed changes in the co-operative legal framework. For example, the working group, while concentrating on the governance of a going concern, also contemplated the governance of liquidation and transfer of engagements. The law currently demands that where a solvent society is dissolved, any surplus should be distributed to members according to their purchases rather than capital stakes. The practical difficulties involved persuaded the working group to propose a change in the law and society rules to require any such surplus to be passed to another society with similar rule provisions. The working group recognised the distinction between its own brief to consider the governance of individual societies, and the related question of the governance of the co-operative movement.

Chapter 8

Directors' Remuneration: Towards some Principles of Substantive and Procedural Review

Chris Riley and Diane Ryland
University of Hull

8.1　Introduction

A number of factors make this an opportune time to address the topic of directors'[1] remuneration. First, corporate governance is now enjoying sustained attention, and the issue of how, and how much, directors should be paid is central to this wider governance debate. A second factor is concern at the recent steep upward trend (rather than the absolute level) of directors' pay,[2] a trend which has been the subject of a near running-commentary in much of the press. This concern has been compounded by a general perception (supported by some empirical evidence)[3] that large pay increases have too often accompanied poor company performances. Thirdly, if we should be concerned about growing inequality within our society,[4] then the growing disparity between the rewards earned by directors and those earned by other workers seems to demand our attention.[5]

The plan of the chapter, and the arguments it seeks to make, are as follows: 8.2 sets the scene by describing the two concerns over directors' pay addressed by this chapter, namely its quantum and its structure; 8.3 examines the importance of a proper process in the determination of remuneration, describing and defending the role which 'remuneration committees' might play in such a process; 8.4 turns to the question of enforcing any such process, and suggests a mixture of regulatory strategies, involving greater shareholder self-help, a more active judicial approach and a new model of disclosure.

1　More precisely, and as will become apparent, our concern here is with the pay of executive directors, but we adopt the shorter description for the sake of brevity.

2　See Conyon and Gregg, '*Pay at the Top: A Study of the Sensitivity of Top Directors' Remuneration to Company Specific Shocks*' (1994) Nat. Inst. of Econ. Rev. 83.

3　See Conyon and Gregg, op cit note 2, and Gregg, Machin and Szymanski, '*The Disappearing Relationship Between Directors' Pay and Corporate Performance*' (1993) BJ of Ind Rels 1.

4　See, for example, Jenkins and Cowell, '*Dwarfs and Giants in the 1980's: Trends in the UK Income Distribution*' (1994) 15 Fisc. Studies 99.

5　Conyon and Gregg op cit note 2.

8.2   Identifying the issues

Much of the debate over the level of directors' remuneration focuses upon the *amount* any particular director receives. The problem is seen as one of distribution: a cake of a given size is to be divided and the task is to determine how large a slice directors should receive. The complaint is that, in large companies with dispersed shareholdings (the sorts of companies with which this chapter is concerned) the directors hold the knife and they choose where to cut. The object of concern, moreover, extends beyond salary to encompass such related issues as the length of directors' service contracts and payments for their termination ('golden handshakes'). All of these problems, then, are but one manifestation of the larger truth that executive directors are in control and use that control to serve their own interests.

There is, however, a second issue, which we might label 'productive efficiency'. How do we ensure that the size of the cake is itself maximised? Part of the answer lies in ensuring that directors perform well – both with competence and without shirking. Of course, company law employs a number of devices to encourage such behaviour, the most obvious being the duty of care and skill to which directors are subject. Paradoxically, however, directors' remuneration might also have a large part to play in achieving productive efficiency. This possibility becomes clearer as attention moves away from the *amount* paid and focuses instead on the *structure* of the remuneration package. For that structure might offer incentives to directors to perform well by linking their pay to their performance. There are, indeed, a whole range of remuneration tools which can be used to encourage and reward good performance in this way: bonus payments, profit related pay, share options[6] and so forth. But the choice of such tools, and in particular the sort of behaviour we wish to encourage, requires us to answer two related questions: how do we measure good performance by directors, and who suffers if directors are over-paid?

The orthodox view, which drives most of UK company law, answers both these questions from the perspective of shareholders. Shareholders are entitled to the residual profits of the company; if directors receive too much, then less is left for them. Similarly, the purpose of the company is to advance the interests of shareholders: so good management is that which, say, maximises profits or shareholder wealth.[7] The orthodoxy is, however, rejected by a number of alternative conceptions of the nature of the company, its purposes,

---

6   Note that many share option schemes were introduced in 1984, after changes were made to the tax system to encourage their use. However, under these tax rules, schemes had to be renewed after, at most, 10 years. This has added to the current attention devoted to directors' pay. See generally Whitehouse and Stuart Buttle, *Revenue Law* (London: Butterworths, 1993, 11th edn) Chapter 36.

7   On the differences between these measures, see Parkinson, *Corporate Power and Responsibility (Oxford: Clarendon Press*, 1993), pp 89-92.

and the relationships which constitute it. We could, for example, conceive of the company as a collection of various groups of actors or stakeholders (investors, creditors, employees, consumers etc), and claim that the task of management is to advance, yet balance, the often conflicting interests of these groups. On this view, excessive rewards for one group (say, directors) means less for all the others (and not merely for shareholders).

Reform to directors' remuneration – or indeed to corporate governance generally – must ultimately choose between different conceptions of the company, and justify that choice. But can we say anything further about the specific issue of directors' remuneration until we have made and justified such a choice? Arguably we can, for the reforms outlined in 8.3 seek to control the rewards earned by directors, and to ensure that such directors are better motivated to advance the interests of the company. How any money saved by such control should be redistributed, and how the interests of the company (and thus what is to count as good management) should be defined, can remain further questions which need not be addressed here. Our only concession to the orthodoxy is in the strategy we suggest for enforcement. As noted in the introduction, we rely heavily upon shareholder self-help. Were shareholders not the main beneficiaries of the reforms we propose, then it is unlikely they would, or should be expected to, play such an active role. The further task then would be to explain how far others – employees, consumers and so forth – could and would take on a greater enforcement role in place of shareholders. This is something which we do not address in this chapter.[8]

8.3   Process and the role of the remuneration committee

We noted above that problems over the quantum or structure of directors' remuneration originate in the ability of directors to determine their own rewards. One solution would be for some third party – say the state itself – to control directly the quantum or structure of directors' remuneration.[9] But if we are committed to the allocation and distribution of resources by markets,[10] then this looks inappropriate. From this viewpoint, our task ought to be to

---

8   One analysis (the so-called 'incentives-residual rights approach') seeks to justify shareholders' entitlement to all residual profits precisely because this gives shareholders the greatest incentive to monitor the company's management and (presumably) because shareholders are best positioned so to monitor: see Alchian and Demsetz, '*Production, Information Costs, and Economic Organisation*' (1972) 62 The Economic Rev. 777. For a variety of criticisms, see L Dallas, '*Two Models of Corporate Governance: Beyond Berle and Means*' (1988) 22 U. of Mich. J. of Law Ref. 19, 53-63.

9   The state already does interfere to some extent through its use of the tax system to provide incentives for share options. See note 6.

10   We do not here have space to address the larger question of whether, or to what extent, resources should indeed be allocated by markets. For an overview of some of the arguments, see Buchanan, *Ethics, Efficiency, and the Market* (Oxford: Clarendon, 1985).

recreate within the company a process for determining directors' pay which mimics market exchanges. If we can do so, then the outcomes of that process – the remuneration agreements[11] which are produced – will enjoy the stamp of legitimacy conferred by market exchanges. And shareholders ought rationally to support this process, directing their efforts into ensuring that it is operating effectively. What form should this market-mimicking process take?

Perhaps the most obvious attribute of a market exchange is the bargaining which parties undertake on a self-interested but arms-length basis. Directors ought not, then, to be in a position whereby they unilaterally stipulate what they shall receive. One way to achieve such bargaining would be through shareholders acting on behalf of the company in salary negotiations with directors, but in a company with more than just a few shareholders this would be plainly impractical. It is for this reason that proposals for reform[12] have focused upon the creation of 'remuneration committees', ie sub-committees of the main board of directors charged with determining or advising[13] upon remuneration. However, one difficulty with presenting such a reform as a solution to the problems of directors' pay is that such committees are already fairly common, both in the US[14] and now in the UK.[15] Moreover, they do not appear to have markedly reduced directors' salaries. Main and Johnston, for example, conclude from their survey of 220 of the UK's largest corporations that:

> '[t]he data examined suggest that, if anything, the disclosed existence of such a committee is associated with higher levels of pay. And ... there is no evidence that they bring about any improved alignment of executive incentives through increasing the proportion of long-term compensation (value of stock options, in this case) in the executive's remuneration package.'[16]

Three points need to be stressed in response to such observations. The first is that we should avoid assuming that a genuine market determination of

---

11 The term 'remuneration agreements' is intended here to encompass remuneration provisions in directors' service contracts, together with 'mid-term' remuneration decisions such as alterations to the quantum or structure of pay or golden handshakes.

12 See, for example, *The Report of the Committee on the Financial Aspects of Corporate Governance* ('the Cadbury Committee') (London; Professional Publishing, 1992). Institutional Shareholders' Committee, *The Role and Duties of Directors: A Statement of Best Practice* (London; 1991), Ramsay, *'Directors and Officers' Remuneration: The Role of the Law'* [1993] JBL 351.

13 One survey found that 54% of UK remuneration committees, and 57 per cent of US committees, directly approved remuneration, as opposed merely to making non-binding recommendations to the board: see PRO NED Ltd, *Remuneration Committees: A Survey of Current Practice* (1992) p 11.

14 In US terminology, 'compensation committees'.

15 Pensions Investment Research Consultants Ltd, *The Committee on the Financial Aspects of Corporate Governance: Current Compliance with the 'Code of Best Practice' among FT-SE 100 Companies* (July, 1992), found that 87 of the FT-SE 100 companies had remuneration committees.

16 Main and Johnston, *The Remuneration Committee as an Instrument of Corporate Governance* (David Hume Institute, 1992), p 35.

directors' remuneration will always result in reduced salaries, or even in salaries which tie remuneration more closely to corporate performance. Salaries will reflect factors outside of the process itself, such as shortages in the supply of managerial labour and competition amongst companies to hire that labour. Changing the process will not change that situation. Indeed, it might intensify such pressures, as a more open, market process generates greater information about high salaries elsewhere and as each company in turn seeks to outbid others to attract 'top' managerial talent.[17]

The second point is that many existing remuneration committees – and the process of which they are a part – appear to be seriously flawed, in a number of ways. Crucially, to be effective, any such committee must have a membership and resources which enable it to preserve its independence from the executive directors[18] whose salaries[19] fall within its remit. It seems self-evident that executive directors ought not to be members[20] of such committees, although it is evident that many remuneration committees do include executives.[21] Less obviously, simply being a 'non-executive' director does not guarantee sufficient independence either. Rather, a more rigorous test of independence, which excludes various relationships with the company, is required.[22] Indeed, the qualities of a good member of the remuneration committee might be rather different from the qualities required for, say, a member of the audit committee. It is common to choose, as non-executive or independent directors, those who are executives of other companies. This often makes good sense, in view of the expertise they will possess. However, if those who are executives of other companies are, for that reason, rather too ready to accept the merits of high awards, and if executive experience elsewhere is less important for effective participation in the remuneration committee, there is a strong argument for restricting its membership to independent directors who lack other executive ties.

---

17   On this so-called 'ratcheting' effect, see Yablon, *'Overcompensating: The Corporate Lawyer and Executive Pay'* (1992) 92 Colum. L. Rev. 1867, 1877-1881 (a review of Crystal, In Search of Excess) (New York: W W Norton & Co, 1991).

18   The remuneration of non-executives raises a whole series of issues which we do not address here. For a brief discussion, see Maw, Lord Lane of Horsell and Sir Craig-Cooper, *Maw on Corporate Governance* (Aldershot: Dartmouth, 1994) pp 40-1.

19   It would seem sensible to include other remuneration related matters, such as golden handshakes, within the committee's remit.

20   This does not preclude the committee talking to executives. Indeed, this seems obviously necessary given that remuneration policy must take account of other corporate policies which directors do properly determine.

21   See *PRO NED Ltd*, op. cit. note 13, pp 4-5, which found that 86 per cent of the remuneration committees surveyed had a majority of non-executive directors and 11 per cent had a majority of executive directors as members. 62 per cent of the committees were chaired by the main board Chairman, 5 per cent by the Chief Executive and 31 per cent by a non-executive director.

22   See, for example, the definition of independence (in terms of the 'absence of a significant relationship with the corporation') in the American Law Institute's *Principles of Corporate Governance: Analysis and Recommendations* (St Paul, Minn: ALI, 1994) §1.34.

More generally, securing a pool of appropriately independent directors takes us into corporate governance more generally, and points to an obvious truth: we cannot simply reform, in isolation, the process for settling directors' remuneration. The structure and role of the board itself, the merits of so-called 'nomination committees' for selecting independent directors, and the resources available to directors, are all implicated in the process advocated here.

Returning to the remuneration committee itself, it clearly needs to be well informed, with adequate data about the 'going rates' of remuneration for comparable executives. And this information ought not to be obtained by, or filtered through, the company's own management. The committee, then, will need the resources to enable it to collect and process such data.[23] Given that the members of the remuneration committee are unlikely themselves to be remuneration experts, it would also seem essential that the committee be served by a remuneration consultant. The committee must be free to choose its own consultant, and that consultant must also have the necessary qualities to ensure that she serves the interests of the company and not those of the executive directors. Crystal,[24] for example, advocates that the committee's consultant should have 'no ties of any sort with the company's management', that she should attend all the committee's meetings and should furnish frequent written opinions.[25] He also advocates protection, similar to that enjoyed by auditors, for the consultant against her removal by the company.

8.4   Implementation and enforcement

The third point to make in response to complaints about the effectiveness of remuneration committees is that designing a process (hereinafter the 'model process') of the type outlined in the previous part is only a start. What are crucial to its success are the mechanisms which exist for its enforcement. The task is both to ensure that an appropriately constituted and resourced remuneration committee is initially adopted, and then to monitor and control the operation of that committee in practice. These are the questions we address in this part. We begin by discussing the capacity which shareholders already enjoy to enjoin the model process directly, ensuring that remuneration committees are adopted and work effectively. We shall argue that, despite a permissive legal regime which does not prescribe the model process,

---

23   The PRO NED survey (op. cit. note 13) notes (p 13) that `[i]t is doubtful whether non-executives and other members of remuneration committees are sufficiently well served with adequate and objective data'.

24   Crystal, *In Search of Excess* (New York: Norton & Co, 1991) chapter 15. Crystal was himself a remuneration consultant in the US, although his observations and recommendations seem to contain much of relevance to the UK.

25   This requirement is part of the new model of disclosure which we discuss below.

shareholders are already able to do much here. However, two sets of problems limit this enforcement strategy. The first is the collective action problem. Shareholder monitoring, without an appropriate infrastructure of legal norms, will be at best partial and often perfunctory in the enforcement it will generate. The second problem is the form of action being relied upon here. We are contemplating steps to enjoin the process. However, if it is the case that efforts to enjoin the process cannot always ensure that the process is perfectly implemented, then we must contemplate that sometimes the company will be harmed by poor remuneration agreements. In such cases, merely changing and improving the process for the future will be an inadequate remedy. Action to compensate the company for its losses – either by challenging the offending agreement, or by holding to account those company agents who have so harmed it – will be required. It is important to see the diversity of responses which these different forms of action represent, a diversity which defeats any attempt to reduce the debate over enforcement to a simple dichotomy between legal – versus self-regulation.

8.4.1   Enjoining the model process and the role of shareholder voice

To what extent do shareholders enjoy the voice to insist that their companies fully implement the model process? Subject to a limited number of exceptions noted below, company law currently leaves it to each company to choose for itself, in its constitution, the process by which the remuneration of directors should be determined. This might seem a doubtful summary of current legal doctrine, for it is trite law that directors must not put themselves in a position in which their personal interests conflict with the interests of their company, a rule which prevents the director from contracting with her company. However, companies can waive the no-conflict rule, and it is generally supposed that most companies now do so. Certainly Table A incorporates such a waiver. Thus, Article 85 does permit directors to contract with their company generally, and Article 84 specifically authorises employment contracts to be given to directors.[26] Most significantly for this chapter, Article 84 makes clear that it is the board itself which has authority to award such contracts.

A few exceptions to the board's right to fix its members' own salaries should be noted. First, articles 94 and 95 respectively preclude a director from voting on any matter in which he has an interest which conflicts with an interest of the company,[27] or from counting towards the quorum for the

---

26   The authority conferred upon the board by article 84 might not cover all aspects of remuneration. So, for example, post-retirement benefits might conceivably not be covered. However, any such limitation is remedied, in the case of Table A, by article 87 which deals with directors' gratuities and pensions.

27   For listed companies, para 20 of Appendix 1 to Chapter 13 of the Listing Rules requires (subject to certain exceptions) a company's articles to contain such a prohibition against directors voting on matters in which they have an interest.

meeting which discusses the matter. These seem to count for little, however, for there is nothing to preclude either the director's presence or participation in the discussion, and reciprocal generosity amongst the board's members seems all too likely. Secondly, in some cases, prior shareholder approval is required for decisions taken by the board. Such cases include, in listed companies, employee stock option schemes involving the issue of new shares[28] and, in all companies, service contracts in excess of five years[29] and compensation payments to a director for loss of office, or in respect of retirement from office.[30] However, these provisions are clearly no substitute for the model process. Too often, a requirement of shareholder approval becomes a mere rubber-stamping of management's decisions.[31] A further problem is that many of the statutory provisions are easily circumvented. The requirement of approval for compensation payments, for example, does not apply to any 'bona fide payment by way of damages for breach of contract or by way of pension in respect of past service.'[32] Whether a payment is being made 'by way of damages for breach of contract' will depend, in part, upon the terms of the service contract under which the dismissed director was employed. And, of course, that contract does not require shareholder approval, save where caught by s 319. But that section is similarly prone to avoidance. Directors can award each other 'rolling contracts' of up to five years' duration. Rather than the unexpired term of the contract (and thereby the cost of its termination) reducing with the passage of time, the contract contains a provision which continuously maintains its term at, or continually restores its term to, five years.

The current legal framework, then, demands very little. Indeed, current practice (in terms of the voluntary adoption of remuneration committees) already goes beyond the law's limited requirements.[33] Within this permissive

---

28 See para 13.13 of the Listing Rules.

29 See s 319 of the Companies Act, 1985. It aims to ensure that directors do not award themselves contracts of such a length that it would be prohibitively expensive for the company to remove such a director during the currency of that contract.

30 See s 312 of the Companies Act 1985.

31 Note that a more active review can be fostered by bodies representing (institutional) shareholders, such as the Association of British Insurers and the National Association of Pension Funds Ltd, issuing guidelines to their members as to acceptable features of schemes which require their approval. See, for example, the following guidelines relating to share option schemes: ABI, *Share Incentive Scheme Guidelines* (1987, with Addenda 1988 and 1991, and amendments 1991); NAPF Ltd, *Share Schemes: A Consultative Approach* (1992); NAPF and ABI, *Share Scheme Guidance* (1993); ABI, *Long Term Remuneration for Senior Executives* (1994).

32 Section 316(3) of the Companies Act 1985.

33 One issue of significance is whether company law even allows remuneration committees which do exist to fix remuneration and bind the board, or whether the whole board must always take the final decision. In principle, there seems to be no reason why the company, in its articles of association, could not confer authority on such an individual or group. It might be, however, that the article conferring authority in this way will need to be clear, and that ambiguities will be construed so as to limit such delegation. See, for example, *Guinness plc v Saunders* [1990] BCLC 402, in which Lord Templeman seemed particularly loathe, on the facts of that case, to construe Guinness's articles to allow a committee of the board to have authority to reward directors.

regime, however, shareholders do still enjoy the 'voice' to demand the implementation of the model process. They could, for example, vote to change the articles, taking away the board's right to determine how remuneration should be fixed. Or they might use their power to hire and fire directors so as to procure a board willing to introduce the model process on the shareholders' behalf. In practice, such open challenges to management are rare, but their threat (rather than realisation) looks a potentially powerful tool.

The major issue here, however, is how far the collective action problem deters this sort of shareholder activism. The essence of the problem is as follows. If a shareholder chooses to become active and seek change, she bears the whole cost of her activism. Any benefits achieved by such activism, however, will belong to all shareholders in proportion to their respective holdings. This discourages activism in two ways. First, it is more likely that an active shareholder's costs of intervention will exceed her share of the benefits resulting from successful intervention (even though those costs may be less than the total benefits to all shareholders). Secondly, she may believe that some other shareholder will take up the battle anyway. She could then 'free-ride' on their effort, at no cost to herself. The logic of the collective action problem seems to be that apathy is rational. Does this threaten to undermine any regulatory strategy which relies upon shareholder enforcement?

Certainly, as one of the authors has argued elsewhere,[34] there are good reasons for thinking that this problem is less formidable where activism is required to enforce structural corporate governance changes, for example changing the composition of the board of directors or introducing board sub-committees. For one thing, such intervention is relatively limited in its nature and demands. It requires one-off intervention, rather than continuous, on-going monitoring, and should in consequence be less time consuming and less expensive. Moreover, it often seeks changes which, by virtue of their appearance in a variety of codes of practice,[35] are already widely accepted as desirable. Again, this reduces the need for individual shareholders to spend time and money researching whether intervention is required, and if so, what form such intervention should take. Finally, it takes advantage of the desire of some institutional shareholders to be seen to be relatively active on 'high-profile' corporate governance issues.[36]

---

34   See Riley, 'Regulating Corporate Management: US and UK Initiatives' (1994) Legal Studies, 244.

35   The promulgation of the Cadbury Committee's Code of Best Practice, which includes a number of (albeit rather weak) recommendations on remuneration committees is merely the latest example of such codes. See also the Institutional Shareholders Committee The Role and Duties of Directors – A Statement of Best Practice (London; 1991), PRO NED Ltd, Remuneration Committees (London, undated).

36   A good example of which seems to be PosTel's current campaign against rolling service contracts in excess of two years. See Lewis, 'Cut the strings on the parachute' Financial Times, 17 August 1994.

However, to point to these grounds for optimism also forces us to acknowledge the inevitable limitations of shareholder voice in enjoining the model process. First, while the structural aspects of that process may be pursued by shareholders, other elements may be enforced in a rather more perfunctory way. Thus, for example, ensuring that the remuneration committee's members are truly independent, enjoy adequate resources and so forth will all require a level of shareholder activism which collective action problems suggest will not be forthcoming. The second difficulty is this: shareholders want the members of the remuneration committee not only to be independent, well-resourced and so on, but also to work diligently and with care and skill. Again, shareholders can seek to ensure this by specifying in advance how the committee is to work – the length and frequency of its meetings, the quantity and quality of the information it must have, and so forth – and then monitoring the committee members' actual behaviour, intervening where appropriate to correct their shortcomings. But this would demand exceptional, and quite implausible, effort by shareholders. The whole point of devising a process involving corporate agents is that such agents actually do the task they are assigned. It is not for shareholders to perform the tasks for them.

8.4.2   Substance reintroduced

To some extent, these problems can be further mitigated by shareholders switching their focus from process to substance, in this sense: if the quality of substantive outcomes (actual remuneration decisions) can be taken as a surrogate measure of the quality of the process which generates them, then monitoring the merits of actual decisions might provide a more reliable guide to the merits of the process adopted, and its conformity with the model process. While it is important to introduce the relevance of the review of the substantive quality of remuneration decisions, however, it would be misleading to exaggerate its contribution. For one thing, monitoring substantive outcomes is likely to be itself relatively time consuming for shareholders. For another, evidence of substantive failures merely tells the shareholders that the process is not working in some respect. It still remains for the fault to be located and corrected.

8.4.3   Increasing the pressure to adopt the model process

Insofar as the failure to enjoin fully the model process lies in the collective action problem, then a number of possible solutions can be suggested. One is to rely more heavily on voluntary codes of practice of the type generated by the Cadbury Committee. There have been complaints about the substance of the Cadbury proposals, but as a technique for avoiding the limitations of self-help, what is the merit of voluntary codes? The obvious problem is their lack of an enforcement mechanism. They do not create their own machinery for enforcing their recommendations, but rely on a mixture of increased market pressure, voluntary compliance by directors and, primarily, shareholder activism. They take us back, then, to the very method of enforcement which led us to consider their utility in the first place. This is not to claim that they serve no purpose. But their contribution as a spur to shareholder activism has already been acknowledged, above, and found to be insufficient.

Perhaps the most obvious and apparently simple solution is to create a mandatory legal norm which insists upon the adoption of the model process by each company to which it is directed. As a mechanism for enjoining the process, however, this too has some obvious limitations. To some extent, directors might choose to adopt the process simply by virtue of the legal norm's existence, but given the possibility that this is not in their self-interest, it seems unlikely they would comply with the norm in a full and effective way. Some agent capable of enforcing the legal norm would remain necessary then, and the obvious candidate for this role remains the shareholders. We seem to be back at our original problem of finding an enforcement agent. In fact, however, this is not quite the case, for the introduction of a legal norm might facilitate shareholder activism by requiring less than majority shareholder action to compel its observance. If individual shareholders, or at least some small minority, were given a constitutional right to insist upon the model process, then this would reduce some of the costs of mounting the sort of campaign which might be necessary to procure change in the absence of such a constitutional right.

It might be useful to recap on the argument to here. We have suggested that shareholders can, and are likely to, do much to enjoin some of the features of the model process. However, insurmountable collective action problems make 'full' enforcement unlikely. These problems can be mitigated by using substantive outcomes as a guide to procedural propriety, and by other techniques such as voluntary codes of good practice, and legal norms compelling compliance with the model process. It is, however, surely clear that we cannot rely on the model process always being fully implemented. Defects in the process will remain. Some of these may be picked up by shareholders, either monitoring the process directly or reviewing its outcomes, and changes can be made in response. However, given the inevitability of such defects, and the equally inevitable time-lag in their discovery, some additional set of remedies is necessary to complement the enjoinment of the model process. In effect, action must be taken both in respect of poor agreements and in respect of poor conduct by the company's agents. It is to such action that we now turn.

8.4.4   Avoiding remuneration agreements

We have noted already how company law currently adopts a permissive regime, treating the process for fixing remuneration as a matter to be dealt with in the company's own constitution: the company can allocate such authority as it pleases. The courts, when asked to rule upon the validity of a remuneration agreement, have tended to treat validity as simply an issue of such authority. Thus, if the person authorised by the company's constitution has taken the remuneration decision, then the company should be bound, without regard to the substantive merits of the decision so taken. Oliver J's comments in *Re Halt Garage* (1964) Ltd, for example, illustrate well this approach. He observed:

> '... *assuming that the sum is bona fide voted to be paid as remuneration, it seems to me that the amount, whether it be mean or generous, must be a matter of management for the company to determine in accordance with its constitution which expressly authorises payment for directors' services.*'[37]

Similarly, for all the hostility shown in *Guinness plc v Saunders*[38] to the amount of the remuneration claimed by Ward, the case was decided on a construction of the articles of Guinness and, in particular, their allocation of authority.

If the argument for the model process is accepted, however, then two consequences would seem to follow. First, the enforceability of a remuneration agreement should *prima facie* depend upon whether it is the outcome of that process. If it is, then it should be valid and binding, however generous or poorly structured. If it is not, then it lacks the legitimacy which, it is claimed, the market process confers on the agreements it generates, and should be voidable.[39] To the extent that directors are risk averse, they are likely to adopt the model process rather than risk having their remuneration agreements set aside. In this sense, then, the process would be self-enforcing. Note also that such a rule seems to spare the courts too onerous a task when called upon to rule on enforceability. To be sure the courts must interpret and apply the rules which constitute the requirements of a bargaining process. But they are not required to consider the substantive merits of a particular remuneration package. Given the traditional reluctance of the courts in this country to become embroiled in disputes over corporate management, this looks obviously attractive.

---

37 [1982] 3 All ER 1016, at 1039.

38 [1990] BCLC 402.

39 One would then require some provision determining the circumstances in which the right to avoid should be lost. For a possible set of circumstances, see s 322A of the Companies Act 1985 (invalidity of certain transactions involving directors etc).

We suggested above that enforceability should *prima facie* depend upon process. There are two qualifications here. First, we noted above that the substantive merits of remuneration decisions might provide shareholders with a surrogate measure of the process which generates those decisions. The same point applies to any judicial review. In judging enforceability, substantive fairness or unfairness in remuneration packages can provide evidence of adherence or non-adherence to the conditions of the model process. Secondly, it might be that we would wish to treat remuneration decisions as enforceable even if they were not the product of the model process, provided they were substantively fair to the company. Imagine the managing director of a major and successful company with a salary as modest as that of a university lecturer. The salary was determined by that director herself, no remuneration committee existing in this company. It would clearly seem perverse to hold such an agreement to be unenforceable. This may seem too unlikely a scenario to trouble us, but this does not negate the principle which emerges: substantive fairness is relevant to enforceability.[40] For each of these reasons, then, substantive criteria of fairness must be developed and employed by the courts.

8.4.5   Directors' liability for breach of duty

It is important to stress here that proceedings for breach of duty are likely to be – and ought to be – rare. The intention is not to haul directors into court at every turn. Nevertheless, directors must face the prospect of having to explain and justify the remuneration decisions they reach. The prospect of being held accountable in this way is one means of encouraging directors to advance the interests of the company. Directors are, of course, subject to duties to act with care and skill and to act bona fide in the interests of the company. To what extent can such actions currently be brought against directors if they harm the company by awarding excessively generous or poorly structured remuneration packages? There are two doctrinal difficulties, both arising from the reluctance of the courts to entertain complaints about corporate mismanagement.

First, the courts have developed these fiduciary duties in a way which defers substantially to management. One sees this clearly in the subjective nature of the two duties mentioned. Thus, directors will generally find little difficulty in persuading a court that they honestly believed that their decisions

---

40   We might, of course, place the onus upon the director to show such substantive fairness. This is the position adopted by the American Law Institute's Principles of Corporate Governance: Analysis and Recommendations op. cit. note 22, §5.03, which essentially requires executive compensation to be authorised by disinterested directors or to be fair to the corporation. Where the executive relies on fairness, she bears the burden of proof (§5.03(b)).

were good for the company. Moreover, company law has traditionally required only that directors act with the care and skill which might be expected of a person possessing the knowledge and experience of the director in question. Most directors are not remuneration experts. More generally, one envisages that the courts will defer to the views of directors on the particular facts of the case before them, accepting their evidence as to the merits of the remuneration decisions they have taken.[41]

Clearly, if the threat of being held liable for negligent remuneration decisions is to be a realistic incentive to good decision-making, this judicial attitude must change. We noted above that the enforceability of remuneration agreements should be determined *prima facie*, but not exclusively, by reference to the process by which the agreement had been reached. A similar approach would apply here. In reviewing the competence of the director's performance, account needs to be taken of how the director made her decision. But again we cannot determine the liability of the director solely by reference to that process. Remember that much of the agent's decision-making will take place unobserved. If review were limited to asking questions about the decision-making process – on what information did the committee base their decisions, how long did the meetings last, were all the members awake, and so forth – then it might be too easy for the agents to 'cover their tracks'. The quality of the decision can, in some respects, be a better judge of their performance.

Thus the courts will again need to judge the substantive merits of remuneration agreements. In fact, despite the general assertion that this is a task which they will not, or cannot, perform, the courts have examined quantum in a number of cases. To date, however, these cases have not been of the type we are addressing here, namely the large corporation in which shareholders claim that their directors' pay is excessive or is poorly structured. Rather, they have usually involved small, insolvent companies, and the courts have intervened in order to protect that company's creditors. So, in *Re Halt Garage (1964) Ltd*,[42] although the court denied that it could interfere with payments which were constitutionally proper, it did order a director to repay remuneration which it found to be a disguised dividend or gift out of the company's capital. Similarly, in a number of cases brought under the Company Directors Disqualification Act 1986, the courts have again considered whether the remuneration paid to directors' was excessive in the circumstances of the case.[43] Now, it is obviously true that such companies

---

41   See, for example, the comments of Knox J in *Smith v Croft (No 3)*, [1987] 3 BCC 218, 236: 'I find the uncontradicted evidence of the very special field in which the company operates and the very high level of remuneration which obtains in that field very much more impressive than the statistics about general levels of professional remuneration which the plaintiffs adduced.'

42   [1982] 3 All ER 1016.

43   See for example *Re Cargo Agency Ltd* [1992] BCLC 686, *Re Moorgate Metals Ltd* (Transcript) 23 March 1994, *Re Keypak Homecare Ltd* [1990] BCLC 440.

(and their financial circumstances) are not akin to the large, solvent, companies with which we are concerned. The crucial point, however, is that the courts felt able to express opinions on quantum.

There remains, however, a second difficulty in relying upon actions for breach of duty. It concerns the mechanism for bringing a complaint. The rule in *Foss v Harbottle*[44] is an obvious stumbling block; it is simply highly unlikely that the board of directors will cause the company to sue themselves for their over-generosity! Theoretically, the derivative action does offer one possible way of outmanoeuvring such a board, but recent case law has surely undermined the efficacy of this strategy.[45] This difficulty demands that we rethink the role of the derivative action in UK company law. If the duty of care and skill is to retain some force as a discipline upon directors, then there must be some realistic possibility of its enforcement.[46]

8.4.6   Substantive criteria

Describing with precision how the remuneration package should be structured to achieve this is clearly not easy, and doing so is not part of this essay. The task of explaining how different remuneration packages influence the behaviour of directors with varying characteristics in the context of a wide diversity of companies is not a task for which company lawyers can claim any particular expertise.[47] The important point here is that criteria must be developed to guide remuneration committees in their task and to provide the benchmark for reviewing the substantive performance of the committee. This is not to claim that there is one 'correct' amount of remuneration for all directors, or one 'right' package. As so many commentators have argued, there is a wide array of possible amounts or packages. But equally this does not mean there is complete indeterminacy. Rather, the question in issue is the level of abstraction at which substantive principles can be developed.

---

44   (1843) 2 Hare 461.

45   See *Prudential Assurance Co. Ltd. v Newman Industries Plc (No 2)* [1982] 1 All ER 354 and *Smith v Croft* (No 2) [1988] Ch 114. See generally Gower, *Gower's Principles of Modern Company Law*, (London: Sweet & Maxwell, 1992, 5th edn) pp 643-62.

46   The US doctrine on the derivative action, together with proposals for reform by the American Law Institute, is informative here. See ALI, op. cit. note 22, part VII, Chapter 1, Boyle, *'The Judicial Review of the Special Litigation Committee: The Implications for the English Derivative Action after Smith v Croft'* (1990) 11 Co. Lawyer 3; Riley, *'The American Law Institute's Principles of Corporate Governance'* (forthcoming, Co. Lawyer).

47   For a review of some of the literature, see Ramsay, op. cit. note 12 pp 357-64; Jensen and Murphy, *'CEO Incentives – It's Not How Much You Pay, But How* [1990] Harv. Bus. Rev. 138, Rehnert, *'The Executive Compensation Contract: Creating Incentives to Reduce Agency Costs'* (1985) 37 Stan. L. Rev. 1147, and generally Armstrong and Murlis, *Reward Management* (London: Kogan Page, 1994, 3rd edn).

8.4.7   The role of disclosure

There remains one further area to address, that of disclosure. As we have
noted already, information is central to the model process. The remuneration
committee would need to obtain sufficient data to be able to bargain
effectively with directors. But information about remuneration decisions is
equally crucial to the review of the committee's own performance. To what
extent can shareholders currently obtain such information?

Although disclosure requirements in relation to directors' pay are
numerous, both within company law proper and in other regulatory codes,
they fail to provide the sort of picture of remuneration which shareholders
require in order to act as effective monitors. We do not intend to describe in
detail here the disclosure requirements, nor their many inadequacies. Those
points are satisfactorily dealt with in other works.[48] It would be tempting to
think that the lacunae in the current disclosure requirements could be easily
remedied through appropriate legislative amendments.[49] However, the
deficiencies in the disclosure regime are arguably more fundamental. First, in
some areas it might be difficult to quantify the cost to the company of
particularly complex parts of the remuneration package. This is well
illustrated by the Accounting Standard Board's refusal to require the cost of
executive share options to be disclosed in the company's accounts.[50] Secondly,
there are problems of confidentiality in making available to the world at large
all details of the director's salary. Thirdly, the current regime is based upon the
publication of a uniform, large body of fairly bland information, leaving
shareholders or other commentators to make whatever use of it they might.[51]
Such public disclosure clearly serves a purpose, not least in that it fuels an
active debate which serves to increase the pressure for reform of the
remuneration process. If the regulation is to work effectively, however,
disclosure must be linked to the enforcement mechanisms of shareholder
voice and judicial review described above. It would surely be better for a
dialogue to develop between remuneration committees and shareholders, with
the form and content of the disclosure reflecting the individual company and
the demands of its shareholders. A periodical report by remuneration
committees to shareholders, both describing and justifying actual
remuneration decisions, seems a minimum requirement. This would help both

---

48   See generally Gower, *Gower's Principles of Modern Company Law*, op. cit, note 45, chapter 17;
     Farrar, Furey and Hannigan, *Farrar's Company Law*, (London: Butterworths, 1991, 3rd edn)
     chapter 28; Ramsay, op. cit. note 12 , pp 355-7.

49   On recent US attempts to improve disclosure in relation to remuneration, see Straka, *'Executive
     Compensation Disclosure: The SEC's Attempt To Facilitate Market Forces'* [1993] 72 Nebraska
     L.R. 803.

50   See Urgent Issues Task Force, *Disclosure of Directors' Share Options* (undated) (para 10).

51   See generally Sealy, *'The Disclosure Philosophy and Company Law Reform'* [1981] 2 Company
     Lawyer 51.

shareholders in their own review of the committee's performance, and would provide meaningful information for the judicial review outlined above. Implicit in any such active dialogue between shareholders and the remuneration committee, however, is a body of members actively involved in obtaining the information they perceive as relevant.

8.5   Conclusions

We have claimed that the remuneration of executives is at once both a potential problem, involving the misallocation of resources, and simultaneously a potential solution to at least some of the problems of managerial misbehaviour and under-performance. A process was advocated which seeks to emulate market exchanges, based upon arms-length bargaining between the company and its executives. Having designed such a process, the more difficult task remained: to ensure that it would be enforced in a meaningful way. We noted that shareholders could do much to enjoin the process, by use of their voice within companies. However, because of collective action problems and the difficulties in enforcing any process which depends upon the actions of agents, such enforcement was envisaged as likely to be perfunctory in many cases. Given the inevitability that the process would sometimes be imperfectly adopted, and that only would be realised on an ex post basis, we then turned to examine how loss to the company caused thereby might be remedied. This, of necessity, involved a process of judicial review.

As we noted at the outset, this chapter also assumed an orthodox framework of analysis, in that we took shareholders as the losers where directors' compensation is excessive, and we took the advancement of shareholders' interests as the benchmark by which to judge good management behaviour. Of course, such orthodoxy requires justification. But even if it cannot be justified, then the basic framework presented here will remain valid. We shall still require something like the model process to determine pay, and we shall still need to review the outcomes of that process. One obvious change will be that the substantive criteria by which we judge good management, and thus good 'incentivising' packages, will be something other than the maximisation of shareholder wealth. The most difficult problem then will be the development of an effective means of enforcement. Our analysis above emphasised the policing role shareholders must play. If they are not the sole, or even main, beneficiaries of such activity, it is at least questionable that they will, or ought to, play such an active role. New models of enforcement will then be necessary.

Chapter 9

The Role of the Non-Executive Director

Janet Dine
Professor of Law and Head of Law Department, University of Essex

9.1   Introduction

The report of the Cadbury Committee on The Financial Aspects of Corporate Governance raised fears that the UK was moving towards an adoption of the two-tier board structure set out in the draft EC Fifth Directive[1] and espoused in a number of Member States of the European Union. This paper explains why such fears are only partially justified, examines the theoretical background to issues of corporate governance and suggests a way forward for consideration.

9.2   The Cadbury view

The make up and function of the board was by far the most controversial area addressed by the Cadbury Committee in their report on *The Financial Aspects of Corporate Governance*. The Committee emphasised that tests of a board's effectiveness include the way in which members as a whole work together.[2] They also felt that executive and non-executive directors were likely to contribute in different and complementary ways. Non-executive directors could make two particularly important contributions which would not conflict with the unitary nature of the board.[3] These were the role of reviewing the performance of the board and executive[4] and taking the lead where potential conflicts of interest arise'.[5]

The optimism of the committee was clearly not shared by contributors who responded to the draft report.[6] A considerable number believed that the

---

1   1988 Com (90) 629; OJ C7, 11.1.91.
2   Page 20, para 4.2.
3   Page 20, para 4.5.
4   Page 20, para 4.5.
5   Page 21, para 4.6.
6   For a more detailed consideration of these responses see Dine and Josiah-Brennan (1994) Company Lawyer, 15(3) 73.

separation of function between the roles of the two types of directors was a source for irreconcilable conflicts, and this split in their functions was a Trojan Horse for the introduction of a two-tier board.[7] Ernst and Young expressed the feelings of a number of contributors:

> *'The Committee's proposals would create a two-tier board within the legal structure of a unitary board. We do not regard this as tenable. If non-executive directors are to assume the responsibilities proposed by the Committee, it will be necessary to bring the law into line with these responsibilities and the implications of this need to be considered.'*

Contributors also argued that the burden placed on non-executive directors was an onerous one which focused attention away from auditors' responsibilities. One of the most commonly expressed opinions was that the pool of persons qualified to fulfil the role set out for non-executive directors was too small, so that the committee's proposals were unworkable.

Although the final report claims that the roles assigned to non-executive directors are not inconsistent with a unitary board,[8] the first role assigned to the non-executives was 'reviewing the performance of the board and the executive' and the second was 'taking the lead where potential conflicts of interest arise'.[9] Both of these reflect the role of a supervisory board in a two tier system. The danger is that the way in which the code has been formulated and will be administered may serve to stifle the debate about the best attribution of responsibilities and impose a 'straightjacket' uniformity on company structures, a move resisted by the UK in response to Community initiatives over many years.

However, the concern that the Cadbury suggestions will lead to a two-tier board in the sense understood in German companies and embodied in the Fifth Directive and the European Company Statute may be overstated. Those adopting that view seem to have underestimated the fundamental differences between the two-tier system, and a unitary system with directors having different outlooks and responsibilities. Two interrelated issues may have been overlooked by those voicing fears concerning the move towards a two-tier board. These are the shift away from shareholder power that the establishment of a true two-tier board represents and the consequences of this shift in the market for corporate control.

---

7   In this respect it is interesting to note the views of Erik Werlauff writing in *'EC Company Law'* Jurist-og Økonomforbundets Forlag (1993), expressing the view that the unitary system 'contains the seeds of cumbersome company legal disputes, which in a dualistic system are resolved in a more robust and simple manner, namely through the dismissal by the supervisory organ of one or more managers from their posts' (p 85).

8   para 4.4.

9   Report, paras 4.5 and 4.6, pp 20–21.

9.3   Shareholder power

The establishment of a true 'dual board' system represents a shift from 'shareholder power' to the power concentrated in other hands. This is fundamental because the residence of the power derives from the underlying conceptual understanding of the nature of companies. The UK espouses a contractual theory of company law. This is made clear by an examination of s 1 of the Companies Act 1985, which envisages the formation of a company by the coming together of the owners of a company in a contractual arrangement. Other Member States have espoused a wider view of companies, laying less emphasis on the ownership of the company and more emphasis on the whole of the commercial enterprise and all the individuals involved in the company as a money making concern. The way in which the shift away from shareholder power occurs can be explained most effectively in the context of the effect which the dilution of the effectiveness of shareholders to control the composition of boards may have in the market for corporate control.

9.4   Barriers to takeovers

In its barriers to takeovers initiative, the Department of Trade and Industry identified the way in which two-tier boards were appointed and dismissed as a barrier to takeovers. Under the heading 'post acquisition integration', the DTI explained that the inability of new shareholders to dismiss incumbent management constituted a significant deterrent to takeovers.

In the two tier board system, possession of an absolute majority of shares may be insufficient to dismiss the supervisory board. In particular, the Fifth Directive provides not only for appointment of supervisory board members by employees, but also (in certain circumstances) for up to one-third of the board to be appointed by a person designated by the memorandum or articles.[10] This leaves a small minority of the board to be appointed by the general meeting. Since certain powers of management are devolved to the supervisory board, including appointment of the management board (the executive directors), this may mean that a new majority shareholder will be unable to change the incumbent management. Further problems are caused by the employee participation rules in some Member States which provide for worker representatives to be elected to the supervisory boards of companies, and further provide that they can only be removed by the employees themselves.

In Germany and the Netherlands, a board elected for a set term may sometimes only be removable for just cause before the expiry of that term.

---

10   Article 4A.

In the UK, s 303 of the Companies Act 1985 provides:

'(1) A company may, by ordinary resolution remove a director before the expiration of his period of office, notwithstanding anything in its articles or in any agreement between it and him.'

This sweeping power apparently given to the general meeting to remove a director is, however, subject to two very significant qualifications.

One appears in statutory form in s 303(5) of the Companies Act, which expressly preserves the right of a director dismissed in accordance with s 303 to damages for any breach of contract of employment that has occurred. The rule is that the director may be dismissed, but because he has been dismissed by the company who is also the other party to his employment contract, he will be entitled to damages on the principle expressed in *Stirling v Maitland* (1864)[11] where Cockburn LJ said:

'if a party enters into an arrangement which can only take effect by the continuance of a certain existing set of circumstances, there is an implied engagement on his part that he shall do nothing of his own motion to put an end to that state of circumstances under which alone the arrangement can be operative.'

Thus, a director's employment contract can only continue to operate when the company refrains from dismissing him by passing a resolution under s 303. If such a resolution is passed, it is effective to dismiss him, but it is at the same time a breach of contract and damages for that breach must be paid. The same principle applies where the company is in breach of such a contract by alteration of its articles.[12] A provision which may in some cases alleviate this liability is to be found at s 319 of the Companies Act 1985. This provides that a director may not be employed for a period exceeding five years unless there is prior approval of the contract by the general meeting. Any term included in a director's employment contract which contravenes this prohibition is void to the extent that five years are exceeded. Unless the general meeting so approve, this will limit the damages payable to the amount payable to the director for what remains of the five-year period at the time of his dismissal. The director will also be under a duty to 'mitigate' the damage; that is, to take any reasonable steps available to him to limit the amount payable to him.

The second qualification to the power to remove a director by using s 303 arises because of the strange decision in *Bushell v Faith*[13] In that case, the articles of a private company provided that 'in the event of a resolution being

11   5 B & S 840.

12   See *Southern Foundries v Shirlaw* [1940] AC 701, *Shindler v Northern Raincoat Co Ltd* [1960] 1 WLR 1038, *Nelson v James Nelson & Sons Ltd* [1914] 2 KB 770, *Read v Astoria Garage (Streatham) Ltd* [1952] 2 All ER 292 (see chapter 4).

13   [1970] AC 1099.

proposed at any general meeting for the removal from office of any director any shares held by that director shall on a poll in respect of such resolution carry the right of three votes per share.' Since only three persons were involved (a brother and two sisters), the situation was that if an ordinary resolution was passed under the predecessor section to s 303, the sisters outvoted the brother by two to one, and he was removed as a director. If his special voting right was taken into account the same resolution was defeated by 3:2. This meant that the director in question was effectively irremovable. It was argued that such a 'weighted voting provision' was inconsistent with s 303, since that section had been intended to prevent entrenchment of directors by inserting provisions in the articles. The relevant section (and now s 303) therefore contains the words 'notwithstanding anything in the articles'. Lord Upjohn said:

> '*My Lords, when construing an Act of Parliament it is a canon of construction that its provisions must be construed in the light of the mischief which the Act was designed to meet. In this case the mischief was well known; it was a common practice, especially in the case of private companies, to provide in the articles that a director should be irremovable or only removable by an extraordinary resolution; in the former case the articles would have to be altered by special resolution before the director could be removed and of course in either case a three-quarters majority would be required. In many cases this would be impossible, so the Act provided that notwithstanding anything in the articles an ordinary resolution would suffice to remove a director.*'

Despite the identification of the 'mischief' at which the section was aimed, and the admission that the device used in the case made the director irremovable, the House of Lords came to the conclusion that it was permissible to have this type of weighted voting provision and that it was not in conflict with the predecessor to s 303. This was said to be because no restriction had been placed on the company's right to specify the voting rights of particular shares. There is much to be said for the dissenting judgment of Lord Morris of Borth-y-Guest:

> '*Some shares may, however, carry a greater voting power than others. On a resolution to remove a director shares will therefore carry the voting power that they possess. But this does not, in my view, warrant a device such as article nine introduces. Its unconcealed effect is to make a director irremovable. If the question is posed whether the shares of the respondent possess any added voting weight the answer must be that they possess none whatever beyond, if valid, an ad hoc weight for the special purpose of circumventing [now s 303]. If article nine were writ large it would set out that a director is not to be removed against his will and that in order to achieve this and to thwart the express provision of [now s 303] the voting*

*power of any director threatened with removal is to be deemed to be
greater than it actually is. The learned judge thought that to sanction this
would be to make a mockery of the law. I think so too.'*

In practice the effect of this case is limited, since such entrenchment would
not be permitted by any company admitted to listing on the Stock Exchange.
Nevertheless, it is an oversimplification for the Department of Trade and
Industry to say (*Consultative Document*, pp 20-21) 'directors may be removed
from office by an ordinary resolution, notwithstanding any provision to the
contrary in the articles of the company or any agreement that the director has
with the company'.

9.5   The concern of corporate governance

Corporate governance strives to provide a balance between the freedom of
management to make commercial decisions and control over that
management. The structures that have been examined achieve control in
different ways. Control may be achieved by opening up a free market in
corporate management so that inefficient management are subject to the threat
of takeovers and replacement. The exact opposite end of the spectrum is
control achieved by the full application of the two-tier structure, where the
supervisory board has the power to hire and fire the executive board but
control over the executives is achieved by the supervision of the supervisory
board. The proposals of the Cadbury Committee are a compromise solution
which envisages more input by non-executives without achieving the
fundamental shift in philosophy and power which would result from the
application of the full rigour of the two-tier structure set out in the Fifth
Directive and European Company Statute and espoused in a number of the
Member States of the European Union.

9.6   The theoretical context

Economists argue that corporate governance is contractual in nature. Thus
relations between individuals working within the company (eg labour
relations) are governed by an exchange (work for money). This holds good of
relationships between the company and outsiders, an example being a loan
granted in exchange for capital and interest. Into this model can be built the
theory that the market will look after vulnerable players, eg a lender could
require a higher interest rate if the risk of not getting capital repaid is seen to
be greater. It is important to examine penal provisions in the light of this
theory because the economists would argue that in many instances the
apparently vulnerable are protected by market forces, so rendering otiose the

intervention of the criminal law. However, economic analysis tends to leave out of account the difference in the bargaining power of the so-called 'contractors'.

The political view of companies sees all relationships in terms of balances of power. This may be useful when identifying the purpose of a penal rule because it may exist to protect a vulnerable group. However, as an analytical tool this theory may be faulty, for while it may enable very general comments to be made about common power blocks, unless a particular company is studied in minute detail, it will fail to take account of unusual circumstances (perhaps a particularly strong personality in a particular power block). An example might be a strong personality with a minority shareholding. Company law generally assumes that minority shareholders are vulnerable to exploitation by the majority. A powerful personality in this position might become a major influence within the company, particularly if s/he was the owner of extensive interests in related business fields.

The autopoietic analysis[14] points to the network of decision-makers as providing the essence of a company or group, extending the analysis to outside decision-makers as well as those within the company. In essence, this theory provides a slightly more realistic 'political' view of the way in which a company works by concentrating on where decisions are in fact made, rather than seeking to identify power blocks. The analysis works well when applied to groups as it emphasises the 'network' of decision-makers rather than viewing a group of companies as a hierarchy with 'top-down' control. This insight may be of particular importance where regulators seek to impose reciprocal duties on companies which are closely linked by cross-shareholdings, or where the issue is a manager's duty to a particular company or its parent/subsidiary.

All of these analyses are valuable in affording insight into the place of a particular provision within the company law context. An evaluation of a rule is impossible until the way in which it affects relationships within and outside a company can be appreciated. The economists may warn, for example, that an injustice is apparent and not real, because the loser has built into his contract with the company adequate recompense for the risk he was taking. Thus a creditor lending money to a company will charge a greater rate of interest if the perceived risk of loss is higher. On the other hand, the political analysis would identify certain creditors who perforce 'lend' money to the company, but are politically in a weak position so that they cannot use the market to provide recompense for the risks they are forced to run. An employee will be an example of a creditor in that position. This political viewpoint identifies the usual 'blocks' of power within a company and

---

14 Teubner, *Regulating Corporate Groups in Europe*, in Sugarman and Teubner (eds), European University Institute, Florence 1990.

suggest ways in which power may be shifted from one block to another. The autopoietic system, with its emphasis on decision-makers, might take a middle course, viewing the employees in their context within the particular company and investigating their power as one part of the network which makes up the enterprise.

To explain the way in which a particular company works, it is necessary to go beyond these theories to combine the good points of each, adding a practical viewpoint which examines the variations according to peculiarities of any particular company. This might be called a 'dynamic relations' system. The importance of the need to combine all three theories in order to obtain a true picture is that although decision-makers make up the essence of the company and its relationships with the outside world, as the autopoietic theory emphasises, nevertheless the relative influence of the decision-maker will depend on his situation within a particular power block and in the particular circumstances of his company and personality. To a degree, the relative influence of both decision-makers and power blocks will depend on the contractual arrangements between them which will have been influenced by conditions prevailing in the market place.

This is very little more than saying that one must look at the particular circumstances in each case, but it has two important lessons for the lawmaker and those seeking to discover the way in which a particular rule influences behaviour patterns within a company. One lesson is that situations vary enormously, depending on a huge number of factors including the particular personalities involved. An example might be that a company whose chief executive is female might espouse radically different policies from a company headed by a male.

Secondly, because of the complex interplay of the relationships, things may change with great rapidity. An application of the system of dynamic relationships would identify the way in which a rule would usually influence the behaviour of those involved in enterprises according to market contractual analysis, taking into account common power blocks and the relative position of decision-makers. It will also see those rules in the light of variations of influence which may affect particular companies. The likelihood is that this theory will tend to suggest a legal approach which minimises the objective rules which seek to control the exercise of responsibilities within companies. To be of use to cover all circumstances, such rules need to be enormously complex. However, if they are enormously complex they cease to be of use. As explained above, this appears to be particularly true when the rule concerned is a penal rule.

Thus, the application of the system would attempt to leave companies to be governed by the marketplace and by internal dynamics. An internal policing system of those involved in the day-to-day running of the company is much more likely to be able to respond with speed and sensitivity to indications of fraud, malpractice or negligence, than outside agencies. The ideal would be not to create a complex regulatory structure but to balance the influences bearing on a company so as to achieve maximum fairness. In circumstances where that ideal is difficult to achieve, a fallback position of flexible regulators should be considered.

9.7   The way forward

What force can be harnessed as a medium of control? The traditional answer is to look to the shareholders in whose interest many of the present rules are said to be justified. This chapter has chronicled the failure of outside mechanisms to provide effective legal control. All the theorists unite in wishing for adequate internal control mechanisms, since only internal control can protect the diversity of the corporate sector and police it simultaneously. Traditionally, investors have been weak and ineffective. Can this be changed?

The Cadbury Committee thought that it could,[15] although their reliance on shareholder power was less than convincing. The committee had very little to say about private individual shareholders and focused on the perceived power of institutional shareholders to ensure that the company complied with the code. The Institutional Shareholders Committee submitted a paper addressing *'The Responsibilities of Institutional Shareholders'*. This was not a specific response to the Cadbury proposals but dealt with some of the issues raised in the draft report. The Institutional Shareholder Committee acknowledge that 'because of the size of their shareholdings, institutional investors, as part proprietors of a company, are under a strong obligation to exercise their influence in a responsible manner'. The paper (published in December 1991) examines ways in which this responsibility should be fulfilled including 'regular, systematic contact at senior executive level to exchange views and information on strategy, performance, Board Membership and quality of management.' They also felt that institutional investors 'should support boards by a positive use of voting rights, unless they have good reason for doing otherwise' and 'should take a positive interest in the composition of Boards of directors with particular reference to:

(i) Concentrations of decision-making power not formally constrained by checks and balances appropriate to the particular company.

(ii) The appointment of a core of non-executives of appropriate calibre, experience and independence.'

The Cadbury Committee clearly accepted these views but there was not universal support expressed for them. Some contributors were against more

---

15   The Financial Aspects of Corporate Governance.

involvement of institutional shareholders. Mr FM McPherson of 3is said that 82 per cent of companies surveyed by 3is were opposed to more involvement of institutional shareholders. Furthermore, some contributors argued that there were ways in which structural changes could be made in order to give individual shareholders a voice. An example of a new approach is to be found in the published submission by Matthew Gaved and Anthony Goodman, in which they argue for Government policies to encourage deeper share ownership.[16] In this work, the authors seek to identify the barriers to investment which make the market a hostile environment for individual investors, and argue that a removal of these barriers would permit individual investors to play an enhanced role in corporate governance.

This author remains unconvinced that individual investors can be consistently motivated to be a controlling force in large companies, but does believe that institutional investors should exercise their *de facto* control and that in smaller companies a review of director's duties could make a significant difference to corporate governance.

Using the combined wisdom of the philosophies examined earlier, the ideal picture would seem to be an enabling law which takes into account market forces (economists) and uses the balance of power between interest groups (politicians and autopoietic theorists). The importance of the individual dynamics of particular companies must be emphasised.

Taking into account these factors, two proposals are advanced for consideration. The second of the proposals focuses on the reform of director's fiduciary duties, but the same approach could be adopted for more far-reaching reforms and could help to eliminate the misuse of penal law in the sphere of corporate governance.

9.8   The duty of shareholders to control

Shareholders should regard the use of their votes as a duty as well as a right. In order to ensure that maximum use is made of voting rights the following scheme should be available. If maximum diversity is to be retained, the scheme should be one which may be adopted in the articles of a company so that where it was considered unsuitable it would not apply. Three different types of shares should be available, for the sake of argument we will call them Shares A, B and C.

*   A Shares will be available for the ordinary 'Aunt Agatha' investor and will have limited liability and no voting rights. This share type is ideal for the individual investor since it is very unlikely that they will ever be motivated to exercise control over management. However, if an individual investor wishes to be involved in control they will be able to purchase B Shares.

16   Gaved and Goodman, Deeper Share Ownership Social Market Foundation 1992.

- B Shares will carry voting rights which must be exercised unless the holder is willing to lose the right to limited liability. The holder's liability for the debts of the company would be double the share value every time the voting right attached to the share was not exercised. The liability for the debts could either be absolute or arise only where there had been a breach of directors' duties. In any event, the liability would arise during the life of the company and not just on insolvency. The liability would be enforceable by any shareholder. Obviously B shares would carry a preference of some kind to make them attractive.

- C shares would be the only shares available to those involved in the management of the company. These would carry voting rights in accordance with the amount of investment made by the shareholder. They would also have limited liability.

The effectiveness of this reform depends on the success of the second proposal explained below.

9.9   Reform of directors' duties

In papers presented at the Institute of Advanced Legal Studies in London in 1994, this author put forward proposals for reforms based on an analysis of property rights in shares advanced by Professor Sheldon Leader. The underlying thesis is that purchase of a share gives a shareholders two rights. One is the right to uphold the value of her shareholding. In defence of this right the shareholder may vote selfishly without any regard to the benefit of the company. If, despite so voting the right is unfairly damaged, the shareholder will be entitled to compensation (probably as a result of an action under s 459 of the Companies Act 1985 for unfair prejudice). A shareholder defending such a right would not be entitled to set aside a decision of the management or company on such grounds.

However, a decision by the company or the management may be struck down if it is not taken bona fide in the interests of the company. This is because decisions which affect the interests of the company must be taken for the benefit of the company as a whole even if some shareholders are damaged in the process. A decision not taken for the benefit of the company as a whole should be challengeable by shareholders seeking to protect the value of the interest they hold in the company rather than the value of the interest they hold in their shares.

This analysis of the difference between a shareholder's rights in his/her shares and his/her rights in the company has practical consequences for a number of aspects of corporate governance. The content of the duty owed by directors to the company is governed by the type of right that the directors are obliged to protect when exercising that duty. Two aspects of this duty follow from the correct analysis of the shareholder's rights. The first is that the duty owed to the company is different from (and, where company decisions are made, should take precedence over) the rights of shareholders to protect the value of their shares. The second is as to the content of the duty.

9.10 Ratification – the improper elevation of majority rule

A number of the practical difficulties facing shareholders seeking to enforce the directors' duty is caused by an imperfect understanding of the rights which are being exercised. Where the harm is done to the company by a *mala fide* act of directors, the majority have no standing and should be unable to release the director from his duty. The company is bigger than 100 per cent of the shareholders. Unless a duty to vote unselfishly in the interests of the company is imposed on shareholders, all a vote will tell us is how they would like their rights in the value of the share to be protected.

In the other situation where shareholders property rights are being infringed, the majority also has no role since a vote by such a majority is merely an assertion that their personal interests lie in one course of action being taken, not that their derivative interests lie in that course. This tells us nothing about the legitimate or illegitimate impact on the minority's rights. The protection of minority rights should therefore focus not on balancing majority and minority rights since this does no more than pit one set of personal interests against another. Instead, the concentration should be on ensuring that no shareholder's property interest is unfairly damaged when directors move forward acting in the best interests of the company, whether the disadvantaged shareholder is in the minority or majority. Such an approach would eliminate the complex calculations which now determine the *locus standi* of a plaintiff and whether there has been a fraud on the minority. It is therefore arguable that ratification can only provide evidence of whether the directors are acting in the best interests of the company (because a number of shareholders agree with their actions), or that the course of action pursued is not an unfair infringement of the property rights of others. In either case a ratification by an 'independent' majority would provide the best evidence. However, ratification provides no justification for depriving a shareholder of *locus standi* to sue; because the votes cast by others can never be conclusive evidence that the company's benefit has been regarded or that an unfair course of action is not being pursued. Ratification ought therefore to be a matter taken into account by the court when determining what, if any, remedies are appropriate, but should be irrelevant to the standing of the plaintiff.

The confusion which has arisen in the case law stems from these misunderstandings as to the true value of a ratification.

9.11 The two property rights and their effect on remedies

Any duty needs to be enforceable if those who are owed the duty are going to benefit. Shareholders are in a curious position – they are often (though not exclusively) instrumental in enforcing the rights of the company as well as their own property interests in shares. It is necessary to look at the procedural mechanisms available to shareholders in the light of the analysis of their rights in order to determine what remedies are appropriate in particular circumstances.

If a right has been infringed which is in law a right belonging to a company (eg the misapplication of company property – *Foss v Harbottle*,[17] or indeed any other breach of director's duties) the only proper plaintiff is the company itself. This rule has come to be known as the rule in *Foss v Harbottle* because this is the case in which the rule was at first clearly established. In *Bamford v Bamford*[18] Lord Justice Russell said:

'... *it would be for the company to decide whether to institute proceedings to avoid the voidable allotment: and again this decision would be one for the company in general meeting to decide by ordinary resolution. To litigate or not to litigate, apart from very special circumstances, is for decision by such a resolution.*'

As a practical restriction on litigation this is admirable, because it has the advantage of avoiding the problem of many actions being commenced simultaneously by all members that believed themselves to be aggrieved by a particular action of the management. However, it is conceptually unsound because it elevates the wishes of the majority by assuming that if 100 per cent of the shareholders voted for a resolution then it would be unarguably right. We have already seen that this cannot be the case where the company controllers are acting dishonestly (as in the theft situation). Other problems occur when the company is sliding towards insolvency and the personal interests of shareholders are becoming less important than those of creditors.[19] Yet another difficulty is that of feeding in the interests of employees, should a shareholder wish to complain that they have not been considered.

All these considerations have led the courts to make exceptions to the rule that ratification is an absolute bar to a shareholder suing on behalf of the company and we thus have the exceptions to *Foss v Harbottle*. The courts have gone further and constructed a qualification to the exceptions which give greater weight to an independent majority.[20] This is a tacit acceptance that a vote by shareholders can only constitute evidence:

---

17 (1843) 2 Hare 461.

18 [1980] Ch 212.

19 *Standard Chartered Bank v Walker* [1992] BCLC 603.

20 *Smith v Croft (No 2)* [1988] Ch 114.

- that the company is being properly run (in the case of an action to protect a shareholders right in her company); or
- that the shareholders' rights in his/her share are not being unfairly damaged.[21]

Where the majority is independent of those who would most benefit from the decision, the evidence is obviously more cogent. Any ratification should therefore be viewed by the court as providing the opinion of a number of people on the way in which the company should be run or interests in shares should be protected. It should never deny *locus standi* to a plaintiff.

9.12 Conclusion

A way of reforming this complex area of the law would thus to abolish the exceptions to the rule in *Foss v Harbottle* and the consequent complications surrounding what can and cannot be ratified. This would be replaced by a statutory derivative action whereby a shareholder could complain of the conduct of the company. Ratification of the conduct would provide evidence of the proper conduct of the company. Would such an approach open the floodgates of litigation? It is most unlikely to do so, since the shareholder would not benefit directly from a finding that the conduct of the company was improper, and would be aware that a ratification would probably prevent a successful outcome, a ratification by independent shareholders even more so.

The alternatives are not attractive. We could retain the current complications or move to a statutory restatement of the exceptions to *Foss v Harbottle* in an attempt to inject an element of certainty. In such a statutory restatement, a possible approach would be to make a ratification an absolute bar to a suit by a shareholder subject to exceptions such as illegal activity, or improper consideration of creditor or employee interests. Not only will these be difficult to define – is a pollution offence carrying a small fine an illegal activity? – but also the whole scheme is based on the idea that apart from the excepted situations the shareholders votes provide conclusive evidence that the company interests are being served. We have already seen that this is a flawed philosophy. The flexibility inherent in permitting actions to be brought despite ratification and permitting the court to evaluate the true value of that ratification in those circumstances is more attractive, and is based on a fundamentally sound view of the interests of the company which go beyond an accretion of the shareholders' interests as represented by their votes.

---

21 This is consistent with the *Movitex* decision because ratification should carry different weight re (a) and re (b). In many cases it may have stronger weight in category (a) decisions.

Chapter 10

The Role of the Chairman and Chief Executive: An Industrialist's View

Sir Peter Walters
Chairman of Blue Circle Industries plc, SmithKlineBeecham plc, Deputy Chairman of Thorn EMI plc and HSBC Holdings plc, Director of Saatchi & Saatchi plc

10.1 Introduction

There are many important elements contributing to the success of a well run company, but the relationship between the chairman and the chief executive is crucial. Get it right and the benefits will flow throughout the whole organisation. Get it wrong and dissent, demotivation and even corporate failure will quickly follow.

The proposition itself seems sufficiently obvious that we need to ask why it has assumed such importance in the current debate on corporate governance and control.

The first reason likely to be suggested is probably the wrong one, namely that a number of recent very large corporate failures have arisen because too much power was concentrated in the hands of one man, be he chairman, chief executive, or indeed the possessor of both titles. By the time the other board members knew what was going on, it was too late to intervene and redress the damage.

When a big company crashes, the spotlight obviously turns onto the parts played in the events by the senior executives, and the likely conclusion is that had the power and responsibilities been more evenly spread, the disaster would not have occurred, or at least been much less significant. There is a lot in that argument and, indeed, all well run organisations have a system of checks and balances that apply to all levels of activity. Small fraud is not as damaging as large fraud and small errors of judgment do not bring a company to its knees. Nonetheless in almost every organisation, regardless of size, it is readily accepted that it is well applied systems that create the skeleton of good corporate governance and control.

Not, however, at the level of the chairman and the chief executive, where there is usually a much more personalised and less formal definition of their mutual responsibilities. Of course, both of them will be fully aware of their legal, Stock Exchange and shareholder responsibilities, and what they do not know can easily be ascertained from advisers within and outside the company.

But it is their relationship with each other which will determine whether their combined efforts dovetail sufficiently well that they make an effective top management duo. If they do not, then either by failing to cover the essential ground or by indulging in bruising ego battles over whose responsibility a particular activity might be, the company will be severely disadvantaged compared to its more effective competitors.

Very considerable evolutionary changes have occurred in UK commercial and industrial companies during the past 20 years which accounts for much of the focus today on the chairman/chief executive officer relationship issue.

Twenty years ago it would be generally true to say that the top executive posts in a typical UK company were that of the chairman and the managing director. Both would be full time executives and both might well have been with the same company for most of their working lives. The chairman was undoubtedly the senior of the two men, and in addition to his board responsibilities (ie corporate governance) it was likely that he would have the finance director reporting directly to him and be responsible for the overall strategic direction of the company.

The managing director, on the other hand, would be responsible for the effective implementation of the strategy and the attainment through his departmental heads of the immediate and medium-term objectives of the organisation. In the more recognisable nomenclature of today, the chairman would be the chief executive and the managing director the chief operating officer. Both of them would probably expect to retire at the age of sixty-five, and as likely as not the managing director would become the chairman on the retirement of his senior colleague.

But if that were the situation 20 years ago, today the process of change has taken us into very different and varied situations. That process is still continuing. Some of the changes can be directly related to what have been established practices in the USA for many years. Others have come from the relentless pressures of globalisation of business and the intense competition that the 'old world' faces from the developing economies.

When I first went to live and work in the USA in the 1960s, two things immediately struck me: first how much better paid, job for job, US executives were than their European counterparts and, secondly, how much more mobile they were between companies and even between industries, due in large part to the much greater extent of formalised management education in the USA at that time, which had created a cadre of problem solving individuals with a knowledge of management techniques that transcended individual company differences. In recent years, these trends have developed increasing momentum in top UK management structures and are now widely accepted, but also often criticised aspects of our corporate culture.

At the same time the physical and mental demands on top management have become increasingly severe. In the drive to meet international competition, mergers, acquisitions and consequent demanning and productivity improvements are the order of the day.

Information technology, electronic mail, Concorde and non-stop flights to almost every corner of the world have doubled the pace at which top management can work and therefore must work in order to stay ahead of the game.

The less able, and the unfortunate, take early retirement and even the most able find that they are ready, and their companies agree, to retire at 60. But therein lies an important element in the current view of the chairman/chief executive officer relationship. By retiring from their mainline jobs at 60, a new pool of talented experienced men and women is being created who can move into non-executive chairman positions in other companies and indeed in other industries.

So we have now reached a stage in this process where the chairman and chief executive officer jobs are more likely than not to be separate and will continue to move in that direction; where either the chairman or the chief executive officer or even both of them will be relative newcomers to the organisation, with the chairman likely to be part-time rather than full-time. All these aspects have been given impetus by the expansion in the number of privatised companies, where the talents needed to run a successful company in a market economy have been headhunted from other industries, particularly at the chairman, chief executive and finance director levels.

But while undoubtedly improving the management capability of companies, and the much higher salaries, bonuses and substantial share options offered have been a great incentive to people to move from their existing organisations and a great fillip to improved performance, a new aspect of the chairman/chief executive officer relationship now arises.

Just as I commented earlier on the corporate downfalls attributed to the dominance of a single powerful individual, we now have the possibility of two powerful people, who probably do not know each other very well, coming into conflict over issues as diverse as personal compatibility, corporate strategy or even the pace at which efficiency improvements entailing large scale plant closures and redundancies should take place.

There have been only very recently a number of high profile departures of very able, highly paid, chief executives with exemplary track records in their former companies who for one reason or another failed to accommodate to the ambience of their new employers. In both public and political interest terms, it is often the disclosure of the seemingly over generous departure compensation that is focused upon, rather than the real reasons from which we might all learn some lessons for the future.

Perhaps it has not been sufficiently acknowledged that bringing capable people into an organisation at the top level, though at times vitally necessary for the company, is nonetheless a high risk strategy. It is easy to imagine the chairman of a company, perhaps prodded by his non-executive directors, concluding that the company needs a 'new broom' from outside as chief executive to effect the large scale changes needed to revitalise the organisation in the face of ever increasing competition. None of his existing executives in the next layer down, the 'brigadier belt', either has the ability or indeed the inclination to bring about such fundamental change. Headhunters are engaged, a suitable candidate produced and an attractive free ranging description of the new chief executive officer's job is outlined by the chairman. But within a few months of the new chief executive officer taking over, problems begin to arise.

It is obvious to the new chief executive officer within the first few months that the main impediment to change is, in fact, the 'brigadier belt' itself. Not only are there too many of them, and a number will have to go, but also there will be substantial redundancies amongst their subordinates who have been loyal friends and colleagues for many years. They take their case to the chairman who is equally shocked that becoming efficient would require such pain. He sides with his old friends and colleagues. The new chief executive officer departs.

An extreme case you might think. But it has happened, and not just once or twice. What better lesson than to take us back to my opening paragraph that the relationship between the chairman and the chief executive is crucial to the effectiveness of any organisation.

In the above example there was no relationship. The chairman did not know the extent of his company's problems and the chief executive officer did not know how the chairman would react to his proposed solutions. Neither of them had the knowledge of the other to enable an effective compromise to be achieved. Not a 'papering over the cracks' compromise, which would in any case come apart before too long for one reason or another, but one based on a better mutual understanding of the sensitive areas in both of their positions.

It would have been much more satisfactory if their respective positions had been explored and established in the interview stage, but interviews are notorious for both sides trying to please each other, leaving the difficult aspects for later resolution. How much more likely would they have established the right relationship had they known each other longer. With foresight regarding future succession this could have been achieved as we will see when discussing the chairman's specific responsibilities.

If we could describe as briefly as possible what the respective roles of the chairman and the chief executive officer should be, it would be that the chairman manages the board and the chief executive officer manages the company. But they would go about their separate work only after discussion and resolution of all those issues which encompass a company's ever widening responsibilities.

10.2 The Chairman and the Board

It used to be said that a company's responsibility was to its shareholders. That, of course, is as true as ever today, but the definition has been widened from 'shareholders' to 'stakeholders' and these would include shareholders, of course, but also employees, customers, the community and suppliers. If any of these feel aggrieved or unsatisfied, the company will suffer also. In this context consider for a moment the difference in viewpoint of the executive and the non-executive directors who comprise the board.

In law, all directors have the same responsibilities but they will bring a very different focus into the boardroom. From years of sitting on both sides of the executive/non-executive divide I know that a divide exists. Not for personal or self-centred reasons, but because of the knowledge, experience and focus which the executives will have in great depth regarding their own company and industry and the non-executives will have in much greater breadth from their wider experience and because they are less likely to be caught up in the personal challenges to meet targets that have become an integral part of international competitiveness.

The first responsibility of the chairman, therefore, is to create a board in which substantial issues of company policy might be properly and constructively discussed.

If we look first at the size and composition of the board, the size aspect should be determined by whether, in a true discussion of a problem, there are enough contributors to bring sufficient points of view to bear or too many sitting around the table who might have insufficient opportunity to contribute to a lively debate. This suggests from experience that anywhere between eight as a minimum and 14 as a maximum would be the ideal number.

As far as composition is concerned, the generally accepted view is that non-executive (independent) directors should be in a majority. The point about the 'independent' qualification is that former executive directors who remain on a board as non-executives are in a somewhat anomalous position in this type of headcount, but probably as a species they are not very numerous in any event. More important, however, than the numeric balance is the quality and experience of the individual directors and the spread of relevant input that they can bring to bear on the company's activities.

The way that they are selected is of crucial importance. The chairman and the chief executive officer should together discuss the relevant input and experience that they would seek in a new non-executive in terms of nationality, industrial, academic or political experience which the company needs and increasingly 'headhunters' are the only way to sort through the maze. The 'old boy network' is much less likely these days to produce the right result because of the increasingly complex conflict of interest issues which arise as the demand for able non-executives grows apace.

In many companies, non-executive directors are allocated specific areas of involvement to familiarise themselves in greater depth with the company's work and people than would otherwise be the case. This and the allocation of directors and tasks to the widening range of board committees of audit, remuneration, nomination, and as is sometimes appropriate, research and environment, will be the chairman's responsibility. But, whatever their specific interests in parts of the activities might be, they should all be involved in ensuring that the chairman and the chief executive officer have plans for successors into their own posts. If there is no identified successor for either of them, steps should be taken to bring on board a non-executive who could in due course be the next chairman and an executive director who would succeed the chief executive officer. Thus potentially avoiding the personality clashes referred to earlier in this chapter.

Ideally, these non-executives will be the extension of the chairman's eyes and ears and either in full board discussions or at other appropriate moments will convey to him the views that are an essential part of his responsibility for assessing the right balance between the company's drive for competitive excellence and its public accountability. The board agenda should be framed by the chairman to reflect all of these issues and also to ensure that the board has contact with potential 'high fliers' in the organisation through presentations to the board on matters of current importance or concern.

The chief executive officer will invariably be the driving force of the company's activities, but the chairman will be its public face and is the one to whom the various stakeholders will look to ensure that the right and equitable balance of each of their own interests is fairly maintained.

10.3   The Chief Executive Officer and the company

At the heart of every company's activities is its strategic plan. In many organisations these days it is based on the 10:3:1 principle whereby, as the first stage, a ten-year look into the future of possible and likely demographic, political, technological, economic, social and cultural trends is portrayed which is translated into conjectural opportunities or threats to the company. Hopefully, with somewhat more precision, a three-year plan is produced in which more immediate corporate objectives and their outcome are postulated, followed finally by the definition for the year ahead of specific targets and sales revenues, operating costs, cash flows, capital expenditure, profits and dividends. It is this one-year set of targets that also is the basis for the rapidly growing linking of executive pay with achieved results. At each stage the board is consulted for their comments and appropriate consent.

This process is the prime and predominant concern of the chief executive officer and his executive colleagues. It represents his vision of the company and the ways in which that vision will be translated into profitable reality.

Sensibly, he will use all the knowledgeable input that he can find. Consultants and academics will often play an important part in the 10-year look ahead, but as the time frame shortens, the plan process is increasingly that of the chief executive officer nailing his colours to the mast. This is, essentially, his definition of the way ahead and he will appropriately be rewarded in due course on the results achieved.

He will, of course, have discussed the plans with his chairman who in the light of his own wider but less specific knowledge will have challenged and debated the salient issues. In many areas the chairman will have very considerable input as, for example, in the political and social implications of major acquisitions and redundancies and shareholder and City attitudes and expectations to high gearing levels and dividend restraint which fundamental restructuring might involve. The final plan will proceed to the board and trigger the next important stage of the chief executive officer's responsibilities, namely, to 'sell' the plan in whatever way is appropriate to his internal employee audience and his external audience of financial analysts and investing institutions. To the extent that the chairman's high level contacts can assist the process, they will be used, but it is the chief executive officer and his executive team whose credibility is being tested in this business arena though, assuming that the chairman has a successful track record and high standing, his public support will be a positive factor.

10.4 Conclusion

I have traced the development and likely continuing pattern of the separation of the chairman's and chief executive officer's roles and responsibilities. In an increasingly demanding regulatory and competitive world there are two distinct functions to be performed at the top level and the old adage of 'two heads are better than one' should prevail.

The physical and mental demands of running a successful international business should not be underestimated. Command in any organisation, corporate, military or political, can be a lonely place, and an ambiguous one, where the wrong order can be carried out with as little questioning as the right one. How much better therefore to have an alter ego in the form of your chairman or chief executive officer colleague to whom you can each entrust your visions, enthusiasms and fears about the way ahead.

Perhaps the spectacular corporate crashes that I mentioned at the beginning of this chapter have pointed us in the right direction after all.

Chapter 11

Reform of the General Meetings

Donald B Butcher
Chairman of the United Kingdom Shareholders' Association

11.1 In the beginning ... 1844 to 1862

> *'The directors ... being the managers of other people's money than of their own. It cannot be well expected that they should watch over it with the same anxious vigilance with which the partners in a private co-partnery frequently watch over their own ... negligence and profusion therefore must always prevail, more or less in the management of the affairs of such a company.'*

Adam Smith wrote those words over 200 years ago. Perhaps his sentiments influenced the drafting of the first Companies Act of 1844 – or to give it its full title, 'An Act for the Registration, Incorporation and Regulation of Joint Stock Companies'. The Act required the 'company to hold general meetings periodically' which no doubt were intended to provide an effective means whereby the 'other people' in Adam Smith's words could inject some 'anxious vigilance' into the management of the company's affairs.

The foundations of UK company law can be seen in three Acts passed in 1844, 1855 and 1862. The 1844 Act was followed by the 1855 Act ('an act for limiting the liability of members of certain joint stock companies') which introduced limited liability. The 1862 Act ('an act for the incorporation, regulation and winding-up of trading companies and other associations') was passed in order to 'consolidate and amend' all the previous legislation. The main structure of our present Companies Acts can be seen clearly in these first Acts and, in particular, the key role given to the general meeting in terms of regulation. Regulation was by 'shareholders' in the 1844 Act but by 'members' in both the following Acts. We focus below on certain features of the Acts which touch on the requirement for general meetings.

11.1.1 The 1844 Act

The Act refers to what the 'company is empowered' to do, what the 'shareholders are entitled' to do and what it was 'lawful for the directors' to do. For example, there were 14 items the company was empowered to do including holding general meetings, making 'bye laws for the regulation of shareholders, members, directors, and officers of the company', and appointing directors and auditors. For the directors it was lawful for them to do just seven things – to conduct and manage the affairs of the company, to appoint the secretary, to appoint and remove the clerks and servants, to remove the secretary, to appoint other persons for special services, to hold meetings and to appoint the chairman.

Individual shareholders were entitled to do just four things:

To be present at all general meetings of the company; and also,

To take part in the discussions thereat; and also,

To vote in the determination of any question thereat, and that either in person or by proxy, unless the deed of settlement shall preclude shareholders from voting by proxy; and also,

To vote in the choice of directors, and every auditor to be elected by the shareholders; subject nevertheless to ... and of the deed of settlement ...

Another interesting stipulation of the Act was:

That every joint stock company completely registered under this Act shall annually at a general meeting appoint one or more auditors of the accounts of the company (one of whom at least shall be appointed by the shareholders present at the meeting in person or by proxy) ...

Does this envisage that companies might appoint two auditors – one by the 'management' and the other by the shareholders? Legal opinion sought on the meaning of this clause averred that a drafting or printing error had most likely occurred.

11.1.2 The 1855 Act

The Limited Liability Act of 1855 was just five pages long. By contrast the 1844 Act was 32 pages and the ensuing 1862 Act 59 pages. Essentially the 1855 Act enabled any joint stock company registered under the 1844 Act to obtain limited liability provided it adopted the word limited as the last word of the name of the company. The intention was that this single word would alert creditors and investors to the risks implied by limited liability. Shareholders now for the first time had protection against acts pursued against the company:

'If any execution, sequestration or other process in the nature of execution ... shall have been issued against the property or effects of the company, and if there cannot be found sufficient thereon to levy or enforce such execution, ... then such execution ... may be issued against any of the shareholders to the extent of the portions of their shares ... not then paid up ...'

11.1.3 The 1862 Act

The 1862 Act which consolidated all previous company legislation was divided into nine parts plus a substantial First Schedule Table A. We note below briefly some provisions from Part III ('Management and Administration of Companies and Associations under this Act') and Table A:

- Part III of the Act included a clause 52 which read 'in default of any regulations as to voting every member shall have one vote ...'. However Table A, clause 44 reads:

  Every member shall have one vote for every share up to ten: He shall have an additional vote for every five shares beyond the first ten shares up to one hundred, and an additional vote for every ten shares beyond the first hundred shares.

- Under the topic of proceedings at general meetings we have the first mention of polls. In Table A, clauses 42 and 43 read very like today's law. Clause 42 reads:

  At any general meetings, unless a poll is demanded by at least five members, a declaration by the chairman that a resolution has been carried, and an entry to that effect in the Book of Proceedings of the company, shall be sufficient evidence of the fact, without proof of the numbers or proportion of the votes recorded in favour of or against such resolution.

  Clause 43 reads:

  If a poll is demanded by five or more members it shall be taken in such a manner as the chairman directs, and the resolution of the result of such poll shall be deemed to be the resolution of the company in general meeting.

- Clause 54 of Table A required the remuneration of directors to be determined by the general meeting:

  The future remuneration of the directors, and their remuneration for services performed previously to the first general meeting, shall be determined by the company in general meeting.

- The auditing requirements set out in clause 84 of Table A do not now suggest the appointment of two auditors as did the 1844 Act:

  The first auditor shall be appointed by the directors. Subsequent auditors shall be appointed by the company in general meeting.

  The provisions are thus now similar to today's requirements.

11.2   Fifty years of reform? – 1945 to 1993 (Cohen, Jenkins, Cash and Cadbury)

Tricker[1] has described the 1855 and 1862 Acts as making UK company law the most permissive in Europe and many would claim that remains the case today. Permissive means that the directors could do more or less what they wanted to do, 'control' by shareholders being noticeable by its absence. Reform clearly proceeds slowly.

There have been two substantial enquiries instigated by Parliament in the last 50 years to examine any necessary revisions to the Companies Acts in the light of the problems as seen at the time. Two committees were appointed to make recommendations – one in 1945, the Cohen Committee,[2] and the other in 1962, the Jenkins Committee.[3] Both committees addressed at some length what they saw as the decreasing 'control' which the shareholders were perceived to wield. This control was seen exclusively in terms of what should happen at general meetings and why it invariably did not happen. This was particularly so in the case of the Cohen Committee. Since the problem remains very much the same today as it was in 1945 and 1962, one can conclude that the changes in the Companies Acts made as a result of the two committees' recommendations achieved nothing. An interesting private member's bill proposed by Mr William Cash MP popped up in 1987 and disappeared quickly. The Cadbury Committee's enquiry was substantial and its recommendations were seized upon by a public evidently hungry for results far more extensive and far quicker than the committee had bargained for. We discuss the findings of these committees below.

11.2.1 Cohen Committee (1945)

The committee's report opens with the following claim:

'We have also sought to find means of making it easier for shareholders to exercise a more effective control over the management of their companies. The result will be to strengthen the already high credit and reputation of British companies. We must emphasise, however, that this object will be attained more by the selection by the shareholders of the right governing body of each company, than by the provisions of any statute.'

Which is really saying it's up to you, the shareholders, to elect the right 'governors' and don't look to the law to help you in any other way. The report then explains why this control will never be exercised:

[handwritten margin note: ⇒ Q: is control really the same or is it profits? achieved by good management?]

---

1   Tricker, RI, *Corporate Governance* (1984) Gower.
2   Report of the *Committee on Company Law Amendments* (June 1945) – The Cohen Committee.
3   Report of the *Company Law Committee* (June 1962) – the Jenkins Committee.

'*The illusory nature of the control theoretically exercised by shareholders over directors has been accentuated by the dispersion of capital among an increasing number of small shareholders who pay little attention to their investments so long as satisfactory dividends are forthcoming, who lack sufficient time, money and experience to make full use of their rights as occasion arises and who are, in many cases, too numerous and too widely dispersed to be able to organise themselves*'.

This was written, of course, before the great onset of institutional shareholding. The report concludes by reminding shareholders that:

'*it is by using their powers at meetings that shareholders can exercise control over directors.*'

but then obligingly explains why this will not happen:

'*The annual general meeting should be the occasion on which the ordinary members can introduce resolutions on their own account or, if they so desire, can oppose the resolutions submitted by the board of directors. This opportunity is under existing conditions largely illusory because with the great increase in the number of shareholders if has become difficult for any single shareholder, or even for a group of shareholders, to seek the support of their fellow members.*'

11.2.2 Jenkins Committee (1962)

The Committee, after explaining why it was:

'*probable that the voting power commanded by the directors at the general meeting, albeit a small fraction of the total potential voting power, will suffice to carry the day.*'

had no doubts as to where the blame lay for this state of affairs:

'*The directors of reputable companies would much prefer that meetings should be better attended and that more interest should be taken by members in the company's affairs. Members on the other hand are persistently reluctant to concern themselves with the management of their companies, and, so long as satisfactory dividends are paid, are content to leave everything to the directors.*'

Despite this the committee rejected the suggestion that the Act should be amended to allow voting on resolutions by postal ballot and, inevitably, falls back on the need for a general meeting despite having paraded, just like Cohen, all the many well-known failings of this long-lived, damned-by-all, institution:

'*Where there is any possibility of there being a difference of opinion between members ... we think there should be a meeting at which it may be discussed.*'

11.2.3 Cash (1987)

Twenty-five years after the Jenkins Committee had deliberated, Mr William Cash MP introduced in 1987 a private members' bill, called the Protection of Shareholders Act,[4] which was intended as an amendment to the Companies Act 1985. The bill, a delightfully short two pages, was to:

> '*Make provision for each public company to establish a shareholders' committee; for the allocation of a director in each public company to such a committee; and to prescribe the functions of the auditor, company secretary and solicitor of each such company in relation to that committee.*'

Clause 4 stipulated that:

> '*The Shareholders' Committee shall be so appointed as to secure a proper balance between the interests of the different classes of member of the company and so as to secure adequate and independent representation for members generally and for individual members in particular and the individual members shall be nominated for appointment solely by other individual members and not by the directors, by a body corporate or trust corporation, or by persons on their behalf of connected with them.*'

Inevitably the bill was 'talked out'. Notably Cash was the first to attempt to carve out a meaningful 'ownership' role for the individual shareholder. The bill was also intended, we believe, to apply only to listed public companies.

11.2.4 Cadbury (1992)

The company law changes made as a result of the deliberations of the Cohen and Jenkins Committees clearly failed to encourage the shareholders – or failed to equip them with the power? – to grasp the elusive baton of control. Thirty years after Jenkins it is perhaps not surprising therefore, that the very same issue – now discussed in terms of 'accountability' of directors to shareholders – engaged the minds of the Cadbury Committee.[5] The committee had a limited brief to enquire into 'the financial aspects of corporate governance'. The committee was set up not by Parliament but by the Financial Reporting Council, the London Stock Exchange and the accountancy profession. 'Concerns about the working of the corporate system' were the reasons reported by the committee for its being set up. The committee's aim was, moreover, to produce a code rather than to change the law. In fact, regulation by the market was seen as eminently more desirable than regulation

---

4   The Protection of Shareholders Act, 1987 – No 58 session 86/87.
5   A Report of the *Committee on the Financial Aspects of Corporate Governance* (December 1992), Burgess Science Press.

by law. The latter was, of course, the aim of the Cohen and Jenkins Committees.

Cadbury saw the issue of accountability in this way:

> 'Thus the shareholders as owners of the company elect the directors to run the business on their behalf and hold them accountable for its progress. The issue for corporate governance is how to strengthen the accountability of boards of directors to shareholders.'

A number of proposals were put forward to the Cadbury Committee aimed at strengthening this elusive control by shareholders. For example, one advocated the formation of shareholder committees which could become more closely involved in the appointment of directors and auditors. This was rejected on the grounds of the difficulty of the committee being 'truly representative of all the company's shareholders'. Many proposals were made aimed at making it easier for 'shareholders, individually or collectively, to put forward resolutions at general meetings'. This also received scant support. Predictably, Cadbury falls back on the general meeting, just like Cohen and Jenkins, and, like Jenkins, sees the shareholders as bearing the main blame for the ineffectiveness of meetings:

> 'In the meantime, shareholders can make their views known to the boards of the companies in which they have invested by communication with them direct and through their attendance at general meetings ... If too many annual general meetings are at present an opportunity missed, this is because shareholders do not make the most of them and, in some cases, boards do not encourage them to do so.'

'In the meantime' presumably means in the 50 years or so that it may take to change the law. Shareholders should, therefore, continue to rely on the much abused general meeting, essentially unreformed for 150 years, and recently described by The Economist[6] as the "Annual General Farce". Perhaps a small advance over Cohen and Jenkins can now be recognised in Cadbury's words attributing responsibility for the 'opportunity missed' nature of the AGM to shareholders and boards, albeit 'in some cases'. Cadbury manfully turns his face away from making any recommendations for reforming general meetings and places the responsibility firmly in the laps of shareholders and boards:

> 'In the committee's view, both shareholders and boards of directors should consider how the effectiveness of general meetings could be increased and as a result the accountability of boards to all their shareholders strengthened.'

The only suggestion Cadbury makes for this strengthening of accountability is shareholders sending in written questions in advance of the

---

6   *The Economist*, 12 March 1994.

AGM. If one sees the AGM as an audit by shareholders (see later discussion of this point in 11.8) written questions actually weaken accountability. It is difficult to believe that any of those making the recommendation have actually sat through an AGM with written questions – a truly lifeless and unrewarding experience.

Cadbury in effect provided the shareholders with a 'Code of Best Practice' and told them to get on with it:

> *'The obligation on companies to state how far they comply with the code provides institutional and individual shareholders with a ready-made-agenda for their representations to boards. It is up to them to put it to good use. The committee is primarily looking to such market-based regulation to turn its proposals into action.'*

11.2.5   Two conflicting themes?

If one follows the trail of thought which starts with Cohen and runs through Jenkins to Cadbury, two opposing themes stand out.

One theme is the consistent view expressed of the desirability of shareholders being the regulators of companies but at the same time rejection by Cohen et al. of any changes in the law which might actually contribute to that desirable aim. One supposes that this can be attributed to an extremely strong alliance between two very powerful 'camps', both of which prefer to maintain the status quo, and have succeeded in so doing for 150 years. One 'camp' can be typified as those wishing to maintain the 'dictatorship of the board', in Professor Gower's words, and the other 'camp' as those whose interests are best served by shares being seen as 'betting slips' and shareholders as 'punters'.[7] Who, it has to be asked, wishes shareholders to assume their ownership role? No such 'camp' exists.

The second, but opposing theme sees the shareholders as needing protection from rapacious, too powerful directors:

> *'A large part of company law exists in order to prevent shareholders' interests from being abused by company directors ... The point of these protective requirements is to give the shareholders the information they require to assess the state of the company's affairs'.[8]*

The idea that a regulator, say of the electricity industry, needs 'protection' from abuse of his interests by those he is supposed to be regulating seems faintly quaint. But the idea that shareholders needed 'protection' was clearly

---

7   'A Survey of Capitalism – Punters or Proprietors?' *The Economist*, 5 May 1990.
8   Mackenzie, *The Shareholders Action Handbook* (1993), New Consumer Ltd.

still very much in the mind of Mr William Cash when he introduced his Protection of Shareholders Bill in 1987.

11.3   The continuing 'annual general farce'?

Professor Gower's interpretation of company law[9] is the most pleaded. After noting that:

> *'General meetings are intended to be the means whereby the members exercise control over the management.'*

he concludes that:

> *'general meetings have proved a singularly ineffective way of making directors answerable to the general body of members and the boards of widely-held public companies are self-perpetuating oligarchies which control the general meeting rather than it controlling them.'*

However, after lambasting the ineffectiveness of general meetings, and this seems to be the crucial point, Gower notes ironically that:

> *'the legislature seems to assume the contrary by adding ever more circumstances where the consent of a general meeting is required.'*

Who now bears the burden of Adam Smith's anxious vigilance? Is farce a fair description for The Economist to use of today's typical AGM?[10] If so, why has it become farcical? Is it in the national interest that it should remain so? What reforms might convert a farcical situation into an effective one? Or has the original purpose of the general meeting, first enacted in 1844 and retained in all company legislation since then, to be finally abandoned as a purpose impossible of achievement? How do we at least weaken what Professor Gower described as 'the dictatorship of the board'?[11] Or adding Gower to The Economist, how do we reform 'an oligarchy controlling a farce?'.

Questions like these need to be addressed when suggesting reforms which will hopefully begin to restore some of the general meeting's original purpose – that is the accountability of directors to shareholders. Given the fundamental importance of these questions, it is surprising to note the lack of practical suggestions as to how general meetings might be reformed. For example, the DTI has some six 'working groups' focusing on various aspects of company law reform. No group is presently addressing the need to reform the general meeting. The only call made in public to do so to our knowledge was a recent

---

9   Gower, *Principles of Modern Company Law* (1992), Sweet and Maxwell.

10   *The Economist*, 12 March 1994.

11   Gower, op. cit., p 512.

speech[12] made by Paul Myners, Chairman of Gartmore Investment Management plc, in which he suggested that it was time to resuscitate the general meeting. His proposal, though, was limited to just making the general meeting an occasion when companies could release price sensitive information to the public. 'The general meeting', he said 'may be the ideal form for announcing new information so as to entice shareholders to attend'. Although a useful step forward, this suggestion is rather narrowly focused given the overall purpose of the meeting.

11.4   Why are general meetings so ineffective?

The reason for effectiveness having well nigh vanished, was pithily put by *The Economist:*[13]

> *'What is wrong with the British and American system is that far too many shareholders, both institutional and individual, do not behave like owners ... It is usually quite rational for most shareholders – whether they be individuals, money managers or arbitrageurs – to take a betting-slip view of their portfolios. None of them has any obvious incentive to behave like the owner of a company, nor any effective way to do so.'*

This begs the question: who does act as an owner? Clearly in the absence of committed owners, boards of companies have increasingly assumed this role in practice. In effect, the directors of large quoted PLCs have become only accountable to themselves. We, therefore, start from the position that what the UK needs is more involved and committed shareholders – more proprietors, less punters, as The Economist put it in the survey quoted above. Our view is that these proprietor shareholders should include private shareholders. Interestingly the case for 'deeper share ownership', as opposed to wider share ownership, has been little argued and government policy over the last 10 years has seemed to be exclusively concerned with creating wide share ownership. However, the case for deeper share ownership has recently been very cogently put by Gaved and Goodman.[14] The nub of their argument is:

> *'Widespread and direct share ownership of company capital is a necessary condition for the emergence of a dynamic and creative market economy whose principles are understood and underwritten by a broad consensus of society.'*

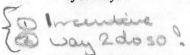

12   *'Corporate Governance – More Than Just a Cliché?'* Speech made to the National Association of Pension Funds Investment Conference, Eastbourne (23-25 February 1992).

13   op. cit., note 7.

14   Gaved and Goodman, *Deeper Share Ownership* (1992), The Social Market Foundation.

11.5 Some basic assumptions

First, we are concerned primarily with listed public limited companies. Although such companies comprise a very small percentage of all those UK companies which are covered by the Companies Acts, they do represent a very significant part of the UK economy and attract a major slice of the investment funds of the institutional investors and the savings of private investors. Being listed means that they have to comply with rules laid down by the Stock Exchange and other regulations aimed at fairness of treatment of the companies' many thousands of shareholders. This means that the general meeting of the typical PLC should be effective and seen to be so.

Secondly, the general meeting provides the occasion when ownership responsibilities can be discharged. Regrettably, as Cadbury reported, general meetings are largely 'an opportunity missed'. For example, institutional shareholders typically vote just thirty per cent of shares owned. The record of private shareholders is no better. Institutional shareholders shun general meetings because they believe they have more (cost) effective ways of communicating their concerns to companies. Any reforms, therefore, have to reflect these different shareholder constituencies while at the same time serving the interests of the company. It is with this in mind that the purpose of the general meeting is discussed below.

11.6 What is the purpose of the general meeting?

The original purpose of the meeting was to provide a forum in which the accountability of the board to the shareholders could be delivered. This required there to be a balance of power which allowed the shareholders to challenge in a meaningful way the board's governance of the company. Today the power lies in the hands of the board.

We suggest that the general meeting has three purposes:

- to provide an open forum in which the board can account for their governance of the company via, for example, the chairman's prepared statement and the answering of shareholders' questions ('accountability');
- to pass various resolutions which legitimise actions which the directors wish to take ('voting and resolutions');
- to convey information about key events touching on the company's recent performance and future trading prospects.

A note of explanation follows about these three purposes.

Accountability will depend primarily on the report and accounts. In this respect shareholders have to rely on the auditing process. Insofar that auditors are now effectively appointed by the board and that they look to the board as their 'clients', shareholders' confidence in what was intended as an independent audit for shareholders has been seriously eroded (see 11.8 below). Accountability also depends very much on the way resolutions are drafted and voted upon and this is further discussed below.

The legitimisation of many of the company's proposed actions is accomplished by the passing of various resolutions. Resolutions and voting thereon, is in theory, a very effective and democratic means whereby shareholders, with perhaps very wide and diverse views, can deliver a decision on any issue. The process fails in practice to satisfy the purposes of the meeting because of the way resolutions are drafted and the way voting is conducted. Both procedures need reform.

The third purpose has been highlighted recently by Mr Paul Myners, Chairman of Gartmore Investment Management plc, who said he believed:[15]

> 'The opportunity exists for a farsighted company chairman to restore the AGM to its rightful place at the nexus of shareholder and management contact. This would be achieved by the company using its AGM to provide a detailed insight into the company's strategy, structure, performance and values.'

Under these circumstances, he suggested:

> 'institutions should be willing to question management in front of their fellow shareholders – they are after all happy to do this at formal analyst presentations so should not feel inhibited by the presence of the private investor.'

His speech is important, first, because it was probably the first time that a major institutional shareholder, of which there are only a small number, has ever suggested that the AGM had any purpose at all and, secondly, because of what it says about the attitude of the institutional towards the private shareholder. Institutional shareholders, it should be noted, very rarely attend general meetings.

11.7 Guiding principles for reformers

Reformers should be guided by four principles:

- The procedure of resolutions and voting thereon is inherently an equitable way of registering the often wide range of shareholders' views on any issue to do with the governance of the company. 'Voting is cheap' as The Economist put it. It might have added that it was effective too.
- Reforms which move shareholders close to the management of the company should be avoided. Large institutional shareholders with too close a relationship with the company are unlikely to improve corporate governance.

---

15 op. cit., note 12.

- Reforms which in any way render the price signal less effective should be avoided. In other words, the danger is that the more you substitute other mechanisms, the less well the price mechanism will work.
- Reforms which reduce 'contestability', as *The Economist*[16] put it, should be avoided. In other words, takeover bids are a very effective way of replacing the management of an under-performing company.

With the purposes of the general meeting in mind as well as the four guiding principles suggested above, we turn to some possible reforms which should be seen as 'first steps' on the road to reform rather than a complete and final menu of reforms. We are, after all, trying to stem a tide which has been flowing strongly in the wrong direction for 150 years! Later reforms should be designed with the experience gained from the results of the first reforms implemented.

11.8   What reforms are now needed?

The task facing avid reformers should not be underestimated. One hundred and fifty years of UK legislation has been drafted on the assumption that directors should be accountable to shareholders. Over the last 50 years, as we have described above, committees appointed by parliament have wrestled with how to 'find means of making it easier for shareholders to exercise a more effective control over the management of their companies' as the Cohen Committee put it. All have failed to find an answer. Have their recommendations then made the problem even more intractable? Possibly they have.

We discuss the first steps towards reform under the following headings:

- Resolutions.
- Voting.
- Auditing.
- Shareholder directors.

11.8.1   Resolutions

The main approach to reform should be:

- a mandatory resolution for all PLCs to obtain shareholders' approval of the board's governance (a 'governance' resolution);
- a mandatory resolution for all PLCs to obtain shareholders' agreement to the remuneration of the board (a 'remuneration' resolution);

---

16   *The Economist*, 1 January 1994.

- to ease the requirement for shareholders to submit resolutions.

There would be a new requirement whereby all listed PLCs must put to each annual general meeting two mandatory resolutions – one to approve the board's governance of the company and the other to approve the board's remuneration. The wording of both mandatory resolutions would be included in a revised companies act. We suggest that several positive outcomes will stem from the adoption of the governance resolution, namely:

- The accountability of the board to all shareholders will be made more explicit.

- The percentage of votes cast for and against the resolution would be required to be announced to all shareholders and this information would provide an invaluable 'league table' of PLCs. This publicity would exert pressure on the boards and shareholders of low ranking companies to improve the governance of the company. Share prices will reflect this new information and exert further pressure for appropriate action by boards. For those companies which failed to win such a resolution, we would expect new duties to be placed on the non-executive directors to make appropriate board changes. However, it may be wise to study the results of this new resolution before proposing what specific action should be required.

- In deciding how they will vote, shareholders will no doubt take a broad view of the performance of the board in its two main roles – first, as custodians of the company's assets and secondly, as being responsible for ensuring that the business of the company was well managed.

- Recognising the different priorities which shareholders legitimately have – for example, private, institutional and employee shareholders may in certain circumstances see the company's future in a different light – this new governance resolution would enable all shareholders to discharge their ownership responsibilities in the only fair and democratic way that is possible. Presently the only occasion when they may have to focus their minds seriously on such a question is at the time of a takeover bid, a relatively rare event in most companies' lives.

- The majority of PLCs would experience no problems in winning such a vote of confidence. This could give boards in some instances a powerful argument for resisting a takeover bid which they saw as being not in shareholders' interests.

- The requirement to have the resolution passed each year should encourage boards to focus even more on the need to communicate to shareholders information about the performance of the company, their plans for the future and thereby to convince shareholders that their companies were in good hands.

A further reform in connection with governance needs to be made. Presently many companies' articles, including many of the privatised utility companies, exempt a number of directors, usually the chairman and the chief executive, from having to retire. This acts directly against accountability and such provisions should be made unlawful. In other words, it must be obligatory for all directors to be appointed by members and for all directors to retire by rotation and to stand for re-election.

Concerning the 'remuneration' resolution, there would again be a simple requirement for shareholders to vote on a resolution approving the board's remuneration, both as directors and as 'officers' of the company.

Information on the board's remuneration would have to be disclosed in full to shareholders. Presently the value of share options awarded to directors are not reported as arguably required by the Companies Act. Another area which is under-reported is that of pension costs for directors, a cost which now often exceeds that of share options which has attracted a great deal of adverse publicity. It is to be hoped that the new requirement for a remuneration resolution will go some way to encourage boards to design remuneration packages, presently seen as opaque by shareholders, which are less complicated and, therefore, easier to convey simply to shareholders. Certainly it is to be expected that shareholders will more readily vote for remuneration packages which they can understand and relate to the company's performance. Should the resolution not be passed, then the board's remuneration would revert to that which was previously approved.

Presently, companies' articles usually set out directors' remuneration and expenses by specifying a 'ceiling' figure for remuneration for their services as directors. The law now needs to be changed so that this 'ceiling' figure includes the total remuneration payable to persons on the board whether this is paid for their services as directors or as officers. This would bring the overall remuneration cost of a board further within shareholders' control.

Finally, the governance of companies would undoubtedly be improved if matters of serious concern to shareholders were submitted as resolutions to be discussed at general meetings. We suggest, therefore, that ten, say, shareholders who can show that they are long-term, committed members of the company should have the right to submit a resolution at the company's expense. The test for long-term and committed could be debated at length. We suggest each shareholder must have owned shares for, say, a continuous period of three years.

11.8.2 Voting

Professor Gower's comments on our proxy voting system point to one
significant weakness:

> 'Although proxy voting gave an appearance of stockholder democracy,
> this appearance was deceptive and in reality the practice helped to
> enhance the dictatorship of the board.'

One simple reform involves changing the proxy card and where it is sent.

First, all discretion should be removed and the proxy card marked 'for',
'against' or 'abstain'. Cards would be void if not so completed. Secondly, all
proxy cards should go to an independent body for counting. After all, when
we vote for our Member of Parliament or local councillor, we do not send the
ballot form to them! It should be noted that the sending out of proxy cards is
not a requirement of the Companies Act. It is a requirement of the Stock
Exchange regulations.

To pursue the analogy, there are, we believe, a number of interesting
similarities between the duties of members (shareholders) and Members of
Parliament. Members of Parliament, if they wish to vote, have to attend
Parliament in person. Both members have to question and to vote.
Government is accountable to Parliament , the board is accountable to
shareholders. The process is one of audit in its most basic form, a point we
pursue further below. Therefore, bearing in mind Professor Gower's criticism
of the proxy system, we believe there is a case to be made for considering
abolition of the proxy system altogether. If we really wish to make the general
meeting a purposeful occasion, would it be too demanding of shareholders to
require them to attend if they wish to vote? A frequent criticism of such a
proposal is that companies may then be encouraged to choose awkward places
and times for meetings. Many do so now. No doubt simple legislation would
put that right.

11.8.3 Auditing

Two requirements were embedded in the first Companies Act which
effectively remain unchanged. First, the directors are accountable to the
shareholders in general meeting, and, secondly, the accounts of the company
must be audited by independent auditors appointed by the shareholders and
reporting to them. Today auditors are effectively appointed by the
management and remunerated by them. They have no meaningful direct link
with shareholders. From a shareholder's viewpoint, the auditor merely recites
a standard incantation about 'true and fair' at each AGM.

Audits often fail to serve shareholders' interests and yet, surprisingly, the
cry goes out, even from shareholders, for more and more auditing. And audits
do not come cheap. A typical PLC may spend £1 million plus on the audit

with a large plc like Hanson spending £6 million. The auditing firm will additionally often be paid fees in excess of the audit fee for 'other services'. Hanson's audit cost of £6 million can be contrasted with the total remuneration of the board at £9 million. In effect, the shareholders are paying the board £9 million to appoint and oversee the management of the company and paying the auditors £6 million, or 66 per cent of the board remuneration, to give them, the shareholders, an independent view as to the financial state of the company. Perhaps the audit as we know it needs some radical re-thinking? Michael Power has done just that.[17] He argues in his recent challenging pamphlet:

> 'Do audits deliver what they promise in the form of greater accountability, efficiency and quality or do they in fact fuel the problems which they address by, for example, exacerbating distrust? Notwithstanding the dominance of audits, there are other ways of achieving accountability.'

Reformers should heed his warning:

> 'It is now more important for an organisation's legitimacy that it is seen to be audited than that there is any real substance to the audit ... the public issue has become the independence of the auditors rather than their competence or relevance. Even with strong guarantees of independence, system-based audits can easily become a kind of ritual.'

Finally, he reminds us of the derivation of the word audit (from the Latin *audire*, to hear) and refreshes our understanding by referring to the audit process as being one in which:

> 'the accountable party defends his actions in person to a relevant audience ... it was the aural as much as the observational intimacy which was the relevant parameter.'

This description of the process of audit adds new understanding to the potential of the general meeting to re-discover its original purpose and serve as a meaningful audit of the governance of the company by the shareholders. Regarding reform, we can best look to the recommendations made by the McFarlane Committee[18] set up in 1993, which sought to enhance the independence of auditors by 'involving shareholders' as the report put it. An 'audit panel', representative of all shareholders, would be established to cover the following:

- the appointment of auditors and the determination of their remuneration;
- the determination of the audit scope;
- the provision of any other services to the company by the auditing firm;
- making recommendations to shareholders concerning all the above.

17 Power, *The Audit Explosion* (1994), Demos.
18 *The Future Development of Auditing* – a Paper to Promote Public Debate, November 1992, The Auditing Practices Board.

The Auditing Practices Board's (APB) recommendations based on the McFarlane report have only just been published in a report entitled The Audit Agenda.[19] The APB argues that 'a mechanism of shareholder panels could merely add another bureaucratic layer of governance'. Instead, the report recommends certain measures to strengthen audit committees which should act as 'proxies for shareholders'.

11.8.4 Shareholder directors

In the light of the APB failing to include the McFarlane recommendations concerning shareholder committees, it is appropriate to summarise briefly the proposals made by Mr Allen Sykes[20] regarding the election of 'shareholder directors'. Although not aimed directly at reforming general meetings, his proposals, if adopted, would have a profound effect on the conduct of meetings in that the proposals address the root problem of the lack of accountability of the board to shareholders. Sykes' starting point is to observe that:

> *'There are no successful systems of corporate governance, past or present, without committed and knowledgeable long-term shareholders, managements with the preconditions and incentives for long-term performance, and with such managements being properly accountable to their shareholders.'*

Without 'effecting discharge of the ownership role', Sykes convincingly argues that corporate governance cannot be effective. If the dominant investment institutions are unwilling or unable to discharge that ownership role which is clearly their responsibility, then it must be procured. Sykes' well-argued proposals involve the creation of 'relationship investors' from the main sixty investment institutions. Each of the FT-SE 100 companies would have five relationship investors who would each appoint a capable businessman as a 'shareholder director'. Such directors would be responsible for the monitoring and remuneration functions on behalf of all shareholders. They would also negotiate five-seven year performance targets with the senior management based on an agreed five-seven year strategic plan. As contrasted with present non-executive directors, shareholder directors would be backed up by a small secretariat, including investment analysts, so that they could effectively discharge their ownership role. In further development of his proposals, Sykes has acknowledged the need for private shareholders to elect a shareholder director.

---

19 *The Audit Agenda*, The Auditing Practices Board, December 1994.
20 Sykes (1994) *'Proposals for internationally competitive governance in Britain and America'*, *Corporate Governance, An International Review*, 2(4), October.

What is convincing about Sykes' analysis is his recognition of the problems stemming from a failure in our present system of corporate governance. In other words, every party in the system acts perfectly rationally, given his own interests. But the overall outcome is widely acknowledged to fall short of what other nations achieve. At the same time, Sykes avoids the trap of simply importing bits of other systems. He has proposed a remedy designed for UK practice and culture. General meetings would be changed radically for the better if his proposals were adopted.

11.9 Summary of reforms

We summarise the reforms briefly as follows:

- Two new mandatory resolutions to be required – 'governance' and 'remuneration'.
- Articles which presently exclude some directors from retiring and standing for re-election to be made unlawful. All directors must be appointed by members, retire and stand for re-election.
- Articles to specify 'ceiling' figure for total remuneration payable to all persons on the board for their services as directors or officers of the company.
- Committed, long-term shareholders empowered to submit resolutions at company's expense.
- Proxy cards to be marked only 'for', 'against' or 'abstain' and sent to an independent body for counting.
- 'Shareholder directors' to be appointed.

11.10 Envoy

After 50 years of attempted reform, the general meeting continues to fail to deliver the results expected of it. Its ineffectiveness, even its farcical nature, is much commented on and yet the law, seemingly regardless of this, has no mechanism other than the discredited general meeting for bestowing legitimacy on many companies' actions. As we have seen from the results of the recommendations made by the various committees over the last 50 years, the basic purpose of the general meeting is as far, probably further, from being realised as ever. The difficulty, we suggest, lies not so much in designing effective reforms as in the absence of a strong enough constituency which wants reform.

However, one spark of hope may lie in the occasional gargantuan abuse of the system as it now is. This may, just, be enough to motivate shareholders to organise themselves and act in a way not hitherto seen so that, even given the much trumpeted difficulties which they face, they do begin to perform their ownership role with increasing effectiveness. After all:

> *'The highest patriotism consists, not so much in altering laws and modifying institutions, as in helping and stimulating men to elevate and improve themselves by their own free and independent action.'*[21]

Alternatively, we can wait for the EC saviour to arrive in the shape of the Fifth Directive. The two tier board will certainly change the present relationship between boards and shareholders in a way which 50 years of avowedly reforming committees have failed to do.

---

21   Smiles, *Self-Help* (1873), John Murray.

Chapter 12

Codes of Conduct and Their Impact on Corporate Governance

Dr Saleem Sheikh and Professor SK Chatterjee
London Guildhall University

12.1 Introduction

Historically, the *laissez-faire* doctrine which has dominated the UK economy seems to have been taken to extremes in many cases particularly in relation to the independence of corporate bodies. Profit maximisation has always been accepted as the sacrosanct principle of business. But the *laissez-faire* doctrine has its own limitations. It cannot be allowed to be implemented at the cost of the public interest and this is where governmental intervention becomes necessary. The tension between corporate business based on profit maximisation, and the interest of the consumers may be identified in the following way: profit maximisation policy may run counter to the interests of the public. Therefore, intervention by the public becomes essential; however, for the purposes of legitimising the public interest, governmental intervention becomes essential. Profit maximisation based on the *laissez-faire* doctrine must compromise with the public interest.

In the UK, the implementation of the *laissez-faire* doctrine in relation to corporate profit maximisation policy has remained intact in the belief that such a policy simply strengthens the economy and at the same time protects the interests of shareholders who invest in the capital of the company. This practice disregards the fact that society's well-being cannot be limited to the benefit of the shareholders. A corporate body's activities may adversely affect the interests of the society in which it operates; from this standpoint, it is not difficult to appreciate that although the general members of the public may not have participated in a company's capital or decision-making, the company's activities may adversely affect their activities. This must be regarded as the limiting factor for a sacrosanct principle of profit maximisation. This issue cannot be effectively dealt with without government intervention or at least by an informal agreement of corporate bodies to follow and implement certain regulatory principles.

The *laissez-faire* doctrine has also been taken to its extreme in the UK by maintaining that even shareholders of a company should not have as much decision-making power as its directors. In other words, the current companies' legislation in the UK tends to promote a pyramidal decision-making structure within the corporate body and thereby diminish the position of shareholders who invest in the corporate capital. Under current companies' legislation, corporate bodies are transformed into narrow institutions for the primary purpose of profit maximisation through managers including directors and executives.

In the UK, efforts at regulating the conduct of corporate bodies remained at a rudimentary stage until the Cadbury Committee's Code of Best Practice in December 1992 was developed, which may or may not be implemented in respect of unlisted companies. This issue has been developed in a subsequent section of this chapter.

This chapter aims to identify the need for corporate social responsibilities which may best be promoted by the implementation of codes of conduct, if not by legislation, and to that effect it briefly traces the history of the growth and awareness of codes of conduct in the UK. The principal purpose of this chapter is to emphasise that where a society is not prepared to accept legislation for regulating the conduct of corporate bodies, codes of conduct may be a better alternative. It is the view of the authors of this chapter that perfect legislation may be very difficult to achieve but a compulsory code of conduct might be an effective alternative to legislation for two purposes:

- to make the society aware of the concept of corporate social responsibilities; and

- to ensure that there persists an understanding in the corporate world that the doctrine of privity is a doctrine of avoiding corporate social responsibilities.

Corporate social responsibilities apply to all corporations including those activities which go beyond the national boundaries. It is to be emphasised that the corporation whose activities go beyond national boundaries may adversely affect societies in foreign jurisdictions. Therefore, the question arises whether it is not the responsibility of the home countries to regulate the conduct of such corporations too. In the absence of coherent national policies in this regard, intergovernmental and international organisations found it necessary to adopt draft codes of conduct in the hope that they would be implemented by their member states in order to regulate the conduct of their respective transnational corporations. This chapter also discusses the effectiveness of such codes of conduct and the responsibilities that they may give rise to, for host countries.

12.2 Development and awareness of Codes of Conduct in the UK

Companies need a framework defining their responsibilities to shareholders and to other 'stakeholders' including employees, consumers, suppliers and the general community as part of their broader social responsibilities. Codes of conduct can provide a general framework for expressing these social responsibilities.[1] Written codes are developed in order to define organisational purpose, establish a uniform ethical climate within the organisation, and to provide guidelines for consistent decision-making. More and more businesses are finding it necessary to write down their corporate philosophies in an attempt to retain confidence in the business organisation and system. Clearly this is a reflection of the fact that, in the UK, the public expects higher standards of conduct and ethical behaviour from the business sector.

According to Manley's[2] research of top executives of 145 UK and multi-national companies, there are eighteen primary benefits of a code of conduct. They are:providing guidance to and inculcating the company's values and cultural substance and style in managers and employees;

- sharpening and defining the company's policies and unifying the workforce;
- codes provide overall strategic direction;
- contributing instruction in interactions with pressure groups from outside the company;
- signalling expectations of proper conduct of suppliers and customers;
- delineating rights and duties of the company, managers and employees;
- effectively responding to government pressures and rules;
- enhancing the company's public image and confidence;
- preempting legal proceedings;
- improving bottom-line results;
- enhancing employees' self-image and recruiting;

---

1   For further consideration of Codes of Conduct, see Ackerman, *'How Companies Respond to Social Demands'* (July-August 1973) Harv Bus Rev; Andrews, *'Can The Best Corporations be Made Moral?'* (May-June 1973) Harv Bus Rev; Bennett, *'Ethics Codes Spread Despite Scepticism'* (15 July 1988) Wall Street Journal; Bowie, *Business Ethics* (1987); Buchholz, *Fundamental Concepts and Problems in Business Ethics* (1989); Cressey & Moore, *'Managerial Values and Corporate Codes of Ethics'*, (Summer 1983) California Management Review; Ethics Resource Center, *Implementation and Enforcement of Codes of Ethics in Corporations and Associations* (1980); Fletcher, *Situation Ethics* (1966); Goodpaster and Mathews, *'Can a Corporation Have a Conscience?'* (Jan-Feb 1982) Harv Bus Rev; Harris, 'Structuring a Workable Code of Ethics' (1978) University of Florida Law Review; Institute of Business Ethics, *Company Philosophies and Codes of Business Ethics*; Opinion Research Centre, *Implementation and Enforcement of Codes of Ethics in Corporations and Associations* (1980); and Sherwin, *'The Ethical Roots of the Business System'*, (Nov-Dec 1983) Harv Bus Rev.

2   Manley, *The Handbook of Good Business Practice: Corporate Codes of Conduct* (1992).

- promoting excellence;
- realising company objectives;
- responding to stockholders' concerns;
- strengthening the UK free-enterprise system;
- nurturing a business environment of open communication;
- integrating the cultures of acquired or merged companies; and
- deterring improper requests of employees by supervisors.

The key to effective implementation of codes of conduct require management involvement and oversight through the supervisory level. Companies need to be constantly conscious of the written, codified values and standards in recruiting and hiring.

Apart from companies drafting their own codes of conduct to regulate their internal affairs, some companies are also subject to national codes of conduct. In the UK, the Code of Best Practice and the City Code on Takeovers and Mergers and SARs and but a few examples of the degree of self-regulation to which some companies are subject. This section considers the Cadbury Code of Best Practice and the Takeovers and Mergers Code, and analyses their impact on the corporate governance debate. There are at present proposals by the Confederation of British Industry to draft a Code of Good Practice on directors' remuneration. A group of top industrialists and company chairmen have been commissioned by the CBI to prepare a Code of Good Practice.[3] The group is expected to report within six months.

12.2.1 The Code of Best Practice

The Code of Best Practice issued by the Cadbury Committee on the financial aspects of corporate governance in December 1992, is the latest to emphasise the importance of following codes of conduct for corporate bodies. The Committee's principal recommendation is that the boards of all listed companies registered in the UK should comply with the code. It also recommended that limited companies should make a statement in their reports and accounts confirming whether or not they complied with the code and the issues in respect of which compliance was not possible and the reasons therefore. The compliance statements should be reviewed by auditors and the London Stock Exchange should publish statements of compliance in order to ensure the implementation of the procedure. The committee also recommended the appointment of a special committee by the end of June 1995 to monitor the progress in relation to compliance with the code. It is a general code which should be followed by individuals and boards of directors

---

3   For further details on the terms of reference for the new group, see chapter 18.

in the light of their own particular circumstances. According to the Cadbury Committee, these individuals and boards are 'responsible for ensuring that their actions meet the spirit of the code and in interpreting it they should give precedence to substance over form'. The Cadbury Committee report can be divided into two parts: whereas part one contains the code of best practice for the board of directors, non-executive directors, and reporting and controls, the other part deals with these bodies, auditors' and shareholders' duties in detail. In writing this chapter, the same division has been followed.

12.2.2 Maw's suggested Code of Practice

Maw describes the Code of Best Practice as a:

> 'commendably brief document ... so far as it goes it is [no doubt] a genuine attempt but, in our view it does not go nearly far enough. There are too many unrealistic requirements and pious hopes, and too much naive confidence. There are holes through which coaches and horses could and no doubt will be driven.'[4]

Maw suggests an alternative code of practice to the Cadbury Committee's Code of Best Practice. Maw's code would be adopted and complied with by the boards of all companies (domestic and foreign) with shares listed on the London Stock Exchange as part of their continuing obligations; of all companies contemplating a listing in the near future; of all companies to which the takeover code applies; and of unlisted companies with a significant shareholding in the hands of banks or other financial institutions; or with a wide spread of shareholders. It should be noted that this suggested code would be of wider application than the Cadbury Code of Best Practice which only applies to public listed companies.

Maw's suggested code would have a minimum number of non-executive directors on its board, namely, one third of the total number of directors and the majority of non-executive directors would be free of any other business or financial connection with the company, apart from their shareholdings. If a listed company falls below the minimum then a reasonable time would be given to fill the vacancy.

His suggested code would require the chairman to be a non-executive director. Neither should the chairman be the chief executive or managing director. The non-executive directors would have the qualities of independence, objectivity, and experience to enable them to evaluate the company's progress and the performance and ability of executive directors. Non-executive directors would be required to contribute in an informed and

---

4   Maw, *Maw on Corporate Governance* (1994) p 143.

constructive approach to broad decisions. They would also have a duty to ensure executive directors comply with the proposed code. They would be appointed for an initial term of three years, subsequently removable by rotation. Each non-executive director would have a letter of appointment setting out:

- his duties;
- his predicted time involvement;
- his fees; and
- the procedure for reimbursement of his expenses on company business, including travel and for seeking independent professional advice.

They would not be eligible to participate in the company's pension scheme, share option schemes, or be included within any class of beneficiaries under a share ownership trust or plan. Their fees should be at a level not only to reflect their predicted time commitment but also the level of responsibility undertaken and the number and nature of board committees on which they serve. The level of fees for non-executive directors should not be so high as to jeopardise their independence. They should not be provided with a company car for their personal use and their letters of appointment must be available for inspection by shareholders on request, and at each AGM.

Maw maintains that non-executive directors should be selected through a formal process. The selection process would be led by the non-executive chairman or a non-executive deputy chairman and primarily be conducted by the remuneration committee. The board would ultimately approve the appointments.

With regard to board committees, Maw's suggested code of practice would require each listed company, upon board resolution, to set up and maintain an audit and a remuneration committee. Neither of these committees would be regarded as a part of management. All members of these committees would be non-executive directors and there would be no fewer than three members on each committee. Each committee of the board would be required to provide a written report of its decisions and recommendations to the full board for circulation through the company secretary. Executive directors not serving on these committees would be able to attend by invitation only.

Members of the audit committee would be required, *inter alia*, to satisfy themselves as to systems of internal financial control; the adopting of appropriate accounting principles; the appropriateness of adopting a going concern basis; compliance with accounting principles; liaison with the auditors as to their audit work; monitoring rotation of the audit partner; discussion with the auditors of all points of principle arising from their audit work including points raised in their management letter; and recommending to the board a fair and appropriate level of audit fees.

The remuneration committee would, *inter alia*, review the levels and basis for remuneration of the executive directors; negotiate the terms of service agreements for executive directors and their severance payments; determine the levels of participation by executive directors in share option schemes; and co-ordinate and manage the selection process for promotion, recruitment and retirement of directors. The remuneration committee would also, at least every three years, commission independent reports from suitable management consultants on executive director appraisals, on the level of executive director remuneration packages, and the rates of non-executive director fees.

Board of directors would have the responsibility for financial accountability, clarity and formal presentation of the company's accounts and annual report. Directors would have a duty to draw attention publicly to matters which materially fell short of proper expectation, for example, the annual accruals. The annual report and accounts would contain a statement by the board as to directors' responsibilities for the preparation of such reports and accounts. Further, Maw's suggested code of practice would require the functioning of the board to be primarily at the initiative of the chairman and company secretary. The functioning of the board would be dependent upon the regularity of its meetings; its circulation of the requisite board papers in advance; firm but sympathetic control from the chair; orderly but free ranging discussion; efficient taking of minutes; a clear understanding of 'reserved' subjects which require board approval prior to action or implementation by the executives.

The director's report accompanying the annual accounts would contain a compliance statement as to the extent to which the mandatory requirements of the code had been adhered to, with explanation of the reasons for non-compliance with some of the provisions of the code. The explanations would be given in sufficient detail for shareholders to understand and evaluate the reasons.

The code would also require boards periodically to commission an environmental audit and a management audit. Shareholders would be informed that it would be the company's policy to do so and the board would implement the results of these audits, where appropriate.

12.2.2.1   The board of directors

According to the committee, a board of directors should meet regularly and retain full and effective control over the company and monitor the executive management. It should also include non-executive directors of sufficient calibre and number, for their views. The recommendations however might provoke controversy with regard to expressions such as 'effective control', 'executive management', and directors of 'sufficient calibre'. It is hoped that the dimensions of these expressions will be determined by judicial interpretation in due course. However, the committee seems to be convinced that meaningful control should be given to the board, and the board is required to be unbiased in order to carry out monitoring of the executive management. In other words, according to the committee, the board should take the supervisory role insofar as monitoring of the executive management is concerned. Full and effective control may perhaps stand for control over the interests of shareholders and the primary aims of the company.

It is to be emphasised that the committee recommended that a clear division of responsibilities at the head of the company would be necessary for ensuring a balance of power, instead of giving any individual unfettered powers of decision. In other words, the Cadbury Committee wanted to see the power structured in a democratic fashion rather than in a pyramidal fashion, which would entail participation of many rather than the one individual in decision-making. It is also hoped that the expression 'directors of sufficient calibre' will stand for those non-executive directors who have had sufficient time in industry and/or the business world to be able to enrich the committee's decision-making power with their wealth of knowledge and experience. The committee's intention is to ensure that directors act in a responsible fashion; it recommends that where necessary, directors in furtherance of their duties should take independent professional advice in accordance with an agreed procedure. This may be ensured by requiring the company to include a clause to that effect in the service agreement. It is interesting to note however that the Cadbury Committee strengthened the position of the company secretary by recommending that all directors should have access to the advice and services of the company secretary who is responsible to the board. On the other hand, the committee suggested explicitly or implicitly that directors should be dependent upon the company secretary for his advice and services. This provokes legal controversy in that directors may shift their responsibilities to their company secretary particularly where they may be accused of negligence or breach of duty. The possibility of directors being involved in criminal action on the advice of their company secretary, whether knowingly or unknowingly, may not be ruled out.

12.2.2.2   Non-executive directors

The primary purpose of appointing non-executive directors is to bring to bear an independent judgment on issues such as strategy, performance, resources, standards of conduct and key appointments. Each of these items needs further interpretation in the light of the objectives of a company. It can easily be surmised that the interrelationship of these items will be different for a company that aims at profit maximisation and the one that aims at profit optimisation. However, the Cadbury Committee appropriately recommended that the majority of non-executive directors should be independent of management and free from any business and other relationship with the company concerned. Indeed, according to the committee, the non-executive directors should be required to disclose their interest in the directors' report.

It is not clear, however, why the committee did not object to their having shareholding rights, although according to the committee, such directors must not participate in share option schemes and not be eligible for any pension scheme operated by a company. This recommendation might provoke controversy in that non-executive directors might not be able to maintain their neutrality sufficiently or at least it may be difficult for them to convince outsiders that they remain totally unbiased.

As to the executive directors, the committee recommended that their service contracts should not exceed three years without shareholder approval. Like the non-executive directors, the executive directors would be required to make a full and clear disclosure of their total emoluments and salaries, including pension contributions and stock options. The committee also recommended that they should be required to give separate figures for salary and performance related elements. Executive directors' pay should be subject to the recommendations of the remuneration committee made up wholly or mainly of non-executive directors. The provision that executive directors' contracts should not exceed three years without shareholders' approval indicates that shareholders, according to the committee, should be given a significant degree of control over such directors' appointments and that such directors must remain accountable to the shareholders. Unless the current companies' legislation is amended to this effect, it is not clear how this recommendation of the committee may in reality be implemented, unless the code is voluntarily implemented by companies along the lines done so by the London Stock Exchange.

12.2.2.3   Reporting controls

The committee, however, attempts to introduce accountability by adopting a system of controls on reporting, whereby it will be the board's duty to present a balanced and understandable assessment of the company's position, that is, the report and accounts should contain a coherent narrative supported by the figures of the company's performance. It is not clear what is meant by 'understandable assessment'. Although the committee has recommended that the board should ensure that an objective and professional relationship is maintained with the auditors, it does not provide any suggestion as to what should be the contents and criteria of this relationship.

It is, however, to be appreciated that the committee recommended that directors should explain their responsibility for preparing the accounts, next to a statement by the auditors. The directors' responsibilities should include preparation of a financial statement for each financial year giving a true and fair view of the company's state of affairs including profits and losses for that period; and the maintenance of adequate accounting records for the purposes of safeguarding the assets of the company and preventing and detecting fraud and other irregularities. Furthermore, they must confirm that they have followed applicable accounting standards and all material departures from them must be justified. It is for the directors to report on the effectiveness of the company's system of internal control and on whether the business is a going concern with justifications and qualifications where necessary.

The code of best practice is an encouraging attempt to regulate the conduct of companies including their officers. It must be regarded primarily as a broad-based guide, the proper implementation of which depends upon each company in accordance with the business in which it is engaged. The code simply demonstrates the aspirations of an influential committee which, if followed, should produce some beneficial results. It will be inappropriate to seek any legally binding effect in the code; nor can it be an exhaustive code in that not all business practices can be embraced in one code. The code at least forms the basis for forwarding ideas which should be considered in amending current companies' legislation.

12.2.3 The City Code on Takeovers and Mergers

The City Code on Takeovers and Mergers was issued by the Panel on Takeovers and Mergers.[5] It was drafted primarily to 'ensure fair and equitable treatment of all shareholders in relation to takeovers'. It is not concerned with the financial or commercial advantages or disadvantages of a takeover nor is it concerned with issues such as competition policy which are the responsibility of the government. Before the code is critically examined, it is appropriate to discuss some of the most important aspects of the code.

The code was primarily devised and is executed by a panel consisting of a chairman, deputy chairman and some non-representative members. On the panel are also represented a number of national institutions.

The panel works on a day to day basis through its executive headed by a director general. The executive employs a broad spectrum of power which includes the conduct of investigations, monitoring of relevant dealings, consultation on issues coming under the purview of the code and giving of rulings on points of interpretation before or during a takeover or merger transaction.

The panel co-operates with regulatory authorities such as the DTI, The London Stock Exchange, Securities and Investment Board, self-regulating

---

5   On the issue of self-regulation and the City Code on Takeovers and Mergers, see Morse, 'The City Code on Takeovers and Mergers – Self Regulation or Statutory Protection?' (1991) JBL 509. See too Johnson, The City Takeover Code (1980). For an independent dimension, see Horn, Legal Problems of Codes of Conduct For Multinational Enterprises (1980); Waldmann, Regulating International Business Through Codes of Conduct (1980); and Donaldson, Business Ethics: A European Casebook: Principles, Cases and Codes (1992). See also 12.3 on international codes of conduct.

organisations, and the Bank of England, in order to develop and employ a system of mutual exchange of information. In fact, this aspect of the panel's activity is most important in monitoring the activities of companies in the City of London. Breaches of the code are reported by the panel to the relevant authority. The panel also works closely with the London Stock Exchange in monitoring dealings.

The code is based on a number of general principles which represent statements of good standards of commercial behaviour. Although such terms are identifiable, both the courts and the commercial world are familiar with them and from this standpoint they should not provoke any controversy. Good standards of commercial behaviour must be interpreted in the context of a business. The code also contains a series of rules, the purpose of which is to expand the general principles, so that the complex issues of takeovers may be dealt with effectively. In the event of any doubt as to whether a proposed course of conduct is in accordance with the general principles or the rules, the parties should consult the executive in advance in order to minimise the incidence of breaches of the code. In giving a ruling on any application of the code, the executive hears the views of all parties involved in the deal. Should a party wish to contest a ruling of the executive, it may ask the panel to review it and the same right is available to an aggrieved shareholder although the panel has the right to reject frivolous cases.

Under the code the executive has the right to institute disciplinary proceedings in the event of a breach having taken place.

The code contains detailed procedure as to conduct of disciplinary proceedings. In brief, it may be stated that the rules of natural justice are observed and the parties are given ample opportunity to present their case. There is a right of appeal to the 'Appeals Committee' in the following cases:

- where the panel upon finding a breach of the code proposes to take disciplinary action;
- where the panel has allegedly acted outside its jurisdiction;
- in respect of any refusal by the panel to recognise, or any decision of the panel to cease to recognise, a market-maker or fund manager as an exempt market maker or exempt fund manager as the case may be.

Appeals to the appeal committee may be made only with leave of the panel. Leave to appeal is not normally granted by the panel against a finding of fact or against a division of the panel on the interpretation of the code. The appeal committee may assume jurisdiction only in the event of material new evidence. If an appeal is dismissed, normally the findings of the panel are published, and stipulated steps must be implemented.

The code applies to offers for all listed and unlisted public companies in the UK, including the Channel Islands and the Isle of Man (and where appropriate, statutory and chartered companies). It also applies to offers for private companies considered to be so resident, but only when:

- their equity share capital has been listed on The London Stock Exchange at any time during the 10 years prior to the relevant date; or
- dealings in their equity share capital have been advertised in a newspaper on a regular basis for a continuous period of at least six months in the 10 years prior to the relevant date; or
- their equity share capital has been subject to a marketing arrangement as described in s 163(2)(b) of the Companies Act 1985 at any time during the ten years prior to the relevant date, eg their shares have been dealt in on an unlisted securities market; or
- they have filed a prospectus for the issue of equity share capital at the companies' registry at any time during the 10 years prior to the relevant date.

In each case the relevant date is the date on which an announcement is made of a proposed or possible offer for the company or the date on which some other event occurs in relation to the company which has significance under the code.

As the code may not be appropriate to all statutory and chartered companies or private companies the panel is prepared to apply it with a degree of flexibility in suitable cases.

The code contains ten general principles which are usually adhered to generally and applied to circumstances not expressly covered by the rules. The general principles may be summarised in the following way:

- all shareholders belonging to the same class of an offeree company must be treated similarly by an offeror;
- in relation to an offer which is in contemplation or already made, an offeror or an offeree company or an adviser must furnish information to all shareholders instead of to some selected shareholders;
- all offers must be carefully and responsibly considered prior to their announcement. Only offers capable of being implemented should be made;
- sufficient information and advice should be provided to allow shareholders to reach a properly informed decision in regard to an offer;
- all documents or advertisements addressed to shareholders containing information or advice must be prepared with the highest standards of care and accuracy;
- efforts must be made to ensure that false markets are not created in the securities of an offer, nor must the parties involved mislead the shareholders or the market by providing unfounded or inaccurate information.

12.3   International Codes of Conduct

12.3.1 Introduction

The issue as to how conduct of transnational corporations may be regulated has been a moot point for a considerable period of time. The UN Draft Code of Conduct on Transnational Corporations has defined a 'transnational corporation' as:

> *'an enterprise, comprising entities in two or more countries, regardless of the legal form and fields of activity of these entities, which operates under a system of decision-making, permitting coherent policies and a common strategy through one or more decision-making centres, in which the entities are so linked, by ownership or otherwise, that one or more of them may be able to exercise a significant influence over the activities of others, and, in particular, to share knowledge, resources and responsibilities with the other.'*[6]

The alternative definition in the code maintains all aspects of this definition save the following variations:

> *'an enterprise whether of public, private or mixed ownership, comprising ...'*

and

> *'that one or more of them may be able to exercise ...'*

The alternative definition obviously fits the structures of transnational corporations in mixed and/or socialist economies.

As has been demonstrated in this chapter, in drafting this code the drafter took into consideration the differing views of both developed and developing countries in respect of all aspects of transnational corporations, including their organisational structures, the system(s) control, ownership, investment policies, their responsibilities towards host countries, the obligations of home countries, and the probable means of exercising control over their activities by host countries. However, the UN Draft Code of Conduct by no means represents the first international effort to consider the probable means of regulating the activities of transnational corporations. The following represent some of the efforts made by other organisations, whether international, or inter-governmental, or regional, or non-governmental, towards the same objective:

- Multinational Enterprises and Social Policy adopted by the International Labour Office (ILO) 1973;

---

6   The text of the Draft Code of Conduct has been reproduced in 23 International Legal Materials (1984) at 626.

- 'The Set of Multilaterally Agreed Equitable Principles and Rules for the Control of Restrictive Business Practices' 1980;[7]
- 'Draft International Code of Conduct on the Transfer of Technology' 1980;[8]
- 'The OECD Declaration on International Investment and Multinational Enterprises' 1976;[9]
- The OECD report entitled International Investment and Multinational Enterprises: Responsibility of Parent Companies for their Subsidiaries 1980;[10]
- 'The Andean Foreign Investment Code' of 1976 and the various decisions passed by the commission of the Cartagena Agreement;[11]
- International Code of Advertising Practice 1986 (ICC);[12]
- International Code of Sales Promotion 1987 (ICC);[13]
- Rules for the ICC International Council on Marketing Practice, 1988 (ICC);[14] and
- ICC Code on Environmental Advertising 1991.[15]

Although transnational corporations contribute very significantly to economies and the economic development process, the adoption of a large number of codes of conduct seems to suggest that in certain respects their conduct and activities need to be regulated. As the OECD guidelines and the UN Draft Code of Conduct are quite comprehensive with regard to this issue, it has been decided to discuss them in this chapter. References to the other codes will be made where necessary.

12.3.2 What is a Code of Conduct and why is it necessary?

A 'code' stands for a person's standard of moral behaviour. In the context of transnational corporations it would stand for the standard of conduct that a

---

7   UN Doc TD/RBP/CONF/10 of 2 May 1980. The text of the document has been reproduced in International Legal Materials (1980) at 813.

8   UN Doc TD/Code TOT/25 of 2 June 1980. The text of the draft code and other relevant documents, including the text proposed by the 'Group of 77', have been reproduced in International Legal Materials (1980) at 773.

9   The text of the declaration has been reproduced in International Legal Materials (1976) at 967.

10 Published by OECD, Paris (1980).

11 16 International Legal Materials (1977) 138 and 21 International Legal Materials (1982) 542. See also Chatterjee, 7 Company Lawyer.

12 This code was adopted by the executive board of the ICC on 2 December 1986, in modification of its 1973 edition. ICC publication No 432B.

13 ICC publication No 432A.

14 Adopted by the executive board at its 53rd session on 11 February 1988, ICC publication No 432C.

15 ICC publication No 509.

transnational corporation is expected to maintain in carrying out its activities in foreign jurisdictions. The movement towards codes of conduct aimed at regulating the conduct of transnational corporations may be traced to the growing awareness of the international community of the need to evaluate the contributions transnational corporations make to economies and the economic development process. This awareness has become manifest in both developed and developing countries. Of course, aspiration to economic self-determination in consequence of attaining independence motivated developing countries in general to reflect on issues such as the ownership of their natural resources and the role of transnational corporations in their jurisdictions. Since the 1970s, in particular, when the decolonisation process was almost over, most of the developing countries have utilised the UN which offered them a platform, primarily through the 'Group of 77' (UNCTAD – the UN Conference on Trade and Development) which prompted them to consider such issues as ownership and control in transnational corporations, participation in the management, prioritisation of investment sectors emphasising their ownership in their natural resources, in addition to formulating policies as to the acquisition of technology from transnational corporations and protection of the environment.[16] Such ideas also formed the basis for public and mixed enterprises. In the developed world, the concept of corporate social responsibility, which predominantly originated in the USA much earlier than the 1970s, started gaining ground in other countries during the 1970s. The OECD responded to the issues promptly, identifying the need for transnational corporations demonstrating corporate social responsibility in their activities in both developed and developing countries. The OECD showed that transnational corporations should not distance themselves from the aspirations of societies. Economic regeneration in the Latin world motivated by the idea of gaining control over the activities of transnational corporations led the Latin countries to abolish the Latin American Free Trade Area (LAFTA) and formulate guidelines for controlling transnational corporations expressed through the Andean Investment Code and other decisions adopted by the Commission of the Cartagena Agreement. The unceasing work of non-governmental organisations such as the World Council of Churches in opposing the investment policies of some of the transnational corporations in South Africa, and the development of various codes of conduct addressed to transnational corporations and other corporations by the International Chamber of Commerce should not be disregarded. The climate of codes of conduct was thus developed.

---

16 See, for example, the Draft International Code of Conduct on the Transfer of Technology, 1980; the UN General Assembly Resolution entitled Permanent Sovereignty over Natural Resources, 1962 (Resolution No 1803), and the opinions expressed by developing countries at the Stockholm Conference of 1972 on the protection of the environment.

The need for codes of conduct was felt for another reason too. Prior to the decolonisation period, in most cases, the activities of transnational corporations were primarily governed by home countries' legislation. It became inevitable that with the emergence of so many newly born countries transnational corporations would encounter restrictions in their investment systems through the host countries' legislation; thus a situation of conflict also became inevitable. The adverse effect of rigid restrictions on investments would be felt by both private foreign investors and host countries. Additionally, the growing awareness of corporate social responsibility in most societies would inevitably make transnational corporations the subject of constant criticism, whether valid or not. Codes of conduct offered a prime opportunity to de-limit the parameters of power, control, management, responsibility etc. for both the actors, the host countries and private foreign investors. It is in this perspective that the necessity and usefulness of codes of conduct should be appreciated. The effectiveness of codes of conduct has received attention in the concluding part of this chapter.

It is immaterial whether any acceptable definition of a code of conduct exists or not. A code of conduct simply attempts to embody in an instrument the guidelines based on consensus of the parties, both home and host countries, and their aspirations as to how private foreign investors may be part of their investment policies. According to Baade:

> 'A code of conduct on transnational corporations, whether in legally binding or non-binding form, represents an effort to formulate expectations which governments collectively feel justified to hold with regard to the conduct of transnational corporations.'

This definition clearly suggests that a code of conduct represents an effort to formulate government's expectations of private foreign investors in fulfilling which they will automatically maintain the standard of ethics adopted by governments collectively. In this situation, the question of a code of conduct having legally binding effect or not, is otiose.

Professor Vogelaar, an OECD consultant on international investment and multinational enterprises, who was actively engaged in the negotiation and drafting of the OECD guidelines, clarified the usefulness of a code of conduct or guidelines in the following way:

> '... it is extremely important that Western countries have laid down amongst themselves a certain philosophy for the phenomenon of international investment; that they have confirmed their belief in a liberal investment climate; that they speak of the positive contributions multinational enterprises may make to the economic and social development of the OECD area and the world as a whole and that they are willing to co-operate with efforts elsewhere.'[17]

---

17   The OECD Observer (1975) No 78 at 17.

A code can therefore stand for a philosophy of the phenomenon of international investment which, if followed, would not only prevent conflict between the actors, but also contribute to the economies and economic development process and develop a climate of harmony between private foreign investors and host countries. This statement also clearly suggests that transnational corporations cannot disregard the phenomenon of social development, which emanates from the concept of corporate social responsibility. In other words, a code of conduct attempts to make a compromise between the extremities of the doctrine of the *laissez-faire*, which has dominated the world economy for many years, and the aspirations of the exponents of corporate social responsibility, which may, in effect, eventually change the nature of corporate governance. It should contribute to avoiding conflicts between private foreign investors and host countries. It should also prompt home countries to adapt their legislation so as to secure the place of transnational corporations in various foreign jurisdictions.

12.3.3 Efforts made by the OECD

The OECD forum is the forum of the developed states. It is the most appropriate forum for recommending measures with a view to regulating the conduct of transnational corporations. The Investment Committee of the OECD is the particular organ which considers issues in order to develop standards for foreign and local investments by transnational corporations. The most important guidelines that the OECD issued in this regard were:

* the Declaration on *International Investment and Multinational Enterprises* 1976; and

* the report entitled *International Investment and Multinational Enterprises: Responsibility of Parent Companies for their Subsidiaries* 1980.

By this declaration the OECD Member States[18] considered, *inter alia*, that:

'... *co-operation by member countries can improve the foreign investment climate, encourage the positive contribution which multinational enterprises can make to economic and social progress, and minimise and resolve difficulties which may arise from their various operations.*'

This statement is indicative of the fact that even in the 1970s many transnational corporations were not making a sufficiently positive contribution to economic and social progress by seeking to minimise and resolve difficulties arising from their various operations. Furthermore, it was necessary for them to improve the foreign investment climate. Lack of initiative in such matters positively damages the relationship between private

---

18   The Turkish government was not in a position to participate in this declaration.

foreign investors and host countries, be they developed or developing countries. The OECD's Investment Committee therefore found it necessary to develop Guidelines for multinational enterprises.[19]

The guidelines stated, *inter alia*, that:

> '... *the advances made by multinational enterprises in organising their operations beyond the national framework may lead to abuse of concentrations of economic power and to conflicts with national policy objectives. In addition, the complexity of these multinational enterprises and the difficulty of clearly perceiving their diverse structures, operations and policies, sometimes give rise to concern.*'

This represents a direct recognition of the economic power transnational corporations enjoy which may be directed to economic domination leading to monopolisation markets. Furthermore, it also recognises that the complexity of their structure makes it difficult to ascertain the control mechanism they operate, and that such complexity in their organisational structures, operations and policies sometimes gives rise to concern. It must be re-iterated that with the growing awareness of the concept of corporate social responsibility, host states will question the governance system applied by various transnational corporations. This issue also hints at the need for more provisions for disclosure of corporate information.

As pointed out earlier in this section, that prior to the 1970s, the governance system of transnational corporations in most cases was home country-based. The remoteness of the host country from the actual governance system operated by the home country to which a transnational belongs gives rise to suspicion and isolationism, which by the 1970s was contrary to the policies of most of the countries, rich or poor. The guidelines further stated that:

> '*Every State has the right to prescribe the conditions under which multinational enterprises operate within its national jurisdiction subject to international law and to the international agreements to which it has subscribed. The entities of a multinational enterprise located in various countries are subject to the laws of these countries.*'

A reminder of these issues was timely and indeed essential, particularly when until the 1970s most of the transnational corporations had the freedom to invest in various developing countries according to their own policies and priorities. It is also interesting to note that the OECD recognised the activities of transnational corporations may be governed by the appropriate rules of international law, that is rules of customary international law expressed in the form of state responsibility. Furthermore, as the paragraph clearly suggests,

---

19   The text of the guidelines has been reproduced in 15 International Legal Materials (1976) at 969.

that the OECD Investment Committee drew to the attention of the member states that transnational corporations were subject to the laws of host countries, implying the developing host countries, as such was already the practice in the developed world.

In addition to laying down certain general principles, the guidelines dealt with the following items: disclosure of information, competition, financing, taxation, employment and industrial relations, and science and technology. The council of the OECD also passed special decisions on the following items:

- inter-governmental consultation procedures on the guidelines for multinational enterprises;
- national treatment of foreign multinational enterprises and exceptions thereto;
- international investment incentives and disincentives.

The Report entitled International Investment and Multinational Enterprises: Responsibility of Parent Companies for their Subsidiaries, 1980, was a follow-up to the OECD declaration of 1976. The 1980 report paid particular attention to certain important issues related to intra-group relations such as law, tax law and law against restrictive business practices, in addition to the controversial question of whether the structures of companies might be responsible for their violating rules of restrictive business practices and the nature of the legal responsibility of parent companies for their subsidiaries. The Report pointed out that:

'In situations where within a group a subsidiary is completely integrated with the parent company, the latter appearing as its alter ego, it would be futile to assume an independent interest of the subsidiary for protective purposes.'

This also suggests that for all practical purposes the units of a transnational corporation together with its headquarters constitute one economic entity, and it is essential that in determining liability and responsibility for any unit, the principal and agency relationship between them must be examined. In this sense, the principle of 'veil lifting' stands for a more theoretical formality. The above-mentioned passage also refers to the issues of ownership and control, which are centrally organised and managed, in consequence of which transnational corporations become centres of economic power which in turn allows them to manipulate markets to their best interests in order to reach their profit-maximisation goal.

In 1984, the OECD's Committee of Experts on Restrictive Business Practices prepared a report entitled Competition and Trade Policies[20] which examined both trade-related competition issues and competition-related trade issues, in addition to dealing with issues relating to the formulation and implementation of trade and competition laws and policies. The report demonstrated its concern as to the methods used by certain transnational corporations in order virtually to form export cartels whose behaviour has a trade-distorting and competition-restricting effect.[21] It stated, *inter alia*, that:

> 'Trading companies vary considerably in size, structure, functions and frequency of use from one country to another. They are tending however to become increasingly significant in the export and import trade of a number of Member countries, accounting for a considerable share of total foreign trade or trade in particular product groups.'[22]

The behaviour of transnational corporations in attaining their profit-maximisation goal has, in general, remained unchanged even during the current decade. Without concerted efforts by the states globally, no effective action plan may be formulated and implemented in an attempt to restrain transnational corporations from engaging in such activities. The report rightly noted that:

> 'Although there seems to be growing observance of moderation and self-restraint, in the absence of multilaterally agreed upon criteria, unilateral approaches are not likely to be successful in resolving all conflicts which may arise.'[23]

The dominating position of transnational corporations is a cause for concern especially for those countries that lack sufficient resources and economic power. Rigid investment legislation and restrictions imposed on private foreign investments in certain jurisdictions are direct results of such concern.

The OECD's guidelines and reports did not directly refer to corporate social responsibility, although a derivative interpretation of many of the issues discussed by these instruments may refer to it. Even during the 1970s and 1980s in most parts of Europe the concept of profit maximisation, which abhorred the concept of corporate social responsibility, reigned supreme. These instruments however concentrated more on the ways and means of allowing the *laissez-faire* doctrine free play, and the avoidance of distortion of markets by monopolies of any nature. However, these instruments clearly revealed that in view of the behaviour of transnational corporations which in

---

20 OECD, *Competition and Trade Policies: Their Interaction*, Paris (1984).

21 op cit, p 15.

22 op cit, p 16.

23 op cit, p 138.

certain cases became a cause for concern, some guidelines as to the standards of conduct would be useful.

12.3.4 Efforts made by the United Nations

As stated earlier, the UN efforts in connection with the issue of regulating the conduct of transnational corporations were reflected in a number of its resolutions; but for the sake of brevity, it has been decided to discuss here only the UN Draft Code of Conduct on Transnational Corporations, 1982. This Draft Code of Conduct, which is, in effect, a resolution of the UN General Assembly, was initiated by the UN Commission on Transnational Corporations, with the UN Centre on Transnational Corporations acting as its secretariat. It seems to have dealt with all possible issues associated with the activities of transnational corporations, including economic, political, socio-cultural, legal etc.

The Draft Code of Conduct is a very comprehensive document, and it has discussed the following issues:

Activities of Transnational Corporations

A. General and Political

i.   Respect for national sovereignty and observance of domestic laws, regulations and administrative practices;

ii.   Adherence to economic goals and development objectives, policies and priorities;

iii.   Review and re-negotiation of contracts;

iv.   Adherence to socio-cultural activities and values;

v.   Respect for human rights and fundamental freedoms;

vi.   Non-collaboration by transnational corporations with racist minority regimes in South Africa;

viii.   Non-interference in internal political affairs;

ix.   Non-interference in inter-governmental relations; and

x.   Abstention from corrupt practices.

B. Economic, Financial and Social

i.   Ownership and control;

ii.   Balance of payments and financing;

iii.   Transfer pricing;

iv.   Taxation;

v.   Competition and restrictive business practices;

vi.   Transfer of technology;

vii.   Consumer protection; and

viii.   Environmental protection.

C. Disclosure of Information

1.   Treatment of Transnational Corporations

i.   General treatment of transnational corporations by the countries in which they operate;

ii.   Nationalisation and compensation;

iii.   Jurisdiction.

2. Inter-Governmental Co-operation

Implementation of the Code of Conduct

i.   Action at the national level;

ii.   International institutional machinery;

iii.   Review procedure.

In view of the differences of opinion among states, many alternative uses of phrases and ideas have been included in the draft code, although the main headings remain unaltered.

In the context of this work, the drafters' particular attention to the following items deserves commendation: adherence to socio-cultural activities and values, ownership and control, consumer protection, environmental protection, and disclosure of information. The provision of general treatment of transnational corporations by the countries in which they operate and the recommendation that host countries should not nationalise or expropriate assets of such corporations on an unjustifiable basis are also important means for maintaining harmony between host countries and private foreign investors. As to ownership and control, the draft code provided, *inter alia*, that:

> '*Transnational corporations should/shall so allocate [endeavour to allocate] their decision-making powers among their entities as to enable them to contribute to the economic and social development of the countries in which they operate.*'[24]

Similar ideas are also advocated by the exponents of modern corporate governance and corporate social responsibility, *mutatis mutandis*, at a national level. Decision-making powers must be held and exercised with full regard to the policy of contributing to the economic and social development of the

---

24   Paragraph 21.

country in which a corporation operates. As to disclosure of information, both developed and developing countries agreed on each issue and no alternative phrases have been included in paragraph 44, the initial part of which provided that:

> 'Transnational corporations should disclose to the public in the countries in which they operate, by appropriate means of communication, clear, full and comprehensive information on the structure, policies, activities and operations on the transnational corporation as a whole.'

As to the implementation of the code, the drafters recommended action at the national level, action by international institutional machinery, such as the UN Commission on Transnational Corporations which has assumed functions for the implementation of the code, and through review procedures. In so far as action at a national level is concerned the drafters recommended four different means, which are not difficult to apply:

- publicise and disseminate the code;
- pursue the implementation of the code within their own territories;
- report to the UN Commission on Transnational Corporations on the action taken at the national level and on the experience gained from its implementation; and
- take actions to reflect their support for the code.

In the event of a country experiencing any difficulty in implementing this draft code, the UN Centre on Transnational Corporations shall provide assistance, inter alia, by:

> '... collecting, analysing and disseminating information and conducting research and surveys, as required and specified by the Commission.'[25]

In other words, the responsibility for the implementation of the draft code lies with the Member States of the United Nations. This is a crucially important issue, in that they are not being subjects of international law, there does not exist any privity between this draft code and transnational corporations. The draft code has been addressed to the members of the United Nations. The same argument applies to the guidelines developed by the OECD. Co-operation of the member states of the United Nations, who are also members of the OECD, is vitally important in order to effectively implement the UN Draft Code of Conduct and the OECD guidelines or any other guidelines that have been adopted by other organisations, be they international, inter-governmental or non-governmental. As stated earlier in this work, social awareness must be the most important factor in bringing about changes in the attitudes of the business community of which corporations are part, and by legislative means, voluntary arrangements for

---

25   Paragraph 70.

inculcating corporate social responsibility must be developed. Corporations may no longer be treated as inanimate legal entities particularly when their activities produce direct effects on societies.

12.4 Conclusions

One of the consistent controversies concerning such guidelines and codes of conduct relates to their legally binding effect. Guidelines are not generally meant to be legally binding in effect; they are mere guidelines. Furthermore, when guidelines are issued by inter-governmental organisations, such as the OECD, they are characteristically non-binding, unless the member states agree to accept them as binding. From a strict legal standpoint, this is the position of the guidelines and reports published by the OECD in regard to regulating the conduct of transnational corporations. Nevertheless, the persuasive effect of such guidelines should not be underestimated. The ICC codes, for example, have been voluntarily accepted by many companies belonging to the member countries of the ICC, and the habit of following these codes spreads. In reviewing the OECD Guidelines for Multinational Enterprises, Blanpain said that:

> 'These guidelines, which take into account the problems which can arise because of the international structures of these enterprises, lay down standards for the activities of these enterprises in the different Member countries. Observance of the guidelines is voluntary and not legally enforceable. However, they should help to ensure that the operations of these enterprises are in harmony with the national policies of the countries where they operate and to strengthen the basis of mutual confidence between enterprises and States.'[26]

In the process of developing mutual confidence between enterprises and states, home states are required to ensure whether by legislation or otherwise that transnational corporations abide by these guidelines, as host states would expect transnational corporations to follow these guidelines.

As to the Draft Code of Conduct adopted by the United Nations, controversy persists concerning the legally binding effect of it. The Draft Code of Conduct is, in reality, a resolution of the UN General Assembly, and academic opinions in abundance question the legal effect of resolutions adopted by the UN General Assembly.[27] Such controversy persists primarily for the reason that the UN General Assembly resolutions have no legally

---

26 Blanpain, *The OECD Guidelines for Multinational Enterprises and Labour Relations* 1982-84: Experience and Review, Davanter, Kluwer Law and Taxation Publishers (1985) at 188.

27 See Tunkin, *'The Legal Nature of the United Nations'* (1966) II Hague Rec 1-68, and Johnson, *'The Effect of Resolutions on the General Assembly of the United Nations'* (1955-56) 32 British Yearbook of International Law 97-122.

binding effect. The perception that the UN General Assembly resolution has no legally binding effect stems from the historical notion that the General Assembly was to be treated as a forum for discussion of matters of international importance, and that the UN has not been given any mandate to make its resolution binding upon any Member State unless it has been adopted by the UN Security Council under Chapter VII of the UN Charter was adopted, the drafters considered the Security Council as the organ that would maintain international peace and security and they armed it with mandatory powers, in disregard of the fact that matters other than of a military nature can also be as important. Nowhere in the charter has it been mentioned that the UN General Assembly resolutions cannot have a legally binding effect. Indeed, the Uniting for Peace Resolution which was adopted by the General Assembly was accepted as a legally binding resolution, so much so that the International Court of Justice, in deciding on the status of the resolution confirmed that the members of the United Nations had an obligation to contribute to the general expenses of the United Nations, over which the General Assembly has the sole authority, whether they voted for such a resolution or not.[28] In this case, France and the Soviet Union refused to accept the validity of the resolution adopted by the General Assembly on the basis of which emergency forces were sent to the Middle East and the Congo. The court confirmed that the expenses incurred on such matters must be regarded as the general expenses of the United Nations, the authority over which rested with the General Assembly.

The UN General Assembly resolutions reflect the aspirations/consensus of the international community, and one should not raise the question whether such resolutions give rise to soft law or hard law. The alternative is not to treat them as sources of soft law either.[29] The uncontroversial provisions of a resolution adopted by the General Assembly signifies their law-making capacity.[30] In examining the legal effect of the General Assembly resolutions, Sloan said that:

> 'It seems clearly inherent in the position of the General Assembly that Members can take steps within the Organisation to reach binding agreements. It also appears true that consent to such agreements may be expressed by a vote in the General Assembly.'

---

28 *Certain Expenses Case*, ICJ Reports (1962).

29 See further Chatterjee, '*The Charter of Economic Rights and Duties of States: An Evaluation After 15 years*', 40 International and Comparative Law Quarterly (1991) 669 at 681; Tepe, Jr '*The Charter of Economic Rights and Duties of States: A Reflection or Rejection of International Law?*' (1975) 9 International Lawyer 295-318.

30 Sloan, '*The Binding Force of a "Recommendation" of the General Assembly of the United Nations*', (1948) 25 British Yearbook of International Law at 22 and 23.

The question whether an affirmative vote cast by a delegation to the General Assembly can itself constitute the consent necessary to give rise to a binding contractual obligation will be subject to greater controversy, but where the intention is to be so bound there is not reason why it should not be given effect.[31]

Higgins maintains that:

'Resolutions of the Assembly are not per se binding; though those rules of general international law which they may embody are binding on member states, with or without the help of the resolution. But the body of resolutions as a whole, taken as indications of a general customary law, undoubtedly provide a rich source of evidence.'[32]

The functions and purposes of the UN General Assembly have changed considerably over the years, particularly since the third decade of the United Nations. It is now involved in almost every important issue of international law, and its discussions and recommendations reflect the general consensus of the international community, and the opinion juris of the said community. An example in point is the UN General Assembly discussion on the Nuclear Tests Ban Treaty, and the judgment of the International Court of Justice in the *Nuclear Tests Ban Treaty* case.[33] It may be irresponsible to dismiss the legal effect of the General Assembly resolutions especially those pertaining to state responsibility, such as the resolution entitled Permanent Sovereign over Natural Resources, 1962, which is a highly regarded resolution-declaration.[34]

There is another was of evaluating the General Assembly resolutions. When the General Assembly adopts a resolution, which is in effect a declaration requesting its member states to adopt it in accordance with their own legal systems, any expectation of a legally binding effect is misconceived. Its sole purpose is to give guidelines to its member states to enable them to adopt it at national levels; in other words, such declarations-resolutions form the corpus of law. In such a situation, to raise controversy as to their legally binding effect is irrelevant.

The UN Draft Code of Conduct is one such resolution-declaration which the states are expected to adopt and embody as far as possible in their national legislation, and which many states, particularly in the developing world, have

---

31 Higgins, *The Development of International Law Through The Political Organs of The United Nations, Oxford: Clarendon Press* (1965).

32 ibid.

33 ICJ Reports, 1974.

34 Chatterjee, op cit at 682. See also for example the Texaco/Libyan Arab Republic arbitration, 53 International Law Reports (1979) at 487.

already adopted.[35] The controversy should centre around the status of the General Assembly, which has been constantly changing, but not the qualitative aspects of the General Assembly resolutions, which are no different from those adopted by the Security Council.

It is also possible to establish the interaction between the guidelines adopted by the United Nations and inter-governmental organisations such as the OECD, and national legislation, by pointing out that the national authorities who are generally members of the United Nations and the OECD tend to respect the guidelines offered by these organisations in drafting their own legislation at a national level.

This chapter has discussed the impact of codes of conduct on corporate governance and transnational corporations as private foreign investors at two levels: first, their impact on a national level such as may be produced on English companies particularly by the City Code on Takeovers and Mergers, and the Cadbury Code of Best Practice; and secondly, the impact of international codes on corporations when they enter into foreign jurisdictions as private investors. There are certain common elements in examining the effects of Codes of Conduct on both types of corporations and their systems of governance. Whether a corporation is local or transnational in terms of its activities, the fact remains that the absence of strict regulatory measures often operates as an unwanted hindrance in pursuing their economic policies.

As has been demonstrated in this work, corporate governance cannot be separated from the concept and operation of corporate social responsibilities which should be examined from both a national and an international perspective.

As far as the UK is concerned, any changes that may be brought about in respect of the corporate governance system would require legislative and societal intervention. In order to have effective legislative intervention, the role of societal intervention based on an awareness of corporate social responsibilities cannot be denied.

The efforts made by the City Code on Takeovers and Mergers and the Cadbury Code of Best Practice are commendable in that they form the basis for a humane corporate governance system in the light of corporate social responsibilities. One should not expect these codes of conduct to be legally binding; they merely represent the aspirations of the community and their primary function is to keep corporations alert to what the stakeholders expect. They form the basis for future law. They also offer guidelines as to how new legislation, if any, should be developed in order to protect the interests of the stakeholders. An appropriate corporate governance system must strike a

---

35 See further UN Centre on Transnational Corporations, *Transnational Corporations in World Development*; Third Survey, UN and Graham Trotman Ltd (1985).

balance between the aspirations of the corporate management and the stakeholders. The interaction between law and codes of conduct is an important factor for achieving that objective.

Chapter 13

Ethical Codes of Conduct: Developing an Ethical Framework for Corporate Governance

Paul Griseri
London Guildhall University

The Cadbury Report, though primarily dealing with the governance of listed companies, raised questions which are relevant to all organisations, small or large, public, private or voluntary. The debate which the report has spawned has highlighted the importance of ethics for a clear understanding of standards of governance, but a clear framework for understanding, measuring and evaluating the values underpinning an organisation's governance has yet to be hammered out. The present contribution to the debate is intended to provide such a framework – one based on a pluralism of values and a broad definition of stake-holding, and offering a strategy for organisations to develop a systematic approach to the ethical element in their governance and operations. The framework will be constructed out of a series of key principles which arise out of an analysis of some of the key conceptual issues involved in the ethics of corporate governance. It presents a structure within which ethical governance can take place, rather than a series of incentives or compulsions to force boards of directors to act more ethically.

13.1 Key concepts for ethical governance

13.1.1 Individual morals and corporate ethics

The term 'ethics' conceals several systematic ambiguities. Perhaps the most apparent is the ambiguity between moral principles and professional standards. More problematic is that between so-called 'normative' and 'analytic' theories of ethics, ie theories which entail specific moral recommendations, as opposed to those which are ethically neutral and merely analyse moral concepts and terminology. While this distinction is dubious in the absolute, its practical application will inform the discussion below.

Much writing concerning business ethics is driven by an overly normative approach, too ready to advance particular ethical judgments rather than examine the form and structure of the framework underlying practices. This ignorance of analytic ethics has led to a narrowly restrictive conception of 'value', illustrated best by the polarisation between the moral sense and what for a better word we shall call the economic: we might very loosely characterise this as the polarisation between goodness and profit. This distinction is, however, misconceived. Productive organisations, whether delivering a service or manufacturing goods, both create and add value. They provide or add features which individuals value, that is, which individuals regard as desirable or worthwhile. The issue is less whether organisations produce value so much as the conflict between one kind of value which might be created at the expense of another.[1]

KEY CONCEPT 1:   the business as a value input/output system

A business inputs elements such as capital and the commitment of the labour force, and puts out finished goods or services. However, it also lives off trust, both of the customer and creditor, and off relationships with suppliers, regulatory officials and share-holders. It may also operate in the light of the perception of the community as to its intentions, for example, concerning the local economy or the local (or national or international) ecosystem. Equally, depending upon what is known about the operations of the business, any or all of the above may be enhanced or damaged by how the business has carried out its activities, ie there is a value output.

The main feature of this idea is that organisations are not simply measurable on a single dimension of ethical worth. All organisations consume some things which are perceived as valuable by some individuals, and create other things which are perceived by some as valuable. Multiple values are involved, at the individual level and at the collective, and at all stages of the processes of the organisation.

The key aspect of viewing an organisation in this way is that the features mentioned above all have a degree of value – the manager or director weighs them all up before making a decision. The issue is not one of how managers can be made to think in terms other than 'merely' profit. It is rather how 'merely' economic considerations can be put into a scale of priorities. It has been commented that unethical behaviour by managers and executives has often been displayed by 'quite ordinary' individuals, leaving unspoken the question as to how such people could be immoral.[2] However, the conclusion of the above argument is that it is quite simple how and why this happens – it happens because financial gain is itself valuable to many people. Whether we like it or not, if an action would result in a significant gain for an individual or company, for very many people that would count as a strong argument in its favour. It is set against other values, such as honesty, or fairness both to investors or employees, but is not intrinsically diametrically opposed to them. Given that decision-making can involve the weighing up of all factors it is unrealistic to hive off moral values as separate kinds of consideration.

---

1   For a different kind of account which reconciles economic conceptions of value with ethical ones, see Sen 1993.
2   cf. Ottoson 1989.

13.1.2 The horizon of responsibility

Clearly the concept of the business as a values input/output system is an open idea until we pin down whose values are to be considered by the system. Many writers on business ethics take a stakeholder perspective on this question.[3] That is, the parties who have a 'stake' in the activities of the organisation are those whose values should be taken into account when judging the ethical outcomes of the organisation's activities. A typical list of such stakeholders might include: owners, employees, customers, creditors, suppliers, the local community, and the government.[4]

There are, however, difficulties with maintaining this as the sole determining factor of whose values to take into consideration.[5] For the purpose of this discussion the key problem with this view is the horizon of responsibility. As Cadbury quoted in discussion of the *Caparo* case, too strong a requirement of responsibility to (in that particular case, a specific set of) stakeholders would lead to '... liability in an indeterminate amount for an indeterminate time to an indeterminate class'.[6] Clearly, this is unacceptable. An organisation cannot function without some conception of the limits within which it is operating.

KEY CONCEPT 2: the definition of a sphere of responsibility

It is moral responsibility which is intended here, of course. Legal duties and responsibilities represent important means whereby interested parties can enforce such values as have been enshrined in legislation. What is needed over and above the legal concept, however, is for organisations – each organisation, in its own way – to make clear to all who deal with it just what it will regard as part of its business, and what it will not.

A definition of the sphere of responsibility of an organisation should include:

- identification of the key foreseen consequences of the activities of the business;

- stipulation of the range of stakeholders' interests which the business will consider as relevant;

- statement of the degree of responsibility the business will accept;

- statement of a process of monitoring the above.

This may appear to be an unusual and unwarranted extension of an organisation's responsibilities, but in fact statements of this kind abound, in the form of customer charters, statements of key organisational values etc. In

---

3   eg Sheridan and Kendall (1992).
4   This list is taken from Cannon (1992), p 44.
5   For example, Donaldson (1992) discusses some of the difficulties in this view.
6   Cardozo, CJ, quoted in the Cadbury Report.

such documents, organisations will often set out what they see as the main interests of those who are regarded as the key stakeholders, and an indication is given of the extent to which the organisation will take responsibility for substandard activities, services or goods. Where the statement is a customer charter, or makes statements concerning owners and shareholders, then there may well be created a legal liability. In the case of charters which mention valuing other stakeholders, such as employees, suppliers, or the local community, this may be less clear.

One area which not all such statements fully deal with is that of the impact of the organisation's activities. It is one thing to promise to support the local economy through employment and using local suppliers, it is quite another to regard this as a binding commitment. However, often a local community may well perceive such a statement in this way. It is essential, therefore, for an organisation to identify the limits of such commitments, if for no other reason than to forestall any misconceptions.

Certain corporate statements of value do clarify such limits. The kind of policy statement required for Investors in People status, for example, requires not merely an assertion of the value of employees, but also an indication of level of commitment, often in concrete cash terms. This represents, in effect, not merely an indication of (a part of) the sphere of responsibility, but also an identification of how the organisation perceives this in relation to its activities. A stakeholder group is identified, a set of interests is recognised, and a stipulation of the horizon of responsibility is also made. Investors in People only relates to a specific area of value – human resource development – but it does represent a good example of the kind of form a well structured 'charter' style statement can take.

Unfortunately, many of the current codes of practice, customer charters, etc, are honoured more in the breach than in the observance, and many others are carefully presented to avoid too great a burden of liability (eg the British Rail passengers' charter offers to reimburse passengers more than half an hour late for their destinations: only a tiny minority of late arrivals fall into this category). However, many others define precise and public standards of quality, thereby creating a stakeholder confidence which operates within well drawn limits. In drawing up such charters, organisations state explicitly both to whom they will be held accountable and for what. Hence the definition of a horizon of responsibility goes hand in hand with that of the range of stakeholders and which of their interests an organisation will take account.

13.1.3 The spectrum of expectations

A further problem arising out of a normative approach to business ethics is that such a view prescribes a uni-dimensional view of the point of ethical behaviour. To the question 'why bother being moral?' the normative view will tend to give a single answer.

In some cases, such an answer will be market or business driven. Laura Nash states:

> '*The reasons for the new elevated place of ethics in business thinking are many. Managers have seen the high costs that corporate scandals have exacted; heavy fines, disruption of the normal routine, low employee morale, increased turnover of employees, difficulty in recruitment, internal fraud and loss of confidence in the firm ... Business leaders and ... many others are emphasising that high personal standards of conduct are a major asset, as economically valuable as ... goodwill.*'[7]

The key phrase in the above is 'economically valuable'. Nash is implicitly giving credence to the view that good morals equals good business. This is a convenient and comfortable view – good will always receive its reward. It is also one which many will feel is too optimistic.

A contrasting view, but still clearly normatively based, is the emphasis on the legal aspect. Thus Clutterbuck emphasises the growth of legal regulation and the increased levels of litigation involving managers and directors, covering environmental issues, corporate governance and employee relations, amongst other areas.[8] This view places the value of prudence above other considerations. It avoids the *naiveté* of the previous view, though hardly creating confidence in the permanence of directors' commitment to ethical values.

Both these and other such approaches advance a single perspective on ethical behaviour. They fail to recognise the intrinsic plurality of values both in our society in general and in the philosophies of corporate governance which drive organisations along different paths.

KEY CONCEPT 3: the ethical stance of the governing body or bodies[9]

By the phrase 'ethical stance' is intended the fundamental prioritisation of key values which each individual is committed to – whether they recognise this or not. By extension of the idea, I am proposing that each organisation has some kind of basic disposition. This represents a kind of meta-ethical standpoint,[10] in that it does not commit an organisation to any specific evaluation in any particular situation. Rather, it provides an overall indication of the kind of choice a board would be likely to make in certain circumstances.

Clearly, this can only be a part of the organisation's strategy if it is properly formulated. Much of the time, organisations – like individuals – do

---

7   Nash (1990), p 2.

8   Clutterbuck *et al.* (1990), pp 14-16.

9   Note the possible plurality – the points being made here are not intended solely as relating to UK or USA companies. They are also relevant to European and other national companies where two-tier boards have been in operation for many years.

10   Though not in the sense in which philosophers talk of meta-ethics.

not recognise explicitly what the real values driving their activities are. Then, often in some moment of crisis, it becomes clear through the choices that are made or rejected what represents their bottom line. If the board of a company, local authority, NHS trust or whatever, intend to manage the values of their organisation, as part of the culture, then some degree of actualisation, through policy is necessary.

A policy statement on an organisation's ethical stance would not make fixed assertions as to the actions and choices to be expected. Rather it would set out the relative priorities between various examples of the two following key concepts:

KEY CONCEPT 4: teleological values: those relating to the promotion of specific kinds of result, such as the promotion of human well being, generation of wealth, reduction in environmental damage.

KEY CONCEPT 5: deontological values: those relating to fundamental imperatives, which might be considered sometimes to over-ride teleological values; for example, a commitment to anti-discrimination whether or not it promotes any particular results, a commitment to a certain level of quality, a policy of 'never knowingly undersold', a policy of never abusing trust, not taking or giving bribes whatever the potential payoff, etc.

It is the balance between these two broad categories of value which will define an organisation's ethical stance. Different organisations exist for quite different purposes, and it is inappropriate to fix them with a single series of moral principles. The trading company formed to facilitate activities by a charity will naturally embody a quite different set of values from a multinational motor manufacturer; the 'ethical' investment house may share some values with an environmentally friendly chemical company, but they will not coincide. The balance of fundamental values will therefore add considerable colour to the stipulation of a sphere of responsibility outlined earlier.

13.1.4 Structural values

Two additional features of an ethical framework need to be considered. These are:

- transparency, and
- consistency.

Transparency has become a vogue term since the publication of the Cadbury report. Broadly it is a re-affirmation, in the context of corporate governance, of the view that justice should be seen to be done. That is, principles and criteria for sound governance should be public, so that all relevant stakeholders can make their own evaluation of the governance of an organisation.

This is not of itself an ethical value. It is rather a tool for achieving an ethically valuable result, namely, the promotion and maintenance of honesty. However, it has to be measured in so far as it can achieve this result. Clearly, an organisation may have a policy of stating explicit criteria for appointment to the board, remuneration principles, rules for re-appointment and/or dismissal of directors, roles for executive and non-executive directors and so on. That in itself cannot ensure that a determinedly corrupt individual or group will be prevented from keeping their old pals and puppets on the board. Nor can it ensure that such a matter would be plainly obvious for the public, shareholders and other stakeholders to see, for often the links between individuals may lie buried at the bottom of the files in Companies House.

Indeed, disclosure could be harmful to the interests of minority shareholders; for, if a company discloses information which reveals an element of ethically dubious governance, shares in that company might lose value – hence, while it is open to the investor to jettison their stake in the company, they may well only be able to do so at a loss. Transparency can work both ways – in this case, potential future investors' interests may be protected at the expense of current investors.

This is not to suggest that transparency is not worthwhile, but it is to emphasise that it represents only a limited mechanism to support good corporate governance. As Cadbury himself acknowledged[11] even from the limited perspective of his report, that disclosure would be supplemented by the various checks and balances in company board structures. The ethical framework advocated here goes further than that – it requires a full scale policy on the ethical aspects of governance. Transparency of operations is a useful tool to help achieve this, but no more than that.

A more wide ranging issue is that of consistency. It is perfectly open to an organisation to make one sort of choice at one time and, at a later date, make a different kind of choice in apparently similar circumstances. So long as no legal responsibilities have been violated the board is free to act in such a manner – there may be some damage to labour or community relations, but nothing *prohibits* the organisation from so acting.[12]

The idea behind consistent corporate behaviour is more complex than it looks – what counts as a relevantly similar circumstance, for example? However, the concept is clear enough. Taking the analogy from accounting, a rule or principle applied in one context is to apply also whenever that context appears again, just as the adoption of a particular policy of depreciation in one

---

11   Speech to the Institute of Management, reprinted in *Professional Manager* November 1993, pp 8-10.

12   But it is worth noting that certain acts taken at one time may have implications for later acts: eg a stated policy for selection of employees for redundancy on one occasion may well be considered to remain applicable at a later date.

year should be maintained in further years, to facilitate realistic comparisons. Several of Cadbury's recommendations, such as the setting-up of nomination committees for the appointment of non-executive directors, and the recommendation of specifying a particular appointee's role, duties, length of service and remuneration on appointment, assume consistency as a central principle for good corporate governance.

Consistency applies to all actions by an organisation. However, this is in its absolute form an unenforceable requirement, since there is always the argument that a particular set of circumstances has not appeared before, because the business environment has changed. Nevertheless, it is measurable, albeit obliquely. For example, where a major acquisition is being considered, a statement of justification, outlining the reason for the decision can be usefully compared with previous acquisitions – while these cannot of necessity be identical circumstances, it can be ascertained how far one justification resembles the other. For example, a manufacturing company may decide to make a bid for a supplier company, on the basis of making effective use of surplus funds and maintaining a key part of the chain of operations. If latterly the same company tries to take over a retail outlet, the justification for this may be compared and contrasted with the previous acquisition. Clearly, this is an imperfect measure of consistency. Also, none of this is being suggested as a legal requirement – no one is bound by these suggestions. All the same, this is one illustration of how a board of directors can demonstrate consistency in practice.

13.1.5   The framework for ethical governance

The framework proposed consists basically in the collection of the principles discussed above.

13.1.5.1   The pluralist system

Organisations should be seen as 'processing' items of value – a plurality of values, moral and non-moral, are both inputs and outputs of the system, and are elements in corporate decision-making.

13.1.5.2   The horizon of responsibility

The organisation's conception of its sphere of operation needs to be clearly stated; this will involve an identification of stakeholder groups, and for what areas the organisation will hold itself accountable.

13.1.5.3   Ethical stance

A broad indication of the balance between impact-oriented (teleological) and self-standing (deontological) values should be stated as part of the organisation's mission.

13.1.5.4   Consistency

A policy toward consistent and transparent corporate behaviour should be adopted, including public justification of major strategic actions.

The following section will briefly offer some indication of how this framework may be used to improve the ethical quality of corporate governance.

13.2   Engineering an ethical approach to corporate governance

13.2.1 Creating ethically informed governance

The above account has leant heavily on the idea of the explicit corporate statement, be it mission statement, customer charter, or some other kind of code, as a key factor in the development of more deeply ethically informed corporate behaviour. These cannot be statements by the Board alone – they need to be treated as any major corporate change in culture would be: via consultation, discussion, and very much owned by the whole workforce. No one internalises an ethic they have been made to accept – only those they choose to accept, and this choice is more easily made when there is a feeling of some degree of ownership.

The construction of codes, then, is but a part in the process. Equally important is the development of a more creative imagination on the part of directors and employees alike.[13] The extent to which the necessary development is of individuals' powers of perception or their powers of feeling is beyond the scope of this paper, raising as it does some large questions of philosophy. The main point here, however, is that the creation of more ethical corporate governance is a cultural change which runs far beyond the boardroom, and as such it should be treated like any other major organisational development.

Extension of the formal regulation of corporate governance has been resisted, certainly so far as the UK has been concerned. Two principles of the UK approach, however, can provide a stimulus to higher standards of

---

13   An interesting account of the role of imagination in Business Ethics is given in Ciulla (1991).

corporate governance. On the one hand there is the principle of voluntarism, explicitly supported by the Cadbury report, and on the other, that of collective responsibility of directors. Where an organisation has taken some steps towards putting in place an ethical framework, along the lines suggested above, then the whole board must be committed to its implementation. Paradoxically, it is the very weakness of the principle of voluntarism which is its strength. Directors cannot avoid their responsibilities – as an employee could – by suggesting that they were instructed to go along with a code of ethics. The director has to make a specific, and voluntary, step, as part of the role of being collectively responsible. If they don't like it, they should terminate their relationship with the company. This is of a different order from the idea that if workers do not like something, they can always get a job elsewhere – for the reality of late twentieth-century capitalism is that they cannot. By contrast, the voluntary – though remunerated – role of a director is a real choice, since it is not an employment in the sense of being the primary means of someone's livelihood.

13.2.2 Monitoring organisational ethics

The first task in monitoring is to measure what is there. The idea of ethical audit (ie carrying out an audit of the extent to which ethical considerations are adopted within an organisation) has gained some credence recently, drawing from the analogy with environmental auditing. Despite its superficial plausibility, however, it has several shortcomings which render it only partially useful in measuring how ethically informed an organisation's activities are.

One of these weaknesses is that of perception. A key feature of ethical audit must be testimony, but questions of significance raise their heads. An organisation may be unpopular, for example – and thus likely to be poorly described by its stakeholders, without having done anything which is morally wrong. It may simply be poor at public relations. A related difficulty is the so-called 'halo' effect. A person or organisation which is perceived positively over one issue may well be perceived more partially over another, and vice versa. This is really a subclass of a broader unclarity: an individual or organisation performs a certain action, but an ethical evaluation of this requires some projection of an intention behind this. In projecting an intention, we may well be reflecting what was truly intended, or we may be fictionalising – doubtless there are many intermediate grey areas. I pass over without further comment the points I have made concerning plural values earlier, except to point out that they raise difficulties for the idea that there is a common language of morality within which we can even construct a measure. The analogy with environmental auditing breaks down. If there are any moves to develop an ethical standard, parallel with the quality and environmental ones (BS5750 and BS7750 respectively), then it will have to involve a much more sophisticated approach to measurement than those standards.

The approach I have been advocating above owes more to the idea of corporate social reporting[14] than to direct audit. An organisation can be more strongly influenced to aspire to higher ethical standards of governance if its own statements, of policy, of achievement, of justification, are used as an indication of its ethical values than if some apparently independent attempt at measurement is made.

Beyond measurement is operational control. If the Board of a company is to be made aware of how far it is meeting or missing its own standards of governance, or if those same standards are to be rationally criticised, then this should issue from within the board rather than from without. An employee may well be too intimidated to provide a thorough critique of the hand that feeds him or her. An external observer may well suffer from the difficulties of lack of a full understanding of the context and history of the organisation.

On a parallel with the idea of audit committees, organisations should set up an ethics committee. While this may draw from the ranks of all stakeholders, there should be a significant representation from the board. Ideally, a non-executive director of some standing should be a figurehead for the rational criticism and continuous improvement of ethical standards, not just within the Board but across the whole organisation. Such a senior non-executive director would be assigned responsibility for ensuring that ethical policy statements are developed and brought to the attention of the whole board at critical times. They would also be responsible for ensuring both that standards of transparency and consistency were met, and that a properly identified sphere of responsibility was defined for the organisation's activity, and that the organisation's own broad ethical stance was recognised.

Such a function would be a major departure for virtually all governing bodies, outside one or two professional institutions. It would require a new kind of non-executive, and would create a significant series of tasks in developing a sensitivity to this area amongst other, more directly commercial, directors. Nevertheless, any company adopting such an approach could demonstrate to customers, suppliers, employees and others the extent of their commitment. This is no small benefit.

13.3   Unitary versus two-tier boards

The issue as to how far corporate governance structures can create and sustain moral value within an organisation is a large question, which raises questions such as the legitimacy of national and multinational corporations, the

---

14   *cf. Gray et al.* (1987) for a persuasive introduction to this concept.

legitimacy of the various forms of capitalism itself, and the future of advanced technological society.[15] One small issue, which has been particularly emphasised since the publication of the Cadbury Report, has been the resurrection of the idea of adopting two-tier boards. One, the main board, would consist of directors much as on the standard UK board – representing the owning stakeholders, by and large. The other would represent additional interests: in Germany, for example, the second tier, or advisory, board represents mainly employee interests, though there is no reason why such a board could not include community and industry representatives as well.

Such a structure clearly works – it has served Germany well for decades. However, it has to be seen in the context of an overall national climate of employer/employee relations. the conflict orientation of the UK industrial relations scene may have reduced, but it has not disappeared. The radical criticism of such an arrangement is that it further enshrines the disparity between capital and labour, and that a more thorough response to the challenge of employee – or broad stakeholder – participation, is seating on the main board. So far as ethical aspects of governance are concerned, there is some substance in this view. Employee interests can be advanced within an advisory board, but there remain in addition a powerful series of other mechanisms for protecting their interests. The situation with ethical concerns is not the same, however. Ethical considerations are not the property of any particular group in any case, but also there is no supplementary way for them to be supported – there is no analogue of the strike. The presence of specifically ethically responsible directors on the main board, however, creates the need for the whole board, the whole governing body of the organisation, to take ethics seriously. It cannot be shelved as being a 'second tier/second class' issue, and collective responsibility forces all directors to confront the issue, once it is on the boardroom table.

The ethical propriety of corporations has been put under scrutiny in recent years, and in many respects has been found wanting. The development of a systematic and substantial ethical framework is no light task. it will involve additional staffing, additional roles for directors, and greater subjection to the public scrutiny. It does, however, offer the possibility for generating greater public confidence in corporate governance. In this contribution I have tried to show that one aspect of business ethics is not dependent on a normative, judgment-based view of moral value, that it is possible to remain neutral over moral specifics, and still outline the key features of sound, morally informed corporate governance. The framework described above has been consciously argued from an explicitly non-normative standpoint. The variety of ethical views, and the diversity of global cultures, make it ever less appropriate to fasten on a small set of concepts, which are not even unanimous in any one

---

15 Several provocative responses to this question may be found in Sutton (1993).

Western nation, let alone around the whole global community, village though we may now be. However, within the village, we need to have a common understanding, a structure to recognise and deal with our differences, corporate or individual.

Chapter 14

The Role of the Institutional Shareholders' Committee

Julian Potter
Former Secretary General, Institutional Shareholders' Committee

In this chapter, Julian Potter, Secretary General of the ISC for three years from April 1991, discusses the role of the ISC and looks at its papers in relation to the Cadbury Report.

In January 1993, institutional shareholders held over 60 per cent of all UK equities. This contrasts with the situation only 30 years ago, when they held just under 30 per cent. The proportion held by private investors has over the same period slipped from 54 per cent to 21 per cent.

The Institutional Shareholders' Committee, set up partly in response to this changing pattern of ownership, is an association of associations. Its five members are:

- The Association of British Insurers (ABI)
- The Association of Unit Trusts and Investment Funds (AUTIF)
- The Association of Investment Trust Companies (AITC)
- The Asset Management Committee of the British Merchant Bankers' Association (BMBA)
- The National Association of Pension Funds (NAPF)

It is not possible to say precisely what proportion of all institutional shareholdings are owned by members of these five associations, since in each of the fields they represent there are a few companies or firms that have chosen to operate independently of any association. But in each case these independent operators are only a small minority, so it is probable that members of ISC member-associations (and for the sake of precision, this long-windedness is unavoidable) are the holders of well over half of all equities in this country. Producing a more accurate calculation is complicated by the fact that most of the shares held by BMBA members are held on behalf of other institutions, such as pension funds or unit trust, so there is a problem of double counting to deal with.

The business of the ISC is that of their members as shareholders, and this is exemplified by the fact that the secretaries of the investment committees (formerly known as the Investor Protection committees) of both the ABI and the NAPF always attend ISC meetings. This is also why it is the Asset Management Committee of the BMBA that is the ISC member, and not the BMBA itself. Other sections of the BMBA and of the ABI have the job of looking after their members' interests as companies, but these corporate interests are not supposed to weigh in the deliberations of the ISC.

With members' members owning over half of GB Limited, it might be thought that, with such a broad constituency, the ISC should be in a position to exert considerable influence on corporate affairs on behalf of shareholders. Representing so many shareholders – albeit indirectly – should it not be in a position to blow the whistle on any company stepping out of line? In its early days, it was indeed thought that the ISC should have an interventionist role and there was some discussion on how its powers should be divided with those of the Bank of England. In 1977, James Callaghan set up a committee to investigate and make recommendations on the financial institutions and the provision of funds for industry. It was chaired by Harold Wilson, who submitted its report to Margaret Thatcher in 1980. It said:

> '*there may be a case for drawing up under the supervision of the Bank of England a more explicit code of practice for cases dealt with by the Investment Protection Committees or The Institutional Shareholders' Committee ... [but] ... the existing mechanism seems to us to be adequate for any collective action that may be needed ... We see no reason to strengthen the ISC and would not wish it to be given an overall monitoring function. We think this is a role more appropriately filled by the Bank of England.*'

In other words, the minimalist view was that the ISC would sometimes intervene in the affairs of particular companies on behalf of shareholders, although it should not have an overall supervisory role. During the 1980s there were occasions when the ISC acted in such a way, although it is impossible to quantify them, since such intervention would normally be carried out behind the scenes. Since 1991, however, the interventionist role has been abandoned and the ISC has not dealt with issues affecting particular companies, believing that these are best resolved by the shareholders of the companies concerned, as indeed has always happened in the majority of cases. If necessary, the investment committees of the ISC's member-associations can be called on for assistance.

There are, however, two major functions of the ISC that persist. Currently, the most active of these is the provision of a forum where member-associations can meet and discuss common problems. It is hardly surprising that five separate bodies of institutional investors should seek the benefit of each others' views on topics of common concern. Not a month goes by in the City without the emergence of a discussion paper from one quarter or another asking those involved for comment. Whether these papers come from the Bank of England, the SIB, the accounting bodies or perhaps some newly established quango, all of them, including white and green papers from government, land on the desks of the five ISC member associations. Even though the responses to these papers will vary according to the particular viewpoint of each association, the opportunity to discuss them at ISC meetings is useful. Last year responses to the CREST proposals were discussed, for example, as were responses to the government's amended regulations on the dissemination of price sensitive information and a Stock Exchange committee's subsequent paper on the same subject.

It may be thought that the ISC should be well placed to synthesise the views of its members on such subjects and issue statements on behalf of all of them. Usually it does not, partly because all the member-associations have substantial numbers of permanent staff, with experts in this or that aspect of the capital markets, to whom any technical matter can be referred. It was never an economic or sensible idea to impose on top of that an ISC secretariat staffed with its own specialists. Consequently, when responses from the institutions are called for, they tend to come from one or other of the five member-associations. Furthermore, a single response on behalf of all member-associations is usually difficult to formulate without recourse to bland generalities, since it has to take account of the different interests and concerns of insurance companies, pension funds, unit and investment trusts.

A second major function of the ISC is to issue its own documents (guidance notes, codes, position statements – the acceptable word for them keeps changing) on behalf of all its members. This is a more high profile but much less frequent activity than the provision of a forum for debate. The documents are not responses to someone else's discussion paper, but statements of views on major contemporary issues on which member-associations feel strongly and about which they all agree. Such documents are usually drafted in the first instance by one member-association and are then sent for comment to each of the other four. They in turn give the paper a democratic airing within their own associations, perhaps through an investment committee. The whole procedure may be repeated with a second draft. Thus by the time the ISC document finally emerges, it may fairly be said to represent the views of institutional shareholders in general.

This consultation process, although admirably democratic, is clearly time-consuming and cannot be used to respond to urgent matters. It is reserved for occasional statements on major on-going issues, on which a consensus among the institutions has gradually built up.

Four documents have been issued so far. The first, Management Buy-Outs, was published in December 1989 and offered guidance on aspects of an MBO that shareholders would be looking at before deciding to accept an offer. The most recent, *Suggested Disclosure of Research and Development Expenditure*, came out in April 1992. This listed all those aspects of R&D that it would be useful for investors to know about, if not in the financial statements (an area where it would be rash to meddle), then in the narrative section of the annual report or through any other means of communication. It suggested that the benefits of disclosure should always be considered before automatically shrouding information in a cloak of secrecy. The plea was for more disclosure.

The two intervening documents were on the responsibilities of directors and of shareholders and covered the same ground as much of the subsequent Cadbury Report. The rest of this chapter will discuss these papers.

The Role and Duties of Directors – a Statement of Best Practice was issued in April 1991. At that time the spotlight was on corporate governance, perhaps in response to the rash of takeovers in the 1980s. With the encouragement of the Bank of England, the ISC and other bodies, Pro Ned had been formed, with the idea of promoting the use of non-executive directors. The Cadbury committee was soon to be established. The ISC document was in some ways a precursor of the Cadbury Report. It is true that both documents dealt with some subjects not covered in the other. For example, the ISC did not touch on the role of the accountants and Cadbury did. Cadbury did not go into borrowing powers, duties to employees or management buy-outs; the ISC did. On the other hand, many of the most highly publicised clauses of both documents are very similar, as is shown by the following quotations:

Appointment and numbers of non-executive directors

ISC para 4.1:

'Institutional shareholders strongly support the presence of independent directors on the boards of companies.'

ISC para 4.5:

'The non-executive directors should be sufficient in number and calibre for their views to carry sufficient weight on the board.'

Cadbury Code, 1.3:

'The board should include non-executive directors of sufficient calibre and number for their views to carry significant weight in the board's decisions.'

Separation of roles of chairman and chief executive

ISC para 3.2b:

'The roles of chairman and chief executive should not, therefore, normally be combined.'

Cadbury Code, 1.2:

'There should be a clearly accepted division of responsibilities at the head of the company, which will ensure a balance of power and authority, such that no one individual has unfettered powers of decision.'

Directors' contracts

ISC para 5.1b:

'... contracts should not run for a period of more than three years and there may be circumstances where a rolling contract should be limited to a period of no more than one year.'

Cadbury Code, 3.1:

'Directors' service contracts should not exceed three years without shareholders' approval.'

On many other issues, including the desirability of audit committees and remuneration committees, the two reports appear to speak with one voice. The Cadbury committee certainly discussed the ISC document and possibly the fact that Mike Sandland (then group investment manager for the Norwich Union) was at the time both chairman of the ISC and a member of the Cadbury committee accounts for some of the similarities. However, Cadbury did not endorse and quote from the *Role and Duties of Directors* in the same way as it did in respect of the ISC's next document, on the responsibilities of shareholders. It may therefore be worth looking for those differences between the ISC and the Cadbury documents that may have restrained the Cadbury Committee from giving the former its unqualified approval.

Such as they are, they are small. One, which may already have been spotted from the above quotes, is that Cadbury makes no reference to *rolling* contracts. (At the time of writing, July 1994, the institutions are becoming more open in their opposition to lengthy rolling contracts.) Another is on the question of what a Board should do in cases where, despite the views of Cadbury and the institutions, the roles of chief executive and chairman are still combined. Cadbury says (Code, 1.2) that in such cases '... it is essential that there should be a strong and independent element on the board, with a recognised senior member.' The ISC says (3.2b) 'In circumstances where they are combined it is unlikely that institutional shareholders will be satisfied unless there is a strong body of independent non-executive directors who are aware of their overall responsibilities to shareholders ...'. The problem was presumably the insoluble one of how to organise opposition to a too powerful chairman without being divisive. It looks as if the ISC thought it would be too divisive to set up 'a recognised senior member' as a counterweight to the chair/CEO; while Cadbury thought it would be too divisive to ask a particular section of the board to report back to shareholders.

That NEDs had a special responsibility to shareholders was spelt out in 4.5b of the ISC document: 'While all directors have a duty to monitor the performance of a company, the non-executive director should acknowledge a particular duty to monitor the performance of the board as a whole, and to report to the shareholders if they are not satisfied after reasonable efforts have been made by them to remedy the causes of their dissatisfaction.' The ISC document was sent to the chairmen of all major companies at the time and a majority of those who responded did so with enthusiastic support. A few disagreed with particular points, including the paragraph quoted. How, it was asked, can NEDs monitor and report on other directors when all directors are in law equally responsible for the conduct of the company? Sir Owen Green, then chairman of BTR, was particularly strong in opposition to this paragraph, thinking it to be divisive. Others thought it was a half-way house to the two-tier board. Cadbury was diplomatic, re-affirming its support for the unitary board but pointing out that (Report, 4.4) 'Whilst it is the board as a whole which is the final authority, executive and non-executive directors are likely to contribute in different ways to its work'. There is no mention in the Cadbury Report or code of a special link between NEDs and shareholders.

These are matters of detail. In all major issues, the Cadbury code and the *Role and Duties* are at one – and in general terms the ISC formally endorsed the code in a press release; and when its own document was re-issued in August 1993 it was amended to include aspects of corporate governance covered by Cadbury but not in the first edition of the ISC document. Minor differences have only been unearthed in an attempt to explain why Cadbury did not specifically endorse and quote from it in the same way as it did for the ISC's next document, *The Responsibilities of Institutional Shareholders in the UK (Dec 1991) (RIS)*.

This document was seen as a companion document to that on the responsibilities of directors. As the title indicates, it was aimed at the ISC's own members, rather than at directors. It contained a number of points covered in the earlier document, such as the appointment of audit and remuneration committees and properly constituted boards, but this time it was putting the onus on shareholders to see that these requirements were carried out. Its main message was that institutional investors should take an interest in the affairs of the companies in which they invest, maintain contact with the management of those companies and exercise their influence through use of the vote or in discussion before the voting stage was reached.

Since the RIS document was published, member-associations of the ISC have been encouraging their own members to vote and in 1993 research by the ISC itself showed that there had been some movement in that direction. It indicated that with major PLCs, on average 34 per cent of all shares were voted, compared with an estimated 20 per cent in 1990. Looking at the twenty largest shareholdings in each of the companies surveyed, the average level of voting was 50 per cent. (However, there is some concern now that with the advent of CREST, this level will drop back, because the new system will lead to a more widespread use of nominees.) Whether the extent of shareholders' involvement at an earlier stage is similarly increasing is not known, as such discussions take place in private. Presumably press reports on the lines that 'pressure from shareholders' have achieved this or that result are based on speculation only.

The Cadbury code makes only one reference to shareholders ('... service contracts should not exceed three years without shareholders' approval'). But the Cadbury Report, which introduces the code, welcomes the RIS document, quotes verbatim the paragraphs dealing with its main message and makes it clear that only shareholders are in a position to see that the code is implemented. This is because there are no sanctions to enforce compliance. The Stock Exchange requires a statement of compliance or non-compliance as one of its continuing listing obligations. But if such a statement shows inadequate compliance, what then? The Cadbury Report (6.16) has the answer:

> *'Because of the importance of their collective stake, we look to the institutions in particular, with the backing of the ISC, to use their influence as owners to ensure that the companies in which they have invested comply with the code ... The obligation on companies to comply with the code provides institutional and individual shareholders with a ready-made agenda for their representations to boards. It is up to them to put it to good use. The committee is primarily looking to such market-based regulation to turn its proposals into action.'*

The Cadbury Report was issued in December 1992. With such a high level of agreement between Cadbury and the ISC on those issues covered separately by both parties, what progress has been seen since then? On the question of NEDs, Colin St. Johnston, managing director of Pro Ned, says approximately 90 per cent of listed companies now have them compared with roughly 50 per cent in 1982. More important now, he thinks, is that they should be selected in such a way as to ensure that they are truly independent, as required by both the Cadbury and the ISC documents. This too is beginning to come right. He estimates that in 1982 up to 80 per cent of NEDs were specialist advisors, former executives of the company or just friends; whereas now up to 80 per cent fulfil the independence criteria.

On this and on other issues, the National Association of Pension Funds (NAPF) is offering shareholders Cadbury's 'ready-made agenda' as part of its voting issues service. This not only advises shareholders of any resolutions at a forthcoming AGM that might be held to be contentious (so making the business of voting intelligently less laborious), but also provides a 'corporate governance checklist', showing the extent of the company's compliance with Cadbury and ISC requirements. An NAPF benchmark check among 250 companies in 1993 showed that already 84 per cent of companies favoured splitting the roles of chairman and chief executive, while remuneration and audit committees had been appointed on the lines prescribed by, respectively, 78 per cent and 76 per cent. Meanwhile the Cadbury committee itself, which still sits and which is due to have appointed a 'successor body' by the time this book is published, has a working party chaired by Professor Andrew Likierman, the purpose of which is to monitor compliance with the Cadbury code. The Association of British Insurers (ABI), which after the NAPF represents the second largest association of institutional shareholders, is involved in this work.

None of the documents discussed in this chapter can claim to have been strong on original ideas. Rather they gave impetus to the prevailing consensus, which was in favour of the sort of proposals they contained. Preliminary indications are that, since the documents were published, there have been substantial changes in corporate governance along the required lines. Meanwhile, since Maxwell, the spotlight seems to have shifted away from corporate governance and moved on to regulation, whether by the old SROs, by the PIA or, failing that, imposed by government.

Chapter 15

Three Faces of 'Corporate Social Responsibility': Three Sociological Approaches

Dr Stephen Lloyd Smith
School of Social Science, Kingston University

15.1 Introduction

Product safety, environmental protection, the removal of gender and racial discrimination, the fair treatment of suppliers, the maintenance of employees' health and safety, and the creation of meaningful and rewarding work, are widespread modern concerns. They are often, though not universally, treated as 'corporate social responsibilities': duties dischargeable by the firm.[1]

However, it is a good deal easier to come up with a common-sense, popular list of issues like these, than it is to specify what corporate social responsibility really is. The difficulties are made worse because the terms 'corporate', 'social', and 'responsibility' carry diverse meanings and connotations. The working definition of corporate social responsibility (CSR) used here is *changing ideologies and practices which allocate the authority for defined problems to an association, and which determine that the authority for dealing with those problems is legitimate, competent, dischargeable, accountable and necessary.* Ideology and practice, the discourse on responsibility, has always been shifting.

The challenge is to explain why certain responsibilities are defined as belonging to the business corporation, while other duties have been taken away from the firm, and allocated to the state, to the family, or to individuals. This chapter will focus on explaining how the allocation of responsibility (or an absence of responsibility) has been determined in three cases. It is written by a sociologist, but aimed at practitioners and policy-makers. For this reason, the discussion of social theory is kept as direct and straightforward as possible, focusing on significant and often surprising findings.

In the past, I balked, as co-writer, at using the expression corporate social responsibility, adopting the less forceful, but vague category: corporate social policy.[2] Indeed sociologists did not invent the expression, rarely think in terms

---

1   For an interesting discussion of the rationales behind selected corporate social responsibilities, see Adams *et al. Changing Corporate Values, a Guide to Social and Environmental Policy and Practice in Britain's Top Companies*, pp 5-59. For a general introduction, see Frederick *et al. Business and Society, Corporate Strategy, Public Policy, Ethics London*: McGraw-Hill.

2   Harvey *et al. Managers and Corporate Social Policy; Private Solutions to Public Problems?*

of corporate social responsibility, and UK sociologists almost never.[3] Our book focused mainly on explaining differences between firms' behaviour, through differences in their 'organisational cultures'. Other approaches are suggested here: principally the historical and the formal. Further frameworks can be imagined; the main claim is not that the approaches taken here are definitive, but that they are worth exposing to criticism.

The sociologist's hesitation over CSR is odd in some ways. The discipline was founded on an 18th century commitment to enlightened social improvement through scientific understanding of social systems, known in conjunction as *positivism*. The promise of scientific social improvement was rhetorical and therefore hard to resist. (Who would favour *unscientific social decline*?) Corporate social responsibility is also a rhetorical device which promises improvement. The acceptance, or forceful imposition of the responsibility for tackling a problem, promises its solution; acceptance of a responsibility is (rhetorically) better than a refusal. The point is that sociologists might have been expected to have shown more interest in CSR as would-be improvers, and as a response to the rhetorical plea that 'something has got to be done about the [x] problem'.

Perhaps sociologists are afraid of 'studying upwards', and shy away from senior managers; or think of social problems as state, professional, or (like Plato and Aristotle) as communal responsibilities, properly belonging anywhere except in business hands. Perhaps sociologists are wary of CSR because it implies the erosion of governmental responsibilities, to which we were allied to through an eighteenth and nineteenth-century positivist commitment to address private troubles through state solutions. The idea that a competitive firm might embrace responsibilities without being forced to do so still seems suspect.

Vagueness perhaps? While CSR is certainly a vague category, there are many research topics which are plagued with definitional problems, but which attract a lot of attention. Besides, the stuff of CSR: private and public troubles, legitimacy, authority, power, the sacred and the profane, continuity and change, order, class, gender, managerialism, is also the stuff of general sociological discourse.

Whatever the reason for avoiding CSR, the importance of the corporation certainly means that all its activities, and the forces that determine the

---

3   The 1992 edition of Sociological Abstracts, a world listing of sociological research, gives 557 entries against 'organisation', of which a mere 16 approximated to a concern with corporate social responsibility (most reflected American concerns). Of these, 14 were on employee issues, mostly discrimination, and health and safety. Only two went outside organisational boundaries – 'Government Regulation of Corporate Violence' (92Y7974) and 'Public Good' (92Z2266). Looking at the 16 entries for 'ethics and ethical decision-making', for the first half of 1994, Abstracts, covers eight on medical and health questions, and eight entries in political philosophy; none are addressed in terms of business ethics. Text-books in organisational sociology generally do not discuss differing standards among organisations in ethical terms.

boundary between private and public responsibility, deserve sociological attention – not just the organisational structures, cultures and labour-processes which attract extensive sociological interest. Sociologists having absented themselves, the balance of business school discourse tends too readily to accept as axiomatic, the proposition that large firms can and should meet responsibilities beyond profit and growth (Friedman, Hayek and Drucker[4] excepted).

15.2   Value conflicts

Although many of my colleagues would recoil from the suggestion that they are positivists, a positivist tendency persists in sociology. For example, there is a tendency to reject the deskilled organisation, where direct managerial control, and workers' boredom prevails, as a retrograde social development, to be opposed. Organisations which are based on workers' skill and autonomy are seen as understandably better and worth fighting for.[5] Gender equality is seen as a very desirable organisational objective.

The problem is, of course, that it is very difficult to establish unequivocal, progressive ethical standards, values and objectives in any area of social life. Skilled workforces often exclude women from skill acquisition.[6] Thus a company that is behaving well by one criteria (meaningful work), often behaves badly against another (gender equality).

Whether or not you think that a given change is an improvement depends on what you value.

These value-conflicts cannot be smoothed over by simplistic, rhetorical appeals to corporations that they should behave responsibly. This simply begs the question 'which value?' The questionable generalisation that big business is 'socialising itself', and evolving into a neutral, technocratic, interest-balancing mechanism, does not appear to get around the 'which value?' question.[7] *Absolute* value-choices cannot be balanced technocratically, because value-choices are not technical in nature.

Indeed, fierce, absolute, value objections have been made against the idea that corporations have any other responsibilities besides profit. For example:

---

4   Drucker, *Management*; Friedman *Monopoly and the Social Responsibilities of Business and Labour*, in Friedman and Friedman (eds) *Capitalism and Freedom*; Hayek 'The Corporation in Democratic Society' in Ashen and Bach (eds) *Management and Corporation in 1985*.

5   For a discussion see Woods, *The Transformation of Work*; Skill Flexibility and the Labour Process.

6   See Cockburn, *Brothers; Machinery of Dominance; Women, Men and Technical Know-How; In the Way of Women; Men's Resistance to Sex Equality in Organisations*.

7   Berle, *Power Without Property*; Berle and Means, *The Modern Corporation and Private Property*; Wright-Mills, *White Collar*. For a critical discussion see *Auerbach, op cit.*

'That managers should [advocate] 'corporate social responsibility', apart from being unnecessary, is also politically objectionable according to this view. Making decisions other than on the basis of profit involves policy choices that should be made by publicly accountable bodies and not private, unelected managers.[8]

Friedman dismisses 'corporate conscience' because it 'would destroy a free society'.[9] Hayek thought that private sector managers should be outlawed from pursuing a public good![10]

Hayek is echoing the ancient concerns found in classical theories of state and citizenship. These imply that a private corporation cannot be said to have responsibilities, by definition. Both Plato and Aristotle argued that private citizens had a responsibility to participate in public life; indeed active citizenship and active statehood were seen as mutually inter-dependent. That a private corporation should intervene between citizen and state, by declaring responsibilities of its own, would seem to challenge the rights, responsibilities and functioning of states and citizens. Yet neither Plato, nor Aristotle, had to face up to the existence of massive corporate entities. So a classical dismissal of CSR is somehow too easy to make.

This neat division between public, business, and citizen responsibilities, also offers little towards a method for solving value-choices that are inherent in business activity. Value-choices occur even at the level of so-called 'bottom line' market issues, let alone wider corporate responsibilities. Value-choices and compromises have to be made between growth and dividends; quality and quantity; accuracy and speed; organisational democracy and demagogy; between security and risk; individual entrepreneurship and bureaucratic routine; niche and mass markets, and so on. 'Which (business) value to pursue?' is as much a question of intrinsic good, as abortion, the death penalty, euthanasia and so on: not simply economic or technical questions. Just as with skill and gender equality, it is not possible to say definitely as a matter-of-fact, that a growing company which produces a cheap and acceptable product is any better or worse than a company which pays high dividends and produces an expensive and excellent product. Value-choices mean that there can be no such thing as the definitive, 'X-efficient' company, because quality and quantity cannot be weighed in on the same balance.[11]

---

8   See chapter 3.

9   Friedman, *Monopoly and the Social Responsibilities of Business and Labour*, in Friedman and Friedman, *Capitalism and Freedom*, p 120. He continues *'Few trends could so thoroughly undermine the very foundations of our free society as the acceptance by corporate officials of a social responsibility other than to make as much money as possible for their stockholders as possible'* (p 133). See also Friedman, *'The Social Responsibility of Business is to Increase its Profits'* in Steiner and Steiner (eds) *Issues in Business and Society*.

10 Hayek, *'The Corporation in Democratic Society'* in Ashen and Bach (eds) *Management and Corporation in 1985.*

11 Liebenstein *'Allocative Efficiency vs. X-Efficiency'* in *American Economic Review* (1960) 56, 392-415. This is an influential, but inherently flawed idea.

There are two conventional methodological routes in social science that can be taken. They are not mutually exclusive opposites (and both have cogent features), nevertheless they do inspire substantively different approaches in practice.

The first route was taken by earlier social scientists. This promises to explain specific values and ideologies by the specific social relationships that give rise to them. Notwithstanding major differences between them, Marx and Durkheim both took this approach. It follows that social scientists ought to be able to pronounce on the 'correctness' a value in terms of whether or not it fits the social structure. Certain values are correct in modern societies, traditional values correct in traditional societies. This method would treat social responsibilities in terms of conformity with, and deviance from, social structures and relationships. The case studies that follow tend in this direction.

The alternative has been hinted at. Max Weber argued that values and facts are distinct; facts can be established empirically (facts are facts), whereas values are 'absolute'. You either accept a given value, or you do not (as with gender equality versus skill, above).[12] Facts and values are not comparable – they are infinitely more different than chalk and cheese. So according to Weber, the correctness of a fact can have no bearing at all on the correctness of a value.

Following Hume and Kant, Weber thought that research could however:
* point-out value inconsistencies within an individual or organisation;
* measure the factual consequences of putting a value into practice;
* point out the unintended consequences of pursuing a value; and
* explore less costly and more beneficial means to a desired end.

He also argued that while research must be carried out objectively, it would be pointless unless the researcher set out with a specific value-preference in mind. This method also differs from both utilitarian judgment (which asks how much does [x] contribute to the pursuit of pleasure, or to the avoidance of pain) and from 'traditional' prescription and proscription (thou shalt do [x] ... thou shalt not do [y]).

It is reasonable to suppose that had Weber been asked to comment on how to approach CSR, he would have said that empirical research is only of limited help in deciding which values the corporation should aim at. For example, the objective, factual question 'how much environmental and social damage does this process cause?' should only be asked once the researcher has established her/his own preference between conserving the environment and existing employment, on the one hand, and free unrestricted, maximum consumption of the product on the other.

---

12   Weber, *The Methodology of the Social Sciences.*

Weber's denial that a value could be scientifically validated makes sense when contemplating the sheer extent of value-conflicts *within* a society. A lot of social life consists of seeking to resolve equally plausible, but nevertheless irreconcilable, value differences – here between conservation and consumption. Weber's reluctance to use social science to judge values seems to make sense where diverse values are held.

Although early sociologists were very optimistic that social science could provide a systematic under-pinning for an *improved* society (route 1), we have retreated from this objective. There is a reluctance to deal head-on with ethical concerns. Corporations cannot be expected to hit upon an optimum set of values any more than individuals or groups (or sociologists) are able to.

But this loss of confidence in their ability to specify correct values cannot wholly explain sociologists' specific aversion for CSR. For every piece of social research goes through a stage during which its (world-improving) values are proclaimed. This stage invariably involves explicit, or thinly veiled, attempts to promote the importance of a particular value – liberty, equality, fraternity, conservatism, sisterhood etc (Weber says, rightly so). The researcher will go on to explore whether or not their cherished value is threatened.

So, it is difficult to explain the contrast between the hot partisanship which fuels so many lively sociological disagreements on the one hand, and sociologist's avoidance of CSR.

This chapter offers some sociologically inspired research approaches which unpick CSR by asking three questions:

- while some social problems are owned by the firm (or imposed on it by the public), many have been abandoned; why?;
- in a negative test case of the 'managerialist thesis': why is it that a privately owned and controlled firm proclaims the most developed set of responsibilities?; and
- some industries are characterised by self-imposed good behaviour, others can hardly avoid behaving badly; what determines the morality and amorality of different markets?

The cases share the working definition given above.

Organised around two dimensions – the public and the private, the sacred and the secular – I offer some explanations for the allocation of problem-ownership through three case studies. These are condensed from some of my idiosyncratic researches. I have revised sociological theories so that they can be applied from a vantage point that sociologists seldom use: the public/private, sacred/secular divides, viewed from within the firm. Each case tends to indicate that different values have to do with different social structures, and that somewhat contrary to Weber, the scope for holding, expressing and implementing values are distinctly bounded by social structures. The reader's values will determine which cases s/he warms to, and rightly so.

15.2.1 Introduction to case studies

15.2.1.1   Case 1

The first case study is historical and local; a reminder that the ownership of problems has shifted over time according to upheavals in the urban social structure. The case describes the social origins of local authority (public) responsibilities, and the decisive impact which these have had, on private competence today. This history contains important paradoxes, whose modern implications are not fully appreciated.

In the last century, local governments were allocated many responsibilities formerly in the private domain; these were distilled into a sacred 'civic gospel', freeing business to attend to profane dividends and growth. Large owners had clear reasons for persuading local authorities to adopt public responsibilities. This explains why there are specific social problems which present-day firms do not want to own, which they need not, should not, will not and cannot embrace as their responsibilities. That is, responsibilities and values that do not belong to the modern firms as a matter-of-fact (or as near as).

15.2.1.2   Case 2

Guardian columnist Will Hutton complains that 'ethics ... find no place in the new [individualistic] enterprise era'. This secularising tendency for business to mind its own business can be put down to structural changes.

The contrary view is that a 'managerial revolution' from owner-management to joint-stock corporate structures, has expanded managers' competence over social problems.[13] I will argue that this is an implausible piece of wishful thinking. While case 1 is about the self-destruction of corporate social responsibility, case 2 draws a similar conclusion by another route.

The most extensive development of residual private responsibilities is found in a large multi-national, *family-owned* business which seeks to increase the world's responsibly-owned dog and cat population; to broadcast scientific

---

13 See Berle and Means, *op cit* For a critical discussion, see Scott, *Corporations, Classes and Capitalism.*

findings on the beneficial effects of pet-ownership, and to set the highest commercial standards. This case runs directly against the managerialist thesis, by indicating that owner-managed corporations like Mars Inc, are better placed to develop corporate social responsibilities, than companies which have passed through a managerial revolution.

15.2.1.3   Case 3

The last case is based on a recent survey of 45 small firms in four markets. Most texts focus on large firms. Yet most firms are small.

By looking at small owner-managed firms in services, it will be seen that there is a striking 'industrial divide' in behaviour between sacred and profane sectors. Plant-hire firms and repair garages are obliged to behave well towards each other; they are enmeshed in a rich network of reciprocity, sharing customers and resources of all kinds. In these industries 'my closest competitor is my best friend'. By these standards, designers, advertisers, employment and training agencies behave badly. Here is fear and loathing; designers are self-professed cut-throats, 'out-to-kill' competing businesses.

The argument is that the presence or absence of spontaneous moral regulation in business is explained by differences in the social organisation of markets.

15.2.2 Case 1

Where did public responsibility come from, and where did private responsibility go to? 'North Homeshire' past and present

Since the late 1970s, governments and several non-governmental charities and agencies[14] have joined in the demand that industrialists should become involved in public policy, hoping for more 'business-like' local government. For example:

'The founding fathers of the great cities of Britain not only built their factories. They also created a community around them to house their labour force. They took out their profits, but put back amenities, schools and parks into an area in which they too lived close at hand. ... I have set myself the task of helping to reverse the drift away from partnership between local authorities and local business communities. I want to

---

14 Business in the Community; Community Projects Foundation; Council for Industry and Higher Education; Per Cent Club; Directory of Social Change.

engender the belief that if the private sector takes on a positive, more assertive role in local affairs, the benefits to the community will be enormous'.[15]

In 1979, I was looking into the history of local 'power structures' in 'North Homeshire', concentrating on business influence over local government and public policy since 1814. This fell into three periods. The first was a period of small business rule characterised by 'economising' and self-help. The second period of 'improvement' was defined by big-business leadership, which advocated the expansion of every facet of the welfare state. In the third period, local authority leadership built on the preceding gospel of civic improvement, but without business involvement.

A follow-up study was made in 1994-5. Had business accepted the responsibility of taking 'a positive ... assertive role in local affairs' in 'North Homeshire' again?

15.2.2.1   Small business rule

North Homeshire's early 19th century ruling class – Anglican brewers, bakers, and candlestick makers, handicraft producers, and shop-keepers – were united only over public order and keeping local property taxes low.

Street lighting was adopted to prevent 'those nightly depredations which are most successfully practised in the dark'. The workhouse, rooted in Elizabethan Poor Law, also aimed to maintain public order. But this otherwise rather fractious class did not envisage much of a role for local government. Wary of the growth of Non Conformism, they reluctantly responded to the Methodist's school (smashed up in a riot), by subscribing to resurrect a moribund grammar school, educating a handful of public scholars (soon re-privatised).

Despite cholera, the Anglicans dithered over public water supply. In the late 1820s the Vestry installed a steam pump to provide safe drinking water, but ratepayers were frightened-off by the cost and refused to pay for it. Therefore the whole cost fell on the churchwarden who had placed the order, 'which is said to have broken his heart'. There were occasional attempts to control cholera by disinfecting open drains. The streets remained full of rubbish, manure and pot-holes, until central government inspection in 1849 began to force a clear-up.

There was some small-scale charitable welfare for the poor, though this was patchy, and prone to fraudulent misappropriation by trustees. Typical of early 19th century industrial towns and cities, North Homeshire's Anglican elite can be summarised as 'economisers' – an ideology and religious

---

15   Michael Heseltine as Environment Secretary.

affiliation which can be linked to the low productivity of handicraft production. Quoting *The Times*, a local small business notable protested that:

> 'The [New Poor] Law affronts men's understanding whilst it picks their pockets, and treats them like fools while it legalises extortion, which out of every shilling it professes to raise for the relief of the poor, gives ten pence to some otiose salaried officer or absentee inspector.'[16]

By contrast, the earliest 'improvers' were Methodists. In the teeth of local opposition, they campaigned successfully to expand public (sic) corporate (sic) responsibilities (sic) through collective local authority. Local government was thus shaped by a bitter mid- to late 19th century 'crisis within the bourgeoisie'.[17] The local line of small business resistance is encapsulated in the following protest:

> 'When he started in business in 1846, the town was in a prosperous condition. They didn't owe a brass farthing, but if they wanted a two and a half penny rate, it was made and paid ... Boards were the greatest curse that could be inflicted on any place. People could manage their own affairs very well without their assistance. When a man died he was entitled to four boards, but unfortunately he had to put up with the same number whilst still alive. (Applause and laughter.) There was not the same sympathy for the tradesman that used to exist. They used to remember when they were all links in a chain and when a pound was to be spent, it was spent at home ... if [anybody] went to a tradesman for anything, it had to go down in the family Bible and very often to be wept over [laughter]. He impressed upon all young men that golden opportunities existed for them to get on in life if they would only take advantage of them and live within their means.'[18]

15.2.2.2   Big business rule

New services displaced or superseded charitable and Vestry responsibilities. Competence in training, education, health, sanitation, housing, transportation, recreation, public safety and civic well-being were wrestled out of private hands, against small business resistance, and handed-over to the state. The point is that the agenda was shifted sharply and decisively away *from the private to the public, by big private interests,* a process reinforced by increasing central government powers in education and health. How was this done in North Homeshire?

---

16 *The Times*, 26 April 1844.

17 See also Foster, *Class Struggle and The Industrial Revolution*; Fraser, *Power and Authority in the Victorian City*; Prest, *Locality and Liberty*; Briggs, *Victorian Cities*; Cannadine (ed), *Patricians, Power and Politics in Nineteenth-Century Towns*. Some of the consequences for business leadership can be traced through Stein, *The Eclipse of Community*; Lynd and Lynd, *Middletown in Transition*; and Marshall, *The History of Lancashire County Council*.

18 Report of a speech by a local small businessman, 1889.

A Free Lecture Society was set up by a newcomer in 1888 – a partner in the town's biggest, most innovative and rapidly expanding engineering works. Under its Methodist founder, the company had always tended to side with 'improvers'. Now that support became marked. The new Society, patronised 'any movement calculated to be for the social and intellectual benefit of the inhabitants ...'. The work's new owner (nicknamed 'Stormy Petrel' for the rows he caused), got elected to the Local Board of Health (meaning to enforce sanitary controls over his employees' rented slums), and was later elected to the district and county councils. He co-founded the Association of Industries (1921), with its progressive 'Brighter and More Beautiful' manifesto. 'Thank God success in business does not only mean good dividends', he is quoted.

'Everything in and about the town, everything relating to the health and content of the community in general, had a deep and abiding interest for him ... he sought every means in his power to find fresh suggestions and improvements for the development of the civic, social and community life of the town and its peoples ...

... when his day's work ended, those energies found a marvellous play time in finding new improvements, new developments, new attractions and new enterprise for the civic, social and general life of the town and its inhabitants. He is essentially a Master Builder and his powers know no limitations, manifesting themselves as earnestly and successfully with men as with engines, with communities as with motors.'[19]

The big business strategy was to match private donations with public funding for capital schemes; political work ensured that services were then adopted by local government, which met current costs through local and central taxation. The technical college originated this way, as did new grammar schools, adult education, ambulance and district nursing services, a cottage hospital and a rheumatism clinic – which claimed cures for eighty per cent of patients – town parks, housing, tramway, library and other services. The Association fielded candidates in local elections and gained a controlling position on the local council. The AI set a high property qualification – presumably to keep out parsimonious small businesses. The local steam brewery, a paper mill and a drug manufacturer were strong supporters: all 'big (owner-managed) businesses'.

A crucial difficulty for the Heseltine manifesto (and for Berle) is that 'responsible' captains of industry were non-government owner-managers. Marx noted big business support for the regulation of the working day,[20] but this is lost on some commentators, who claim that 'industrial capitalists were staunch advocates of [Adam] Smith's economic philosophy [of competition,

---

19   Press reports, 1938, 1911.
20   Marx, *Capital* Vol I, pp 222-86.

and therefore] ... had little concern for social responsibility'.[21] The US view that 'corporate political power diminished as a result of governmental restraints, and the emergence of countervailing power blocs.'[22] overlooks the state-creating role which big business played in Europe's industrial cities, and in US cities, particularly after the Civil War.[23]

North Homeshire's large firms stood for:

> *'... the full benefits of local government ... pride in township in the hearts of inhabitants ... a model industrial town ... homes of a class suitable to the comfort and convenience of the industrial population ... [and a] carefully thought out town planning scheme ... to leave a very much more attractive place than we have today.'*[24]

Against a background of unrest following the First World War, and probably with one eye on the October Revolution, the Association supported the creation of bigger local authorities for more effective service provision and better co-ordinated industrial development policy. They promoted major roads, public housing, unemployment relief, the expansion of public tramways and municipal power and gas generation. This manifesto was essentially the same as organised labour's.[25]

15.2.2.3   The essence of local *authority*

The greater difficulty for those who wish for a return to this level of business involvement is that, paradoxically, business leadership in civic affairs was destroyed by its own success. Over time, perhaps unwittingly, large capitalists worked themselves out of corporate social responsibilities, and virtually right out of the urban political scene, by pressing the state to implement the civic manifesto of the big bourgeoisie. Local governments are rightly known as local authorities. In large part, their authority was constructed and handed over to them by authoritative business leaders. Large firms' present-day indifference towards civic problems therefore is a direct result of past business commitment to solving them. The socially indifferent, disengaged firm is often the latter-day international, joint-stock, managerial incarnation of an older, politically engaged, enterprise.[26] The social transformation of what counts as their responsibility is complete. The libertarians have got it wrong.

---

21 Luthans and Hodgetts, pp 7-8

22 Jacoby, *Corporate Power and Social Responsibility*, p 264.

23 Among other social forces, the ascendancy to state power of the Union seems linked to the ascendancy of big business; the defeat of Confederacy, linked to the destruction of earlier capitalist arrangements: a crisis-within-the-bourgeoisie played out on a vast and bloody scale.

24 AI Handbook, 1921.

25 A neighbouring authority was proclaimed *'the First Soviet in England!'*, on the basis of an ambitious public housing programme.

26 See also Harvey *et al. op. cit.*, pp 67-85.

Firms have been freed to get on with minding their own business, by the state interventions which they demanded.

The old order might lament the 'eclipse'[27] of business leadership; welcome or not, they played a big part in change. The political power and authority of the 'improver' capitalists self-destructed; business leadership undid itself by succeeding.

Would present-day directors be willing to joust (in full armour) at a

'... great pageant [in which] class hatred and religious differences and many points which go to make up friction in each country are forgotten, and there develops from this friendly intercourse of persons, and one class with another, a spirit of friendliness and comradeship which will bind the social life of the district together more than any effort yet known.'[28]

... as they did in the early 1930s? Or stand alongside the local Labour and Liberal MPs, the local colonel (steam brewery) and some members of the House of Lords, to express public optimism at a shopping carnival in 1922, and defend capitalism? 'It was no use trying to imagine the capitalist as an ogre' stressed a mill-owner. 'If we did we were doomed'.

By the 1930s there was a worry within the Association that the scale of local government would end the 'voluntary tradition' in service provision – and with it their role. In 1937, the chair of the county council defended service centralisation in terms of the extent of the health, educational and transport problems to be dealt with – if private provision could not respond to these needs, then 'criticism of local government was unjust', he told the AI. Unemployment relief, power generation, urban transport, hospitals and district nursing, education, technical training, unemployment relief and road construction were taken out of *district* control. From 1945, legislation set out the clearest-ever standards for the remaining district planning and housing functions. These tendencies had the complimentary effect of undermining business leadership: on the one hand, important services were no longer in the local ambit, and standards in remaining services were much less subject to local determination. Moreover, the powers of the welfare state were probably beginning to exceeded the imagination of the association.

By 1945 business leadership ended. Although the local engineering works encouraged the council to 'get cracking on council housing' in the 1950s – with Labour in local control, this was simply pushing at an open door. Among branch managers there was a general 'reluctance to devote business hours to [public] pursuits' (1963). The Multiple store 'had meant the disappearance of much of the chamber's usefulness to traders in the town'[29] and, the council

---

27 Stein, *op cit.*

28 Pamphlet: *Wide Awake,* July 1932.

29 Small traders had been allowed to join the *Association of Industries/Chamber of Commerce.* Presumably the Association was confident that small businesses had given up the fight with the industrial capitalists, against statism.

was 'failing to consult business' over the town plan (1965). The chamber hired an ex-civil servant to analyse the plan, which suggests acknowledgment of a technocratic rather than sectional rationale in policy. In 1967 the council allowed business 'a preview' of the plan, but there were not any meetings of its retail section that year. In 1969, low attendance was 'horribly embarrassing'.

By 1979, later-day managers at the old engineering plant definitely eschewed 'benevolent attitudes'.[30] Company restructuring and merger meant they 'were in no position to make substantial donations to the town ... a park, cottage hospital, support for the Sea Cadets, and the Easter parade'. Mayoral visits were seen as 'ceremonial'. 'I'm a nine-to-five person really', said a senior manager, 'I don't want to get involved.' Many employees commuted from outside the area – so there was little point, he said. The practical benefits of taking up county invitations to debates on the structure plan were 'difficult to assess'. Only two local firms went. The firms' response to a new town-plan, lacked its former civic vision. They merely asked for a bus stop to be resited a few yards nearer the works for the convenience of employees; and they recommend increasing the radius of the corner to the works entrance, to enable lorries to get round it easily.

Had there been any 'business involvement', it should have been found here. These interventions do not constitute involvement. The exception was a semi-retired manager, active chamber member, and chair of the local magistrates bench, who had 'been an understudy' to the earlier regime of business leadership. He was attempting to re-establish the Association –perhaps on Heseltine's cue – however, other firms reported that they could not see what its agenda might usefully set out to achieve. The attempt folded.

15.2.2.4   1994

Private efforts to create *public* responsibilities have abated.[31] By 1994, the MD at the engineering firm saw it as 'part of an international firm that just happens to be in [North Homeshire]'. The locality was not relevant and he took no interest in it. The company's large social club, and an excellent training department, were recently handed-over to the *public sector* – continuing the process of public-isation begun around the 1860s and 1870s.

---

30 See also Harvey *et al. Managers and Corporate Social Policy*, pp 67-85.

31 Nevertheless, firms continue to attempt to get the state to under-write their viability. For example commercial property developers seeking the public investments which compliment urban renewal schemes; local boosterism; the Jubilee Line Extension into Docklands; housing landlords who maximise income by drawing high rents off the poor via welfare payments; privatised utility companies whose regulators are forced to sanction prices which guarantee profits, because privatisations cannot be allowed to fail; local authority 'partnership schemes' which are gold-plated by tax payers; private school fee-paying trust funds (which form the largest, tax-exempt, registered charities in the UK), and other trusts which benefit from heavy tax exemptions.

It was already clear in 1979, and clearer still in 1994, that autonomous local authority leadership was still growing from its own logic. This has thrown up the most counter-intuitive of all North Homeshire's tendencies: a public drive to expand the private sphere. At first sight, this looks like the state's attempt to un-make itself, and bring business back into partnership. But this is something of a myth, which must be broken down carefully into two processes.

First, and easiest to dispel, is the notion that privatisation means 'rolling back the state'. Despite service privatisation, the civic functions which big nineteenth-century capitalists envisaged as state responsibilities, largely remain state responsibilities. Private sub-contracting leaves the state perfectly intact as a structure of authority. Where public responsibilities are not executed properly, this still constitutes news and 'public outcry' follows (for example over badly-run state-subsidised private homes for the elderly). Private contractors do not assume a social responsibility by working for the state; contractors are bound by profitability. Where a charity persuades the state to use its services as a 'provider', this is a classic, and probably welcome continuation of the Association's former strategy: to set private funds to chase public funds.

It remains to be seen whether the public will tolerate, for instance, the abandonment of state responsibility for the elderly. At the time of writing, Health, Transport, and Home Office ministers were seeking to distance themselves from various public service failures, on the grounds that politicians are 'responsible for policy rather than practice'. So far, history has not run backwards. Despite major efforts, the state has failed to eradicate the nineteenth-century legacy of collective social responsibility and civility.

Secondly, is the deceptive issue of 'local authority responsiveness' to business. It seems that public policy is being subordinated to private business interests. Homeshire's County and District authorities are competing to represent and repackage local public policy as if it was a response to business demands.[32] Throughout the county, local authorities are attempting to get markets to work, to create new markets, and to persuade existing firms to vocalise an interest, or express some enthusiasm for, plans for the future. Politicians and officials have envisaged North Homeshire as European Connection – an idiomatic device for organising discourse and assembling

---

32 For similar new findings, see Caufield and Minnery, *'Planning as Legitimation: a Study of the Brisbane Strategy Plan'* in *International Journal of Urban and Regional Research*, 184, 1994, pp 673-89. The authors see the globalisation of capital, and inter-authority competition for foot-loose, firms as the cause of local authority behaviour. However my approach is more historical. Autonomous local authority pro-activity is hardly new: see the chapter on the legitimating function of the Citizen's Action Commission in Dahl's study of Newhaven, USA, in the mid-1950s (Dahl, *Who Governs?*). Dahl's 'pluralist' approach could not be more different to mine, however the data on the CAC is robust and clear enough - local authorities lead, control and manipulate business opinion, not follow it.

public and private consent and monies, for the wholesale restructuring and eventual transformation of North Homeshire's economy and society. This is an ambitious extension of the old responsibility to make North Homeshire 'Brighter and More Beautiful' – inherited from the Association.

Because the government's cue is that 'business involvement' is to the good, local governments gain a good deal of legitimacy by association with business. The reorganisation of local government also threatened to abolish some authorities. The two pragmatic objectives of 'business-like' local authorities in North Homeshire are therefore:

- to defend themselves against abolition by demonstrating their business-relevance; and
- to maximise central funding for public infrastructures, again by presenting them as business needs. Inter-authority competition has intensified the pressure to be seen to embrace business interests.

Industrial forums have been established (eg Homeshire Industrial Liaison Group, North Homeshire Industrial Forum) – the latest in a long line – at which public policy ideas and texts are rehearsed before invited business guests. It is clear from interviews that the intention is to use the forums to persuade industrialists to adopt and use these themes. If, subsequently, a senior manager can be quoted as having sounded a keynote, then his or her apparent 'intervention' carries the weight of a private demand for action, to which public policy is a seeming response. In this round-about way, local governments promote an emerging economy and society and staves-off abolition threats.

There is little evidence that the private sector has progressive ideas of its own. It is reluctant to move beyond minding-its-own-business. For example most of Homeshire's chambers of commerce, are weak. Two are financially viable, all the remaining forty-three chambers are dependent on local government sponsorship. A county-wide, Core Chamber has been set up and jointly funded (again from public funds) by the County authority and Homeshire Training and Enterprise Council.[33] However, because business registration is not compulsory in the UK, membership rates will be low, and fees very high, to compensate – probably rendering the new Core Chamber non-viable as a strictly private enterprise.

Inter-authority competition has further undermined this 'initiative'. In hot rivalry with the County's Core Chamber, the Districts in North Homeshire sponsor the Federation of North Homeshire Chambers. Both Chambers are portrayed as giving 'a strong voice to business'; yet the voice of business, such as it exists, is divided, and state-dependent.

Furthermore, local officers report that business has been slow to join the process of public policy-making, confirming that industrialists have difficulty

---

33 TECs are presented as private 'market' organisations, despite obvious dependence on state finance.

in understanding its relevance, and that they dislike public exposure. In a neighbouring county, said a County official, this shyness had lead to a bungle. The forums had met and rehearsed their scripts with industry, a deputation to central government was arranged.

> *'All the industrialist had to do was say his lines. But he didn't ask the questions! The senior civil servants, the minister, the politicians were all there, well-briefed and ready with the funds. But he fluffed it. He just didn't ask THE questions. The meeting collapsed. And they all went home empty-handed.'*

Occasional, negative business reactions are registered. North Homeshire District Council has avoided many of these demands, probably due to the lasting effects of earlier consensus-building by the Association. But neighbouring authorities have faced them. A local branch of the Confederation of British Industry recently objected to a plan for an ambitious business park on redundant industrial land, claiming it would increase competition in the labour market, and raise wages. 'Can you believe it', exclaimed a County officer, 'the CBI against development!', adding that the County was working hard to 'change this attitude'. In the 1970s, local businesses pleaded against allowing new skill-based businesses into Homeshire. They were ignored. During the worst breakdown in 1980, a disgruntled small business owner initiated a Scotland Yard police investigation into local suspicions that a big urban renewal contract –which was seen as a major threat to existing businesses - had been pushed through by bribes from the developer. The owner could not understand why a local council would act against local, represented, business interests, in favour of interests *which had no local representation*.

> *'Just look at it ... I mean they must have paid somebody off. It's a disgrace. I say there is something they are not telling us. They say they're not hiding anything, but yes they are! ... There must be something fishy. There's a police investigation. Just wait!'*[34]

The District motive was, of course, an extension of the old civic gospel of public good. As the chief executive said, to 'put the town on the map!' Local

---

34 The police exonerated both the developer and council officials. No substance could be found to local notables' claims that a senior officer's house 'had been built with bricks left over' from the development, nor that the finance officer had collapsed, drunk, on the railway station platform, having 'signed away all the council's money for a hundred-and-twenty-five years'.

However, disquiet among local politicians and businesses over the unfavourable terms of the renewal contract –which effectively committed the council to underwriting the developer's risk – and the impact of the development on local traders, forced a symbolic sacrifice. With a change in local political control, most of the planning department staff, was 'massacred' to the delight of some notables. The new leadership committed itself to a 'market-driven', rather than the past approach which they characterised as 'planning'. Yet these changes were largely symbolic. After the 'night of the long knives', the new council continued to pursue boosterism on big scale, and continued with the primarily of attracting 'outsider' companies. Local business influence was therefore very much weaker than it appeared to be.

businesses were 'just lashing out'. The 'inducements' which flowed were largely from the authority to the developer and large stores, in the form of profit guarantees, rent and tax relief, and large public investments in car parks and other infrastructures. These maximised the viability of the scheme, ensuring that 'footloose outsiders' came to the city.

A far bigger out-of-town shopping centre is taking shape in North Homeshire, threatening town-centre businesses. The District has grouped central businesses into a Town Centre Committee, providing it with a budget to investigate and propose ways of making the town-centre more attractive.[35] A District officer is also seconded to the Chamber of Commerce, to promote economic development, again with public financial support.

It is suggested that these measures help to secure local authority control of agenda-setting and conflict management. There is sufficient local authority to exclude unwanted businesses interests from policy formation and agenda-setting. The interests of non-local, non-represented, prestige sectors generally do best, because these are equated with the primary objective of local policy which is, broadly, to make life better for as many people as possible. This surely represents an extension of the state, and a further erosion of business' civic role.

In Homeshire and elsewhere, the capitalists are not in a position to lead their communities.

Finally, it is striking to find that local political leaders drawn from the small bourgeoisie, are enthusiastic interventionists today. In theory, and historically, the sworn enemies of statism, they have fallen under the spell of civic gospel.

The state is the market's 'vicarious champion'.[36] The benefits of attracting inward investment are arguable, but here is good evidence that business activism is not a pre-requisite for thriving communities, nor for effective industrial and commercial development policies. Indeed, the effect of expressed business demands in Homeshire would have been to slow down economic and social change, had they been accepted. Business and state have devised interesting social arrangements for the distribution of authoritative responsibility, in which business roles are minimised.

---

35 But a similar strategy of incorporation failed to contain business disaffection in the neighbouring city just described.

36 Lamarche, 'Property Development and the Economic Foundations of the Urban Question' in Pickvance, Urban Sociology: Critical Essays; Castells, The Shek Kip Mei Syndrome: Economic Development and Public Housing in Hong Kong.

For comparable findings, see also Caufield and Minnery, 'Planning as Legitimation: a Study of the Brisbane Strategy Plan', op. cit., pp 673-89. The authors argue that the globalisation of capital, and inter-authority competition for foot-loose firms determine pro-active local authority planning. However the approach taken in the Homeshire case study is historical. Local authority pro-activity is hardly new: see the chapter on the legitimating function played by the business members of the Citizen's Action Commission in Dahl's classic 1950s study of Newhaven, USA (Dahl, op. cit.). Dahl's 'pluralist' approach could not be more different to mine, however the data on the CAC is robust enough - local authorities lead, control and manipulate business opinion, not follow it.

15.2.3 Case 2: How far can private responsibility be taken?

During the inter-war period, Berle claimed to be witnessing a 'managerial revolution', brought about by the creation of joint-stock companies. This familiar hypothesis holds that the shift from concentrated, private owner-control, towards dispersed, publicly-quoted share-ownership and autonomous, professional management, would enable managers to be both more responsive to popular demands, and better placed to meet them.[37] Share-holder power would recede, and corporate social responsibility would grow, Berle promised.

This case study concerns a company which adopts the highest standards of corporate social responsibility (defined common-sensically), but which remains unquestionably in private ownership and control. It is therefore an important 'counter-factual' or negative test case for Berle's hypothesis. Directed by Brian Harvey at Nottingham University (now at Manchester Business School), the author and co-researcher, Barry Wilkinson (now at Cardiff University), visited Pedigree Petfoods one day a week, over an eighteen-month period, carefully logging hundreds of hours of interviews in the early 1980s. Considerable updating was provided by Pedigree Petfoods in 1995.[38]

Pedigree Petfoods is one of many subsidiaries within Mars Incorporated, a family-owned US multi-national,[39] and world leader in each of its main businesses – snack foods, petcare products, main meal foods, electronic coin mechanisms and drinks vending. Pedigree Petfoods is the UK part of Mars' petcare business with manufacturing plants in the East-Midlands at Melton Mowbray and Peterborough.

Every Mars business operates to a common set of beliefs, the Five Principles Of Mars, which evolved from the late-1960s. One of these, Mutuality, states that company activities should be 'mutually beneficial', providing a 'good deal' for consumers, associates (employees), the local community, and the trade. A manager explained:

'The belief that a business cannot flourish or progress in isolation from the community in which it exists is fast gaining wide acceptance. The community comprises people and people are in turn our customers, suppliers and associates. Our active help and support in creating a healthy and prosperous environment therefore is a basic obligation we cannot afford to ignore. Investment in the community is not only good sense and good citizenship but also a sound investment in our own future.'

---

37 Berle *et al.* op cit.

38 This case appears with kind permission of Pedigree Petfoods. The author expresses his thanks for managers' extensive help.

39 In 1991 Mars was valued at over $12 bn (Adams, op. cit., p 357; also *The Washington Post Magazine*, 12 April 1992, p 11) with an annual global turnover of £5 bn (Adams).

The principles include 'maintaining independence' by growing from internal resources through a high return on total assets – 'efficiency makes all other things possible'. Mars rejected growth by share issue, and debt-financing as 'restrictive'. Private ownership and full control of Mars Inc therefore passed intact to Forrest's children: Forrest junior, John and Jacqueline. A Pedigree Petfoods manager explained that:

> 'The Mars family are very involved in the business and take a keen interest in helping the community. It all stems from the principles that they developed: wherever we are, there should be a benefit to the community.'

This occurs at a number of different levels. Locally, the company supports several charities, self-help, sporting and volunteer groups, with cash, material support and advice. It also encourages its own suppliers to participate. Several associates contribute, by acting as officers or governors on charitable and school boards. Pedigree Petfoods is the main supporter of Melton Day, contender for the largest free show in the UK. He continued:

> 'We are developing in Central and Eastern Europe; the philosophy is that as you develop a new market, you get involved with the local community, wherever your office or factory may be. And we start to look at ways in which we can offer some benefits, and explain to them what the benefits to them will be. I have been talking to my colleague in Poland. There is quite a Polish community in Melton and they are very interested in twinning; so because one of the links we have is with the Twinning Association, I agreed to support a trip out for a delegation to Poland, and my Polish colleague covered the cost of the trip back. I arranged for a trip 'round our factory, for clearly, if we are building a factory in Poland, they want to compare; and we were able to share with them some of the things we do with the local community and the local council were obviously talking about some of the things we've done. There is this general feeling, or ambience of benefit that they accrue. It is a world-wide approach wherever we are.'

These links are described as 'partnerships'. For example, a local school[40] wanted to design a room to meet the special needs of disturbed children. The company contacted a firm of designers and architects to:

> 'work with them on drawing up some plans, which gave them that tremendous impetus of getting their thoughts down, professionally, on paper. We covered a little bit of the time and the company charged at cost for the materials, so it was a very beneficial way of doing something that was practical ... Probably more practical at that time than handing over cash.'

A partnership was struck with Melton's Council for Voluntary Services, who were encouraged to develop their 'care and repair' scheme through a

---

40   Pedigree Petfoods has links with all 32 local schools.

local partnership with Pedigree Petfoods, Melton Borough Council and Leicester County Council. This put them in a position to bid for additional central government funding. The company explained that a broader partnership was the best way to secure the future of the scheme. Long-termism characterises Mars Inc organisations generally.[41]

'The relationships we establish with a supplier, or a local charity, we try and do for the long term. The best way of getting these commitments to run is on a partnership basis, so that it is not solely down to us. It is one of the benefits of mutuality.'

Similarly, the company gave Melton's River Improvement Society financial help in drawing up a plan to put to the borough for a grant. Pedigree Petfoods provided Melton Volunteer Bureau with a car and fuel allowance to run out-patients to hospital. They helped equip a van for a local health-care advisory service, and the company pays for advertising space, providing registered charities with a 'notice board' in the local press. 'It is extremely well used. It is not a high profile thing, but people who use it do appreciate it.'

Some schemes have been handed on. The Melton Industrial Development Advisory Service was begun in the early 1980s to promote confidence in the local economy, by helping to attract small new businesses to the locality. Local authorities provided industrial units and Pedigree Petfoods gave free advice and cash prizes for the best business propositions – later joined by a bank and an accountancy firm. Leicestershire Chamber of Commerce have taken on the scheme.

The scientific expertise behind all Mars' petcare companies is provided by Waltham, 'The World's Leading Authority on Petcare and Nutrition'. Together with Mars petcare companies, Waltham has developed a specific set of self-professed corporate responsibilities around pet animals. These include promoting responsible pet ownership, substantiating nutritional claims, behavioural research, and exploring the benefits of animal companionship.

Waltham undertakes, or manages research on behalf of all Mars Incorporated units, worldwide, trialing and substantiating the nutritional claims. It also has a record of funding independent scientific research into the human social, mental and physical health benefits of pet ownership at a number of universities. Waltham runs prestigious international conferences on animal nutrition, health, behaviour and human/companion-animal interaction, and is equivalent to a well-funded, university research department; it employs animal scientists with world-reputations, providing 'the science behind our products world-wide'. All final year veterinary students in the UK are invited to Waltham.

---

41   See Harvey *et al.* op cit pp 86-108. See also *Adams et al.* op cit, pp 356-60.

Waltham has evaluated two recent projects which have been supported by Pedigree Petfoods. A manager explained:

'One is at Papworth looking at angina sufferers and comparing people who have a pet and people who don't, [in terms of] recovery rates. The second is at Southampton where they are doing a study on the use of a dog to help the communication development in downs syndrome children, having completed a successful pilot on the increasing confidence that is given to a child. I'm happy to support this, but I use the Waltham link because they need to scientifically approve the work and then say to me, "Yes this is sound and this would be beneficial". Apart from the fact that I think its wonderful what they're doing anyway – I need some help in understanding the science ...'

Pedigree Petfoods:

'Feels that it is very important to contribute to the business it operates in and consequently has long held a commitment to promote responsible pet ownership. For example we look at the issue of dogs in the community; clearly there is a lot of emotion about stray dogs, particularly about dog-fouling and the nuisance factor, which we recognise and respond to with our 'Good Dog Campaign', started in 1974.'

... specifically geared to try and help local authorities understand the issues and to address them in a balanced way – an informed and educated way – within their local communities.

'We have strong and productive links with the Dog Warden Association. The use of our materials has increased over the years ... materials produced in consultation with users: 'The Dog Warden Hand Book', ... guide-lines on 'How to Use your Local Media', 'How to Plan Campaigns'. We have run a number of regional seminars, so authorities who have a good campaign will become a model. We get wardens in and we share best practice, by running a workshop. That is something which I feel is of great benefit long term to communities.'

Pedigree Petfoods has various links with national organisations, through the Petfoods Manufacturers Association, to the Pet Advisory Committee, which includes environmental health officers, the RSPCA, SSPCA, BVA, BSAVA, NOA, the Dog Warden Association, and police authorities. 'The PFMA can participate in putting a sensible point of view across ...' The company sees it as 'very important that theses are independent and credible groups'.

'We also have good working relationships with a lot of pet or animal-related charities ... again we will try and work on a practical basis. We don't just make a donation to the RSPCA, [we] work on activities or events or something tangible where we can see a benefit. We have extended this in a couple of cases, to our brands. We have a brand which was involved with guide-dogs, and did some work with hearing

dogs. We helped to fund an advertisement for Guide Dogs For the Blind, where they acknowledged that the space was paid for by us.'

Earlier work with an hospice, and links with the Society for Companion Animal Studies, led to contact with a local hospice for terminally ill children. The company has offered to establish an aviary, supply feeds and form a 'partnership with the local budgerigar society who will look after the birds'. They will also produce a video to aid hospice fund-raising, mindful of the need to show the hospice's work, without the intrusion of visitors. The company seeks 'practical ways you can offer help in a non-intrusive way'.

Pedigree Petfoods has run an Education Centre since 1970, supplying a wide range of materials to schools and youth groups on pets and responsible pet ownership. This 'helps people understand their role as responsible owners, and is allied to the national curriculum'. The Education Centre is 'clearly marked as Pedigree Petfoods, because it is very popular, and something we want to contribute to schools.'

'I'm sensitive to the commercial ethics question very much. The important thing is that we care about pet care ... it's the future of the business. ... The work of our schools programmes has increased, and is widely acknowledged.'

At the level of the industry, the company acts as a co-operative market-booster, rather than aggressive competitor, spreading technological and organisational innovations to as many firms it can reach. It has developed a competitive edge by collaborating. Close involvement with suppliers derives partly from Just-In-Time manufacture: because Petfoods carry no more than a few hours inventory, reliable supply is critical. Suppliers receive a premium in return for their commitment to invest in new production technology. They are also encouraged to widen their pool of customers, avoiding reliance on Pedigree. This promotes the growth of the petfood industry as a whole, by raising the long-run viability of suppliers and competitors. The Principles are pursued in a vigorous, systematic, and determined way. Managers can reasonably claim that 'No one has ever done badly out of Petfoods'.

'Although the petcare market is a highly competitive one, Pedigree Petfoods acts a co-operative partner within its trade association (PFMA) to promote the growth and reputation of the petcare industry as a whole. We focus on what we do best – viz. developing, manufacturing and marketing our products. We leave other functions such as distribution and storage to others which promotes a good network of suppliers within our communities.'

The company's commitment to corporate social responsibility is substantial. It manufactures socially useful products to the highest nutritional standards (which it has shaped, and which are typically much stricter than for tinned food for human consumption). Pedigree Petfoods has minimised the environmental impact of its plant in a number of ways. It only uses materials from animals inspected and passed as fit for human consumption.

15.2.3.1   Private ownership and control

An explanation for these practices is found in the company's ownership and control. The family owners are known for their missionary-like commitment to socially responsible business. But instead of imposing direct control over managers, Mars insist on a devolved system of open management. 'We regard all associates in an equal light and avoid divisive privileges.' This means that major decisions are only taken after wide consultation, and careful, reasoned and plausible justification. This also ensures overall coherence.

'No doors on offices' is a family dictum. Indeed, open-plan offices are an architectural manifestation of a system which reinforces, rather than loosens owner-control. The status symbols associated with managerial hierarchies are absent. The managing director's desk is indistinguishable from the secretaries'. There is little to distinguish different layers of management. The family, managers, directors, and associates all clock-in; all levels share the same facilities and pension scheme.

What is distinctive, is that there are no significant conflicts of interests, and practices, within management. The organisation has a complete and seamless quality which is rare. There are non of the informal patronage systems which tend to plague conventional, hierarchical organisations; no conflicts between older and younger managers, nor between divisional functions; no muddles. Free speech is central to this:

'We're very good at being open ... over everything. We recognise that different functions may have some conflicting interests. But because we have an open management style we can sort out these differences in a constructive manner. And yes, there are different views about styles. We encourage open discussion in order to achieve a resolution.

'We believe in setting objectives and being accountable. Having to justify your objectives openly [means] you can't [be unreasonable] ... You have to have a good rational argument otherwise you get shot down in flames ... It has to be justifiable for the whole team to go for it.'

Another manager stressed the pace of work.

'... the whole philosophy is to get things done – disagreements quickly get resolved ... Get problems sorted out, that's the thing ... and make things happen. You get swept along with it.'

The results is that managers were often unable to identify where decisions had originated. Yet all insisted that they were 'really at the heart of things' ... 'Everybody here [is] at the heart of things'. As another manager pointed out, 'By the time you do anything, people have all moved with you. The corporate conscience will have changed'. Over the period of observation, we found quiet and polite 'consultation'. Respondents were sometimes interrupted by offers of help to problems they did not know they had.

The sense in which this is an open organisation should now be clearer. It should also be clear that private ownership and managerial control are not incompatible; on the contrary, control occurs with managers' full participation. Corporate Social Responsibility is easier to understand, once the thorough-going sense of purpose, which is built into the organisational structure, is appreciated. The Mars family concern is relayed through the organisation without having to jump hierarchical or professional boundaries. Conflicting divisional and professional aims, which often introduce contrary layers of meaning and purpose to the strategies of more conventional organisations, are not found here.

This case represents some striking continuities with past notions of corporate responsibility. This is an owner-controlled corporation that has successfully exported an early twentieth-century US business ideology – using exemplary behaviour as a way of avoiding unwanted governmental restrictions on pet-ownership, for marketing, and as a way of boosting the industry. The heightened sense of responsibility has something in common with the civic urgency and commitment shown by late nineteenth-century business leaders in the UK (above). There is continuity in the attempt to stimulate certain innovations in public policy by corporate-giving, for example, around the therapeutic use of pets. The company is single-minded about promoting 'mutual benefit' throughout its dealings. As in earlier times, CSR is associated with defending business virtues.

Although far more externally-linked than most firms, Petfoods (and Mars) shared some of the outward reticence typical of managers in joint-stock corporations. Managers clearly accepted Mars' 'profane' need for profit and the 'sacred' duty of bringing wider benefits.

This means that Hayek and Friedman cannot be applied very easily. CSR at Mars is mindful of the owners' interest in profit and growth – something which would win approval from classical economists. However it is also clear that there is an intrinsic commitment to public good, which seems to be part of the family's identity, which contributes to managerial morale, but which is not encompassed by classical models.

The main point is that it is not possible to reconcile Berle's model of managerial enlightenment with:

- Mars' continuing, extensive, private family commitment to public good;
- the civic reticence typical of most modern joint-stock firms, or
- bygone civic activism of large owner-managers in the earlier period of 'business leadership'.

Berle predicts that private ownership and control would be associated with the blinkered pursuit of profit, while managerial control would be associated with a strong sense of public obligation. In my extensive researches into large corporations, neither was not found, indeed exactly the opposite to Berle's prediction on all counts.

15.2.4 Case 3: Why are some markets 'friendly' and others 'cut-throat'?

Among the supposed duties of the 'socially responsible' firm is the ambiguous requirement that they should 'compete freely and fairly'. Practices differ wildly. We have seen in the Mars case, that long-term competitiveness may involve co-operation with competitors by promoting the viability of common suppliers. Competition and co-operation are not opposites.[42] But can sociologists predict the form which so-called 'competition' will take?

Research was carried out on the market behaviour of 45 small firms in the service sector.[43] Advertising and design firms, employment and training agencies, plant-hire firms and repair garages each differ in rather obvious ways. But an important hidden social contrast was found, which separates them into two camps.

On one side of an 'industrial divide in services' there is a fiercely competitive ideology. Advertising and design, employment and training agencies, are *competitive, combative, predatory, individualistic, unruly and unstable*. They welcome the death of competing firms. On the other side, garages and plant-hire firms are morally-regulated, distinctly trust-based, and mutually supportive. They are conscious of a *binding responsibility* for each others' survival.

To explain this important contrast it helps to think of markets as social systems – sets of relationships – and not, as economists tend to think, as the sum effect of an interaction between atomised economic agents. A social conception of markets makes them accessible to the rest of social science; in this way a good deal of economic theory can be discarded.

For example, the 'industrial divide' exists despite the fact that all the firms studied occupy equally 'free' markets. Orthodox competitive market models would have some difficulty in explaining why some markets should behave so completely differently to others.

But some major social theories can be discarded too. For example these differences in ways of doing business also cut across these men and women's common '*petty-bourgeois class-position*'. Conventional class analysis is unhelpful, because common class membership is supposed to lead to broadly similar ideologies and practices within a class, which is clearly not the case

---

42 Hayek consistently describes markets as arenas where agents co-operate (sic) to secure mutual gains. See also Auerbach et al. '*The Dialectic of Market and Plan*' New Left Review, July/August 1988; also Aoki, *The Co-operative Game Theory of the Firm*; Carlisle & Parker, *Beyond Negotiation*; or Fransman, *The Market and Beyond*; *Co-operation and Competition in Information Technology in the Japanese System*.

43 Acknowledgments to Keith Dickson and Adrian Woods, Brunel University, and to James Curran, Kingston University, for their help with project management and statistical analysis.

here. And while much has been written about co-operation and competition in terms of 'organised' and 'disorganised capitalism'[44] and through 'Fordism' and 'Post-Fordism', these categories are little use in this case.[45]

A more fitting explanation for the way these markets generate different levels of responsibility, can be based on Simmel's formal theory of social relationships within groups, developed over 90 years ago.[46] Coser offers a concise description:

> *'[Simmel] uncovers the new properties that emerge from the forms of association among individuals, properties that cannot be derived from characteristics of the individuals involved.*
>
> *Because [dyads depend] on only two participants, the withdrawal of one would destroy the whole: 'A dyad depends on each of its two elements alone – in its death though not in its life: for its life it needs both, but for its death, only one.'*
>
> *Hence the dyad does not attain the superpersonal life which, in all other groups creates among its members a sense of constraint ... The dependence of the whole on each partner is obvious; in all other groups duties and responsibilities can be delegated, but not in the dyad, where each participant is immediately and directly responsible for any collective action ...*
>
> *When a dyad is transformed into a triad, the apparently insignificant fact that one member has been added actually brings about a major qualitative change ... The dyad relies on immediate reciprocity, but the triad can impose its will upon one member through the formation of a coalition between the two others ...'[47]*

---

44 Offe, *Disorganised Capitalism*; Lash and Urry, *The End of Organised Capitalism*.

45 Fordism is associated with large, 'vertically integrated' mass production companies and their supply-chains. That is large customer domination of smaller hard-pressed component suppliers. Fordism is also linked with 'rational-bureaucratic', centralised organisational structures which impose deskilling and direct control on workers.

    Small garages and plant-hire firms have not entered the Fordist stage in any sense. They are pre-Fordist. Advertising, design and employment agencies are post-Fordist, in that they perform functions which used to be carried out 'in house' – tasks which used to be vertically-integrated within large organisations. Now these are contracted out. But these agencies do not behave as the theory of post-Fordism predicts; for they are very wary of forming the 'strategic alliances' which are supposed to typify post-Fordism (Teece, *'Profiting from Technological Innovation: Implications for Integration, Collaboration, Licensing and Public Policy'*, Research Policy (1986) 15; Sayer, 'Post-Fordism in question', The International Journal of Urban and Regional Research, 134, 1989). For a wider discussion see Gilbert *et al.* (eds) *Fordism in Question; Divisions and Change*.

46 Simmel, *'Quantitative Aspects of the Group'*, in Wolf (ed and trans) *The Sociology of Georg Simmel*.

47 Coser, *Masters of Sociological Thought*, pp 184-5; see also Wolf (ed and trans), *The Sociology Of Georg Simmel*, op cit.

From this simple, but elegant perspective, it is deduced that triads (and larger 'multiplex' groups) are more resistant to destructive behaviour by members – an immunity based on the numbers involved. Transgressions within a triad meet with majority mobilisation in defence of the norm. Deviants can be controlled in larger groups in a way impossible within dyads. The greatest instabilities occur in the dyad, which, 'for its life needs two', but, in Simmel's memorable words, 'for ... its death, needs only one' to act treacherously.[48]

In short-hand, 'A-Type' companies are forced into the competitive idiom because most of their links are dyadic and prone to breakdown (high-gain/high-threat, pair-relationships). 'B-Type' companies are forced *into co-operation because they have multiplex, multipurpose relationships among many firms, who can therefore impose stability and customary standards* (low-gain/low-threat, multiple-relationships).

Simmel's thinking is formal and ahistoric: stripped of any references to the concrete entities involved, to the subject matter, to history.[49] This ahistorical quality is a strength and a weakness. Simmel is just as easily applied to other entities, as it is small firms, regardless. The model applies equally to friendships – dyadic, intense, unstable friendships; multiplex, gentler and more dependable friendships – to inter-national relations, coalition governments, households, etc. according to the same general rules, in any historical period.)

But because Simmel is ahistorical, he cannot be used to explain why specific industries (friendships, governments etc.) have adopted particular idioms. Why are market relations in design typically dyadic, while among plant-hire firms, multiplex relationships have emerged? Why no multiplex relations among designers; why so few dyadic relations in plant-hire? Recently Casson has a similar approach to co-operation and competition, using game theory to explain types of economic behaviour.[50] He too admits to being unable to explain why certain kinds of relations should characterise one

48   Simmel, *The Metropolis and Mental Life*', (1903) in Wolf op cit.

49   The formal sociological theory applied to this third case-study is quite different to the approach taken in Cases 1 and 2 (which are concrete, historical and specific). Strictly speaking, because Case 3 has a different underpinning, it is not wholly comparable to Cases 1 and 2. The readers will make his or her own judgment about whether this amounts to a serious methodological flaw or not. My view is that as long as the difference is recognised and is open to discussion, then there is no need to reject the findings as a whole. Methodologies are not perfectible, just like bridges, chairs or motor cars. So imperfection need not imply automatic rejection.

50   Casson, *The Economics of Business Culture*; Game Theory, Transaction Costs and Economic Performance.

51   Human Science external seminar paper, Economics as an Imperial Social Science, Kingston University, 1994.

market as a whole, but not another.[51]

In the material to follow, note that the level of 'responsibility' varies between industries, giving individuals little choice in the way they do business. As their scope is limited, no ethical evaluation of their actions seems appropriate. Like Cases 1 and 2 this material tends towards the proposition that values are relational: 'correct' insofar as they accord with the relationships which generate them.

15.2.4.1   Designers

Type-A1 'jobbing' designers undertake varied, labour-intensive, short-term work. Type-A2 designers specialise in 'high specification' work for large corporate clients on a longer term basis. Some agencies (A3), design very little: acting as co-ordinators and brokers, finding clients, agreeing specifications, and subcontracting to specialists.

Most designers use subcontractors to some degree. They are specifically dependent for colour printing, graphic design, desk-top-publishing, photography, layout etc. The puzzle is that *industrial interdependence is high*, yet independence is the prized value. Why? The solution may lie in the 'geometry' (Simmel) of the links involved. Designers depend on the specific, dissimilar skills of others: each link is dyadic and heterogeneous.

'Rip-offs' and disappointments are likely. Designers are bound to prize their 'independence', because they have good reason to be wary of betrayal. Dyadic instability also characterises design partnerships, which are often compromised when a partner 'steals' clients, splitting away to form a new business.

True to dyadic laws, there was little informal interaction within the sector. Contacts among designers were avoided. The research found no (Type-B) collaborators in design. Table 15.1 indicates that there is a significant (0.00669) difference between the sectors in terms of their expressed willingness to 'co-operate with others in the trade'.[52] The industrial divide is suggested by the heavier line.

---

52 Significance is a measure of the probability that obtained results could have been produced by random chance – ie by spinning a roulette wheel. The minimum acceptable level of significance in sociology is usually set at one-in-twenty, the '0.05 level'. This means that there must be less than a one-in-twenty chance that a result is a fluke, before it can be accepted as an indication of a correlation. The smaller the number, the greater the significance.

Table 1 The Level of Co-operation in Each Table

	Advertising & Design	Employment & Training	Garages	Plant Hire	Total
Co-operate a Lot or a Fair Amount	2	3	8	9	22
Co-operate a Little	4	2	4	2	12
Co-operate a Little	6	4	0	0	10
Total	12	9	12	11	44

(1 Non-Response)

Eight out of 12 garages said they co-operated 'a fair amount, or a lot'. All garages or plant-hire firms said they co-operated. Table 15.1 also shows that on the other side, co-operation is rarer. The majority of designers and employment agencies said that they do not co-operate; on their side of the divide, links are fewer and less permanent.

Designers are urbanites. They have:

'a matter-of-fact-attitude in dealing with men and with things; ... often coupled with an inconsiderate hardness ... an unmerciful matter-of-factness ... repulsion ... aversion ... [and] atrophy.'[53]

This shows in their comments:

Respondent A was an A3-Type (design broker). Commenting on an impromptu visit to a competitor in the area by chance:

'I tried, *once* – but he slammed the door in my face ... I think *perhaps* we ought to [co-operate] with a company ... [so] similar to us. [Yet] I don't ever see the time when I'd want to lay-off business to a competitor as an

---

53 Simmel, '*The Metropolis and Mental Life*', in Wolf op cit.

option rather than expanding, becoming more selective or raising our prices and making a bit more out of it. The next stage would be to recruit another consultant ... [But] I am very wary of attracting any further fixed overheads ... 'Would need an extra 25-30K [of annual business] to justify it. Collapsed order books have caught a lot of people out.'

Growth is ruled by lack of trust - some 'farming-out' might have enabled more contracts without increasing overheads.

Did he 'withhold advantageous information?'

'Yes [confidential information] is worth its weight in gold. It is very important to know when a [client] is becoming ripe for a new [job].'

Respondent B was an A1-Type (jobbing designer) 'How has trade been?'

'Getting more cut throat!'

Did he 'discuss with others?'

'We don't want other people to know what our business is ... We don't talk direct. It is as simple as that! It is very very competitive. We don't want other people to know who we are dealing with. It is not just us being unfriendly ... With customers of course [links] are very important ... because they know their business.'

Did he 'discuss with competitors?'

'The sad thing about not talking to each other is that knock ups [outline designs] cost everybody more – 100 to 200 [each time]. So it's cutting off your own nose if you don't talk to each other. We spend twenty hours on knock-ups, but we [can] only charge for ten! Business is very much cut throat at the moment. Trust went out the window because customers want the lowest price. This is happening more and more.'

Were 'any changes planned?'

'It is just so much hassle now. The enjoyment's gone out of it ... We have ... decided that it is just not worth trying to push for the money ... It is not so much the economic climate on its own, as the attitude of other people. So many big companies ... have got financial constraints, they don't care who they tread on ...'.

Respondent C was also an A1. What were the 'sources of suggestions?'

'... Just don't talk to each other. We are all out to kill each other rather than speak to each other ... [Yet] We are now more uncertain about future growth, and we cant grow much more from internal resources. The ideal is to offer even more services perhaps linked in with a printer (sic) or another design group. We would welcome any such approach, not to sell out, but to realise a special type of service.'

Respondent D, Type-A2 (specialist, high spec.) Did he 'discuss industry?'

'Discuss with friends ... not very close ... I don't go out of my way to talk.'

Respondent E, Type-A2 Did he 'co-operate with designers?'

'No! They are the enemy!'

But high-technology design could bring greater independence. Continued respondent C:

'New technology is throwing everything into turmoil ... There are two ways to go ... You can either not bother with it, and be trapped in a safe trading position, probably losing 20 per cent of your staff, not invest in the new technology and have a fairly comfortable life style, or we can expand and take on board the new technology. It is the latter we have done ... It is affecting relationships with suppliers because it means that more of the business is being done [without] outside suppliers.'

Respondent E thought:

'Over the next five-ten years, studios are going to install computers that will take design through from conception straight through to making films, taking a whole stage out – reprographics.'

Technologies which cut out subcontractors are attractive within a competitive idiom (CAD, photocomposition systems, desk-top-publishing, 'intelligent' photocopiers linked to PCs). But capital intensive design demands continuous, high levels of asset utilisation, while designers are loathed to pool customers (unlike plant-hire). Paradoxically, reluctance to co-operate means that the level of custom required to finance independence through technology, cannot be had.

15.2.4.2   Employment and training agencies

Type-A1, general (white- and blue-collar agencies), and Type-A2 specialist (professional legal, computer, management, and accountancy) agencies, are also independent-minded. Competitor links were non-existent for Type-A2 firms and minimal for Type-A1. Type-A1 secretarial agencies used 'an army' of roving, self-employed, freelance trainers and instructors. As in design, new companies form, when an agent corners a large enough contract to attract footloose freelancers into partnership.

Respondents:

'Talk with competitors?'

A'I haven't got one!' Links were deliberately avoided, except for 'clients or friends of clients' – Type-A2.

B'I've only got one, indirect, competitor. Sometimes [we] talk very generally about business and about the industry.' – Type-A2.

C 'There is a lot of competition in the recruitment business. The industry has got a bad name and has got worse. We are trying to distance ourselves from the tarnished image of recruitment.' 'Passing on information?' 'Only to clients. Never to competitors!' – Type-A1.

D 'Links can be useful, but whether or not they are telling the truth ... hiding the facts? ...' – Type-A1.

E There is an 'exception that proves the rule'. Unique among our final sample of employment and training agencies, she co-operated a very great deal (the Type-B idiom). Why? The company provides secretarial, WP, assertiveness and awareness training, and acts as a consultant in personnel management. The respondent stressed that because the company is a workers co-operative, and holds many public contracts, they wish to be seen to operate in a public, transparent and reputable way. For these reasons (obeying Simmel) they had developed many links:

We get help from BBB. They are likely to help – so we are affiliated to them ... Colleagues in the Co-op movement. We talk to them quite a lot; a lot comes from that.

'Importance of business links?'

Links are crucial. We have quite a few formal and informal links. It is crucial to keep them up to date with any changes – not so much technological changes as what's wanted with the product. We have almost no links at all with the private sector. We see them, and recruit from there on women's courses – we ... wouldn't really get into a dialogue with them. We do have links with the FE. college. We also have good links with Community Business Network. So we take up links where they are going to be of use to the business ... the federation for workers co-ops.

'Quality of links with local businesses?'

The people we are in competition with ... they would be quite similar organisations to us and we feel we have quite friendly arrangements. And if it was something that we knew we couldn't do, either by date or by content, we would just pass that on its way. There is usually no mileage in hiding anything. The competition really doesn't work that way. The competition happens within the tender if you like. The co-ordinator is actually choosing what would be most suitable for them, rather than we providing exactly the same service as everybody else.

We have a different style. We tend to do a lot of sharing of information. If it is not really for us, we say why not try X?

15.2.4.3   Plant-hire

Four types of businesses were seen in our sample of plant-hire firms. The sector exists because construction companies do not own the equipment they need.

Established, generalist plant-hire operators (B1) carry overlapping ranges of equipment (trucks, mixers, skips, excavators, space heaters, screed pumps etc). Their survival depends on a remarkable network. Maximum equipment utilisation comes through contracts which are passed on via a resilient networks, governed by established, unwritten rules, which result in price stability. Sharing equipment, exchanging customers, and technical information, is commonplace:

The telephone rings. A builder wants a dumper-lorry of a given size, on a given date, at the market rate. The hire firm agrees immediately – knowing they cannot provide it. The contractor then telephones around the trade, re-cycling the contract only fractionally under the charge agreed with the builder. Just £1 per hour under the market rate would be usual, cutting the contractor's margin on the job he's passing on virtually to zero. The benefits are long term; the reputable trader will shortly receive contracts in return. The telephone could ring with a similar offer from any 'competitor' in the network. Thus reciprocity leads to maximum asset utilisation.[54] Normative regulation of plant-hire was withstanding the recession. Owners express sadness when 'competitors' go bust.

Young firms work differently. One-person (Type-A1) plant-hire firms, have perhaps one or two trucks. Described as ruthless, competitive, opportunistic, 'breakaways' from larger, reputable (B1) firms, Type-As did not have networks. A's were viewed with disdain, dismissed as 'cowboys' 'bad boys' and 'naughty boys' by B1s – certainly as boys. Plant-hire firms make use of two-way radio networks. Lorry movements are instructed over the air and builders may be offered contracts in this way. Boys listens-in; if he thinks that he can get his truck to a site faster than anybody else, he will cut corners to get there. On arrival he will under-cut the market rate without compunction, stealing the business.

Type-A1 plant-hire firms have something in common with Type-A1 designers (above). The reason now becomes clearer. They have low overheads, therefore they do not need to co-operate in order to maximise the use of their equipment. There is no pressure to act reputably. They are free to act outside the 'moral economy' of plant-hire. But with expansion, overheads grow, and Type-As are compelled to acquire the reputable, co-operative disposition of the mature firm. A 'Type-B' admitted to being a cowboy once.

Specialist firms with large overheads including crane hire (Type-B2) behave somewhat like B1 firms, but only on their 'own patch'. Specialisation means that the network of similar companies is thinner: perhaps just three or

---

54 Adam Smith had the following to say about business association: 'People of the same trade seldom meet together, even for merriment and diversion, but the conversation ends in a conspiracy against the public or some contrivance to raise prices.' (Smith, *Wealth of Nations* 1930 Book 1, Ch 10, p 11, cited by Friedman op. cit., p 130.) What would Smith have thought about plant-hire?

four other similar firms in the region, all behaving responsibly, passing subcontracts around the regional network. But, comments suggest that B2s revert to Type-A (predatory) behaviour when winning contracts outside their own, customarily regulated area, where they are unknown, and unconstrained. Finally Type-B1 general tool-hirers appeared moderately co-operative.

Small plant-hire firms avoid dealing with the few large hire operators, regarding them as 'the major threat to all independents'.[55] A recent large entrant to the UK industry had just collapsed, to the clear satisfaction of small firms.

There is a Simmelian logic to the competitive/co-operative dynamic in each sub-sector of plant-hire. How this sector acquired its logics is unknown. Plant-hirers typically said of co-operation:

Respondent A was a Type-B2 (ie relatively specialised) and logically, only a moderate collaborator. Did he 'Pass on information?'

'Some, relating to our four similar companies in the region. But [I] do not pass on 'valuable' information. We have contacts if we are desperate for a machine to do a job.' Discuss the industry? 'If a job is in London, or Scotland [ie far from here] then [our] company will locally subcontract.'
The quality of inter-firm relations?

'Two or three of us will get together ... it does help get the word around on the quality of new machines.'
Links with suppliers?

'They will pull the stops out if I'm desperate.'
Customers?

'Whatever advice I give, he'll take my word for it because he trusts me.'
Respondent B (Type-B1, tool hire).

'I try and involve other people ... keep in touch, find out what is going on. [Competitors] warn each other if there are thefts or frauds [going on].'
Respondent C (Type-B1) is involved in 'lots of cross-hiring'.
Respondent D (Type-B2):

'[It is] very important to keep friends. The competition all use each other especially ZZZ and YYY. No poaching. There is a 'naughty boy' who is undercutting. Was a driver [with us] until two years ago. I helped to get him started. Now he's got two or three cranes, and he's the naughty boy.'

---

55 *Independent* is a misnomer. The 'independents' are highly inter-dependent.

Respondent E (Type-B1) will:

'cross-hire with competitors for regular customers ... [but] you have to be careful who you deal with.'

Respondent F has a unique business and effectively, has no competition – a rule-proving exception. There are some comparable firms a long way off, and he is a member of the relevant national association. He has few informal links and declares himself to be 'very secretive about new developments' he is making. He could make no comment on 'making contacts in the industry?'

15.2.4.4   Garages

Informal, long-standing, co-operative networks abound in this sector, covering technical and trade information, borrowing or swapping of parts, equipment and custom. A significant amount of subcontracting takes place, like plant-hire, that is, circulation of customers.[56] MOTs, panel beating, welded repairs, fitting helicoils, resprays were all cross-contracted. Links are integral to business. The reliability of these links has allowed them to be treated as friendships. A seriously injured garage owner's creditors were prepared to 'wait as long as it took' for payment. Without their valuable support, the business would have collapsed.

Garages and plant-hire firms appear to be significantly more open to mutual discussions than designers or employment agencies. Table 15.2 shows that all garages and plant-hire firms regularly discusses their industry with competitors (sig .01407). The divide is indicated in bold.

---

56   Customers may remain unaware that their vehicle was fixed by a second, or third garage.

Table 2: Discussing the Industry with Competitors by Sector

	Advertising & Design	Employment & Training	Garages	Plant – Hire	Total
Discuss with Competitors	8	4	12	8	32
Do Not	3	4	0	0	7
Total	11	8	12	8	39

(6 Non-Responses)

Most small, Type-B2 specialist garages, such as vintage and classic car restorers, nevertheless had extensive networks of suppliers and competitors. Specialist garages were like specialist (B2) crane hire firms.

Some garages have car hire, car sales, roadside cafe and breakdown-recovery services. They maintained extensive links, but the impression is that the 'sister' businesses were conducted with more formality and less reciprocity. For example a very genial local garage owner also had a formalised breakdown-recovery contract with the AA and formal membership of the national vehicle recovery association.

Garage owners said about co-operation:

Respondent A

'You've got to share to survive! We have all got bits and pieces we can share off each other. There are four or five garages around that if I've got something I'll tell them and if they've got something they'll tell me. [It] saves us each going out to buy it. Basically we've got a little co-op here. We share info[rmation] as well.'

Respondent B Any lending?

'I expect them to put trade my way [and I] send passing trade elsewhere, regularly.'

Said C:

'In restoring [cars], other garages are colleagues you see. We help each other out if we can – certain things I can do which other restorers cannot, and vice versa ... delicate measuring equipment, staff that [one] wouldn't use very often, heavy pulling and lifting gear; swap things around as it were. Modern garages [do not] see me as a threat and are more than happy to send me the odd things they don't want to do.'

And D

You must have the respect of colleagues to survive.

Was advantageous information ever withheld?

'I can't think that at the end of the day it would work to your advantage.' The interviews were interrupted by a stream of trade 'phone calls visits, leg-pulling and amusing banter.'

Garage E is an exception which proves the rule: his technology is all supplied by a franchiser, who tightly controls the way he works. Passing on information?

'Yes, to others in the XX service network. But we don't go shouting it around ... that is giving our blood away, ... our reserve away ... and ... certainly, I won't tell another garage who is not in the XX network about [ideas] ... except those in another town!'

15.2.4.5   Urban/rural differences?

Sociologists have often suggested that rural areas are more morally regulated than urban areas. Can 'urban' businesses get a way with 'irresponsible' behaviour that wouldn't be possible in a rural setting? No significant differences could be found. Analysis of a much larger sample of firms, failed to find any significant differences between urban and rural firms in 'lending to others' (0.71050), 'borrowing instead of buying' (0.85201), 'contacts counted as friends' (0.56287), 'long-term compared with short-term relationships' (0.25140), 'friendly relations' (0.56287), 'formality and informality' (0.48322), nor 'the quality of relations between local businesses' (0.51900). There was no significant variation in the 'amount of subcontracting' (significance 0.92305, almost random chance). But many of these issues showed significant sectoral differences.

By all means define a locality in terms of its small firms; but do not define a small firm in terms of its locality. The locally-connected sectors – garages, plant-hire – that were the most co-operative, and spontaneously-regulated, regardless of location.

Table 15.3 shows how firms felt about the 'quality of relations between local businesses'.

Table 3: The Quality of Local Business Relations by Sector

	Goods	Reasonable	None	Bad
Employment & Training	2	2	3	0
Advertising & Design	0	6	5	6
Plant – Hire	7	3	0	1
Garages	10	2	0	0
Totals	19	13	8	1

4 Non-Responses

The divide is clear and highly significant (0.00536). Virtually all garages, and most plant hire-firms enjoy reliable local relations, enmeshed in 'supra-individual constraint'. The quantitative evidence underlines garage owners' descriptions of the way they operate.

Nobody in advertising and design described their local business links as good, underlining their *ad lib* comments. Here are Simmel's dyadic, unregulated, and unstable relationships. Moreover, when asked to describe business relations as 'formal' or 'friendly' sixteen garages and plant-hire firms answered 'friendly', but only four design and employment agencies thought this.

15.2.4.6   Personality differences by sector?

Are standards of behaviour connected to the personal disposition of individual owners? Or does business behaviour reflect its sector? The questionnaire contained a section on attitudes; eight of 39 attitudinal questions aimed to distinguish 'individualists' from 'collectivists'. Personality tests typically use far more items, so the following conclusions are provisional. There was little evidence that differences between Type-A and Type-B firms, could be explained by the migration of different personalities to different sectors. The eight items showed no significant sector differences. Individualist and collectivist traits were fairly randomly distributed across the divide. ('I like to go to social functions a lot' scraped a sectoral significance of 0.087).

The suggestion is that sectors constrain individuals to act in particular ways, regardless of individual traits. The experience of working in Type-A or Type-B sectors has no apparent cumulative effect on the owner's underlying self. Some advertisers' and designers' expressed disliking for the treacherous competitiveness of their industries. These may have been the would-be collectivists. Small business behaviour is not a reflection of its owner, though this is still being explored.[57]

15.3 Discussion and conclusion

All three cases establish that the allocation of specific responsibilities, both towards and away from the firm, is the results of social relationships, for which transparent, testable, theoretical and empirical accounts, can be offered. The challenge to researchers is to refute these cases with counter-factual evidence. Whether the distribution of public and private responsibility is as it *should* be, is much less easy to say.

This chapter closes first by summarising what may be concluded from the case studies, and by establishing what the counter-factual cases would look like. Secondly, I will offer a provisional set of critical comments on the logic of the values which may lie behind corporate social responsibility as *ideals*.

15.3.1 Case 1: Homeshire

The first conclusions about 'business involvement in the community' are clear cut:

- Business influence over local public policy making, has been very weak in the post-war period. Public officials were largely in control of the agenda. [Counter-factual: public policy initiated by private interests.]

---

57 Dickson *et al.* *'Type 'A' or Type 'B'? Explaining Sector Differences in Co-operative Networking'*, paper to the British Academy of Management Conference, September 1994.

- It is very striking that, at the local level, *non-represented business interests did best in terms of local economic policy* (ie 'outsider' companies – prestige chain stores, national construction companies, international manufacturing and commercial corporations). Local policy tends to suit outsiders without them having to make any political interventions. [Counter-factuals: successful local business resistance to outsiders. National and international business lobbying overturning local resistance to outsiders.]

- Such local businesses participation as there is, tends to be *stage-managed and controlled by the state*. Business influence and community involvement is a chimera. Business forums were convened by local government officials and politicians, as a convenient way of promoting local authority thinking to business audiences, and as way of controlling business disquiet. Business demands that are heterodox to the plan, are rejected implicitly, if not explicitly. [Counter-factual: the existence of effective business lobbies wholly set up, wholly financed and wholly run by business.]

- Private and public officials would *rather avoid conflict* between them, finding it acutely embarrassing. Public agents seek to avoid conflict by initiating dialogue; most private sector managers are inclined to avoid conflict by not participating at all. [Counterfactual: unconcealed business hostility towards the state.]

- This cannot be explained by orthodox political models. The normal expectation is that competing demands are initiated by classes or interest-groups, and that these get translated into subsequent government policies. Yet in North Homeshire, locally represented, conservative business interests tend to be rejected, while public policy tends to anticipate the interests of non-represented outsiders. This puzzle can *only be resolved historically ... in terms of the triumph of the 'big bourgeoisie' over the 'small bourgeoisie' in the mid-, to late-19th-century.* [Counter-factual: policies which originate from business demands.]

- Paradoxically, by demanding increases in state responsibility, *the 'big' bourgeoisie had worked both itself and small business out of a local political role by World War Two. A period of local business leadership led directly to the creation of local institutions which deprived business of leadership.* [Counter-factual: social movements among large and small firms, which curbed the role and responsibilities of the (local) state.]

15.3.2   Case 2: Pedigree Petfoods

This centred on the development of responsibilities which remain private. Pedigree Petfood's contribution to public responsibilities through the taxes it pays, certainly exceeds its visible expenditure on the responsibilities which it has chosen to discharge, by a large margin. Nevertheless, the firm's direct engagement with public troubles is considerable, especially in comparison with other large firms.

*   Mars is an important test: a socially responsible yet private multi-national corporation. The notion that a managerial revolution has extended CSR does not apply here. Berle's model of dispersed ownership associated with enlightened, public-minded management, does not fit Mars' global corporate commitment to public good. Neither does Berle fit the civic reticence of most modern joint-stock firms, nor the civic activism of large owners during the period of business leadership. Berle would predict that private ownership and control would be associated with the blinkered pursuit of profit, and managerial control with a strong sense of public obligation. My researches into large corporations, has never found anything to support the managerialist thesis. The managerialists' academic credibility is out of all proportion to the evidence in a UK setting.

    Corporate social responsibility is much more strongly associated with owners, than with managers. This is not a moral indictment of the managerial class. Managerial ascendancy coincided with state take-over of the firm's 'sacred' responsibilities, leaving managers in charge of mostly profane business matters. It is a good deal easier for them to ignore public troubles than it was for preceding owner-managers, not least because remarkable progress has been made towards eliminating mass disaffection with capitalism, which once stimulated progressive nineteenth-century capitalists into political action. [Counter-factual: private sector managers acting as official representatives of joint-stock companies, who appoint themselves to promote a public good.]

15.3.3 Case 3: Competition and co-operation

Differences in the ways markets behave can be explained by treating them as social systems rather than the net outcome of individual needs, preferences, ethical codes etc. Of course many have urged this, before, during, and since the break-up of social science into disciplines.[58] There is inadequate space to outline, let alone discuss the range of available explanations.

---

58   Marx op. cit.; Durkheim, *The Division of Labour and Society*; Simmel op. cit.; Weber, *The Protestant Ethic and the Spirit of Capitalism*; Weber, *The Theory of Economic and Social Organisation*; Weber, *Economy and Society; Parsons & Smelser, Economy and Society*; Solow, *The Labour Market as a Social Institution*; Polanyi, *The Great Transformation*; Scott, *The Moral Economy of the Peasant*; Holton, *Economy and Society*; Locke (1993) 'R J Holton "*Economy and Society*" reviewed in Capital and Class, 51 pp 204-206; Auerbach, op. cit.; Wellman and Berkowitz, *Social Structures a Network Approach*; Thompson *et al. Markets Hierarchies and Networks*; *The Co-ordination of Social Life*.

- However, an explanation based on Simmel accounts for moral and amoral behaviour among small firm. Type-A firms are forced by their dyadic relationships to behave amorally. Type-B firms are constrained by their multiplex relationships to behave well. [The counter-factual would be stable dyads, and unstable multiplexes.]

- The evidence suggests that entire sectors may operate one way rather than the other. Why industries acquire particular idioms, cannot be explained by formal methodologies like Simmel's. [Therefore counter-factual not applicable.] Historical work is needed.

15.3.4 Values, rhetoric and reality

This chapter has described and explained three examples of the allocation of responsibility, arguing theoretically, empirically, historically and formally, that there is not (and cannot be) a definitive set of corporate social responsibilities.

But sociologists must also attend to the use of definitions, pick-over and scrutinise, the meaning and implications of definitions and categories. These closing notes consider some of the outer-limits of what private corporate social responsibility might mean and to argue a rhetorical counter-case for conserving the social democratic values, practices and relationships which define the current boundary between public and private responsibility.

First a sense of contrast and proportion:

Consider the list of responsibilities which heads this chapter: product safety, the acceptance of responsibility for environmental damage, the adoption of practices which counteract gender and racial discrimination, and the maintenance of employees' health and safety. Note that this list is defined by shared public concerns over firms' private behaviour.

In contrast, larger nineteenth-century owners were troubled by private anxieties about the quality and sustainability of public life. They converted semi-private charitable responsibilities into systematic state services, so that troubles could be dealt with efficiently (Case 1).

To strike a sense of proportion, note that in 1988, UK company-giving was estimated at £285 million[59] – a modest, tax-allowable and selective contribution to solving public troubles, often subservient to private marketing and PR. objectives.[60] This is a very small sum; barely enough to cover the

---

59 Directory of Social Change, Estimate, 1988, cited in Fogerty and Christie, *Companies and Communities; Promoting Business Involvement in the Community.*

60 Clutterbuck *et al. Actions Speak Louder than Words.*

education budget of a county council, and less than half the cost of running the UK's local public lending-library service.[61]

Contemporary claims made for CSR as effective private solutions to public troubles, seem:

- blissfully ignorant of the essential limits set by the nineteenth-century revolution in responsibilities; and

- wholly disproportionate to the amount of giving.[62] This provokes the suspicion that CSR is being used as a vehicle for questionable ideological work.

The term 'corporate (sic) social (sic) responsibility (sic)' is an unfortunate one. Some meanings behind 'corporate', especially in juxtaposition with 'social' and 'responsibility', are disturbing. As there are other happier phrases which could have been coined, this suggests that 'corporate social responsibility', has an agenda-setting, discourse-altering function.[63] The uncritical promotion of corporate social responsibility could let loose some metaphorical 'old devils'. These demons are axiomatic to the concept of corporatism:

'Corporate' has many layers of meaning. 'Corporate' may refer to the collective concern of civil society as a whole, implying the existence of a community of shared values, common interests and common purpose. Essential to the idea of community, is the root notion that the interests of the individual and those of the group are shared with the wider community as a whole, and that there are few if any conflicts to be faced – outsiders excepted.[64] A community 'is as one'.

The logic of a unity-of-interests-of-a-society-as-a-whole is 'agreement; no distinction between public and private spheres; no imaginable objections; all-for-one and one-for-all; common-purpose.' This strikes at something important. The strength and perhaps stability of modern association, depends on the weakness of social ties. In a modern Western society, where conflicting individual, group and class interests abound, the scope for the development of unifying 'corporate' institutions and practices is limited. Therefore to speak as if we were 'we', is to repudiate real differences of interest, which in turn,

---

61 UK total net expenditure on local public libraries was £727 million in 1992/3 (source: Library Information Statistical Service, Loughborough).

62 Fogerty *et al. op cit.*

63 Why not refer to 'responsiveness', 'non-owner interest protection', or 'non-owner guarantees'? These expressions would be as easy on the tongue, and more transparent.

64 Indeed in ultra-communitarian systems, individuals are recognised less as individuals, than as clan members, brothers, sisters, uncles, daughters etc. - that is in relation to others. Their absorption by the community involves some loss of individual separateness and interests. Some communal societies are reported as not having a word for 'I' and 'me' (Heelas, *'Introduction: Indigenous Psychologies'* in Heelas and Lock (eds) *Indigenous Psychologies*; Harre, *Personal Being*.

implies the erosion of hard-won political spaces where different interests are fought out. There is something anti-democratic about CSR, especially the rhetorical elimination of objections by treating them as unreasonable.

In past usage 'corporate' has also meant 'to do with church and state'. The medieval world was corporate. The distinction between church and state, between the sacred and the profane, and between public and private would be alien to us. State coercion and religious imperatives went hand-in-hand. Church and state were sometimes allied, sometimes fierce and bloody rivals, but nevertheless, closely linked.[65] Economic activity was neither public nor private, as it was regulated through guilds which were themselves part of a corporate social structure.[66]

This is hinted at in corporate social responsibility. De-secularisation; new, transcending goals binding on the firm; business to mind more than its own business? I have argued that most companies still treat the public sphere (meaning everything outside their walls) as an open system to be bargained with if necessary, and avoided if possible. The majority of managers are disinclined to involve themselves in the pursuit of public good, seeing no point in it – a distraction, or indefensible meddling in other peoples' business.

The Mars case is more ambiguous. The 'philosophies' adopted by the family seem to have something in common with corporatist pre-texts. The company does treat its interests and those of the community as one. It pursues transcending, unitarist goals.[67] And it is difficult to see what could be objectionable about a company which meets such high standards. What is wrong with promoting responsibility? Scientifically tested mental and physical health benefits from pet ownership are surely worth sponsoring. Why should work not be engrossing, the product, safe and socially useful? As with garages and plant hire, why should firms not co-operate to mutual advantage?

The lack of conflict is partly what troubles. But the absence of a vigorous sociological debate over the way in which the processes identified here, structure public and private corporate responsibility, is also regrettable. In the study of what determines the relationship between the state and civil society and the allocation of responsibilities, why the invariable focus on the state?

'Some sociologists have contributed to the Journal of Business Ethics, to the Employee Responsibilities and Rights Journal and to the Business and

---

65 Take Louis XIV of France and Pope Innocent XI, in the 1680s. Louis (like Henry VIII) tried to wrest the church from the control of Pope Innocent and failed; nevertheless Louis remained a zealous Catholic throughout. Similar quarrels took place throughout Europe to the 1690s.

66 The Hanseatic League is a celebrated, if well-worn example of this. Described in modern terms, the League set closely governed international 'public' standards of 'business', as well as exhaustively detailed rules and punishments to govern the 'private' behaviour of 'employees'. However, none of these modern terms would really make any medieval sense, because the degree of separation denoted between the entities, did not apply in a corporate world.

67 There are clear parallels with large Japanese corporations.

Professional Ethics Journal. But the discipline would not recognise these as prestigious platforms for sociological debate. In contrast, among economists, business historians, and in business schools generally, CSR is covered more extensively. (For a list of teaching centres, see Adams op cit 562-563.)'

Chapter 16

Going Concern and Internal Control

Tony Scott
B. Com, B. Compt(Hons), CA(SA), ACMA, FCCA; Director VFL Limited;
Director of Education & Training, Littlejohn Frazer, Accountants

16.1 Introduction

An article in the July 1994 issue of *Management Today* states 'Hindsight is the best of all management tools. A major corporate crisis never fails to provoke – from journalists, investment managers and fellow businessmen – a chorus of exemplary wisdom after the event. The writing was on the wall months ago, the pundits will claim, you had only to walk down the high street to see it.'

Going concern and its reporting is an important issue in the corporate governance debate.

16.2 The going concern concept

There are four fundamental accounting concepts used in financial reporting. These concepts have been developed over a number of years are formally set out in a *Statement of Standard Accounting Practice – SSAP2 Disclosure of Accounting Policies* issued in 1971.

16.2.1 The going concern concept

The assumption is made that the reporting entity will continue in operational existence for the foreseeable future. In particular, the profit and loss account and balance sheet assume no intention or necessity to liquidate or curtail significantly the scale of operations.

16.2.2 The accruals concept

Revenue and profits recognised are matched with the related costs and expenses incurred in earning the revenues. In order to achieve the matching revenues, profits, costs and expenses are recognised as they are earned or incurred, ie accrued, not as cash is received or paid. Income and expenditure is dealt with in the profit and loss account for the period to which they relate.

16.2.3 The consistency concept

There is a consistency of accounting treatment of like items within each accounting period and from one period to the next.

16.2.4 The prudence concept

Revenue and profits are not anticipated, but are recognised by inclusion in the profit and loss account only when realised in the form of cash or other assets, the ultimate cash realisation of which can be assessed with reasonable certainty. Provision is made for all known liabilities, ie expenses and losses, whether amount of these are known with certainty or is a best estimate in the light of information available.

The above four concepts were incorporated in law by the Companies Act 1981, now consolidated as the Companies Act 1985. On going concern, the legislation states 'the company shall be presumed to be carrying on business as a going concern' (Companies Act 1985, Schedule 4, para 10).

16.3 Capital markets and financial reporting

Information is central to the operation of effective capital markets. Financial reporting has the unique role of reducing risks and uncertainties that investors and creditors must deal with by providing relevant and realisable information about transactions and events.

Users of financial statements have different expectations of the audit product than those of auditors. These differences need to be addressed and identified in order to ensure that financial statements and the audit continue to be relevant.

A report prepared in 1993 by the AICPA Special Committee on Financial Reporting on the information needs of today's users states that 'over a time, a financial reporting process that fails to meet the information needs of investors and creditors results in less effective capital markets. Uninformed markets misallocate and misprice capital – to the detriment of almost everyone.'

Reporting on going concern is an important part of the information requirements of users.

16.4 At what point does the going concern assumption stop being appropriate?

Going concern uncertainties arise from the possibility that the company will cease to exist. Due to business risks, there is always some degree of possibility that a company will not be able to continue indefinitely.

Conditions giving rise to a company's failure develop over a period of time. A number of studies have been undertaken on methods for predicting corporate failure, eg work undertaken by Argentini[1] and Taffler & Tisshaw.[2]

The 'pre-failure stage' is caused by a number of adverse conditions, eg the general state of the economy including the company's individual segment, changes in markets including technology and competition and significant management weaknesses.

The adverse conditions can lead to a number of 'management errors' which, over a period of time, can result in major cash problems and shortages. The cash shortage can drive the management to increase borrowings, selling assets and 'down sizing' the operation to remedy the cash problems. Ultimately, the problems can lead to defaults on loan payments and bankers refusing to extend overdraft and other loan facilities.

16.5 Stages of business failure: warning signs that the going concern basis may not be appropriate

There are a number of warning signs that can indicate that the going concern basis may not be appropriate. It is a good idea to keep the indicators under review and act on any major changes. In practice, it is not possible to anticipate all business failures. The various stages of the going concern scenario are set out in the decision chart in Figure 16.1.

Going concern problems are often linked to the general state of the economy (macro-economic) industry and individual company problems. A decision chart of the factors is set out below in Figure 16.2.

---

1 'Predicting Corporate Failure' and 'Spot the Danger Signs Before it is too Late', published in
   Accountancy (ICAEW) (February 1986), 157-8 and (July 1986), 101-102.
2 'Going, Going, Gone – Four Factors Which Predict', Accountancy (ICAEW) (March 1977), 50-4;
   A study in Canada shows a failure pattern developing over a 10-year period (Hanbrick and
   D'Aveni, 'Large Corporate Failures as Downward Spirals', Administrative Science Quarterly
   (1988) 33, 1-23.

FIGURE 1

STAGES OF A COMPANY'S FAILURE

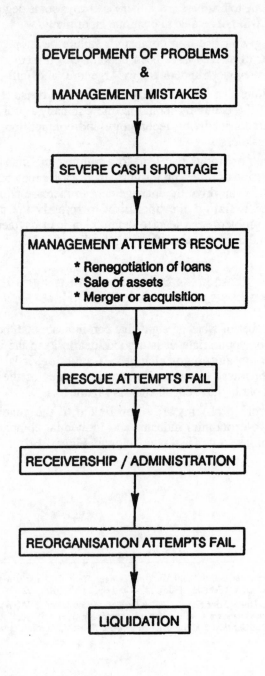

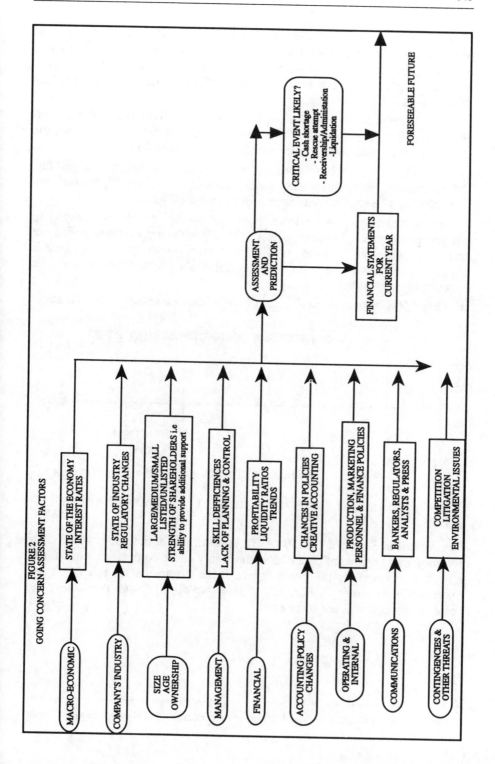

FIGURE 2
GOING CONCERN ASSESSMENT FACTORS

At key points, the directors and auditors must consider the indicators and assess whether the degree of doubt about the company's viability has reached a level sufficiently high to require disclosure of that doubt or abandoning the use of the going concern basis in favour of an alternative appropriately disclosed basis of accounting.

With hindsight, it is often easy to identify that the going concern basis was not appropriate. Events in the foreseeable future will determine whether the accounts were based on an invalid going concern assumption.

Research in approaches to dealing with risk and uncertainty[3] suggest that the expressions about uncertainty such as 'remote', unlikely', 'possible' and 'probable' can be set out on an approximate probability scale.

As an example. the various 'levels of doubt' can be expressed in percentage terms and 'decision points' inserted on the graph. These points can in turn be related to decision chart 1, for example when the management is attempting rescue actions there is substantial doubt whether the plans will be successfully concluded.

Graph 16.1: Examples of degrees of uncertainty expressed as percentages

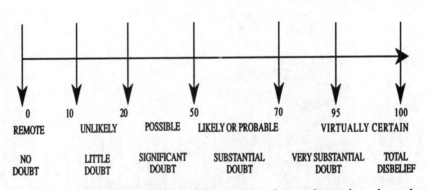

EXAMPLES OF DEGREES OF UNCERTAINTY EXPRESSED AS PERCENTAGES

0	10	20	50	70	95	100
REMOTE	UNLIKELY	POSSIBLE	LIKELY OR PROBABLE		VIRTUALLY CERTAIN	
NO DOUBT	LITTLE DOUBT	SIGNIFICANT DOUBT	SUBSTANTIAL DOUBT		VERY SUBSTANTIAL DOUBT	TOTAL DISBELIEF

The American Standard SAS59 (AICPA) states that at that point where there is a substantial degree of doubt about the ability of the company to continue as a 'going concern', is the point at which the disclosure of going concern uncertainties is required. The AICPA does not specify what probability the point of substantial doubt represents.

---

3   Published by the Canadian Institute of Chartered Accountants in 1990 (Research Report by Boritz, Toronto CICA 1990).

The middle point of a 100 point probability scale can be considered to represent the point of maximum uncertainty. In estimating the degree of likelihood, the directors and auditor need to take into account both quantitative and qualitative factors.

16.6 Large company failures as downward spirals

The study on large corporate failures by Donald C Hanbrick and Richard A D'Aveni[4] examines large company failures in the USA. The study reviewed four areas, namely:

- domain initiative: the extent to which a company changes its price in markets should be a central part of any enquiry into failure;
- environmental carrying capacity: the environment provides the companies resources and creates certain contingencies with which the organisation must deal;
- slack: a cushion on actual or potential resource, eg financial slack, human resources and technology;
- performance: are large business failures, relative to survivors, typified by long or short periods of performance deficiency in the years before failure?

16.6.1 Domain initiative

The firms that failed were on average, no more or less inertial in the 10 years proceeding failure than those that survived.

16.6.2 Environmental carrying capacity

There were no significant differences in the demand growth of bankrupts and survivors in any years.

16.6.3 Slack and performance

The finding regarding slack and performance are the most striking result of the research. It puts the others in context and indicates that the failures show signs of relative weakness very early. The failures, on average, had significantly lower equity to debt ratios than the survivors for every year examined as far back as ten years before they failed. The failed companies' operating performance, measured by return on assets, also significantly lagged with survivors in all the years observed. Poor profits limit any increases in

---

4 *Administrative Science Quarterly* (1988), 33.

shareholders equity via retained profits and causes the company to take on more debt to finance its operations.

The ratio of working capital to sales showed a relative deficiency for the bankrupt companies only in year 10 (ie the year the company failed). From years two-nine, the failed companies maintained cushions of slack comparable to firms that survived for meeting current obligations, at the same time as profitability was suffering and their potential slack was reducing.

16.6.4 Conclusion of study

A central finding of the study is that the weakness in failed firms showed up reasonably early. All subsequent behaviours must be taken potentially as both quarters and effects of decline. In practice, this can be portrayed as a downward spiral.

16.7 Accountancy profession guidance

The accountancy profession issued guidance to auditors on going concern in 1985 in the form of an auditing guideline.[5] The guideline sets out suggested procedures for auditors to follow in forming an opinion on whether the going concern basis is an appropriate method for preparing the financial statements. In determining whether the basis is appropriate, the auditor has to take into account the foreseeable future. The guideline states 'while the foreseeable future must be judged in relation to specific circumstances, it should normally extend to a minimum of six months following the date of the audit report or one year after the balance sheet date, whichever period ends on the latter date. It will also be necessary to take into account significant events which will or are likely to occur later.'

Where the going concern basis is not appropriate, the financial statements will have to be prepared on the liquidation basis. Using this basis, adjustments have to be made to reduce the value of assets to their recoverable amount, and provide for any further liabilities which might arise and reclassify fixed assets and long-term liabilities as current assets and liabilities. In most cases, this results in major write downs to assets.

The above guidance has been replaced in November 1994 with an auditing standard issued by the Auditing Practices Board.

---

5   The auditors considerations in respect of going concern.

16.8 Auditing Practices Board Guidance

The Auditing Practices Board (APB) was established in 1991 to advance standards of auditing and associated review activities in the UK and the Republic of Ireland. In addition to practising auditors, members of the APB include representatives from the business and academic worlds, the public sector and the legal profession.

The APB issued an exposure draft of a new auditing standard on going concern in May 1993. It is intended that, when finalised, the new standard will replace the existing auditing guideline issued in 1985.

The proposed standard suggested extending the period to be considered by the auditors to a period of 12 months after the date of the audit report. Current guidance provides for the later of 12 months after the year end, or six months after the date of the audit report (whichever the later). The proposals on the period, and also the audit evidence required, have been subject of considerable contentious debate.

The exposure draft of this standard was re-issued in December 1993 with minor amendments and examples of the audit evidence that should be obtained by the auditor. The periods in the original exposure draft for assessing going concern have been retained. The new exposure draft has been subject to a considerable amount of criticism, including that from the financial accounting and reporting group of the Institute of Chartered Accountants (ICAEW). The institute considers that guidance on the accounting aspects of going concern should be developed by the Accounting Standards Board and not the APB.

The APB has considered the responses it received and the new standard was published in November 1994. The standard SAS 130 (Statement of Auditing Standards – The Going Concern Basis in Financial Statements) applies to financial statements for financial periods ending on or after 30 June 1995. Earlier adoption is encouraged by the APB. The new standard replaces the existing auditing guideline issued in 1985.

The standard requires auditors, *inter alia*, to assess the adequacy of the means by which the directors have satisfied themselves that:

- it is appropriate for them to adopt the going concern basis in preparing the financial statements; and
- the financial statements include disclosures, if any, relating to going concern as are necessary for them to give a true and fair view.

If the period to which the directors pay particular attention in assessing going concern is less than one year from the date of approval of the financial statements, and the directors have not disclosed that fact, the auditors are required to mention this fact within the section of their audit report setting out the basis of their opinion, unless the fact is clear from any other references in their report. The audit report should not be qualified on these grounds alone.

16.9   Criticism of the auditor

Recently, auditors have come under increasing criticism where they have issued unqualified audit reports on the financial statements and, shortly after issuing their report, the company has gone into liquidation.[6] This criticism has led to the term expectation gap. This gap may be defined as 'auditors are performing in a manner at variance with the beliefs and desires of those for whose benefit the audit is being carried out'.[7]

16.10   Contentious areas

The whole area of going concern raises a number of contentious issues, including foreseeable future, evidence from bankers, increased responsibilities for directors, and self-fulfilling prophecies.

The issue that has raised the most debate is the question of the foreseeable future period. The APB retained the period of 12 months after the date of the signing of the audit report, as this is considered to be an important part of the work in closing the 'expectation gap'. In terms of the Companies Act, public companies are required to publish their accounts within seven months of the year end and for private companies the period is ten months. In practice, this means that auditors could be looking at periods of 19 months (public companies) and 22 months (private companies) after the year end of the company concerned. Under the terms of the Stock Exchange listing agreement, listed companies are required to publish their accounts within six months of the year end.

16.11   Evidence of going concern

The amount of evidence available on going concern depends on the nature of the company, its size and complexity. In practice, it is up to the directors to decide what information is necessary to establish that a business can continue as a going concern.

Large companies have sophisticated reporting systems that provide budgets, cash flow forecasts and particulars of borrowing facilities. Companies operating in complex and volatile environments are more likely to have procedures for identifying risks and uncertainty to which the company may be subject. At the other end of the scale, for a small company operating in uncomplicated environment, the directors may consider that all that is needed is that they should keep abreast of developments within their business and

---

6   For example Polly Peck plc.

7   *Current Issues in Auditing*, Sherer and Turley (eds), (2nd edn) p 7, London: Paul Chapman Publishing Ltd.

industry as a whole. Where the business is stable, the directors might not consider it necessary to prepare cash flow forecasts and other budgets as a matter of course.

16.12 Evidence from bankers

The majority of businesses in the UK are financed by means of bank overdraft facilities. These facilities are, by their very nature, short-term and subject to review on an annual basis. What evidence of continuing support will the auditor be able to obtain from the banker? Discussions have taken place between the APB and the British Bankers Association in order to establish the from of comfort bankers will be prepared to provide.

16.13 Increased responsibilities for directors

Concern was expressed in a recent article[8] that companies could, if they did not take legal advice on the contents of the directors' statement on responsibilities, run the risk of extending the legal liability of directors unnecessarily. The article implies that there is an element of shared responsibility between directors and auditors for the preparation of financial statements. However, the legal position is that directors have sole responsibility for the preparation of the financial statements.

The code will require directors to state in the report and accounts (financial statements) that the business is a going concern, with supporting assumptions or qualifications as necessary, and the auditors will be required to report on the directors' statement. Is the statement and the auditor's report on the statement going to increase the liability of both auditor and directors?

16.14 Current auditor's report

The auditing standard on Audit Reports[9] applying to accounting periods ending on or after 1 September 1993 already includes reference to a statement of directors' responsibilities. The statement, if not included in the financial statements (in the directors report, the notes or on a separate page), is inserted in the audit report.

An example of the directors' responsibility statement from the Auditing Standard as set out below:

'Company law requires the directors to prepare financial statements for each financial year which give a true and fair view of the state of affairs of

---

8   *Law Society Gazette*, 3 November 1993.
9   SAS 600.

the company and of the profit or loss of the company for that period. In preparing those financial statements, the directors are required to:

- *select suitable accounting policies and then apply them consistently;*
- *make judgments and estimates that are reasonable and prudent;*
- *state whether applicable accounting standards have been followed, subject to any material departures disclosed and explained in the financial statements;*
- *prepare the financial statements on the going concern basis, unless it is inappropriate to presume that the Company will continue in business.*

The directors are responsible for keeping proper accounting records which disclose, with reasonable accuracy at any time the financial position of the company and to enable them to ensure that the financial statements comply with the Companies Act 1985. They are also responsible for safeguarding the assets of the company and hence for taking reasonable steps for the prevention and detection of fraud and other irregularities.'

One of the reasons for the revised auditing standard is to attempt to narrow the 'expectation gap' by explaining the directors' and auditor's responsibilities in the report.

16.15 Cadbury and going concern

One of the contentious issues in the Cadbury Report is the requirement for companies to report that the business is a going concern. The code states that 'the directors should report that the business is a going concern, with supporting assumptions or qualifications, as necessary'. The code notes that companies will not be able to report on this aspect until guidance has been developed. The report recommended that the guidance should be developed by the accountancy profession, together with representatives of preparers of accounts.

The committee emphasises that new guidelines must strike a careful balance between drawing proper attention to the conditions on which the continuation of the business depends, and not requiring directors to express unnecessarily cautious reservations that could of themselves jeopardise the business. Directors should be required to satisfy themselves that the business is a going concern, on the basis that they have a reasonable expectation that it will continue in operation for the time period which the guidelines define. Directors should not be expected to give a firm guarantee about their company's prospects because they can never be completely certain about future trading. The guidelines should also recognise the position of smaller companies.

16.16 Joint working group on going concern

As a result of the Cadbury Report, a joint working group on going concern was formed, consisting of individuals put forward by The Hundred Group of Finance Directors, the Institute of Chartered Accountants in England and Wales, including its Board for Chartered Accountants in Business and the Institute of Chartered Accountants of Scotland.

The working group published draft guidance in May 1993. Final guidance was published in November 1994 at the same time the APB issued the auditing standard on going concern. (Going Concern and Financial Reporting – Guidance for directors of listed companies registered in the UK.)

The guidance has three objectives, namely:

- to explain the significance of going concern in relation to the financial statements;
- to describe the procedures that an explicit statement may entail; and
- to recommend appropriate disclosure.

The recommendations are intended to codify best practice.

The going concern concept referred to above is a fundamental accounting concept and, as such, underlies the financial statements. In practice it is very unusual for accounts not to be prepared under the going concern concept. The going concern concept is unlikely to be compatible with the intention or the necessity to:

- enter into a scheme of rearrangement with the company's creditors;
- make an application for an administrative order;
- place the company in administrative receivership or liquidation.

Doubts over the application of the going concern concept do not automatically mean that the company is insolvent, however there may be an effect on the company's solvency if doubts on going concern are disclosed in the financial statements.

The specific factors the directors will need to consider will vary from company to company and from industry to industry. The guidance sets out a number of procedures under the following headings:

Forecasts and budgets

Borrowing requirements

Liability management

Contingent liabilities

Products and markets

Financial risk management

Financial adaptability

Other factors including sensitivity (ie how sensitive the company has been to past events).

After following the procedures, the directors will need to assess the information and consider whether the going concern basis is appropriate, taking into account the likelihood of the various outcomes. After weighing up the results, the directors can come to one of three basic conclusions:

- There is a reasonable expectation that the company will continue in operational existence for the foreseeable future and have therefore used the going concern basis.

- factors have been identified which cast some doubt on the ability of the company to continue in operational existence in the foreseeable but they have used the going concern basis

- The company is unlikely to continue in operational existence in the foreseeable future and therefore the going concern concept is not an appropriate basis.

It is important to note that the Cadbury Report does not expect directors to give a guarantee about their company's prospects.

The guidance recommends that disclosure about going concern should be made in the operating and financial review statement (Accounting Standards Board Guidance). Alternative locations are in the directors report or in the statement on compliance with the Cadbury Code. Examples of suggested disclosures are:

After making enquires, the directors have a reasonable expectation that the company has adequate resources to continue operations for the foreseeable future. For this reason, they continue to adopt the going concern basis in preparing the accounts.

The company is in breach of certain loan covenants at its balance sheet date. As a result, the company's bankers could recall their loans at any time. The directors continue to be involved in negotiations with the company's bankers and as yet no demands for repayment have been received. The negotiations are at an early stage and, although the directors are optimistic about the outcome, it is as yet too early to make predictions with any certainty.

In the light of the other measures described elsewhere in the OFR, the directors consider it appropriate to adopt the going concern basis in preparing the accounts.

It is important to note that the statement on going concern is the responsibility of all the directors. In practice, the audit committee should review the statement and supporting work on behalf of all the directors.

16.17 The Auditing Practices Board and Cadbury Requirements

The APB has issued a revised bulletin on disclosures relating to corporate governance (Disclosures Relating to Corporate Governance (Revised) – November 1994). The bulletin includes a section on 'Going Concern'. The auditors are required to consider the 'directors statement on going concern' and assess whether the statement may be misleading. The assessment includes considering whether the statement is inconsistent with other information they have become aware in considering, as part of the audit of the financial statements, the appropriateness of the going concern basis and the adequacy of related disclosures in the financial statements.

The APB considers that it is not practical, although it would be possible, for auditors to 'give an opinion on the directors report' on going concern as mentioned in the Cadbury Report (Para 5.19). In order to give such an opinion the APB considered that the additional work required in addition to the normal audit would not justify the additional burden on preparers of financial statements. Burden in this scenario means additional audit and accontancy costs.

The bulletin therefore only requires auditors to consider whether the directors statement is consistent with other information as mentioned above. If the information is inconsistent the bulletin describes the action auditors should take. The action includes a qualification on their report on the directors statement of compliance.

16.18 Recommended action for companies

Recommended action for directors in the companies to ensure compliance with the proposal includes:

- Maintaining proper accounting records – this is, of course, a requirement of company law and essential for the management of the business.

- Maintaining proper forecasting, budgeting and management accounting systems – these systems are essential for demonstrating that the company is a going concern. If the auditor is reporting on the directors' statement on going concern, he will need to examine audit evidence. For listed and large companies this will encompass examining the company's budgeting and cash flow forecast and cash management systems, eg is the company's budgeting procedure reliable? For example, taking into account past experience.

The board should ensure that at least one of their members is following the going concern debate. Reporting procedures should be reviewed and the need for any changes considered in the light of the proposed guidance.

16.19 Qualified audit reports

There is significant divergence of views regarding the nature and purpose of the going concern qualification. It is unclear whether the qualification is designed to forecast future liquidity problems, to act as a disclaimer on the financial statements, or to bring to the attention of readers possible losses on assets in the event of a future forced sale.

The auditor faces a dilemma in deciding whether or not the financial position of the company warrants a going concern qualification. If he does not report, users may be financially damaged by relying on the financial statements which do not warn of the going concern problem, however, if he reports a going concern problem, this may contribute towards the financial collapse of the company and the resulting losses to shareholders and other stakeholders. The auditor may also become the subject of litigation.

Directors and other senior management can exert substantial pressure on the auditor not to qualify on going concern. The auditor may be faced with the loss of his client as a result of the client changing auditors. This potential loss has to be balanced against the potential loss arising from litigation should the auditor not qualify and the company subsequently fail.

A qualified report can insulate auditors from liability and meets users' expectations in being told by the auditor that there is doubt about the company's ability to operate in the foreseeable future.

16.20 Current reporting practice during 1994

Companies are reporting compliance with the provisions of the Cadbury Committee's Code of Best Practice in their financial statements other than those relating to going concern and internal control, as the required guidance has not yet been produced.

The APB issued a bulletin in December 1993 on disclosures relating to corporate governance. The bulletin provides preliminary guidance for auditors on the new responsibilities under the Cadbury Committee's Code of Best Practice. The auditors are required to report on compliance with the code, as the Stock Exchange has amended the listing rules to take this into account. The bulletin includes examples of letters setting out the terms of their engagement for reporting on the code, audit reports for reporting, and examples of audit procedures.

16.21 Consequences of requiring a director's statement on going concern

Requiring the directors to make a specific assertion or statement on going concern may have the affect of requiring management to pay more attention to this area of the companies operations. Directors will need to ensure that the going concern basis is appropriate and in order to be able to consider this, will require budgets cash flows and other analytical reports. It may mean that directors are warned earlier that their company is in the downward spiral mode and this may result in remedial action being taken before it is too late.

16.22 Short-termism

UK management has been criticised for its short-termism approach compared to the medium to long-term approach used by a number of our EU competitors. Many managements only look forward to the next financial year end.

The Cadbury requirements and the auditing standard on going concern will require management to look forward at least one year after the date of the auditor's report. The question to be addressed is will this, in some small way, help management to look further forward? Any move away from the short-termism approach should assist the medium to long-term development of the economy.

Chapter 17

The Cadbury Committee Report –
Implementation and Influence

Gina Cole
Secretary to the Cadbury Committee on the Financial Aspects of
Corporate Governance

The Committee on the Financial Aspects of Corporate Governance was set up in May 1991 by the Financial Reporting Council, the London Stock Exchange and the accountancy profession, who were concerned at the lack of confidence in financial reporting, and the value of audits in particular. The underlying factors were perceived as looseness of accounting standards and the lack of a clear framework within which directors could keep their business controls under review. The concerns were heightened by some well-publicised failures of prominent companies, whose financial statements appeared to give shareholders no advance warning of the real state of their affairs. Against this background, it is pertinent to draw attention to the fact that the committee's remit did not extend to the general corporate governance of companies but was restricted to the financial aspects, especially when any assessment is made of the effectiveness of the committee's work.

The committee recognised early on that there was a need for consensus on any proposals that it put forward, and that by giving the business and financial community a chance to comment on its draft report in May 1992, a high level of acceptance was achieved. In fact over 13,500 copies of the draft were distributed, and around 200 written submissions received in response. In addition, many chose to make their views known to the committee through less formal channels. This gives the measure of interest in the committee's work, which was of course fuelled by such events as the collapse of the BCCI Bank and the Maxwell affair. More recently the committee's work has come under the microscope in relation to directors' pay.

It was important to retain a balance when considering such a large number of responses to the committee's draft. There was of course dissension with some of the finer detail, but the committee felt that there was enough general support for the principles and the approach adopted for the recommendations to be accepted by companies. There will be those who scrutinise written submissions made to the committee and make criticisms about points which were not acted on, or on the approach adopted by the committee on particular issues. They can do this with the benefit of hindsight and the freedom that comes from not having to take heed of any counter arguments put forward by other parties, or the acceptability to the accountancy profession or the companies themselves of proposals made. Through its broad-based membership, the committee was able to get a very accurate feel as to whether a proposal, for all its merits on paper, would be practicable to implement and gain a consensus of acceptance amongst the majority of those parties affected by it, be they directors, shareholders, company secretaries, auditors or accountants.

The committee recognised that the introduction of a code could not ensure integrity or competence. It could not, for example, prevent another Maxwell. The strength of the report and code lies in the fact that they provide reference points which will concentrate minds to aim for high standards of corporate governance.

All listed and USM companies reporting in respect of years ending after 30 June 1993, should make a statement in their report and accounts about their compliance with the code and identify and give reasons for any areas of non-compliance. The publication of the compliance statement, reviewed by the auditors, is a continuing obligation of listing by the London Stock Exchange.

Immediately after publication of the report and code, enquiries to the committee's office from companies related in the main to the scope of the listing requirement, its date of implementation and a need to talk through some of the points in the code. Two common examples would be the role and number of non-executive directors (NEDs) and how their independence could be defined. Sometimes to the consternation of the enquirer, no hard and fast definition of independence was given from the committee's office. It is the committee's view that it is the responsibility of the chairman of the company (after relevant consultation with the board) to decide on the independence of his NEDs - only he will have all the relevant information as regards the interests of the company and the interests of the individual, and whether these might at any time come into conflict. It is, of course, up to the directors to declare openly any financial or other interests which they have which could affect their independence, but the final decision should rest with the chairman. Guidance on what other bodies regard as independent in this context is readily available (ie from the Association of British Insurers and the National Association of Pension Funds). It is up to the company to make the judgment and to justify it to its shareholders, should they question it. We hope that by adopting this approach companies will all address the independence issue themselves and that shareholders will retain the option of questioning the company's judgment, should they so wish. It was not felt that the committee could ever be better placed than the actual company to make such a judgment.

The issue of independence is a good example of the committee's non-prescriptive approach. Non-prescription was seen as the wisest course for a number of reasons. Firstly, the principle that directors are responsible for the governance of their companies, subject to laws, regulations and the endorsement of shareholders in general meeting.

The committee set out a framework for what they perceived as good corporate governance relating to financial reporting, thereafter it is the responsibility of the directors to work within that broad framework. It is essential that directors really address corporate governance issues as they affect their own companies, and not just comply with a checklist of detailed regulations. It is recognised that standards cannot be raised overnight and it is much more important that companies comply with the spirit of the code and not simply with its letter, by making a boiler plate compliance statement.

An unwieldy bureaucracy could have developed, had the committee decided to adopt a prescriptive approach. This in turn would have given rise to further questions – for example, would the committee's judgments remain effective after it handed over to its successor body in 1995? Would companies be prepared to meet the cost of the committee taking on an expanded advisory role, or would its current sponsors be expected to extend their funding? Companies remain answerable to their shareholders for their standards of corporate governance and the committee continues to hold the view that it is not advisable to act as an intermediary

Some companies, especially smaller ones, have expressed worries about making statements of non-compliance. The committee has always maintained that statements of compliance or non-compliance are equally acceptable, provided that one or the other is made. There should be no real or imagined black mark against a company which makes a statement of non-compliance. Such a situation might occur, for example, where a smaller company has only two non-executive directors. They would therefore have to declare non-compliance with paragraph 4.3 of the code which states that: 'The board should establish an audit committee of at least three non-executive directors with written terms of reference which deal clearly with its authority and duties.' Having made that statement, the shareholders would be in a position to decide whether they would want to question it further with the company. The committee considers it unlikely that investors would lose confidence in a company solely on the basis of a non-compliance statement. Indeed, there are examples of very successful companies in the FT-SE Top 500 who have made non-compliance statements. Further research will be needed to establish whether there is a significant correlation between non-compliance statements and company performance, or vice versa.

Much press and media attention has rightly been focused on whether companies are complying with the code. The committee itself is participating in a monitoring exercise to establish levels of compliance with the aim of providing the committee's successor body, due to be convened by the Financial Reporting Council in June 1995, with evidence as to whether the code needs refining or amending.

The London Stock Exchange is monitoring all listed companies' compliance with its continuing listing obligation. The committee are hopeful that both institutional and private investors will also be taking an active role in monitoring those companies in which they have an interest. Evidence to date suggests that there is increasing activity in this area. However, instead of taking compliance statements at face value, investors will have to assure themselves that overt compliance with the code has made a substantive difference to a company's direction and control.

Detailed research, funded by the ICAEW, is being undertaken into the changing role of institutional investors and its results (together with other corporate governance-related research projects) will be made available to the committee's successor body in 1995.

To quote paragraph 3.1 of the report:

'The Code of Best Practice is directed to the boards of directors of all listed companies registered in the UK, but we would encourage as many other companies as possible to aim at meeting its requirements.'

I do not think that when this paragraph was drafted the committee envisaged the extent to which its proposals would be taken up by other organisations, well outside the original target area of the code. Although there is no requirement to comment on the extent of compliance with the Code of Best Practice until their first annual report and accounts, some companies coming to the market are now including in their share prospectuses a paragraph on corporate governance, together with justifications for any areas of non-compliance. There have been suggestions that the code should be applied to unlisted companies, not so much for its affect on public accountability but more as a means of achieving effective control and direction. Even small and unlisted companies need to ensure that there is a balance of power at the top and that proper debate is encouraged, together with the introduction of procedures to ensure that the board can make informed and timely decisions.

Beyond the company sector, the building societies have introduced measures, prompted by the publication of the code, aimed at drawing attention to best standards of corporate governance in their field. And in April 1994, the National Health Service published its own Codes of Conduct and Accountability for NHS Boards. There are calls in the press for similar measures to be taken elsewhere in the public sector, especially where there is currently perceived to be a lack of accountability.

There has been much interest expressed from overseas on reactions to the introduction of the report and code and the extent to which companies are complying with them. The processes followed by the committee in drawing up its recommendations were called on by the Toronto Stock Exchange Committee on Corporate Governance in the development of its draft report. Interestingly, this draft recommends that listed companies should be required to disclose annually in their information circulars whether they comply with the proposed guidelines, and if not, provide an explanation of any departures from the guidelines. Like the Cadbury Committee, they are not suggesting that compliance with the guidelines themselves should be mandatory.

The King Committee on Corporate Governance in South Africa has very broad terms of reference, but many of the points covered are not dissimilar to those considered by the Cadbury Committee, for example, 'The question of the appointment of audit, remuneration and nomination committees of a board, their composition and their role.'

In Australia, the Australian Stock Exchange has decided that it should take a leadership role in establishing standards of corporate governance for listed companies. It has proposed that it should not impose corporate governance standards as a condition of listing but, again following the Cadbury lead, it is envisaged that listed companies would be required to disclose in their annual reports whether they comply with recommended corporate governance practices, and if not, to explain why not.

One cannot say that if the Cadbury Committee had not existed that these developments, and others overseas, would not have occurred. However, it does not seem unreasonable to suppose that the fact that they have chosen to follow the line taken by the committee and the London Stock Exchange on disclosure and compliance is recognition of the strong influence of the committee's work.

Chapter 18

Corporate Governance and Corporate Control – Self-Regulation or Statutory Codification?

Dr Saleem Sheikh, London Guildhall University
and Professor William Rees, University of Greenwich

18.1 Background

The Committee on the Financial Aspects of Corporate Governance under the chairmanship of Sir Adrian Cadbury, was established in May 1991 by the Financial Reporting Council (FRC), the London Stock Exchange and the accountancy profession.[1] These sponsors of the Committee were concerned about the perceived low level of confidence in financial reporting and in the ability of auditors to provide the safeguards which the users of company reports both sought and expected. They saw the underlying factors as:

- the lack of a clear framework for ensuring that directors kept under review the controls in their business;

- the looseness of accounting standards; and

- competitive pressures on companies and auditors, which have made it difficult for auditors to stand up to demanding boards of directors.

The harsh economic climate was partly responsible for the establishment of the Committee heightened by concerns about standards of financial reporting and scrutiny and the financial scandals concerning BCCI, Maxwell and excessive directors' remuneration. The Committee was of the opinion that changes to the corporate governance system were needed with an opportunity to raise standards in the system. Its proposals were aimed at restoring trust and

---

[1] The Committee's membership was extremely distinguished including what *The Independent* aptly called 'the great and the good from well-established companies': see *'Will Cadbury Mean Real Change?'* Business and City Commentary, *The Independent*, 28 May 1992, p 25. The membership included the Senior Partner of KMPG Peat Marwick, the accountant, Mr Jim Butler; the chairman of the London Stock Exchange, Sir Andrew Hugh Smith; the chairman of the FRC, Sir Ron Dearing; the president of the Law Society, Mr Mark Sheldon; the chairman of the Institutional Shareholders Committee, Mr Mike Sandland; the adviser to the governor of the Bank of England, Mr Jonathan Charkham; Professor Andrew Likierman of the London Business School; Mr Hugh Collum, chairman, Hundred Group of Finance Directors; Mr Ian Butler, council member, former chairman, CBI Companies Division; Mr Nigel Macdonald, vice president, Institute of Chartered Accountants of Scotland; and Sir Dermot de Trafford Bt, chairman, Institute of Directors. In addition, Sir Christopher Hogg, chairman of Reuters Holdings plc, Courtaulds plc and Courtaulds Textiles plc, acted as an adviser to the Committee. It is regrettably noteworthy that no woman sat on the Committee. It is to be hoped that this exclusively male dominance will not be continued in the membership of 'Son of Cadbury'. What price a woman chairperson of the successor body so that it can be appropriately nicknamed 'Daughter of Cadbury'?

confidence in the corporate system and to ensure shareholders were given a more effective voice within the governance system. The chairman of the Committee, Sir Adrian Cadbury stated:

> '*We are relying on what might be called market regulation to turn our recommendations into real improvements in the way companies are run ... Compliance, therefore, will result primarily through a combination of the self-interest of boards and shareholder action.*'[2]

Accepting the premise that directors must be given the autonomy to drive their companies forward to achieve efficiency and to maintain a competitive position, the Committee argued that the exercise of that freedom must be within a framework of effective accountability. This was the essence of any system of good corporate governance. There were two basic assumptions underlying the Committee's recommendations:

- self-regulation, rather than statutory regulation and enforcement, was the optimum way to improve corporate governance; and
- financial markets, rather than independent regulators, provided the most appropriate means of dealing with those companies which fell below the acceptable standards of corporate governance.

The Committee addressed its main recommendations on the control and reporting functions of boards and the role of shareholders and auditors. The Committee will remain responsible for reviewing the implementation of its proposals until a successor body is appointed in 1995 to examine progress and to continue the ongoing governance review. It would be for the sponsors to agree the remit of the new committee and to establish the basis for its support. The Cadbury Committee has been responsible for monitoring the implementation of its proposals since it published its final report in 1992.[3]

The process of bringing greater clarity to the respective responsibilities of directors, shareholders and auditors will also strengthen the trust in the corporate system. The Committee's aim has also been to strengthen the unitary board system and to increase its effectiveness. The strengthening of this system requires all directors to be responsible for the stewardship of the company's assets. All directors have a monitoring role and are responsible for ensuring that the necessary controls over the activities of their companies are in place and are working.

The Committee published its draft report on 7 May 1992 which was issued for public comment. It received over 200 written submissions in response to its proposals. According to the Committee, a great majority of the submissions from interested parties broadly supported the Committee's approach towards reform of the corporate governance.

---

2   Sir Adrian Cadbury, '*Restoring Trust and Confidence in The Corporate System*' [1992] ICCLR 403.

3   See chapter 17.

The need for standards to be raised and for clarification of responsibilities had also clearly emerged from another working party set up by The Institute of Chartered Accountants of Scotland in April 1991, under the chairmanship of Nigel Macdonald, who was also a member of the Cadbury Committee on The Financial Aspects of Corporate Governance, a month before the Cadbury Committee was established. This working party was concerned with 'striking the appropriate balance between the responsibilities of the company directors and those of the auditing profession'.[4] Whilst our analysis concentrates upon the Committee's final report proposals, we will refer, where appropriate, to the working party's report by way of comparison.

The Committee's formal terms of reference were to consider the following issues in relation to financial reporting and accountability and to make recommendations on good practice:

- the responsibilities of executive and non-executive directors for reviewing and reporting on performance to shareholders and other financially interested parties; and the frequency, clarity and form in which information should be provided;

- the case for audit committees on the board, including their composition and role;

- the principal responsibilities of auditors and the extent and value of the audit;

- the links between shareholders, boards and auditors; and

- any other relevant matters.

These terms of reference were regrettably relatively narrow as they were geared quite simply to seeking to restore confidence in financial reporting and auditing practice.[5] Similarly, the Scottish working party only considered the corporate governance debate in isolation by limiting its discussions to the financial aspects of corporate governance.

Regrettably, some of the Committee's recommendations were unoriginal. They appear to have been inspired by a combination of the radical proposals made in 1973 in the Conservative Government's White Paper *Company Law*

---

4   See the *Introduction to Corporate Governance –Directors' Responsibilities for Financial Statements –Recommendations of the Working Party* (1992). The working party identified three main corporate governance issues of importance to the accountancy profession, namely: directors' responsibilities for financial statements; the requirement for companies to maintain adequate internal control systems; and the implications of these issues for the role of audit committees.

5   According to a report in the Financial Times, dated 10 August 1992, the Cadbury Committee's draft report, issued for public comment, had received a majority backing by its respondents. An analysis of the 70 respondents to the report revealed that at least 64 per cent were in favour of the proposed recommendations. 16 per cent opposed its recommendations against 20 per cent who were 'very supportive'.

Reform[6] and, in the same year, in the CBI's publication *The Responsibilities of the British Public Company.*[7] Although the CBI's terms of reference 20 years ago were wider than those of the Cadbury Committee,[8] its recommendations were very similar to those now made by the Committee. The CBI was also anxious to 'raise the general level of business conduct to that already practised by leading firms large and small'.[9] This is very much like paragraph 2.8 of the Cadbury Report whose stated objective is 'to help raise the standards of corporate governance ...'[10] The only difference from the work of 1973 is that the term 'corporate governance', which hails from the USA, is now a 'buzz word' and accordingly has become centre stage in the discourse.

A central question in the debate is whether a self-regulatory system of corporate governance is preferable to legislation which would have to be obeyed to the letter but perhaps not in spirit. The Cadbury Committee appear to have considered that this would be the negative outcome of taking the legislative route. This debate as to which regulatory system is preferable has never been decisively resolved. The 1973 CBI publication regularly reminded us that the voluntary self-regulatory approach was preferable to statutory codification:

'Business today operates in a time of change; it must therefore show itself capable of the degree of evolution and self-reform necessary to cope efficiently with the new circumstances in which it has to operate.'[11]

Yet the very fragmentation of the UK self-regulatory framework has once again renewed demands for a statutory codification of the system of corporate governance in the 1990s.

6   Department of Trade and Industry, *Company Law Reform* (1973) Cmnd 5391. This was concerned primarily with effective accountability by the board of directors towards other potential claimants on the company as well as balancing the interests of shareholders: 'ownership involves responsibilities as well as rights. This requires company directors, on behalf of shareholders, to discharge their social responsibilities as well as to protect their legitimate interests', p 5.

7   Confederation of British Industry, *The Responsibilities of the British Public Company – final report of the Company Affairs Committee* endorsed by the CBI Council on 19 September 1973. The committee, which was established under the chairmanship of Lord Watkinson, had, inter alia, the support of the governor of the Bank of England. The final report was the product of an interim report circulated by the CBI to the public for their comments in January 1973.

8   The CBI's terms of reference were: to examine the factors which might be expected to assist the direction and control of public companies and corporations; to examine the role and responsibilities and structure of the boards of public companies and corporations; and to consider corporate behaviour towards interests other than those of shareholders and providers of finance, including employees, creditors, customers and the community at large.

9   *CBI, op cit* note 7, p 2.

10   *The Committee on The Financial Aspects of Corporate Governance: Final Report*, 1 December 1992, p 15.

11   *CBI, op cit*, note 7, para 6, p 2.

18.2　Reinforcing the traditional theory of the firm

One of the main drawbacks of the Committee's discussion of corporate governance has been its failure to challenge the traditional theory of the firm.[12] As with previous law reform committees, the Cadbury Committee reinforced the traditional company law philosophy on corporate governance in which the main *'dramatis personae'* are yet again the directors, shareholders and auditors. This is made clear in paragraph 1.6 of the report where the Committee is determined to bring 'greater clarity to the respective responsibilities of directors, shareholders and auditors [which] will also strengthen trust in the corporate governance system'.

The Committee and its sponsors missed the opportunity to consider the wider aspects of corporate governance. By strengthening the tripartite relationship between directors, shareholders and auditors, the Committee believed that companies would be able to raise their standards of governance. The issue of corporate governance is a much wider one than that suggested by the Cadbury Committee. The interests of employees in particular deserve recognition in their contribution to raising the standards of corporate governance. The role of employees is briefly mentioned in paragraph 4.29 ('Standards of Conduct') where the Committee believed it was important that all employees should be aware of what standards of conduct were expected of them. The Committee maintained that it was good practice for boards of directors to draw up codes of ethics or statements of business practice and to publish them both internally and externally. The role of employees was, therefore, strictly limited to receipt of information on a company's code of ethics rather than any formal participation by employees in the corporate governance system.

In Chapter 1, Dr Saleem Sheikh and Professor Chatterjee argued that the concept of corporate governance embraced a wide range of constituencies other than shareholders and auditors. To the interests of shareholders and auditors should be added the interests of other potential claimants on the corporation. These include the interests of employees, creditors, consumers and the general community. Although the Committee's terms of reference were confined to the financial aspects of corporate governance, it is arguable that employees may claim to be entitled to disclosure of financial information concerning the company's performance. There is at present no obligation under the Companies Acts for companies to disclose financial information to employees. Disclosure of such information is restricted to shareholders only. An effective corporate governance system requires close interrelationship between different stakeholders who should have a common objective in ensuring the future survival and success of the corporation.

12　See especially chapter 1.

We suggest that the new committee, which is taking over from the Cadbury Committee in mid-1995, should be charged not only with the responsibility for monitoring and implementing the recommendations of the Cadbury Committee, but also should consider the future role of employees within the corporate governance system and how employees could effectively participate in the corporate governance system. In English company law, directors are required to consider the interests of employees in the performance of their duties.[13] However, in considering the employees' interests, directors are also required to take account of shareholders' interests. This duty, however, is owed to the company and to the company alone. In practice, this means that in the event of a conflict between the interests of shareholders and employees, the interests of shareholders will always prevail. There is clearly now a recognition that other stakeholders have a role to play in the future direction of the corporation. It is maintained that there should be a representation of other stakeholders' interests on company boards. This could take the form of an advisory or strategic planning capacity. Representatives of company employees, environmental groups, local communities or informed public opinion should assume a more active role. They could serve as joint participants with corporate directors on committees reporting to the board or senior management. The Companies Acts will require amendment to reflect the modern roles of directors in discharging their duties towards the stakeholders and to consider the interests of these groups in the performance of their duties.

18.3 Strengthening the composition and structure of the board of directors

As part of its aim to achieve an effective system of corporate governance, the Cadbury Committee attributed significant importance to the role of the board of directors within the company. The Committee believes that every public company should be headed by an effective board which can both lead and control the business. The board should comprise executive directors and non-executive directors. The latter would strengthen the board by bringing a broader view to the company's activities under a chairman who accepts the responsibilities and obligations of the post of chairman.

According to the Committee, the test of 'board effectiveness' would include the way in which the members of the board as a whole work together under the chairman and whose position in the corporate governance system is perceived as particularly important. The board should, therefore, provide collective responsibility by providing effective leadership and checks and balances in the governance system. Since shareholders elect directors, they

---

13   Section 309 Companies Act 1985; see too s 719 Companies Act 1985; s 187 Insolvency Act 1986; and *Parke v Daily News Ltd* [1962] Ch 927.

must ensure that the governance structure is effective and that no one individual dominates the corporation.

The Committee recognised that occasions may arise whereby the board may require legal or financial advice in the furtherance of their duties. Apart from consulting the company's advisers, the Committee recommended that the board should also consider taking independent advice where this was felt necessary and at the company's expense through an agreed established written procedure. This procedure could be set out in the company's articles of association or in a board resolution or in a letter of appointment. This would be a matter for the board to determine. Further, the board should also have access to the advice and services of the company secretary and it should recognise that the chairman is entitled to the strong and positive support of the company secretary in ensuring the effective functioning of the board. The company secretary would also be a source of advice to the chairman and the board on the implementation of the Code of Best Practice.

18.3.1 Establishing nomination, audit and remuneration committees

According to the Cadbury Committee, the effectiveness of the board could be determined by reference to its structures and procedures. The board should consider the appointment of 'audit', 'nomination' and 'remuneration' committees.

Nominations committees should be established to make board appointments. The nominating committee would have the responsibility of putting to the board any proposed new appointments of executive or non-executive directors. This committee should comprise a majority of non-executive directors and it should be chaired either by the chairman or the chief executive.

The Committee recommended that all listed companies should have an audit committee. They should be formally constituted to ensure that they have a clear relationship with the boards to whom they are answerable and to whom they should report regularly. The audit committee should be given written terms of reference which deal with their membership, authority and duties and that they should normally meet at least twice a year. It should comprise a minimum of at least three members. Membership should be confined to the non-executive directors and a majority of the non-executive directors serving on the committee should be independent. Further, membership of the committee should be disclosed in the Annual Report.

The Committee recommended that the external auditor should normally attend audit committee meetings as well as the finance director. Other board members should also have the right to attend these meetings. It recommended that the audit committee should have discussions with the external auditors at least once a year, without executive board members present, to ensure that there were no unresolved issues of concern. Further, the audit committee should have explicit authority to investigate any matters within its terms of reference, the resources which it needs, and full access to information. The committee should be able to obtain external professional advice and to invite outsiders with relevant experience to attend meetings. The Committee believed that the audit committee's duties should include making recommendations to the board on the appointment of the external auditor, the audit fee, and any questions of resignation or dismissal; to review the half-year of the company's performance and to review annual financial statements before submission to the board. The audit committee's duties would also include a discussion with the external auditor about the nature and scope of the audit, co-ordination where more than one audit firm was involved, any problems or reservations arising from the audit, and any matters which the external auditor wished to discuss, without executive board members present; to review the external auditor's management letter; to review the company's statement on internal control systems prior to endorsement by the board; and to review any significant findings of internal investigations. The Committee recommended that the chairman of the audit committee should be available to answer any questions about the audit committee's work at the annual general meeting.

The issue of directors' remuneration has been the subject of much debate and controversy. The Committee was of the view that the overriding principle in respect of board remuneration was that of openness. Shareholders were entitled to full and clear statement of directors' present and future benefits and how they had been determined. The Committee recommended that in disclosing directors' total emoluments and those of the chairman and highest-paid UK director, separate figures should be given for their salary and performance-related elements and that the criteria on which performance was measured should be explained. Information about stock options, stock appreciation and pension contributions should also be given.

The Committee recommended that a remuneration committee should be appointed by the board of directors. It would comprise wholly or mainly of non-executive directors and be chaired by a non-executive director. Its task would be to recommend to the board the remuneration of executive directors in all its forms, drawing on outside advice, where necessary. Executive directors should play no part in decisions on their own remuneration. The directors' report should disclose the membership of the remuneration committee.

Although the Cadbury Committee had received written submissions suggesting that shareholders should be permitted to determine the amount of directors' remuneration, it did not see how the suggestions could be made workable:

'A director's remuneration is not a matter which can be sensibly reduced to a vote for or against. Were the votes to go against a particular remuneration package, the board would still have to determine the remuneration of the director concerned.'[14]

Further:

'Shareholders require that the remuneration of directors should be both fair and competitive. Striking this balance involves detailed consideration of the kind which a remuneration committee, whose members have no personal interest in the outcome, can give to the matter. Remuneration committees need to have the interests of the company and the shareholders always in mind in coming to their decisions.'[15]

The chairman of the remuneration committee should be available to respond to any concerns of shareholders at the annual general meeting. The AGM would provide an opportunity for shareholders to make their views known to the board on directors' remuneration. This would be the most effective way according to the Cadbury Committee for influencing board policies.

On the issue of directors' service contracts, the Committee recommended that these should not exceed three years without shareholders' approval and accordingly the Companies Act should be amended. The effect would be to strengthen shareholder control over levels of compensation for loss of directors' office.

In attempts to further strengthen the board procedures, the Committee was of the view that boards should have a formal schedule of matters specifically reserved to them for their collective decision, to ensure that the direction and control of the company remains firmly in their hands and as a safeguard against misjudgments and possible illegal practices. A schedule of matters should be given to directors on their appointment and kept up to date. The schedule of matters would, as a starting point, contain information on the acquisition and disposal of assets of the company or its subsidiaries that were material to the company and investments, capital projects, authority levels, treasury policies and risk management policies.

In January 1995, the CBI requested Sir Richard Greenbury, chairman of Marks and Spencer plc, to chair a group to review the structure within which pay and conditions for plc directors are determined and disclosed, and seek to propose a Code of Good Practice.

Sir Bryan Nicholson, president of the CBI, stated that it was clear that public confidence in the fairness and openness of the procedures that companies used to determine directors' pay had taken a knock. It was in the interest of business to seek to rebuild that confidence. He argued, however,

---

14   p 31 para 4.43.
15   p 32 para 4.44.

that it was not a problem which could or should be resolved by legislation. Governmental interference in pay determination, at any level, had always created more problems than it solved. He maintained:

> '*The prime responsibility must rest with boards and shareholders. But they need to discharge that responsibility in a clear and defensible manner. The group's aim will be to seek out good practice and draft a code which will be put to business bodies and shareholder representatives for consultation. In due course, it may be appropriate for it to become part of the Cadbury guidance.*'[16]

The new group includes nominees from the Institute of Directors, the Association of British Insurers, the National Association of Pension Funds and the Stock Exchange. In addition, a number of other senior corporate chairmen will take part, including Sir Michael Angus, chairman of Whitbread, Sir Denys Henderson, chairman of ICI, and Sir David Simon, group chief executive of BP. The group's terms of reference are to identify good practice in determining directors' remuneration and prepare a code of such practice for use by UK plcs. In fulfilling that remit, the new group is, *inter alia*, considering, : the constitution and effectiveness of remuneration committees; remuneration practices such as the issue of share options, bonus schemes and contract lengths; the appropriate methods of communicating remuneration policies and practices to shareholders; and the disclosure of remuneration packages of the board as a whole and individual directors. The new group is now likely (as at May 1995) to report at the end of June 1995.

The Institute of Directors has recently published its proposals on the remuneration of directors which provide some guidance for remuneration committees in their assessment of directors' pay.[17] The Institute invites companies and other interested institutions to adopt the guidance it provides. It maintains that its guidelines would provide a benchmark against which shareholders could decide whether they were satisfied with the actions of the remuneration committee and the board. The guidelines are largely addressed to large quoted plc companies where the arrangements for scrutiny and control of directors by shareholders are less clear cut. However, the Institute believes that high remuneration packages for directors should be justified in appropriate circumstances:

> '*Where directors are taking responsibility for risk, exercising leadership and using talent so that wealth is created, thereby enhancing shareholder value, high remuneration packages are justified. In many of the professions and in other walks of life, such as entertainment and sport,*

---

16 CBI, *New Group on Executive Pay* (press release) 16 January 1995.

17 Institute of Directors, The Remuneration of Directors: A Framework For Remuneration Committees (1995). See too S Sheikh, '*Curbing Top Pay Bonanza*' (1995) The Company Lawyer; S Skeikh, '*Directors Remuneration*' (1995) April, ICCLR.

people with exceptional talent are highly rewarded. There should be no difference in the commercial world.'[18]

The Institute endorsed the Cadbury Committee's recommendations that boards should appoint remuneration committees consisting wholly or mainly of non-executive directors. Since directors were responsible to their shareholders, they had a responsibility to justify to the shareholders directors' remuneration arrangements. The first duty of remuneration committees was to act on behalf of the board in the interests of shareholders collectively.

The Institute maintained that shareholders had power to take action in relation to excessive directors' remuneration and that they should be encouraged to exercise that power if necessary. If the shareholders were not satisfied with the performance of members of the remuneration committee or the board, they could remove members of the remuneration committee or the board as an ultimate sanction. In this regard, institutional shareholders would have greater ability than individual shareholders to take effective action. However, institutional shareholders could not be expected to monitor the day-to-day actions of directors.

The Institute has, therefore, proposed a set of principles which provide a framework of best practices within which shareholders can expect the remuneration committee to act in recommending directors' remuneration. Companies would be required to state in their Annual Report and Accounts whether or not their remuneration committee have adopted this framework, and if not why not. The Institute has argued that shareholders should not be required formally to approve reward arrangements at an AGM:

'This would go against the basic principle that the running of a company is delegated by the shareholders to the Board of Directors. It would be inflexible and would make the recruitment and retention of directors an uncertain process for both companies and individuals. It would also place upon shareholders a burden which most of them would not be interested in exercising and may not be qualified to exercise.'[19]

Remuneration committees established by companies would require some guidance in determining and fixing directors' remuneration. There should be an encouragement of enterprise and long-term commitment. The Institute believes that the extent to which directors perform in the interests of shareholders collectively is likely to be strengthened if there is an identity of interest between them. As the shareholder is risking capital, directors must share this burden. There should also be a significant connection between reward of directors and the long-term performance of the company. This could be achieved by enabling directors to have a financial interest in the company

18   ibid, p 1.
19   ibid, p 1.

such as shares, share options or bonuses. Longer term holdings of shares and share options, and longer term bonus arrangements, of a minimum of three years' duration in each case should be encouraged. The Institute, however, maintained that remuneration packages which were structured to reward improvements in performance should also penalise deterioration. Directors' holdings should be a matter for individual boards to determine and for remuneration committees. It should also be explained in the Annual Reports and Accounts.

According to the Institute, the following matters should be considered by remuneration committees in respect of individual directors:

*   The nature of the work being undertaken by the director.
*   The pay of the individual director.
*   The range and weight of responsibilities held by the director.
*   An assessment of the risk to which the director is exposed both in relation to the director's own job security and the risks and competitive pressures facing the company.
*   The market comparisons appropriate to the position in question.
*   The limits on the extent to which market comparisons, especially international comparisons, are relevant.
*   the progressive ladder of remuneration levels within the company.
*   Other factors, including salary and employment conditions affecting staff generally and the trading activities of the company in the market place.

The shareholders should be given sufficient information concerning the company's remuneration arrangements. The Institute, therefore, proposed that the company should state in its Annual Report and Accounts the following matters:

*   that it has adopted this framework, or the reasons for not doing so;
*   the full cost to the company of each director's remuneration package, giving separate details of

    - fees

    - salary

    - bonuses

    - pension arrangements

    - other benefits such as cars or private health insurance;
*   each director's shareholding in the company, distinguishing between shares acquired by directors in the normal way and those acquired as part of a remuneration package, as well as share options.
*   the length of each director's contract. Notice periods should be of a limited

duration. Rolling contracts should be for a maximum period of two years. Fixed term contracts should be for no more than two years' duration except in certain circumstances, which must be explained to shareholders, where a longer term may be appropriate.

18.3.2 Reforming directors' duties – towards a statutory codification

Traditionally, directors' duties have been regulated by various mechanisms, namely, the common law duty of care and skill; fiduciary duties; statutory duties; and regulation under the City Code on Takeovers and Mergers and the Admission of Securities to Listing. Without doubt, the law on directors' duties is fragmented and unclear. Recently, a survey by the Forum of Private Business, revealed that 79 per cent of the respondents (namely company directors) supported a proposal to clarify directors' responsibilities and duties.[20] The need for reform of directors' duties is now urgent. In the UK, directors' duties and responsibilities need to be clarified so that clear guidance can be given to directors as well as the company's stakeholders on the roles, duties, responsibilities and accountabilities of directors. Although judicial guidelines have been useful in setting parameters for directors' duties, there has also been a traditional reluctance by the judiciary to encroach into managerial decision making.[21] In 1977, however, the UK Labour government published a White Paper entitled *The Conduct of Company Directors*.[22] The government was of the view that the duties of directors under common law and their fiduciary duties needed to be codified. It maintained that it was desirable to include a general statement of directors' duties under statute law. For a statutory definition of 'fiduciary duty', the government at that time proposed to introduce a provision requiring a director to observe the utmost good faith towards his company in all of his actions and to act honestly in the exercise of his powers and in the discharge of the duties of his office. The government also intended to provide that a director should not make use of any money or property belonging to his company to benefit himself. Also, the director would be prohibited from using any information acquired by him, or opportunity afforded by him by virtue of his position as a director of a company, if by doing so he gains an advantage for himself where there may be a conflict with the interests of the company.

With regard to the common law duty of care and skill, the law requires directors to perform their duties with reasonable care, exercising that degree of skill and standard of care. The standard of care is an objective test, namely that to be expected of a reasonable person. The standard of skill is a subjective test under which the level required depends upon the knowledge and

---

20 Forum of Private Business, *A Report Into Business Legal Structures* (1991).
21 See chapter 1.
22 Department of Trade, *The Conduct of Company Directors* (1977) Cmnd 7037, HMSO, London.

experience of each director. The government of the day decided that there was a case for the requirements of the common law should be codified in legislation. This would require directors to exercise that degree of care and diligence that a reasonably prudent person would exercise in comparative circumstances and the degree of skill which may reasonably be expected of a person of his knowledge and experience.

Recent well reasoned proposals put to the President of the Board of Trade for codification of director's duties apparently did not find favour with him. It is thus unlikely that the present government will legislate on this subject in its instructive lifetime. It is nevertheless instructive to return to what the last Labour government proposed as a starting point for guidance as to what might happen later this decade in relation to directors' duties.

In 1978, the Labour government published a Companies Bill which provided, *inter alia*, for directors' duties to be codified.[23] Clause 44(1) of the Bill provided:

General Duties

'44(1) A director of a company shall observe the utmost good faith towards the company in any transaction with it on its behalf and owes a duty to the company to act honestly in the exercise of the powers and the discharge of the duties of his office;

(2) A director of a company shall not do anything or omit to do anything if the doing of that thing or the omission to do it, as the case may be, gives rise to a conflict between his private interests and the duties of his office.

(3) Without prejudice to subsections (1) and (2) above, a director of a company or a person who has been a director of a company shall not, for the purposes of gaining, whether directly or indirectly, an advantage for himself:

(a) make use of any money or other property of the company; or

(b) make use of any relevant information or of a relevant opportunity;

(i) if he does so while a director of the company in circumstances which give rise or might reasonably be expected to give rise to such a conflict; or

(ii) if while a director of the company he had that use in contemplation in circumstances which gave rise or might reasonably have been expected to give rise to such a conflict.'

The term 'relevant information' in relation to a director was defined as any information which he obtained while a director or other officer of the

---

23 On the criticisms of the 1978 Bill with specific reference to directors' duties, see Birds, '*Making Directors Do Their Duties*' (1979) Co Lawyer 67.

company and which it was reasonable to expect him to disclose to the company or not to disclose to persons unconnected with the company. The term 'relevant opportunity' in relation to a director of a company, means an opportunity which he had while a director or other officer of the company and which he had:

- by virtue of his position as a director or other officer in the company; or
- in circumstances in which it was reasonable to expect him to disclose the fact that he had that opportunity to the company.

Clause 44(5) of the Bill provided that if any of the provisions on directors' duties were contravened, the directors would be liable to account to the company for any gain which they had made directly or indirectly from the contravention or, as the case may be, would be liable to compensate the company for any loss or damage suffered directly or indirectly by the company in consequence of the contravention.

A person would not be liable for any act or omission which was duly authorised or ratified. However, this would be without prejudice to any remedies which may be available for a breach of any fiduciary duty and to any other provision of the Companies Acts imposing duties or liabilities on such directors, or defining their duties or liabilities. Compliance with any requirement of these Acts would not of itself be taken as relieving a director of a company of any liability imposed by clause 44 of the Bill.

The common law duties of care and skill would be codified under statute law. Clause 45 of the Bill provided that:

'In the exercise of the powers and the discharge of the duties of his office in circumstances of any description, a director of a company owes a duty to the company to exercise such care and diligence as could reasonably be expected of a reasonably prudent person in circumstances of that description and to exercise such skill as may reasonably be expected of a person of his knowledge and experience.'

Clause 45 would prevail over any other rules of law stating the duties of care and diligence and of skill owed by a director of a company to the company. There are some fundamental issues on this topic which we must now address.

It has been questionable for some years whether directors' legal responsibilities and duties bear much resemblance to reality. According to Mace, USA directors have a very minor role within the corporation. In his book *Directors - Myth and Reality*, Mace observed that the typical board was largely a 'vestigial legal organ which included merely subservient and docile appointees of the owner-manager'.[24] In short, the duties and responsibilities ascribed by law to directors have no resemblance in reality to what directors

---

24   Mace, *Directors: Myth and Reality* (1971), in the introduction to his book.

actually did in practice. He found that in practice, directors provided advice and counsel to the company's president/chairman rather than engage in decision making functions. According to one company president, the board of directors served as 'a sounding board - a wall to bounce the ball against'.[25] Another president thought that 'the board rubber-stamps the actions of management'.[26] Most of the directors did not devote substantial amounts of time to the boards on which they served. They were reluctant to ask inquisitive questions of their president. In reality, they acted in a crisis situation in only two circumstances: first, where the president had died or became incapacitated, the board would appoint a successor; and, secondly, where the president's performance was so unsatisfactory that the board would require the president to resign: the directors would then appoint a new successor. Mace, therefore, concluded that it was a myth to suppose that directors established objectives, strategies and policies for their companies. The board merely resembled a 'ritualistic performance'.

Indeed, it is now becoming highly fashionable in corporate governance circles to ask whether directors serve any useful function at all. According to Axworthy, modern studies in North America have decisively shown that directors 'not only do not do what the law envisages of them but ... cannot fulfil the law's requirements'.[27] He concluded that there was no role for directors to serve on company boards and company law should dispense with their requirements without 'any deleterious impact'.[28]

A recent survey in the USA by the Conference Board has revealed that many boards of US corporations have made definite strides towards greater independence in their memberships.[29] Many companies had eliminated directors whose connection with the company could conflict with their ability to exercise independent judgment on corporate matters before the board. A majority of the companies surveyed had nominating, audit and compensation committees to ensure fairness and openness in the disclosure of information to the shareholders. A majority of the board chairmen, however, were also the company's chief executives. There have been demands from activist shareholders there for a separation of these two roles in order to clarify the

---

25   ibid , p 14.

26   ibid , p 15. See also Mace *Directors: Myth and Reality – Ten Years Later* (1979), Vol 32 *Rutgers Law Review* p 293, where Mace concluded that little had changed in the system of corporate governance since his original study in 1971: 'The reluctance of business leaders to develop affirmative and constructive ideas for improving corporate governance is somewhat understandable' (p 307) but he suggested that any changes would gradually evolve over time.

27   Axworthy, '*Corporate Directors – Who Needs Them?*' (1988), Vol 51 No 3 Modern Law Review 273. See also the *Canadian study* by McDougall and Fogelberg, *Corporate Boards in Canada: How Sixty–Four Boards Function*, (1968); The Conference Board in *Canada, Canadian Directorship Practices: A Critical Self-Examination* (1977); and Haft, '*Business Decisions by the Board: Behavioural Science and Corporate Law*' (1981) 880 Mich. L. Rev 1.

28   ibid , 275.

29   The Conference Board, *Corporate Boards and Corporate Governance* (1993).

board's role as overseer and monitor of management and strengthen the board's hand in its dealing with the chief executive. Some activist institutional shareholders have begun to focus their attention on boards of directors of underachieving portfolio companies. A primary emphasis in most cases was on recommendations that would strengthen the independence of the board, so that it would monitor the company's management better. Discussions with managements and directors of targeted companies have been effective in getting agreement to desired changes. This form of activity should be encouraged in the UK, given the UK companies traditional desire for voluntary self-reform rather than statutory regulation.

18.4   Company chairman and chief executive

The Cadbury Committee attached some considerable importance to the respective roles of the company chairman and chief executive (who may well be one and the same person) and vitally to the interrelationship between the two roles. It considered that the chairman's role is fundamental within the system of corporate governance. The chairman has the task of accepting overall responsibility for the board. The chairman is primarily responsible for the working of the board, for its balance of membership subject to the board's and shareholders' approval, for ensuring that all relevant issues are on the agenda, and for ensuring that executive and non-executive directors are enabled to play a full part in corporate decision making. The Committee was of the view that chairmen should be able to stand back sufficiently from the day-to-day running of the business to ensure that their boards were in full control of their company's affairs and to consider their obligations to their shareholders. According to the Committee, chairmen ensure that their non-executive directors receive timely information concerning the company on whose board they sit. Non-executive directors are encouraged to make full contribution to the board's work.

The Committee recommended that the roles of chairman and chief executive should be split: if the two roles were combined in one person, it would represent a considerable concentration of power. There should therefore be a clearly accepted division of responsibilities at the head of the company which would ensure a balance of power such that no one individual would have unfettered powers of decision.

The CBI reached similar conclusions in 1973 when it stated that 'the whole tone of the company and its public image must be set by the board and in particular, by the positive leadership by the chairman. No company can be successful unless the chairman is of a calibre to provide this leadership and to represent the company properly to the outside world'.[30]

---

30   CBI, op cit, note 7 para 99 p 34; see too chapter 10.

Although the Committee usefully recommended that the chairman's role should be separated from that of the chief executive,[31] this recommendation again is unoriginal. It was, for example, suggested 20 years ago by the CBI which was then emphatic that there ought to be a clear distinction between the roles and responsibilities of the chairman and the chief executive. The CBI concluded:

What is necessary in a substantial company is that the chairman has executive functions, he should have with him, on an equal or a near equal level, one or more colleagues who will share with him the executive responsibility and thus avoid too much concentration of power.[32]

This thinking represents a sensible compromise and the separation of roles would, therefore, be a safeguard against abuse and misuse of power by the chairman.

18.5 Non-executive directors

One of the Cadbury Committee's main recommendations has been for companies to appoint non-executive directors to their boards. The Committee believes that their 'independent judgment' and monitoring of corporate performance strategy will raise standards of good corporate governance. It recommended that the calibre and number of non-executive directors on the board should be such that their views should carry sufficient weight in the board's decisions. It recommended that there should be a minimum of three non-executive directors, one of whom may be the company's chairman provided he or she was not also its executive head. Two of the three should be independent of the company. This means that apart from their directors' fees and shareholdings, they should be independent of management and free from any business or other relationship which could materially interfere with the exercise of their independent judgment. However, in order to safeguard their position, non-executive directors should not participate in share option schemes and their service as non-executive directors should not to be pensionable by the company.

---

31 Apparently some companies including Guinness plc, Grand Metropolitan, Kingfisher plc and Thorn EMI did defy the trend to split the roles of the company chairman and chief executive. However, recent examples of the difficulties associated with combining the two roles have been the experiences of Mr Gerald Ratner of Ratners, the jewellers, and Mr Jim McAdam, formerly deputy chairman of Coats Viyella. According to Mr Mike Sandland (a member of the Cadbury Committee), chairman of the Institutional Shareholders Committee: 'As chairman you are meant to arbitrate between the non-executive and executive elements on the board, and provide a balance. As chief executive you must be an advocate of your company in a more committed way. It can prove very difficult to take off one hat and put on another.'

32 ibid pp 35-6.

The Committee suggested that boards should provide non-executive directors with information on the company on which they sit. The board is, therefore, recommended to review regularly the form and the extent of information which is provided to all directors. The board is given the responsibility for deciding whether this definition has been satisfied. Information about the relevant interests of directors should be disclosed in the directors' report. Non-executive directors should have equal access to corporate information and should share decision making powers with the other directors; this would go some way towards reducing instances of abuse and misuse of power by other directors and should lessen the potential for a conflict of interest, especially in the context of takeovers and mergers.[33]

The task of selecting non-executive directors would be a matter for the board as a whole and there should be a formal selection process, which will reinforce the independence of non-executive directors, and make it evident that they have been appointed on merit and not through any form of patronage. The task of selection would be delegated to a 'nomination committee', which will be required to report back to the board on its recommendations for appointment. The nominating committee will consist of a majority of non-executive directors chaired by either a non-executive director or the company chairman. Non-executive directors would be appointed for specified terms and their reappointment would not be automatic. Their letter of appointment should set out their duties, term of office, remuneration and its review. The Committee suggested that the reappointment of the non-executive directors should not be automatic but that a conscious decision for continuation had to be made by the board and the director concerned.

The Conservative Government's 1973 White Paper was convinced of the desirability of appointing non-executive directors onto company boards. It suggested that the non-executive director could play a powerful and useful role on the board 'partly by his concern for the interests of the shareholders and partly by obliging executive members to look beyond their immediate concerns to the longer future and to the wider stage upon which the individual company must operate'.[34] The White Paper recommended that every company over a certain size would benefit from their presence and concluded that shareholders might reasonably rely on the non-executive director to be

---

33 The Scottish working party also strongly recommended that the board of every listed company and substantial economic entities should have some non-executive directors but surprisingly did not consider the role and duties of non-executive directors in any depth. For a detailed consideration of the nature and proposed functions of a non-executive director, see: Institute of Chartered Accountants in England and Wales, *The Changing Role of the Non-Executive Director* (1991). This report was compiled by a study group of the Institute of Chartered Accountants, PRONED, and the Institute of Directors. See especially its conclusions in para 4 of the report.

34 DTI, *op cit*, note 6 para 61 p 21. The White Paper suggested that in particular non-executive directors could exercise 'a detached and impartial judgement' on the board: para 61 p 21.

particularly sensitive to their interests, since he would be 'less committed' to the managerial view and hence would be better able to discharge the 'stewardship' function'.[35]

Later in 1973 the CBI agreed that the appointment of non-executive directors would be 'highly desirable'. They would exercise an independent and objective approach to corporate policies and would bring to the company the benefit of their wider knowledge and experience. However, the non-executive director would need to be familiar with the company's management and financial dealings and although not expected to be an expert in all areas, he would need to ensure that the company was operating efficiently. Another recommendation by the CBI was that non-executive directors should have access to all corporate information. Further, as a means of expressing their dissatisfaction with the board, non-executive directors would be required to prepare a memorandum for circulation and discussion by the board. If no change was effected by the board as a result of the recommendations in the memorandum, the ultimate resort would be to resign from the company. Non-executive directors would be under a duty to provide a statement in connection with their resignation taking into account the 'best interests of the company and the shareholders'.[36] It is suggested that this statement should be registered at Companies House on resignation, which would be similar to the procedure for auditors in connection with their cessation from office under s 394 Companies Act 1985.

PRO-NED, an organisation established in 1982, has recommended that companies should appoint independent non-executive directors. It has formulated a Code of Recommended Practice on Non-Executive Directors. The code defines an 'independent non-executive director' as one who has integrity, independence, personality and experience to fulfil the role of a non-executive director effectively. As a guideline, the code suggests the duties and responsibilities of a non-executive director should include the contribution to an independent view of the board's deliberation; to help the board provide the company with effective leadership; to ensure the continuing effectiveness of the executive directors and management; and to ensure high standards of financial probity on the part of the company. They would be appointed for a specific term and would be subject to re-election by rotation.[37]

In our view, the role of non-executive directors ought to go further than that suggested by the Committee and PRO-NED. In the light of the American

---

35   ibid , para 61 p 21.

36   CBI, *op cit*, note 7 paras 106-114 pp 37-38. The CBI thought that the appointment of non-executive directors would restore confidence in the system of corporate governance.

37   See PRO-NED, *Code of Recommended Practice on Non-Executive Directors*, April 1987. PRONED also provides in the code that non-executive directors should be consulted on major issues of audit and control and that these directors should also serve on audit committees set up by companies.

experience, consideration should be given to the appointment of public directors. Stone[38] has, for example, proposed two types of public directors who could usefully serve on company boards: The first type are 'General Public Directors' ('GPDs') who would operate with a board mandate and devote at least half their time to the company boards on which they have been appointed to serve. The GPDs would have a 'superego function', whereby they would be expected to enhance the company's image in society and to consider the interests of the community. 'Special Public Directors' (SPDs) who, however, would only be appointed in exceptional circumstances, as where expert assistance was required in specialist areas of technological innovation, product safety and environmental pollution. Their appointment could be triggered in two situations. Firstly, in a 'demonstrated delinquency situation', they would be appointed if a company had been in frequent violation of the law and where it was apparent that the traditional legal mechanisms would be inadequate to ensure compliance by the company. Secondly, in a 'generic industry problem', SPDs would be appointed if an event of serious social concern had arisen and where the company had not been involved in a repeated violation of the law. The appointment of SPDs would be by the court or an agency/commission before which the company would have to appear through its directors. We suggest that specific duties should be assigned to these public directors to reflect their importance in and to society.

18.6 The role of shareholders in the corporate governance system

The role of shareholders is given some prominence by the Cadbury Committee. The relationship between shareholders and directors is that the shareholders elect directors who report on their stewardship to shareholders. The shareholders appoint auditors to provide an external check on the directors' financial statements. Directors are, therefore, accountable to shareholders for their actions. According to the Committee, however, the issue for corporate governance is how to strengthen the accountability of boards of directors to shareholders.

In the preparation of its final report, it was suggested to the Committee that shareholders could become more closely involved in the appointment of directors and auditors through the formation of shareholders' committees. Other proposals were directed at making it easier for shareholders to put forward resolutions at general meetings. The Committee, however, considered

---

38 Stone, *Where the Law Ends – The Social Control of Corporate Behaviour (1975)*. See especially Chapters 13-16.

these proposals impractical. It thought that shareholders could make their views known to the boards of the companies in which they have invested by communicating with them directly and through their attendance at general meetings. The Cadbury Committee wished to see shareholders participate more actively in the corporate governance process:

> *Shareholders have delegated many of their responsibilities as owners to the directors who act as their stewards. It is for the shareholders to call the directors to book if they appear to be failing in their stewardship and they should use this power. While they cannot be involved in the direction and management of their company, they can insist on a high standard of corporate governance and good governance is an essential test of the directors' stewardship. The accountability of boards to shareholders will, therefore, be strengthened if shareholders require their companies to comply with the code [of best practice].*

One way of improving shareholder effectiveness would be to reform general meetings so as to allow shareholders more participation at such meetings than they have at present. This could be done by providing forms in Annual Reports on which shareholders could send in written questions in advance of the meeting, in addition to their opportunity to ask questions at the meeting itself, and the circulation of a brief summary of points raised at the annual general meeting to all shareholders after the event. Consideration should also be given to the ways of boards keeping in touch with their shareholders, outside the annual and half-yearly reports. The Committee has encouraged boards to experiment with ways of improving their links with shareholders and for shareholders to put proposals to their boards to the same end.

The role of institutional shareholders is becoming increasingly important in the corporate governance debate. The Committee has, therefore, endorsed the statement recently published by the Institutional Shareholders' Committee entitled The Responsibilities of Institutional Shareholders in the UK. These were:

- Institutional investors should encourage regular, systematic contact at senior executive level to exchange views and information on strategy, performance, board membership and quality of membership.

- Institutional investors should make positive use of their voting rights, unless they have good reason for doing otherwise. They should register their votes wherever possible on a regular basis.

- Institutional shareholders should take a positive interest in the composition of boards of directors, with particular reference to concentrations of decision-making power not formally constrained by appropriate checks and balances, and to the appointment of a core of non-executive directors of the necessary calibre, experience and independence.

The Institutional Shareholders' Committee advises its members to use their votes positively and the Cadbury Committee recommended that institutional investors should disclose their policies on the use of voting rights.

Boards of directors have a duty to ensure institutional shareholders and shareholders generally have full disclosure of information to ensure that any significant statements concerning their companies are made publicly available to all shareholders. Shareholders, too, have a role in the communication process by informing companies if there are aspects of the business which given them cause for concern. Both shareholders and directors have to contribute to the building of a sound working relationship between them.

18.7   The Code of Best Practice

At the very heart of the Cadbury Committee's recommendations is the proposal for a 'Code of Best Practice' ('the code'). This is specifically designed to achieve the necessary high standards of corporate behaviour. The key question which we now wish to address is: how likely is it that this code will achieve this admirable objective?

The Committee has enlisted the support in this enterprise of the London Stock Exchange and unsurprisingly its other sponsors, convened by the FRC, who in 1995 have taken the joint initiative to appoint the group to examine the progress to date and to establish an ongoing review of the code. More immediately, the Stock Exchange now requires all listed companies registered in the UK, as a continuing obligation of listing, to state whether they are complying with the code, and if not, why not?[39] This new listing requirement (beginning with companies' 1992 accounts) is a rare exception to the predominantly voluntary nature of the proposed reforms. The threat that the Stock Exchange would delist companies which chose not to disclose their degree of compliance with the code is unlikely to cause considerable fear amongst such deviant directors on the basis of the Stock Exchange's track record, given that it has rarely used such a sanction. Such delisting for non-disclosure would also have the knock-on effect of making it more difficult for investors to get rid of their shares in the offending company by selling them. The Stock Exchange has planned to draw public attention to cases of inadequate disclosure; a programme of disclosure will also be undertaken to assist future monitoring of the code.

---

39   The Cadbury Code has been criticised as being 'too vague' by the Chartered Association of Certified Accountants. It argued that the objectives established by the Cadbury Committee required far more clearly defined responsibilities and methods of compliance by bodies including the Stock Exchange and the Financial Reporting Council. Further, the association has called for more weight to be given to internal audit and compliance systems and for less reliance on non-executive directors. See *Financial Times* 12 August 1992.

The Committee believed that by adhering to the code, listed companies would strengthen both their control over their business and their public accountability. In so doing, companies would be striking the right balance between meeting the standards of corporate governance and retaining the essential spirit of enterprise. The Committee considered that voluntary reform to corporate governance was far preferable to statutory codification:

> 'We believe that our approach based on compliance with a voluntary code coupled with disclosure, will prove more effective than a statutory code. It is directed at establishing best practice, at encouraging pressure from shareholders to hasten its widespread adoption, and at allowing some flexibility in implementation.'

The Committee recognised that if companies did not accept its recommendations, the government may introduce legislation to ensure companies were complying with their obligations: statutory measures would impose a minimum standard and there would be a greater risk of boards complying with the letter, rather than with the spirit, of their requirements.

According to the Committee, the general principles of the code are those based on 'integrity', 'openness' and 'accountability'. Openness on the part of companies was the basis for the confidence which needed to exist between business and all those who have an interest in its success. By 'integrity', the Committee meant both straightforward dealing and completeness in the making of statements by companies. Financial reporting should be honest and it should present a balanced picture of the state of the company's affairs.

The Committee was of the view that the code should be followed by companies for two main reasons. First, a clear understanding of responsibilities and an open approach to the way in which they have been discharged would assist the board of directors in framing and winning support for their strategies. It would also assist the efficient operation of capital markets and increase confidence in boards, auditors and financial reporting and the general level of confidence in the business. Secondly, the Committee believed that if standards of financial reporting and of business conduct more generally were not seen to be raised, a greater reliance on regulation may be inevitable.

Public companies are now required to comply with paragraph 12.43(j) of the Stock Exchange's Listing Rules. This states that a public company listed on the Stock Exchange and incorporated in the UK, must provide a statement as to whether or not it has complied throughout the accounting period with the Code of Best Practice. A company that has not complied with the code, or complied with only part of the code or (in the case of requirements of a continuing nature) complied for only part of an accounting period, must specify the paragraphs with which it has not complied, and (where relevant) for what part of the period such non-compliance continued, and give reasons for any non-compliance.

18.8 Auditing[40] and the disclosure philosophy

The Committee is principally concerned with the financial aspects of good corporate governance and to raise the standards of the present financial reporting and accountability procedures.

One of the main weaknesses in the present system of financial reporting in the UK has been the existence of various sets of accounting principles and procedures and the inconsistent results derived from the same set of facts in arriving at a true and fair view.[41] The Committee was concerned that this resulted in a distortion in the financial reports presented to shareholders and recommended that the company's reports and accounts should be presented with greater clarity to the shareholders than at present. The financial reports should be supported by statistics indicating the company's performance and future prospects. This will entail directors displaying a high level of disclosure of their financial dealings to the auditors as well as the shareholders. The Committee also recommended that any interim statements on the company's position should be drawn to the shareholders' attention. Further, the chairman's report should refer to the company's financial position and there should be a shortened version of the company's accounts.[42]

In order to regulate the company's financial position, the Cadbury Committee recommends that all listed companies should have an audit committee on the board of directors. The audit committee would act to safeguard the interests of both the shareholders and creditors against unlawful depletion of corporate funds by directors. They would be formally constituted and their relationship with the board of directors would need to be clarified with specific terms of reference stating their membership, authority, rules and duties. They would be required to meet at least three times a year to assess the

---

40 On the role, duties and responsibilities of auditors see *Caparo Industries plc v Dickman* and others [1990] 1 All ER 568; also see appendix 4 of the Cadbury Committee's report on the auditors' liability in the *Caparo* case. According to the Committee, the *Caparo* case 'involved a careful and complex balancing of interests' of the auditors and the wider public. It agreed with the House of Lords' decision and concluded that the decision should not be altered by statutory intervention. However, see especially pp 57-8 on the Committee's views on the possible ways of extending the auditors' duty of care without creating an open-ended liability.

41 For a controversial view of the accounting techniques employed by some major companies, see Smith, *Accounting for Growth: Stripping the Camouflage from Company Accounts* (1992).

42 The Scottish working party similarly concluded that the annual report should include a statement by directors explaining their duties in relation to financial statements and limits its proposals to listed companies and substantial economic entities. At present, there is no requirement under the Companies Acts for directors to specify their responsibilities towards financial statements. The working party further recommended that in preparing the financial statements directors must satisfy themselves that it is reasonable to make the assumption that the business will continue as a going concern.

company's financial position. They would be comprised exclusively of non-executive directors of the company and a majority of these non-executive directors would be independent of the company. Their role would be to consider areas of corporate concern and to exercise their independent judgment as committee members. The Cadbury Committee believed that an audit committee should be given full access to corporate information with authority to seek external professional advice at their discretion. Their duties would include making recommendations to the board on the appointment of external auditors; reviewing the half-year and annual financial statements before submission to the board; discussing with the external auditors the nature and scope of the audit with a view to resolving any problems; and reviewing the internal audit programme and findings of an internal investigation. However, the chairman of the audit committee would only be accountable to the shareholders at the annual general meeting. This is unsatisfactory and we recommend that a good system of corporate governance entails regular accountability of the chairman of the audit committee to the shareholders.[43]

The proposals for establishing audit committees were also promulgated by the Labour Government in its 1977 White Paper, which referred to the developments and experience of audit committees in North American companies. The White Paper recommended that audit committees should consist of non-executive directors and their main duties would include reviewing the financial statements and monitoring the company's internal governance controls. The North American experience revealed that audit committees were useful in strengthening the influence of non-executive directors and auditors within the company. Although the Labour Government in its White Paper favoured the establishment of audit committees, it did not propose legislation in this area:

'The time may come when it will be appropriate to legislate in this field, but the government believes initially at least it will be better for companies, investors and their representative bodies to work out schemes which can benefit from a degree of flexibility which the law could not provide.'[44]

---

43 The Scottish working party's terms of reference did not allow it to make formal recommendations as to the desirability or statutory requirement for companies to establish audit committees. However, the working party is unanimous in supporting the nature of such committees. It believes that the audit committee should have written terms of reference agreed by the board of directors. Further, the audit committee would be constituted as a sub-committee of the board and a majority on the sub-committee should comprise non-executive directors.

44 Department of Trade, *The Conduct of Company Directors* (1977) Cmnd 7037 para 21 p 6. Further, the White Paper observed: 'It has been found in North America that one of the conditions for the successful operation of audit committees is that the board should contain a sufficient number of strong and independent non-executive directors to serve on them.'

A notable omission by the Cadbury Committee was its lack of consideration of corporate social audits. Company law currently makes no provision for the reporting of non-financial information on the companies' social activities. The social audit may be regarded as an American concept. It measures a company's social performance in areas such as environmental pollution, waste, misleading advertisements, unsafe consumer products, and product quality. This issue should be placed on the statutory agenda. In our view, as part of good corporate practice, companies should be required to identify areas of their social activities and then to measure them. In this way, companies can compare the current results with their past performance with a view to raising the standards of corporate performance. This task could ideally be allocated to public directors.[45]

Consideration should also be given to implementing the recommendations made by the Boothman Committee in 1977, which was set up to 're-examine the scope and aims of published financial information in light of the modern needs and conditions'.[46] That report recommended, inter alia, that financial reports should seek to satisfy the information needs of various users and should not be limited to shareholders. Those claimants with a right to wider financial information would include employees. The employment report would be incorporated in the financial report. It would be concerned primarily with information about the number of employees employed; the age distribution and sex of employees; the main functions of employees; the geographical location of major employment centres; major plant and site closures; disposals and acquisitions by the company during the past year; and the identity of trade unions recognised by the company for the purposes of collective bargaining.

18.9   Towards company law reform: conclusions and recommendations

The present system of corporate governance, self-regulation and the monitoring and control of corporate affairs is inadequate and unsatisfactory to protect the interests of shareholders, creditors and other 'stakeholders' of the corporation.

At the heart of the major reforms should be a consideration of a statutory

---

45 We would highlight the 1973 White Paper proposals, which recommended that 'a useful step forward would be to impose a duty on directors to report to the shareholders on specific parts of the company's response to the social environment': para 58 p 20. This would require additional disclosure in the directors' report. The government clearly viewed the social audit as a mutually beneficial exercise for both the companies and the community. However, for a contrary view see the 1973 CBI report para 98 p 34.

46 Boothman Committee, *Corporate Report: A Report for the Accounting Standards Steering Committee* (1977).

codification of directors' duties which are, at present, fragmented. There should be a statutory codification of directors' fiduciary duties and the common law duty of care and skill. The Companies Bill 1978 is a useful starting point and model for the suggested reforms in this area. A new Companies Act should identify the general role of directors and their function within the corporate governance system. At present, there is lack of clarification as to the role and function of directors. A new Act should specify that the role of directors is to act in good faith in the best interests of the company. This should clearly refer to acting in the interests of their shareholders collectively as a group. However, there should also be a recognition that directors have duties towards individual shareholders. The role of the board of directors should also be clarified. It is suggested that primarily boards are responsible for the effective governance of their companies. Their responsibilities should be defined to include the following:

- setting the company's strategic aims;
- providing the leadership to put the strategic aims into effect;
- supervising the management of the business;
- reporting to the shareholders on their stewardship;
- considering the interests of other 'stakeholders', such as consumers and suppliers, when deciding on corporate policies;
- setting financial policy and overseeing its implementation;
- using financial controls where necessary; and
- effective reporting on the corporate activities and progress to the shareholders.

Company law should make provision for the recognition of 'corporate social responsibilities' as an important feature of corporate governance. There is now a growing recognition in the UK that companies have social responsibilities and are perceived as 'trustees' for the various stakeholders. The law in this area is very fragmented and requires codification as one chapter in the Companies Act 1985 as already amended. This would include s 309 of the Companies Act 1985 (directors to have regard to employees' interests) and the provisions under schedule 7 of the Companies Act 1985 on disclosure of information in the Directors' Report. The information would provide details of the political and charitable gifts made by companies to various institutions, disclosure concerning the employment of disabled persons, and on the health, safety and welfare at work of the company's employees. A new Companies Act should also include Part V of Schedule 7 to the Companies Act 1985 on employee involvement, in one whole chapter, dealing with the social responsibilities of companies. The company would be required to state how it provides information on matters of concern to employees; on matters such as consulting employees or their representatives on a regular basis so that the views of employees could be taken into account in making decisions which are likely to affect their interests; encouraging the involvement of employees in the company's performance through an employees' share scheme; and achieving a common awareness on the part of all employers of the financial and economic factors affecting the company's performance. Company law should, therefore, make provision for more disclosure of information to the company's employees.

Wider participation by non-executive directors serving on company boards should be encouraged. A new Companies Act should require non-executive directors to consider, *inter alia*, the interests of other 'stakeholders' on the corporation. There may very well also be a case for appointing 'public directors' to serve on company boards as representing the 'voice' or interests of various stakeholders.

Consideration should also be given to introducing the concept of 'advisory resolutions'. Where shareholders were not satisfied with the effective corporate governance by directors, shareholders should seek external advice and prepare advisory resolutions which would compel directors to consider these resolutions at a board meeting. The board would then be required to state whether or not it would adopt the advisory resolution and if not, why. The effect of an advisory resolution would compel directors to reflect on their policies and the future direction of the company in discharging their duties collectively, towards shareholders. It is suggested that an advisory resolution would only be put to the board upon a requisition by shareholders holding one tenth paid up capital. This would prevent abuse of the system and save time and expense.

Although we do not advocate a total abolition of the self-regulatory system of corporate governance, there is a strong case for statutory regulation of some of the areas we have considered. We believe that a statutory codification in these areas will raise standards and would provide greater clarification to boards, directors and other interested parties than do law and 'best practice' at present.

Postscript

Sir Adrian Cadbury
Chairman of The Cadbury Committee to Investigate the
Financial Aspects of Corporate Governance

I remain astonished at the pace at which corporate governance has become a public issue internationally. Even the French now refer to 'le corporate governance', in defiance of their country's uncompromising stand against such debasements of their language.

The recession has played its part by exposing corporate weaknesses and focusing attention on issues of financial reporting and control. Another factor has been the inexorable rise of the institutional investor. Corporations now own nearly two-thirds of British equities. Pension funds are major shareholders in most public companies and their growth at home and abroad reflects an ageing population. Consequently, the institutions collectively can no longer sell out when they have doubts about a company's future. As Georg Siemens of Deutsche Bank once said, 'If you cannot sell, you must care.'

A further factor, for the rest of the world, has been the example of shareholder activism in the US. Investors there moved forcefully into governance when the free market in the control of assets – the takeover process – failed to deliver its promised benefits.

Whatever the precise cause, corporate governance has moved from the business to the public agenda and has done so internationally. At the same time, there have been subtle shifts in the balance of power within the Anglo-American governance system. Shareholders have increased their influence, the position of outside, non-executive, directors has strengthened and boards have taken a somewhat tighter grip on the affairs of their companies.

In all this, it is important to keep the limited role of our own Committee in mind. We were set up to consider the financial aspects of corporate governance, not corporate governance as a whole. Our remit was to recommend ways of restoring confidence in the trustworthiness of reports and accounts and the audit statements which accompany them, not to overhaul the British system of corporate governance. We worked on the evidence presented to us, our only full-time member was our hard-working secretary, we had no research capability and our sponsors expected a report within 12 months.

The Committee, therefore, concentrated on recommending ways in which existing structures and processes could be made more effective and robust. An important and probably undervalued aim was to clarify precisely where the responsibilities for financial reporting and accountability lay. Directors and boards were not clear what was expected of them and there was confusion over the respective duties of directors and auditors in the matter. The extent of the lack of agreement and understanding of the financial governance rules, as they stood, has to be appreciated before the significance of the clarification task can be assessed.

The Code of Best Practice provides boards of directors with a check-list against which to measure their standing in matters of governance and shareholders with an agenda for their dialogues with boards. It will be in the interests of boards to comply with the code, because it will improve their standing in the market place. It will equally, and for the same reason, be in the interests of their shareholders to press them to comply. In sum, the Committee is looking to market regulation to bring about compliance with its recommendations.

It is significant that only one submission to the Committee, out of over two hundred, advocated an SEC type of regulatory approach to governance. The problem with statutory regulation is that it is not well-suited to some of the key issues addressed by the Committee, such as the structure and working boards of directors.

There is an obvious point that there is no one pattern of direction and control which could fit the wide diversity of company situations. More fundamentally, more governance requires appropriate board structures, directors of integrity and openness about the working of the governance system. A statutory approach to governance has to concentrate on what can be defined and measured. Not only may this miss the essence of the matter, but also it can serve to obstruct those seeking to discover what the pattern of governance really is in a particular company.

To give an example, the Code of Best Practice does not make the split between the posts of chairman and of chief executive mandatory, although the report makes it clear that, in principle, they should be divided. The code recommendation, however, is that 'there should be a clearly accepted division of responsibilities at the head of a company, which will ensure a balance of power and authority, such that no one individual has unfettered powers of decision.'

A statutory requirement to give different job titles to two members of a board could comfortably be met without any effect on the balance of power in the board. More inhibitingly, meeting the official criterion could close the matter to questioning. By adhering to principles, the code enables shareholders and others to probe precisely what the division of responsibilities is at the head of a company, and so confront a central governance issue.

What is important about structure is that it should assist those responsible for governance to discharge their increasingly demanding duties effectively. It is, however, the quality of those who operate the structure which counts above all. Thus, the code addresses both board structure and board membership. The recommendations, therefore, on how directors should be nominated are fundamental, as are the definition of independent outside (non-executive) directors and the proposal that, when the two top posts in a company are combined, there should be a recognised senior member among the outside directors.

The distinction between those outside directors who are truly independent and those who are not, and the senior member proposal, were both new concepts in terms of British board practice. There are examples of strengthening the checks and balances within the existing framework of boards. Taken with the proposals for the formation of committees of the board, which buttress the position of the outside directors, they enable present board structures to operate more effectively without altering their basic form.

It is logical to aim to make the most of the existing governance system before seeking to change it. The debate does, however, now need to move forward and this involves considering structural changes of the kind adumbrated in this collection of essays. I am cautious about structural change in answer to governance problems. Structure is important, but the way in which it is implemented in practice and the character and calibre of those responsible for so doing are more important still.

There will be a tendency for governance systems to converge internationally, driven by the need for large enterprises, wherever they are domiciled, to seek to raise capital from the same world-wide pool. I would expect convergence to be a slow process, since governance systems are but part of wider economic and social systems. Change, however, will come and so all contributions to the form which it might take are to be encouraged.

By mid-1995, a new committee will have been formed, which will provide an opportunity to review the way in which the recommendations of our Committee have worked out in practice and to decide whether the code needs updating in the light of issues which have emerged since our report was written. More basically, it will raise the question of whether a governance body of some kind has a continuing role and, if so, what its nature and status might be.

All of us on the original Committee were surprised at the degree of public attention, at home and abroad, which our somewhat technical report aroused. Our recommendations received prominence, because a lead in these matters was being sought and because of the ground swell of public interest in matters of governance. We did not cause that interest, but we were carried along by it.

The essential point is that the governance debate should continue. As we said in our report, 'the adoption of our recommendations will mark an important step forward in the continuing process of raising standards in corporate governance.' *Corporate Governance and Corporate Control* contributes constructively to that continuing process.

Adrian Cadbury
31 January 1995

Appendix

REPORT OF THE COMMITTEE ON
THE FINANCIAL ASPECTS OF CORPORATE GOVERNANCE
THE CODE OF BEST PRACTICE
1 DECEMBER 1992

INTRODUCTION

1. The Committee was set up in May 1991 by the Financial Reporting Council, the London Stock Exchange, and the accountancy profession to address the financial aspects of corporate governance.

2. The Committee issued a draft report for public comment on 27 May 1992. Its final report, taking account of submissions made during the consultation period and incorporating a Code of Best Practice, was published on 1 December 1992. This extract from the report sets out the text of the Code. It also sets out, as Notes, a number of further recommendations on good practice drawn from the body of the report.

3. The Committee's central recommendation is that the boards of all listed companies registered in the United Kingdom should comply with the Code. The Committee encourages as many other companies as possible to aim at meeting its requirements.

4. The Committee also recommends:

   (a) that listed companies reporting in respect of years ending after 30 June 1993 should make a statement in their report and accounts about their compliance with the Code and identify and give reasons for any areas of non-compliance;

   (b) that companies' statements of compliance should be reviewed by the auditors before publication. The review by the auditors should cover only those parts of the compliance statement which relate to provisions of the Code where compliance can be objectively verified (see note 14).

5. The publication of a statement of compliance, reviewed by the auditors, is to be made a continuing obligation of listing by the London Stock Exchange.

6. The Committee recommends that its sponsors, convened by the Financial Reporting Council, should appoint a new Committee by the end of June 1995 to examine how far compliance with the Code has progressed, how far its other recommendations have been implemented, and whether the Code needs updating. In the meantime the present Committee will remain responsible for reviewing the implementation of its proposals.

7. The Committee has made it clear that the Code is to be followed by individuals and boards in the light of their own particular circumstances. They are responsible for ensuring that their actions meet the spirit of the

Code and in interpreting it they should give precedence to substance over form.

8. The Committee recognises that smaller listed companies may initially have difficulty in complying with some aspects of the Code. The boards of smaller listed companies who cannot, for the time being, comply with parts of the Code should note that they may instead give their reasons for non-compliance. The Committee believes, however, that full compliance will bring benefits to the boards of such companies and that it should be their objective to ensure that the benefits are achieved. In particular, the appointment of appropriate non-executive directors should make a positive contribution to the development of their businesses.

The Code of Best Practice

1   The Board of Directors

1.1   The board should meet regularly, retain full and effective control over the company and monitor the executive management.

1.2   There should be a clearly accepted division of responsibilities at the head of a company, which will ensure a balance of power and authority, such that no one individual has unfettered powers of decision. Where the chairman is also the chief executive, it is essential that there should be a strong and independent element on the board with a recognised senior member.

1.3   The board should include non-executive directors of sufficient calibre and number for their views to carry significant weight in the board's decisions. (Note 1)

1.4   The board should have a formal schedule of matters specifically reserved to it for decision to ensure that the direction and control of the company is firmly in its hands. (Note 2)

1.5   There should be an agreed procedure for directors in the furtherance of their duties to take independent professional advice, if necessary, at the company's expense. (Note 3)

1.6   All directors should have access to the advice and services of the company secretary, who is responsible to the board for ensuring that board procedures are followed and that applicable rules and regulations are complied with. Any question of the removal of the company secretary should be a matter for the board as a whole.

2.   Non-Executive Directors

2.1   Non-executive directors should bring an independent judgment to bear on issues of strategy, performance, resources, including key appointments, and standards of conduct.

2.2 The majority should be independent of management and free from any business or other relationship which could materially interfere with the exercise of their independent judgment, apart from their fees and shareholding. Their fees should reflect the time which they commit to the company. (Notes 4 and 5)

2.3 Non-executive directors should be appointed for specified terms and reappointment should not be automatic. (Note 6)

2.4 Non-executive directors should be selected through a formal process and both this process and their appointment should be a matter for the board as a whole. (Note 7)

3. Executive Directors

3.1 Directors' service contracts should not exceed three years without shareholders' approval. (Note 8)

3.2 There should be full and clear disclosure of directors' total emoluments and those of the chairman and highest-paid UK director, including pension contributions and stock options. Separate figures should be given for salary and performance-related elements and the basis on which performance is measured should be explained.

3.3 Executive directors' pay should be subject to the recommendations of a remuneration committee made up wholly or mainly of non-executive directors. (Note 9)

4. Reporting and Controls

4.1 It is the board's duty to present a balanced and understandable assessment of the company's position. (Note 10)

4.2 The board should ensure that an objective and professional relationship is maintained with the auditors.

4.3 The board should establish an audit committee of at least 3 non-executive directors with written terms of reference which deal clearly with its authority and duties. (Note 11)

4.4 The directors should explain their responsibility for preparing the accounts next to a statement by the auditors about their reporting responsibilities. (Note 12)

4.5 The directors should report on the effectiveness of the company's system of internal control. (Note 13)

4.6 The directors should report that the business is a going concern, with supporting assumptions or qualifications as necessary. (Note 13)

Notes

These notes include further recommendations on good practice. They do not form part of the Code.

1. To meet the Committee's recommendations on the composition of sub-committees of the board, boards will require a minimum of three

non-executive directors, one of whom may be the chairman of the company provided he or she is not also its executive head. Additionally, two of the three non-executive directors should be independent in the terms set out in paragraph 2.2 of the Code.

2. A schedule of matters specifically reserved for decision by the full board should be given to directors on appointment and should be kept up to date. The Committee envisages that the schedule would at least include:

(a) acquisition and disposal of assets of the company or its subsidiaries that are material to the company;

(b) investments, capital projects, authority levels, treasury policies and risk management policies.

The board should lay down rules to determine materiality for any transaction, and should establish clearly which transactions require multiple board signatures. The board should also agree the procedures to be followed when, exceptionally, decisions are required between board meetings.

3. The agreed procedure should be laid down formally, for example in a Board Resolution, in the Articles, or in the Letter of Appointment.

4. It is for the board to decide in particular cases whether this definition of independence is met. Information about the relevant interests of directors should be disclosed in the Director's Report.

5. The Committee regards it as good practice for non-executive directors not to participate in share option schemes and for their service as non-executive directors not to be pensionable by the company, in order to safeguard their independent position.

6. The Letter of Appointment for non-executive directors should set out their duties, term of office, remuneration, and its review.

7. The Committee regards it as good practice for a nomination committee to carry out the selection process and to make proposals to the board. A nomination committee should have a majority of non-executive directors on it and be chaired either by the chairman or a non-executive director.

8. The Committee does not intend that this provision should apply to existing contracts before they become due for renewal.

9. Membership of the remuneration committee should be set out in the Director's Report and its chairman should be available to answer questions on remuneration principles and practice at the Annual General Meeting. Best practice is set out in PRO NED's Remuneration Committee guidelines, published in 1992.

10. The report and accounts should contain a coherent narrative, supported by the figures, of the company's performance and prospects. Balance requires that setbacks should be dealt with as well as successes. The need for the

report to be readily understood emphasises that words are as important as figures.

11. The Committee's recommendations on audit committees are as follows:

(a) They should be formally constituted as sub-committees of the main board to whom they are answerable and to whom they should report regularly; they should be given written terms of reference which deal adequately with their membership, authority and duties; and they should normally meet at least twice a year.

(b) There should be a minimum of three members. Membership should be confined to the non-executive directors of the company and a majority of the non-executives serving on the committee should be independent of the company, as defined in paragraph 2.2 of the Code.

(c) The external auditor and, where an internal audit function exists, the head of internal audit should normally attend committee meetings, as should the finance director. Other board members should also have the right to attend.

(d) The audit committee should have a discussion with the auditors at least once a year, without executive board members present, to ensure that there are no unresolved issues of concern.

(e) The audit committee should have explicit authority to investigate any matters within its terms of reference, the resources which it needs to do so, and full access to information. The committee should be able to obtain outside professional advice and if necessary to invite outsiders with relevant experience to attend meetings.

(f) Membership of the committee should be disclosed in the annual report and the chairman of the committee should be available to answer questions about its work at the Annual General Meeting.

Specimen terms of reference for an audit committee, including a list of the most commonly performed duties, are set out in the Committee's full report.

12. The statement of directors' responsibilities should cover the following points:

• the legal requirement for directors to prepare financial statements for each financial year which give a true and fair view of the state of affairs of the company (or group) as at the end of the financial year and of the profit and loss for that period;

• the responsibility of the directors for maintaining adequate accounting records, for safeguarding the assets of the company (or group), and for preventing and detecting fraud and other irregularities;

- confirmation that suitable accounting policies, consistently applied and supported by reasonable and prudent judgments and estimates, have been used in the preparation of the financial statements;

- confirmation that applicable accounting standards have been followed, subject to any material departures disclosed and explained in the notes of the accounts. (This does not obviate the need for a formal statement in the notes to the accounts disclosing whether the accounts have been prepared in accordance with applicable accounting standards.)

The statement should be placed immediately before the auditor's report which in future will include a separate statement (currently being developed by the Auditing Practices Board) on the responsibility of the auditors for expressing an opinion on the accounts.

13. The Committee notes that companies will not be able to comply with paragraphs 4.5 and 4.6 of the Code until the necessary guidance for companies has been developed as recommended in the Committee's report.

14. The company's statement of compliance should be reviewed by the auditors in so far as it relates to paragraphs 1.4, 1.5, 2.3, 2.4, 3.1 to 3.3, and 4.3 to 4.6 of the Code.

Bibliography

Aaronovitch, S & Smith, D, *The Political Economy of British Capitalism* (1984).

ABI, *Long Term Remuneration For Senior Executives* (1994).

ABI, *Share Incentive Scheme Guidelines* (1987) (Addenda 1988, 1991, amendments 1991).

Ackerman, H 'How Companies Respond to Social Demands' (July-August 1973) *Harv Bus Rev.*

Adams, Carruthers & Hamil, *Changing Corporate Values, a Guide to Social and Environmental Policy and Practice in Britain's Top Companies* (1991).

AICPA, *The Information Needs of Investors and Creditors - A Report on the AICPA Special Committee's Study of the Information Needs of Today's Users of Financial Reporting* (November 1993).

Alchian, A & Demsetz, H, 'Production, Information Costs and Economic Organisation' (1972) 62 *The Economic Rev* 771.

Allen, D R, *Socialising The Company* (1974).

Allen, J, *The Company Town in American West* (1966).

American Law Institute, *Principles of Corporate Governance: Analysis and Recommendations* (1994).

Anderson, J, *Corporate Social Responsibility* (1989).

Andrews, K, 'Corporate Governance Eludes The Legal Mind' (1983) 37 *Uni of Miami L Rev* 213.

Andrews, K, 'Can The Best Corporations be Made Moral?' (May-June 1973) *Harv Bus Rev.*

Bebchuk, L, Symposium 'Contractual Freedoms in Corporate Law' (1989) 89 *Col L Rev* 1395.

Aoki, *The Co-operative Game Theory of The Firm* (1984).

Argentini, D, 'Predicting Corporate Failure' and 'Spot The Danger Signs Before It Is Too Late' (February 1986) *Accountancy* 157-158 and (July 1986) 101-102.

Armstrong, P & Murlis, R, *Reward Management* (1994).

Arsht, S, 'The Business Judgement Rule Revisited' (1979) 8 *Hofstra L Rev* 93.

Association of Industry, Press reports 1921, 1938, 1911.

Association of Industry, *Handbook* (1921).

Auditing Practices Board, The, *Exposure Draft of The Auditing Standard on Going Concern* (May 1993).

Auditing Practices Board, The, *Exposure Draft on The Auditing Standard on Going Concern* (December 1993).

Auditing Practices Board, The, *Statement of Auditing Standards - The Going Concern Basis in Financial Statements* (November 1994).

Auditing Practices Board, The, *Disclosures Relating to Corporate Governance* (Revised) (November 1994).

Auditing Practices Committee, The, *Auditors' Considerations in Respect of Going Concern* (1985).

Auditing Standards, The, *The Auditing Standard on Audit Reports* (undated).

Auerbach, Desai & Shamsavari, 'The Dialectic of Market and Plan' (July/August 1988) *New Left Review*.

Axworthy, A, 'Corporate Directors - Who Needs Them?' (May 1988) 51(3) *Modern Law Review* 273.

Baddon, L *et al*, *People's Capitalism? A Critical Appraisal of Profit-Sharing and Employee Ownership* (1989).

Baldi, D, 'The Growing Role of Pension Funds in Shaping International Corporate Governance, Benefits and Compensation' (October 1991) 21(3) *International Magazine*.

Baldwin, F, *Conflicting Interests* (1984).

Baran, P & Sweezy, P, *Monopoly Capital* (1966).

Barity, J E, *The Going Concern Assumption: Accounting and Auditing Implications* (1991).

Barry, N, *The Morality of Business Enterprise* (1991).

Batstone, E & Davies, P, *Industrial Democracy: European Experience* (Two Research Papers) London: HMSO (1976).

Bauer, R & Fenn, D, *The Corporate Social Audit* (1975).

Baumol, W, *Business Behaviour, Value and Growth* (1966).

Baums, R, 'Corporate Governance in Germany: The Role of The Banks' (1992) 40 *Am J Comp L* 503.

Baysinger, B & Butler, H, 'The Role of Corporate Law in The Theory of The Firm' (1985) 28 *Jour of Law and Econ* 179.

Bean, C, 'Corporate Governance and Corporate Opportunities' [1994] 15 *The Company Lawyer*.

Beard, M, *A History of Business* (1962).

Beck, C, 'The Quickening of Fiduciary Obligation: Canaero v O'Malley' [1975] 53 *Can Bar Rev* 771.

Becker, G, *The Economics of Discrimination* (1957).

Bennett, T 'Ethics Codes Spread Despite Scepticism' (15 July 1988) *Wall Street Journal.*

Berger, P L, *The Capitalist Revolution* (1987).

Berle, A A, 'Non-Voting Stock and "Bankers" Control' (1925) 39 *Harv L Rev* 673.

Berle, A A, *Studies in The Law of Corporation Finance* (1928).

Berle, A A, *The Equitable Distribution of Ownership: A Symposium on Business Management as a Human Enterprise* (1930).

Berle, A A, 'Corporate Powers in Trust' (1931) 44 *Harv Law Rev* 1145.

Berle, A A, *The Twentieth Century Capitalist Revolution* (1954).

Berle, A A, *Power Without Property,* New York: Harcourt Brace (1959).

Berle, A A, *Power* (1969).

Berle, A A & Means, G, *The Modern Corporation and Private Property,* New York: Harcourt Brace (1933).

Biendenkopt Report, *Co-determination in The Company, Report of The Committee of Experts* (1970).

Birds, J, 'Making Directors Do Their Duties' (1979) *Co Lawyer* 67.

Blackstone, W, *Commentaries on The Laws of England Vol I* (1768).

Blanpain, R, *The OECD Guidelines for Multinational Enterprises and Labour Relations 1982-84: Experience and Review* (1985).

Blumberg, P, 'Reflections on Proposals For Corporate Reform Through Change in The Composition of The Board of Directors: "Special Interest" or "Public" Directors' (1993) 53 *Boston Univ L Rev* 547.

Blumberg, P, Goldston, E & Gibson, G, 'Corporate Social Responsibility Panel: The Constituencies of the Corporation and The Role of The International Investor' (1972) 28 *Bus Law* 177.

Board of Trade, *Report of the Committee on Company Law Amendment* (1945) Cmnd 6659 ('Cohen Committee').

Board of Trade, *Report of the Company Law Committee* (1962) Cmnd 1749 ('Jenkins Committee').

Boothman Committee, *Corporate Report: A Report for the Accounting Standards Steering Committee* (1977).

Boulding, K, 'Implications For General Economics of More Realistic Theories of The Firm' (May 1952) *American Economic Review supplement* 29.

Bowie, D, *Business Ethics* (1987).

Boyle, A, 'The Judicial Review of The Special Litigation Committee: The Implications For The English Derivative Action After Smith v Croft' (1990) 11 *Co Law* 3.

Bradley, C, 'Corporate Control: Markets and Rules' (1990) 53 *ML Rev* 170.

Branson, D, 'Progress in The Art of Social Accounting and Other Arguments For Disclosure on Corporate Social Responsibility' (1976) 29 *Vanderbilt L Rev* 546.

Branson, D, 'Countertrends in Corporation Law: Model Business Corporation Act Revision, British Company Law Reform, and Principles of Corporate Governance Structure' (1983) 64 *Minnesota L Rev* 53.

Bratton, R, 'The New Economic Theory of The Firm: Critical Perspectives From History' (1989) 41 *Stanf L Rev* 1471.

Bratton, R, 'The Nexus of Contracts Corporation: A Critical Appraisal' (1989) 74 *Cornell L Rev* 407.

Briggs, T, *Victorian Cities London: Odhams* (1963).

British Institute of Management, *The Board of Directors: A Survey of Its Structure, Composition and Role* (1986).

Brudney, V, 'The Role of The Board of Directors: The ALI ands Its Critics' (1983) 37 *Uni of Miami L Rev* 223.

Brudney, V, 'Corporate Governance, Agency Costs and The Rhetoric of Contract' (1985) 85 *Colum L Rev* 1403.

Brudney, V & Chirelstein, M, 'Fair Shares in Corporate Management Takeovers' (1974) 88 *Harv L Rev* 297.

Brudney, V, & Clark, J, 'A New Look at Corporate Opportunities' (1981) 94 *Harv L Rev* 997.

Buchanan, T, *Ethics, Efficiency and The Market* (1985).

Buchholz, V, *Fundamental Concepts and Problems in Business Ethics* (1989).

Bullock Committee, Report of The Committee of Inquiry on Industrial Democracy (1977) Cmnd 6706 London: HMSO.

Burnham, J, *The Managerial Revolution* (1962).

Business in the Community, *Direction for the Nineties* (1992).

Business in the Community, *The Business of Change* (1993).

Business Management Record, *Report on Company Contributions* (1992).

Buxbaum, R, 'Corporate Legitimacy, Economic Theory and Legal Doctrine' (1984) 45 *Ohio St LJ* 515.

Cable, J, 'Capital Market Information and Industrial Performance: The Role of West German Banks' (1985) 95 *Econ J* 118.

Cadbury, Sir Adrian, *Speech to the Institute of Management*, (1993) reprinted in Professional Manager November 8-10.

Cadbury, Sir Adrian, 'Restoring Trust and Confidence in The Corporate System' [1992] *ICCLR* 403.

Cadbury Committee, *Financial Aspects of Corporate Governance* (December 1992).

Canadian Institute, *The Going Concern Assumption*.

Chartered Accountants, Accounting and Auditing Implications Research Report by Boritz, *Toronto CICA* 1990.

Cannadine (edn) *Patricians, Power and Politics in Nineteenth-Century Towns* London: Pinter/Leicester University Press (1982).

Cannon, R, *Corporate Responsibilities* (1992).

Cantillion, R, *Essay on The Nature of Trade in General* (1964).

Carlisle, R, & Parker, T, *Beyond Negotiation,* Chichester: John Wiley (1985).

Carnoy, M & Shfarer, D, *Economic Democracy - The Challenge of The 1980s* (1980).

Carroll, A, *Business and Society* (1981).

Carsburg, B V & Gwillam, D, *A Survey of Auditing Research* (1987).

Cary, W L, *Cases and Materials on Corporations* (1974).

Cary, W L, & Goldschmid, H, 'Forward to The Corporate Social Responsibility Symposium: Reflections on Directions' (1978) 30 *Hastings LJ* 1247.

Casson, E, *The Economics of Business Culture; Game Theory, Transaction Costs and Economic Performance Oxford*: Clarendon (1986).

Castells, *The Shek Kip Mei Syndrome: Economic Development and Public Housing in Hong Kong Pion* (1990).

Catala, N, *L'Entreprise* (1980).

Caufield, S & Minnery, A, 'Planning as Legitimation: a Study of the Brisbane Strategy Plan' (1994) 18(4) *International Journal of Urban and Regional Research* 673-689.

CBI, *The Responsibilities of The British Public Company: Final Report of Company Affairs Committee* (1973).

CBI, *Pension Fund Investment Management* (1988).

CBI, *New Group on Executive Pay* (press release) 16 January 1995.

Central Statistical Office, *Studies in Official Statistics*, No 34 (1979).

Centre for Employment Initiatives, *Seconds Out: Business Secondment in Theory and Practice* (1988).

Chamberlain, N, *Forces of Change in Western Europe* (1980).

Chandler, A D, *The Visible Hand: The Managerial Revolution in American Business* (1977).

Charities Aid Foundation, *Charity Trends* (1990) (13th edn).

Charkham, J, *Corporate Governance and the Market for Corporate Control* (1989).

Charkham, J, *Keeping Good Company* (1994).

Chatterjee, S K, 'The Charter of Economic Rights and Duties of States: An Evaluation After 15 years' (1991) 40 *International and Comparative Law Quarterly* 669-684.

Chirelstein, M, 'Corporate Law Reform' in McKie (edn) *Social Responsibility and The Business Predicament* (1974).

Ciulla, J, 'Business Ethics as Marvel Imagination' in R E Freeman (edn) *Business Ethics* (1991).

Clutterbuck, D, Dearlove, D & Snow, D, *Actions Speak Louder,* London: Kogan Page (1990).

Coase, R, 'The Nature of The Firm' (1937) 4 *Economics* 386.

Cockburn, D, *Brothers,* London: Pluto (1983).

Cockburn, D, *In the Way of Women; Men's Resistance to Sex Equality in Organisations,* Basingstoke: MacMillan (1991).

Cockburn, D, *Machinery of Dominance; Women, Men and Technical Know-How,* London: Pluto (1985).

Coffee, J, 'Regulating the Market for Corporate Control: A Critical Assessment of the Tender Offer's Role in Corporate Governance' (1984) 84 *Colum L Rev* 1145.

Coffee, J, 'Shareholders Versus Managers: The Strain in The Corporate Web' (1986) 85 *Mich L Rev* 1.

Coffee, J, 'Liquidity Versus Control: The International Investor as Corporate Monitor' (1991) 91 *Colum L Rev* 1277.

Cole, A H, *Business Enterprise in Its Social Setting* (1982).

Coleman, J, 'Efficiency, Utility and Wealth Maximisers' (1980) 8 *Hofstra Law Rev* 509.

Collins, H, 'Ascription of Legal Responsibility to Groups in Complex Patterns of Economic Integration' (1990) 53 *ML Rev* 731.

Companies & Securities Law, *Enforcement of the Duties of Directors.* Review Committee, and Officers of a Company by Means of a Statutory Derivative Action (Report No 12, 1990).

Conard, A, *Corporations in Perspective* (1976).

Conard, A, 'Response: The Meaning of Corporate Social Responsibility - Variations on a Theme of Edwin M Epstein' (1979) 30 *Hastings LJ* 1321.

Conard, A, 'The Supervision of Corporate Management: A Comparison of Developments in European Community and United States Law' (1983) 82 *Mich L Rev* 1459.

Conference Board, The, *Corporate Boards and Corporate Governance* (1993).

Conference Board in Canada, The, *Canadian Directorship Practices: A Critical Self-Examination* (1977).

Conyon, P & Gregg, J, 'Pay at The Top: A Study of Sensitivity of Top Directors: Remuneration to Company Specific Shocks' (1994) *Nat Inst of Econ Rev* 83.

Cooney Report, The, *Report of the Australian Senate Standing Committee on Legal and Constitutional Affairs* (November 1989).

Cooper, A & Schlegelmilch, B, 'Key Issues in Ethical Investment' (1993) 2 *Business Ethics: A European Review* 213.

Coopers & Lybrand, *Barriers to Takeovers in The European Community: A Study by Coopers & Lybrand For The DTI* (1981).

Cooter, M & Freedman, P, 'The Fiduciary Relationship: Its Economic Character and Legal Consequences' (1991) 66 *NY Univ L Rev* 1045.

Corina, J & Rees, W, *Disclosure of Company Information to Trade Union and Employees* (1981).

Cork Committee, Report of The, *The Report of the Review Committee on Insolvency Law and Practice* (1982) Cmnd 8558.

Corporate Consulting Group, *The Non-Executive Director in The UK* (1980).

Corson, J & Steiner, G, *Measuring Business's Social Audit* (1974).

Coser, T, *Masters of Sociological Thought,* New York: Harcourt Brace Jovanovich (1971).

Cosh, J, *et al, Takeovers and Short-Termism in The UK* (1990).

Cressey & Moore, 'Managerial Values and Corporate Codes of Ethics' (summer 1983) California Management Review.

Crosland, C A R, *The Future of Socialism* (1956).

Crystal, P, *In Search of Excess* (1991).

Cubbin, J & Leech, D, 'The Effect of Shareholders Dispersion on the Degree of Control in British Companies: Theory and Measurement' (1983) 93 *Econ J* 351.

Culler, A, Hindess, B, Hirst, P, & Hussain, A, *Capital and Capitalism Today* (1977/78) Vols 1, 2.

Cyert, E & March, B, 'Organisational Factors in the Theory of Oligopoly' (1956) Vol XX *Quarterly Journal of Economics* 15.

Dahl, R A, *Who Governs?* New Haven: Yale University Press (1958).

Dahrendorf, R, *Class and Class Conflict in Industrial Society* (1959).

Dallas, P, 'Two Models of Corporate Governance: Beyond Berle and Means' (1988) 22 *U Mich J L Rev* 19.

Davies, P, 'Institutional Investors in The United Kingdom' in Prentice & Holland (edns) *Contemporary Issues in Corporate Governance* (1993).

Davis, E, 'The Case For and Against Business Assumption of Social Responsibilities' (1973) 16 *Academy of Management Journal* 312.

Davis, S, & Kay, F, 'Corporate Governance, Takeovers and The Role of The Non-Executive Director' in Bishop & Kay (edns) *European Mergers and Merger Policy* (1993).

Demb A, & Neubauer, G, 'Corporate Governance: A Burning Issue' in Sutton (edn) *The Legitimate Corporation: Essential Readings in Business Ethics and Corporate Governance* (1993).

Demb, A, & Neubauer, G, *The Corporate Board: Confronting The Paradoxes* (1992).

Demsetz, P, 'The Structure of Ownership and The Theory of The Firm' (1983) Vol XXVI *Journal of Law and Economics* 375-390.

Demsetz, P & Lehn, H, 'The Structure of Corporate Ownership: Causes and Consequences' (1985) 93 *Journal of Political Economy* 1155.

Department of Employment, *Boards of Directors in British Industry* (1979).

Department of Prices and Consumer, *A Review of Monopolies and Mergers Protection*, (1978).

Department of Trade & Industry, White Paper, *Company Law Reform* (1973) Cmnd 5391.

Department of Trade & Industry, *The Conduct of Company Directors* (1977) Cmnd 7037.

Department of Trade & Industry, *Guidance Notes to Office Holders* (March 1986).

Department of Trade & Industry, *Reform of the Ultra Vires Rule* (1988).

Department of Trade & Industry, *Ownership and Control of Firms of Auditors Under the Companies Act 1989.*

Department of Trade & Industry, *Amended Proposal For A Fifth Directive on The Harmonisation of Company Law in The Economic Community: A Consultative Document* (1990).

Department of Trade & Industry, *The Law Applicable to Private Companies* (November 1994).

Derrick, P, *The Company and Community* (1964).

Derrick, P & Phipps, J, *Co-ownership, Co-operation and Control: An Industrial Objective* (1969).

Dertouzos, Lester & Solou, *Made in America: Regaining the Productive Edge* (1989).

Dickson, S, Smith, P & Woods, J, 'Type 'A' or Type 'B'? Explaining Sector Differences in Co-operative Networking' paper to the *British Academy of Management Conference* (September 1994).

Dickson, L, 'Ballot Box Crusaders Ride to Foreign Wars' *The Financial Times* 3 March 1993.

Dill, W, *Running The American Corporation.*

Dimock, J & Hyde, P, *Bureaucracy and Trusteeship in Large Corporations* (1940).

Dine, J, 'The Governance of Governance' [1994] 15 *The Company Lawyer* 73-79.

Directory of Social Change, *Company Giving* (1991).

Directory of Social Change, Estimate (1988) in *Forgarty, M and Christie, I, Companies and Communities; Promoting Business Involvement in the Community* (1990) London: PSI.

Dodd, E M, 'For Whom Are Corporate Managers Trustees?' (1932) 45 *Harv Law Rev* 1145.

Dodd, E M, 'Is Effective Enforcement of Fiduciary Duties of Corporate Management Practicable?' (1935) 2 *University of Chicago Law Review* 194.

Donaldson, J, *Business Ethics: A European Casebook* (1990).

Donaldson, T, *Corporations and Morality* (1982).

Douglas, W, 'Directors Who Do Not Direct' (1933) 47 *Harv L Rev* 1305.

Drake, G (1989) *JBL* 474.

Drucker, P, *Concept of The Corporation* (1946).

Drucker, P, *The New Society* (1952).

Drucker, P, *Management* (1974).

Drucker, P, *The Unseen Revolution: How Pension Fund Socialism Came to America* (1976).

Durkheim, E, *The Division of Labour and Society Basingstoke*: Macmillan (1984).

Dworkin, P, 'Is Wealth a Value?' (1980) *J of Legal Studies* 191.

Easterbrook, F & Fischel, D, 'The Proper Role of a Target's Management in Responding to a Tender Offer' (1981) 94 *Harv L Rev* 1161.

Easterbrook, F & Fischel, D, 'Corporate Control Transactions' (1982) 91 *Yale LJ* 697.

Easterbrook, F & Fischel, D, 'Limited Liability and The Corporation' (1985) *Uni of Chicago L Rev* 89.

Easterbrook, F & Fischel, D, 'The Corporate Contract' (1989) 89 *Colum L Rev* 1416.

Easterbrook, F & Fischel, D, *The Economic Structure of Corporate Law* (1991).

Ecsim, T, *Values and Limitations of Codes of Conduct as Regulating Instruments for Multinational Corporation*, Brussels: European Centre for Study and Information on Multinational Corporations (1978).

Eisenberg, M A, 'The Legal Roles of Shareholders and Management in Modern Corporate Decision-Making' (1969) 57 *Cal L Rev* 4.

Eisenberg, M A, *The Structure of The Corporation* (1976).

Eisenberg, M A, 'The Modernisation of Corporate Law: An Essay For Bill Cary' (1983) 37 *Uni of Miami L Rev* 187.

Eisenberg, M A, 'The Structure of Corporation Law' (1989) 89 *Colum L Rev* 1461.

Elkington, J, *The Environmental Audit: A Green Filter for Company Policies, Plants, Processes and Products* (1990).

Elliott, J, *Conflict or Co-operation: The Growth of Industrial Democracy* (1978).

Emerson, F & Lanham, F C, *Shareholder Democracy: A Broader Outlook for The Corporation* (1954).

Engel, D, 'An Approach to Corporate Social Responsibility' (1979) 32 *Stan Law Rev* 1.

Epstein, E, 'Societal, Managerial and Legal Perspectives on Corporate Social Responsibility - Product and Process' (1979) 30 *Hastings LJ* 1287.

Estes, R, *Corporate Social Accounting* (1976).

Ethics Resource Centre, *Implementation and Enforcement of Codes of Ethics in Corporations and Associations* (1980).

Ewing, K D, *The Conservatives, Trade Unions and Political Funding* (1983).

Ewing, K D, *The Funding of Political Parties in Britain* (1987).

Ewing, K D, *Money, Politics and Law: A Study of Electoral Campaign Finance Reform in Canada* (1992).

Fairburn, D, 'The Evolution of Merger Policy in Britain' in Fairburn and Kay (edns) *Mergers and Merger Policy* (1989).

Fama, E, 'Agency Problems and the Theory of The Firm' (1980) 88 *J Pol Econ* 288.

Fama, E & Jensen, P, 'Agency Problems and Residual Claims' (1983) 26 *J Law & Econ* 327.

Farrar J H, 'Ownership and Control of Public Listed Companies: Revising or Rejecting The Concept of Control' in Pettet, B (edn) *Company Law in Change* (1987).

Farrar, J, Furey, N & Hannigan, B, *Farrar's Company Law* (1991, 3rd edn).

Fidler, J, *The British Business Elite: Its Attitude to Class, Status and Power* (1981).

Finch, V, 'Directors' Duties Towards Creditors' (1989) *Co Law* 23.

Finch, V, 'Directors' Duties: Insolvency And The Unsecured Creditor' in Clarke (ed) Current Issues in *Insolvency Law* (1991).

Finch, V, 'Company Directors: Who Cares About Skill And Care?' (1992) 55 *MLR 179*, 202-204.

Finch, V, 'Disqualifying Directors: Issues of Rights, Privileges and Employment' (1993) *ILJ* 35.

Finch, V, 'Personal Accountability and Corporate Control: The Role of Directors' and Officers' Liability Insurance' (1994) 57 *MLR* 880.

Finn, P D, *Fiduciary Obligations* (1977).

Finn, P D, *Equity and Commercial Relations* (1987).

Fischel, D, 'The Corporate Governance Movement' (1982) 35 *Vand L Rev* 1259.

Fishman, D & Cheraiss, C, *The Human Side of Corporate Competitiveness* (1990).

Fisse & Braithwaite, 'The Allocation of Responsibility For Corporate Crime: Individualism, Collectivism and Accountability' (1988) 11 *Sydney L Rev* 468.

Fletcher, *Situation Ethics* (1966).

Florence, P S, *The Logic of British Industry and American Society* (1953).

Florence, P S, *Ownership, Control and Success of Large Companies* (1961).

Fogarty & Christie, *Companies and Communities: Promoting Business Involvement in the Community* (1990).

Ford, M, *Employee Share Ownership and Corporate Efficiency* (Working Paper No 9 July 1991 - University of Manchester).

Forum of Private Business, *A Report Into Business Legal Structures* (1991).

Foster, *Class Struggle and The Industrial Revolution*, London: Methuen (1974).

Franks & Harris, 'Shareholder Wealth Effects of UK Takeovers: Implications for Merger Policy' in Fairburn & Kay (edns) *Mergers and Merger Policy* (1989).

Franks & Mayer, 'Capital Markets and Corporate Control: A Study of France, Germany and The UK' (1990) 10 *Econ Policy* 191.

Franks & Mayer, 'European Capital Markets and Corporate Control' in Bishop & Kay (edns) *European Mergers and Mergers Policy* (1993).

Fransman, *The Market and Beyond; Co-operation and Competition in Information Technology in the Japanese System*, Cambridge: University Press (1990).

Fraser, *Power and Authority in the Victorian City*, Oxford: Basil Blackwell (1979).

Frederick, Post & Davies (eds), *Business and Society, Corporate Strategy, Public Policy, Ethics* (1992).

Friedman, M, *Capitalism and Freedom* (1962).

Friedman, M, 'The Social Responsibility of Business is to Increase Its Profits'
     New York Times Magazine 13 Sept 1970.

Friedman, M, *An Economist's Protest* (1972).

Friedman, M, 'Monopoly and the Social Responsibilities of
     Business and Labour' in Friedman and Friedman (edns)
     Capitalism and Freedom.

Friedman, M, 'The Social Responsibility of Business is to Increase Its Profits'
     inSteiner & Steiner (edns) Issues in *Business and Society* (1977).

Friedmann, W & Garner J F, *Government Enterprise: A Comparative Study*
     (1970).

Frug, D, 'The Ideology of Bureaucracy in American Law'
     (1984) 97 *Harv L Rev* 1276.

Galbraith, J K, *American Capitalism: The Concept of Countervailing Power*
     (1957).

Galbraith, J K, *The New Industrial State* (1967).

Gaved, J & Goodman, S, *Deeper Share Ownership* (1992).

Gilson, R, 'A Structural Approach to Corporations: The Case Against
     Defensive Tactics in Tender Offers' (1980) 33 *Stanf L Rev* 819.

Gilson, R & Kraakman, P, 'Reinventing the Outsider Director: An Agenda For
     Institutional Investors' (1991) 43 *Stan L Rev* 863.

Gilson, R & Roe, T 'Understanding the Keiretsu: Overlaps Between
     Corporate Governance and Industrial Organisation'
     (1993) 102 *Yale LJ* 871.

Goo, S H, *Minority Shareholders Protection: A Study of Section 459 of The
     Companies Act 1985,* London: Cavendish Publishing (1994).

Goode, *Principles of Corporate Insolvency Law* (1990).

Goodpaster, M & Mathews, T, 'Can a Corporation Have a Conscience?'
     (Jan-Feb 1982) *Harv Bus Rev.*

Gordon, R A, *Business Leadership in The Large Corporation* (1961).

Gordon, R A, 'Corporations, Markets and Courts' (1991) 91 *Colum L Rev*
     1931.

Gould, W B, *A Primer on American Labor Law* (1982).

Gower, L C B, *Gower's Principles of Modern Company Law* (1992)
     (5th edn).

Gower, L C B, & Loss, L *New Trends in Company Law.*

Sommer, A A Jr, *Disclosure - Insider Dealings, Take Overs, Mergers and
     Corporate Management Obligations* (1980).

Goyder, G, *The Future of Private Enterprise* (1951).

Goyder, G, *The Responsible Company* (1961).

Goyder, G, *The Responsible Worker* (1975).

Goyder, G, 'Ought Company Debt to be Permanent?' in Sethi, P (edn) Trusteeship: *The Gandhian Alternative* (1986).

Graham, H, 'Regulating the Corporate Form' in Hencher & Moran (edns) Capitalism, *Culture and Economic Regulation* (1989).

Grantham, R, 'Directors' Duties And Insolvent Companies' (1991) 54 *MLR* 576.

Grantham, R, 'The Judicial Extension of Directors' Duties to Creditors' (1991)*JBL* 1.

Gray, R, Owen, D & Maunders, K, *Corporate Social Reporting* (1987).

Green, N, Hartley, T C & Usher, J A, *The Legal Foundations of The Single European Market* (1991).

Green, Sir O, 'Why Cadbury Leaves a Bitter Taste' *The Financial Times*, 9 June 1992.

Green, Sir O, *Pall Mall lecture*, 24 February 1994.

Greene, E & Junewicz, J, 'A Reappraisal of Current Regulation of Mergers and Acquisitions' (1984) 132 *Uni of Pennsylvania L Rev* 647.

Gregg, Machin & Syzmanski, 'The Disappearing Relationship Between Directors' Pay and Corporate Performance' (1993) *B J of Ind Rels* 1.

Griffiths, A, 'The Best Interests of Fulham FC: Directors' Fiduciary Duties and Long-Term Contracts' [1993] *JBL* 576.

Hadden, T, *Company Law and Capitalism* (2nd edn) (1977).

Hadden, T, *The Control of Corporate Groups* (1983).

Hadden, T, 'Regulating Corporate Groups: An International Perspective' in McCahery, Picciotto & Scott (edns) *Corporate Control and Accountability* (1993).

Haft, R, 'Business Decisions by The New Board: Behavioural Science and Corporate Law' (1981) 80 *Mich L Rev* 1.

Hahlo, H R J, Smith, G & Wright, R, *Nationalism and The Multinational Enterprise* (1974).

Halpern, Trebilcock & Turnbull, 'An Economic Analysis of Limited Liability in Corporation Law' (1980) 30 *Univ Toronto LJ* 117.

Hamer, B, 'Serving Two Masters: Union Representation on Corporate Boards of Directors' (1981) 81 *Colum L Rev* 639.

Hamilton, W, *The Politics of Industry* (1957).

Hanbrick & D'Aveni, 'Large Corporate Failures as Downward Spirals' (1988) 33 *Administrative Science Quarterly* 1-23.

Hansmann, T, 'Ownership of The Firm' (1988) *J Law Econ & Org* 267.

Harre, M, *Personal Being,* Oxford: Blackwell (1983).

Harris, S, 'Structuring a Workable Code of Ethics' (1978) *University of Florida Law Revue.*

Harvey, B, Smith, S & Wilkinson, B, *Managers and Corporate Social Policy - Private Solutions to Public Problems?* Basingstoke, Macmillan (1984).

Hayek, F, *The Road to Serfdom* (1944).

Hayek, F, Law, *Legislation and Liberty. A New Statement of The Liberal Principles of Justice and Political Economy* (1982) Vols 1-3.

Hayek, F, 'The Corporation in a Democratic Society: In Whose Interests Ought It And Will It Be Run?' in Anshen & Bach (edns) *Management and Corporations in 1985* (1985).

Heald, M, *The Social Responsibilities of Business: Company and Community, 1900-1960* (1970).

Heelas, A & Lock, D (edns) *Indigenous Psychologies,* London: Academic Press (1981).

Herman, E S, *Corporate Control, Corporate Power* (1981, 1982).

Herman, E S & Lowenstein, P, 'The Efficiency Effects of Hostile Takeovers' in Coffee, Lowenstein & Rose-Ackerman (edns) Knights, Riders and Targets: *The Impact of The Hostile Takeover* (1988).

Herzel, S & Shepro, T, *Bidders and Targets: Mergers and Acquisitions in The US* (1990).

Hessen, R, *In Defence of the Corporation* (1979).

Hessen, R, 'A New Concept of Corporations: A Contractual and Private Property Model' (1979) *30 Hastings LJ* 1327.

Hetherington, J A C, 'Fact and Legal Theory: Shareholders, Managers and Corporate Social Responsibility' (1969) 21 *Stan L Rev* 248.

Hetherington, J A C, 'When The Sleeper Wakes: Reflections on Corporate Governance and Shareholder Rights' (1979) 8 *Hofstra L Rev* 183.

Higgins, N, 'Elements of Indeterminacy in the Theory of Non-Profit Competition' (September 1939) *American Economic Review* 31.

Higgins, N, *The Development of International Law Through The Political Organs of The United Nations* (1965).

Hillmer, C, 'The Governance Research Agenda: A Practitioner's Perspective' (1993) 1 *Corporate Governance* 26.

Hirsch, F, *Social Limits to Growth* (1977).

Hirschman, P, *Exit, Voice and Loyalty: Responses to Decline in Firms, Organisations and States* (1970).

Hirst, P, *On Law and Ideology* (1979).

Hitch, A, 'Price Theory and Business Behaviour' (May 1939) *Oxford Economic Papers* 15.

HMSO, White Paper, *A Revised Framework for Insolvency Law,* Cmnd 9175.

Holdsworth, W, *A History of English Law* (1909) (Vol 3 and 4).

Holland, S, *The Socialist Challenge* (1975).

Holton, *Economy and Society,* London: Routledge and Kegan Paul (1992).

Hopt, K, *Groups of Companies in European Laws: Legal and Economic Analyses of Multinational Enterprises* (1982) Vol 11.

Hopt, K, 'New Ways in Corporate Governance: European Experiments With Labour Representations on Corporate Boards' (1984) 82 *Mich L Rev* 1338.

Hopt, K, 'Directors' Duties to Shareholders, Employees and Other Creditors: A View From the Continent' in *Commercial Aspects of Trusts and Fiduciary Obligations* McKendrick (edn) (1992).

Hopt, K & Teubner, G (edns), *Corporate Governance and Directors' Liabilities* (1985).

Horn, N, *Legal Problems of Codes of Conduct for Multinational Enterprises* (1980).

House of Representatives Standing Committee on Legal and Constitutional Affairs, 'Report on Corporate Practices and the Rights of Shareholders' (1993)

Hower, R, *History of Macy's of New York: 1885-1919 Chapters in The Evolution of The Department Store* (1943).

Humble, J, *Social Responsibility Audit - A Management Tool for Survival* (1973).

Hunt, B, 'Avoidance of Antecedent Transactions - Who Foots The Bill?' (1992) 6 *Ins Law & Practice* 184.

Hurst, J W, *The Legitimacy of The Business Corporation* (1970).

Hussey, R & Marsh, A, *Disclosure of Information and Employee Reporting* (1983).

ICC, *International Code of Advertising Practice* (1986) ICC publication No 432B.

ICC, *International Code of Sales Promotion* (1987) ICC publication No 432A.

ICC, *Rules for the ICC International Council on Marketing Practice* (1988) ICC publication No 432C.

ICC, *Code on Environmental Advertising* (1991) ICC publication No 509.

Institute of Business Ethics, *Company Philosophies and Codes of Business Ethics* (1988).

Institute of Directors, *Standard Boardroom Practice* (1961).

Institute of Directors, *Guidelines for Directors* (1973).

Institute of Directors, *Professional Development of and for the Board* (January 1990).

Institute of Directors, *The Remuneration of Directors: A Framework For Remuneration Committees* (January 1995).

Institute of Management, 'When The Wheels Come Off' (July 1994) *Management Today* 32-35.

Institute of Manpower Services, *Stimulating Jobs: The Charitable Role of Companies* (IMS Report No 166) H Metcalf, R Pearson & R Martin (1989).

Institutional Shareholders Committee, *The Role and Duty of Directors: A Statement of Best Practice* (1991).

International Labour Office, *Multinational Enterprises and Social Policy* adopted by the International Labour Office (1973).

Irvin, A (edn), *Readings in Price Theory* (1952).

Jackson, M, 'Bankruptcy, Non-bankruptcy Entitlements And The Creditors' Bargain' (1982) 91 *Yale LJ* 857.

Jackson, M, 'Avoiding Powers in Bankruptcy' (1984) 36 *Stan L Rev* 725.

Jackson, M, *Logics and Limits of Bankruptcy Law* (1986).

Jacoby, N, *Corporate Power and Social Responsibility,* London: Macmillan (1973).

Jenkins, T & Cowell, D, 'Dwarfs and Giants in the 1980s: Trends in the UK Income Distribution' (1994) 15 *Fisc Studies* 99.

Jenkinson, A & Mayer, B, 'The Assessment: Corporate Governance and Corporate Control' (1992) 3 *Oxford Review of Economic Policy*.

Jensen & Meckling, 'Theory of The Firm: Managerial Behaviour, Agency Costs and Ownership Structure' (1976) 3 *J of Fin Econ* 305.

Jensen & Murphy, 'CEO Incentives - It's Not How Much You Pay, But How' (1980) *Harv Bus Rev* 138.

Johnson, T, 'The Effect of Resolutions on the General Assembly of the United Nations' (1955-56) 32 *British Yearbook of International Law* 97-122.

Johnson, T, *The City Takeover Code* (1980).

Jones, T, 'Corporate Governance: Who Controls The Large Corporation?' (1978) *Hastings LJ* 1261.

Katona, G, *Psychological Analysis of Economic Behaviour* (1951).

Kearney, R, 'The Ubiquitous Director' (1938) 12 *Uni of Cincinnati L Rev* 399.

Kendall, W, *The Labour Movement in Europe* (1975).

Kennedy, T, *European Labor Relations* (1980).

Kester, L, 'Independent Groups as Systems of Corporate Governance' (1992) *Oxford Review of Economic Policy*.

Keynes, J M, *Essays in Persuasion* (1951).

King, M, *Public Policy and The Corporation* (1977).

Kingston University, Human Science external seminar paper, *Economics as an Imperial Social Science* (1994).

Kirkman, P & Hope, C, *Environmental Disclosure in UK Company Annual Reports* (1992).

Kluwer, O, 'Derivative Actions and The Rule in *Foss v Harbottle*: Do We Need a Statutory Remedy?' (1993) *CSLJ* 7.

Kreps, T, *Measurement of The Social Performance of Business*, 'An Investigation of Concentration of Economic Power for The Temporary National Economic Committee' (1940).

Kripke, H, 'The SEC, Corporate Governance and The Real Issues' (1980-81) 36 *Bus Law* 173.

Kuhn, J W & Shriver, D W, *Beyond Success: Corporations and Their Critics in the 1990s* (1991).

Labour Party, Industry and Society: *Labour's Policy on Future Public Ownership* (1957).

Labour Party, *Industrial Democracy*: Report of Working Party (1967).

Labour Party, *The Community and The Company*: *Reform of Company Law* (Report of a Working Group of The Labour Party Industrial Policy Sub-Committee) (Green Paper) 1974.

Lamarche, P, (1976) 'Property Development and the Economic Foundations of the Urban Question' in Pickvance (edn) *Urban Sociology*: *Critical Essays*, London: Methuen.

Lamberton, A, *The Theory of Profit* (1965).

Landers, A, 'A Unified Approach to Parent, Subsidiary and Affiliate Questions in Bankruptcy' (1975) 42 *Univ Chic L Rev* 589.

Landers, A, 'Another Word ...' (1976) 43 *Univ Chic L Rev* 527.

Lash, B & Urry, J, *The End of Organised Capitalism Cambridge*: Polity Press (1987).

Law Commission, The, *Fiduciary Duties and Regulatory Rules*: A Consultation Paper (1992) London: HMSO.

Lee, T A, *Corporate Audit Theory* (1993).

Leech, N, 'Transactions in Corporate Control' (1956) *Uni of Perry L Rev* 725.

Leech, N, 'Corporate Ownership and Control: A New Look at The Evidence of Berle and Means' (1987) 39 *Oxford Economic Papers* 534.

Lewis, P, 'Cut the strings on the parachute' *The Financial Times* 17 August 1994.

Liebenstein, C, 'Allocative Efficiency vs X-Efficiency' (1960) 56 *American Economic Review* 392-415.

Lipton, M & Rosenblum, S, 'A New System of Corporate Governance: The Quinquennial Election of Directors' (1991) 58 *Uni of Chicago L Rev* 187.

Lipton, M & Panner, 'Takeover Bids and United States Corporate Governance' in Prentice & Holland, *Contemporary Issues in Corporate Governance* (1993).

Livingston, J, *The American Shareholder* (1958).

Locke, J, *Some Considerations of The Consequences of Lowering of Interest and Raising The Value of Money* (1969).

Locke, J, 'R J Holton "Economy and Society"' (1993) 51 *Capital and Class* 204-206.

Loomis, P & Rubman, B, 'Corporate Governance in Historical Perspective' [1979] 8 *Hofstra L Rev* 141.

Lundberg, L, *Public Relations in The Local Community*.

Luthans, F, Hodgetts, R & Thompson, K, *Social Issues in Business* (1987) (3rd edn).

Lynch, G & Steinberg, M, 'The Legitimacy of Defensive Tactics in Tender Offers' (1979) 64 *Cornell L Rev* 901.

Lynd, M & Lynd, C, *Middletown in Transition,* New York: Harcourt-Brace.

Mace, M, Directors: *Myth and Reality* (1971).

Mace, M, 'Directors: Myth and Reality - Ten Years Later' (1979) 32 *Rutgers Law Review* 293.

Mackenzie, C, *The Shareholders' Action Handbook* (1993).

Macneil, 'Contracts: Adjustment of Long-Term Economic Relations Under Classical, Neo-Classical and Relational Contract Law' (1978) 72 *NW Univ L Rev* 854.

Main, H & Johnston, M, *The Remuneration Committee as an Instrument of Corporate Governance* (1992).

Manley, W, *The Handbook of Good Business Practice*: *Corporate Codes of Conduct* (1992).

Manne, H, 'Some Theoretical Aspects of Share Voting' (1964) 64 *Columbia L Rev* 1427.

Manne, H, 'Mergers and The Market For Corporate Control' (1965) 73 *J Pol Econ* 110.

Manne, H, 'Our Two Corporation Systems: Law and Economics' (1967) 53 *Virginia Law Review* 259.

Manne, H & Wallich, *The Modern Corporation and Social Responsibility* (1972).

Marris, R, 'A Model of The "Managerial" Enterprise' (May 1963) *Quarterly Journal of Economics* 45.

Marris, R, *The Economic Theory of 'Managerial' Capitalism* (1964).

Marsh, R, *Short-Termism on Trial* (1990).

Marshall, T, *The History of Lancashire County Council Robertson* (1977).

Marx, K, *Capital Vol I London*: Lawrence and Wishart (1974).

Mason, E S, *The Corporation in Modern Society* (1959).

Mason, S, French, D & Ryan, C, *Company Law* (1991).

Maw, N, *Maw on Corporate Governance* (1994).

McCarthy, W, *The Future of Industrial Democracy* (1988).

McConnell, L P & Muscarella, R, 'Corporate Capital Expenditure Decisions and The Market Value of The Firm' (1985) 14 *J Fin Econ* 399.

McDaniel, J, 'Bondholders and Corporate Governance' (1986) 41 *Bus Lawyer* 413.

McDaniel, J, 'Bondholders and Stock-holders' (1988) *J of Corporations Law* 205, 236-237.

McDougall, C, & Fogelberg, A, *Corporate Boards in Canada: How Sixty-Four Boards Function* (1968).

McGuire, Chiu & Elbring, 'Executive Incomes, Sales and Profits' (September 1962) *American Economic Review* 51.

McKendrick, E, (edn), *Commercial Aspects of Trusts and Fiduciary Obligations* (1992).

McKie, J W, *Social Responsibility and The Business Predicament* (1974).

Means, G, *The Corporate Revolution in America: Economic Reality Versus Economic Theory* (1962).

Melrose-Woodman, J & Kverndal, I, *Towards Social Responsibility* (Report No28 British Institute of Management) (1976).

Melrose-Woodman, J & Kverndal, I, *Towards Social Responsibility: Company Codes of Ethics and Practice* (1977).

Middleton, D, 'Wrongful Trading And Voidable Preference' (1992) *NLJ* 1582.

Midgley, K, *Companies and Their Shareholders - The Uneasy Relationship* (1975).

Miliband, R, *The State in Capitalist Society* (1969).

Mitchell, N J, *The Generous Corporation: A Political Analysis of Economic Power* (1989).

Mofsky, J & Rubin, R, 'A Symposium on The ALI Corporate Governance Project' (1983) 37 *Uni of Miami L Rev* 169.

Monks, T & Minnow, S, *Power and Accountability* (1991).

Monsen, R & Downs, 'A Theory of Large Managerial Firms' (June 1965) Vol LXXIII *The Journal of Political Economy* 221.

Marris, A, *The Economic Theory of 'Managerial' Capitalism* (1964).

Marris, A, *The Economics of Discretionary Behaviour: Management Objectives in a Theory of The Firm* (1964).

Morrison, S E, *The Ropemakers of Plymouth: A History of The Plymouth Cordage Company 1824-1949* (1950).

Morse, B, 'The City Code on Takeovers and Mergers – Self Regulation or Statutory Protection?' (1991) *JBL* 509.

Myners, P, 'Corporate Governance - More Than Just a Cliché?' Speech made to the *National Association of Pension Funds Investment Conference, Eastbourne* (23-25 February 1992).

Nader, R, *The Consumer and Corporate Accountability* (1973).

Nader, R & Green, M, *Corporate Power in America* (1973).

Nader, R, Green, M & Seligman, J, *Taming The Giant Corporation* (1976).

NAPF & ABI, *Share Schemes Guidance* (1987, 1988, 1991 & 1993).

NAPF Ltd, *Share Schemes: A Consultative Approach* (1992).

Nash, L, *Good Intentions Aside* (1990).

Neal, A C, *Business Power and Public Policy* (1979).

New Zealand Law Commission, Discussion Paper No 5 on Company Law (1987).

New Zealand Law Commission, Company Law Reform and Restatement *NZLC* R9, June 1989.

Newton, A, 'Agents For The Truly Greedy' in Bowie & Freeman (edns) *Ethics and Agency Theory: An Introduction* (1992).

Nichols, T, Ownership, *Control and Ideology* (1969).

Nielsen, R & Szyszezak, E, *The Social Dimension of The European Community* (2nd edn) (1993).

Northrup, H R & Rowan, R L, *Multinational Bargaining Attempts: The Cases and The Prospects* (1979).

Nyman, G & Silberston, B, 'The Ownership and Control of Industry' (1978) 30 *Oxford Economic Papers* 74.

OECD, (1975) 78 *Observer* 17.

OECD, Investment Committee, guidelines (1976) 15 *International Legal Materials* 969.

OECD, *International Investment and Multinational Enterprises: Responsibility of Parent Companies for their Subsidiaries* (1980).

OECD, *Competition and Trade Policies: Their Interaction* (1984).

Offe, L, *Disorganised Capitalism,* Cambridge: Polity Press (1985).

Ogus, A, 'The Trust as Governance Structure' (1986) 36 *Univ Toronto LJ* 186.

Opinion Research Centre, *Implementation and Enforcement of Codes of Ethics in Corporations and Associations* (1980).

Ottoson, G, *Winning The War Against Corporate Crime* (1989).

Oxford Analytica Ltd, *Board Directors and Corporate Governance: Trends in The G7 Countries Over The Next Ten Years* (1992).

Parkinson, H, *Ownership of Industry* (1951).

Parkinson, J, *Corporate Power and Responsibility* (1993 & 1994).

Parsons, T & Smelser, D, *Economy and Society,* London: Routledge and Kegan Paul (1956).

Peacock, M & Bannock, A, *Corporate Takeovers and The Public Interest* (1991).

Per Cent Club, *Annual Report* (1989).

Petty, Sir W, 'A Treatise of Taxes, Contributions' in *The Economic Writings of Sir William Petty* (1889).

Polanyi, T, *The Great Transformation,* Boston Massachusetts: Beacon Press (1944).

Posner, A, 'The Rights of Creditors of Affiliated Corporations' (1976) 43 *Univ Chic L Rev* 499.

Posner, A, *The Economics of Justice* (1981).

Power, M, *The Audit Explosion* (1994).

Prais, S J, *The Evolution of Giant Firms in Britain* (1976).

Prentice, D, 'Effect of Insolvency on Pre-Liquidation Transactions' in Pettet (edn) *Company Law in Charge* (1987).

Prentice, D, 'The Theory of The Firm: Minority Shareholder Oppression: Sections 459-461 of The Companies Act 1985' (1988) 8 *OJLS* 55.

Prentice, D, 'Shareholders Actions: The Rule in *Foss v Harbottle*' (1988) 104 *LQR* 341.

Prentice, D, 'Some Aspects of The Corporate Governance Debate' in Prentice & Holland (edns) *Contemporary Issues in Corporate Governance* (1993).

Prentice, D, 'Creditors' Interests and Directors' Duties' (10) *OJLS* 215.

Prest, F, *Locality and Liberty,* Oxford: Clarendon Press (1990).

Preston & Post, *Private Management and Public Policy: The Principle of Public Responsibility* (1975).

Pritchett, M J, 'Corporate Ethics and Corporate Governance: A Critique of The ACI Statement on Corporate Governance' (1983) 71 *Calif L Rev* 994.

Pro Ned, *Code of Recommended Practice on Non-Executive Directors* (April 1987).

Pro Ned Ltd, *Remuneration Committees: A Survey of Current Practice* (1992).

Radice, G & Lewis, R, *Workers in The Boardroom* (1976).

Ramsay, B, 'Corporate Governance, Shareholder Litigation and The Prospects For a Statutory Derivative Action' (1992) 15 *UNSW LJ* 149, 165-166.

Ramsay, B, 'Directors and Officers' Remuneration: The Role of The Law' (1993) *JBL* 351.

Ratner, D, 'The Government of Business Corporations: Critical Reflections on The Rule of "One Share, One Vote"' (1970) *Cornell L Rev* 1.

Rehnert, R, 'The Executive Compensation Contract: Creating Incentives to Reduce Agency Costs' (1985) *Stan L Rev* 1147.

Reith, R, 'Corporate Accountability and Regulatory Reform' (1979) 8 *Hofstra L Rev* 5.

Richards, M, *Organisational Goal Structures* (1978).

Richardson, J J, *The Development of Corporate Responsibility in the UK* (1983).

Riley, C, 'Directors' Duties And The Interests of Creditors (1989) *Co Law* 87.

Riley, C, 'Contracting Out of Company Law' (1992) 55 *MLR* 82.

Riley, C, 'Contracting Out of Company Law: Section 459 of The Companies Act 1985 and The Role of The Courts' (1992) 55 *ML Rev* 782.

Riley, C, 'Regulating Corporate Management: US and UK Initiatives' (1994) *Legal Studies* 244.

Robertson, D H, *The Control of Industry* (1928).

Rockfeller, D, 'Ethics and The Corporation' (1979) 8 *Hofstra L Rev* 135.

Roe, F, 'Some Differences in Corporate Structure in Germany, Japan and The United States' (1993) 102 *Yale LJ* 1927.

Rohvlich, C, 'Corporate Voting: Majority Control' (1932-33) 7 *St John's Law Rev* 218.

Romano, E, 'Metapolitics and Corporate Law Reform' (1984) 36 *Stanf L Rev* 923.

Romano, E, 'A Guide to Takeovers: Theory, Evidence and Regulation' in Hopt & Wymeersch (edns) *European Takeovers: Law and Practice* (1992).

Romano, E, 'A Cautionary Note on Drawing Lessons From Comparative Corporate Law' (1993) 102 *Yale LJ* 2021.

Rostow, E, 'To Whom and For What Ends is Corporate Management Responsible?' in Mason E (edn) *The Corporation in Modern Society* (1959).

Rubner, A, *The Ensnared Shareholder* (1965).

Ruder, D, 'Protections For Corporate Shareholders: Are Major Revisions Needed?' (1983) 37 *Uni of Miami L Rev* 243.

Sappideen, R, 'Fiduciary Obligations to Corporate Creditors' (1991) *JBL* 365.

Sayer, G, 'Post-Fordism in Question'(1989) 13 *The International Journal of Urban and Regional Research* 4.

Schumpeter, J, *The Theory of Economic Development* (1934).

Schumpeter, J, *Capitalism, Socialism and Democracy* (1942).

Schwartz, D, 'Response: Some Thought on The Directors' Evolving Role' (1979) 30 *Hastings LJ* 1405.

Scitvisky, T, 'A Note on Profit Maximisation And its Implications' in Irvin (edn) *Readings in Price Theory* (1952).

Scott, J, *The Moral Economy of the Peasant,* Newhaven: Yale University (1976).

Scott, J, *Corporations, Classes and Capitalism,* London: Hutchinson (2nd edn) (1985).

Scott, J, *Capitalist Property and Financial Power* (1986).

Sealy, L S, 'The Disclosure Philosophy and Company Law Reform' [1981] 2 *Co Law* 51.

Sealy, L S, *Company Law and Commercial Reality* (1984).

Sealy, L S, *Company Law Reform* (1985).

Sealy, L S, 'Directors' "Wider Responsibilities" – Problems Conceptual, Practical and Procedural' (1987) 13 *Mon LR* 164.

Sealy, L S, *Cases and Materials in Company Law* (4th edn) (1989).

Sears Inc, *The New Place of The Stockholder* (1929).

Sen, A, 'Does Business Ethics Make Economic Sense' in P Minus (edn) *The Ethics of Business in a Global Economy* (1993).

Sethi, S P, *The Unstable Ground: Corporate Social Policy in a Dynamic Society* (1974).

Shanks, M, *European Social Policy: Today and Tomorrow* (1977).

Sheikh, S, *The Social Responsibilities of Companies* (October 1994, unpublished PhD).

Sheldon, O, *The Philosophy of Management* (1924).

Sherer, M & Turley, S, *Current Issues in Auditing* (1991).

Sheridan, T & Kendall, N, *Corporate Governance* (1992).

Sherwin, A, 'The Ethical Roots of the Business System' (Nov-Dec 1983) *Harv Bus Rev*.

Sherwood, K, 'Are Going Concern Reports Required by Statute?' (March 1993) *Accountancy* 84.

Sherwood, K, 'Auditors Liability: Its Role in The Corporate Governance Debate' (1993) 23 *Accounting and Business Research* 412-420.

Shonfield, A, *Modern Capitalism* (1965).

Simmel, P, 'Quantitative Aspects of the Group' in Wolf (edn and trans) *The Sociology of Georg Simmel*, New York: Free Press.

Simmonds, K, *Multinational Corporation Law* (1979).

Simon, A, 'Theories of Decision-Making Behaviour in Economic and Behavioural Science' (1959) 49 *Am Econ Rev* 253.

Simon, A, 'Contract Versus Politics in Corporate Doctrine' in Karrys (edn) *The Politics of Law* (1990).

Simon, J, Powers, C & Gunnemann, J, *The Ethical Investor: Universities and Corporate Responsibilities* (1972).

Simpson, K, 'Price Theory and the Theory of Profit' (1919-20) Vol XXXIV *The Quarterly Journal of Economics*.

Sioman, M, *Socialising Public Ownership* (1978).

Sloan, L, 'The Binding Force of a "Recommendation" of the General Assembly of the United Nations' (1948) 25 *British Yearbook of International Law* 22-23.

Small, M, 'The Evolving Role of The Director in Corporate Governance' (1979) 30 *Hastings LJ* 1353.

Smiles, S, *Self Help* (1873).

Smith, I, *Accounting for Growth: Stripping the Camouflage from Company Accounts* (1992).

Smith, A, *Wealth of Nations* (1930 edn), London: Cannan (1776).

Smith, A, *An Inquiry Into The Causes of The Wealth of Nations* (Random House edn) (1937).

Smith, B, 'Corporate Governance: A Director's View' (1983) 37 *Uni of Miami L Rev* 273.

Smith, N C, *Morality and the Market: Consumer Pressure for Corporate Accountability* (1990).

Snyder, F, *New Directions in European Community Law* (1990).

Social Audit, 'The Case For a Social Audit' (1973) *Social Audit* 4.

Social Science Research Council, *Advisory Panel on The Social Responsibilities of Business* (1976).

Solomon, L, 'Restructuring The Corporate Board of Directors: Fond Hope - Faint Promise?' (1977) 76 *Mich L Rev* 581.

Solow, T, *The Labour Market as a Social Institution,* Oxford: Basil Blackwell (1990).

Sommer, A, 'The Impact of The SEC on Corporate Governance' (1977) 41 *Law and Contemp Problems* 115.

Stegemoeller, M, 'The Misapplication of The Business Judgement Rule in Contests For Corporate Control' (1982) *Northwestern Uni L Rev* 76.

Stein, A, *The Eclipse of Community,* New York: Harper (1964).

Steinberg, M, 'The American Law Institute's Draft Restatement on Corporate Governance: The Business Judgement Rule, Related Principles and Some General Observations' (1983) 37 *Uni of Miami L Rev* 295.

Steiner, G, *Selected Major Issues in Business's Role in Modern Society* (1973).

Steiner, G, *Business and Society* (1975).

Steiner & Steiner (edns) (1977), *Issues in Business and Society.*

Steinmann, G, 'The Enterprise as a Political System' in Hopt & Teubner (edns) *Corporate Governance and Directors' Liabilities* (1985).

Stevenson, R, 'The Corporation as a Political Institution' (1979) 8 *Hofstra L Rev* 39.

Stevenson, R, *Corporations and Information: Secrecy, Access, and Disclosure* (1986).

Stigler, G & Boulding, K, *Readings in Price Theory* (1975).

Stock Exchange, *Listing Rules* (1993).

Stokes, M, 'Company Law and Legal Theory' in Twining (edn) *Legal Theory and The Common Law* (1986).

Stone, C D, *Where The Law Ends: The Social Control of Corporate Behaviour* (1975).

Straka, K, 'Executive Compensation Disclosure: The SEC's Attempt to Facilitate Market Forces' [1993] 72 *Nebraska L R* 803.

Streek, E, *Social Institutions and Economic Performance* (1992).

Sutton, B, *The Legitimate Corporation* (1993).

Swope, G, *What Big Business Owes The Public Worlds Work* (1927).

Sykes, A, 'Proposals For International, Competitive Governance in Britain and America' (1994) *Corporate Governance, An International Review.*

Taffler & Tisshaw, 'Going, Going, Gone – Four Factors Which Predict' (March 1977) *Accountancy* 50-54.

Tawney, R H, *The Acquisitive Society* (1922).

Teece, C, 'Profiting from Technological Innovation: Implications for Integration, Collaboration, Licensing and Public Policy' (1986) *Research Policy* 15.

Tepe, Jr, 'The Charter of Economic Rights and Duties of States: A Reflection or Rejection of International Law?' (1975) 9 *International Lawyer* 295-318.

Teubner, G, 'Corporate Fiduciary Duties and Their Beneficiaries: A Functional Approach To The Legal Institutionalisation of Corporate Responsibility' in Hopt & Teubner (edns) *Corporate Governance and Directors' Liabilities* (1985).

Teubner, G, 'Regulating Corporate Groups in Europe' in Sugarman & Teubner (edns) (1990).

Thompson, Wright & Robbie, 'Buy-Outs, Divestment and Leverage: Restructuring Transactions in Corporate Governance' (1992) Vol 8 No 3 *Oxford Review of Economic Policy: Corporate Governance and Corporate Control* 58.

Thompson, Frances, Levacic & Mitchell, Markets Hierarchies and Networks; *The Co-ordination of Social Life London: Sage/The Open University* (1991).

Tolmie, L, 'Corporate Social Responsibility' (1992) 15 *UNSW LJ* 268.

Tricker, R J, *Corporate Governance: Practices, Procedures and Powers in British Companies and Their Boards of Directors* (1984).

Tunkin, V, 'The Legal Nature of the United Nations' (1966) II *Hague Rec* 1-68.

Turgot, A, *Turgot on Progress Sociology and Economics* R Meek (edn) (1923).

Turnbull, S, 'Re-inventing Corporation' (1991) 10 *Human Systems Management* No 3.

Turnbull, S, *Should Ownership Last Forever?* (1992).

Turnbull S, 'Improving Corporate Structure and Ethics: A Case For Corporate Senates' (1993) 17 *Directors' Monthly* No 5.

United Nations, *General Assembly Certain Expenses Case ICJ Reports* (1962).

United Nations, *General Assembly Resolution Permanent Sovereignty over Natural Resources* (1962) (Resolution No 1803).

United Nations, Doc TD/RBP/CONF/10 of 2 May 1980 'The Set of Multilaterally Agreed Equitable Principles and Rules for the Control of Restrictive Business Practices' (1980) *International Legal Materials* 813.

United Nations, Doc TD/Code TOT/25 of 2 June 1980 'Draft International Code of Conduct on the Transfer of Technology' (1980) *International Legal Materials* 773.

United Nations, *Conference on Trade and Development Draft International Code of Conduct on the Transfer of Technology* (1980).

United Nations, 'Draft Code of Conduct on Transnational Corporations' (1984) 23 *International Legal Materials* 626.

United Nations, *Centre on Transnational Corporations Transnational Corporations in World Development; Third Survey* (1985).

Urgent Issues Task Force, *Disclosure of Directors' Share Options.*

US Dept of Commerce, *Corporate Social Reporting in The United States and Western Europe*: Report of The Task Force on Corporate Social Performance (July 1979).

Vagts, D, 'Reforming The "Modern" Corporation: Perspectives From The German' (1966-67) 80 *Harv L Rev* 23.

Van Luijk, 'A Vision of Business in Europe' in Mahoney & Vallance (edns) *Business Ethics in a New Europe* (1992).

Veblen, T, *The Theory of Business Enterprise* (1904).

Veljanovski, 'The New Law-And-Economics: A Research Review' in Ogus & Veljanovski (edns) *Readings in the Economics of Law and Regulation* (1984).

Vernon, R, *Storm Over The Multinationals* (1979).

Votaw, D, *Modern Corporations* (1965).

Waldmann, *Regulating International Business Through Codes of Conduct* (1980).

Wardle, M, 'Post Employment Competition – Canaero Revisited' (1990) 69 *Can Bar Rev* 232.

Weber, *The Protestant Ethic and the Spirit of Capitalism* (Parsons, trans), London: Allen and Unwin.

Weber, *The Theory of Economic and Social Organisation* (Henderson and Parsons, edns and trans) (1947).

Weber, *Economy and Society,* Berkeley: University of California Press (1948).

Weber, *The Methodology of the Social Sciences,* New York: Free Press (1949).

Webley, S, *Corporate Social Responsibility* (1975).

Webley, S, *Company Philosophies and Codes of Business Ethics* (1988).

Webley, S, *Business Ethics and Company Codes* (1992).

Wedderburn, K W, 'Control of Corporate Litigation' (1976) 39 *ML Rev* 327.

Wedderburn, K W, 'The Social Responsibilities of Companies' (1982) 15 *Melbourne University Law Review* 1.

Wedderburn, K W, 'Trust Corporation and The Worker' [1985] 23 *Osgoode Hall Law Journal* 1.

Wedderburn, K W, 'The Legal Development of Corporate Responsibilities: For Whom Will Corporate Managers be Trustees?' in Hopt and Teubner (edns) *Corporate Governance and Directors' Liabilities* (1985).

Wedderburn, K W, *The Worker and The Law* (1989).

Wedderburn, K W, 'Control of Corporate Actions' (1989) 52 *ML Rev* 401.

Wedderburn, K W, 'Companies and Employees: Common Law or Social Dimension?' (1993) 109 *LQR* 220.

Weiss, E & Schwartz, D, 'Using Disclosure To Activate The Board of Directors' (1977) 41 *Law and Contemp Problems* 63.

Welling, B L, *Corporate Law in Canada* (1984).

Wellman & Berkowitz, *Social Structures a Network Approach,* Cambridge: University Press (1988).

Werlauff, E, *EC Company Law* (1993).

Weston, F, 'Enterprise and Profit' (1949) Vol XXII *The Journal of Business of the University of Chicago.*

Wheeler, D, 'Disqualification of Directors' in Rajak (edn) *Insolvency Law: Theory and Practice* (1993).

Wheeler, D, 'Swelling the Assets for Distribution in Corporate Insolvency' (1993) *JBL* 256.

Williams, H, 'Symposium on Corporate Governance' (1979) 8 *Hofstra L Rev* 1.

Williamson, O, *The Economics of Discretionary Behaviour: Managerial Objectives in The Theory of The Firm* (1964).

Williamson, O, 'On The Governance of The Modern Corporation' (1979) 8 *Hofstra L Rev* 63.

Williamson, O, 'Corporate Governance' (1983) 93 *Yale LJ* 1197.

Williamson, O, *The Economic Institutions of Capitalism: Firms, Markers, Relational Contracting* (1985).

Wolf, G (edn and trans), *The Sociology Of Georg Simmel* (1950).

Woods, P, *The Transformation of Work; Skill Flexibility and the Labour Process.*

Woodward, J, *A Study of The John Lewis Partnership* (1968).

Wootton, R, 'Creditors' Derivative Suits on Behalf of Solvent Companies' (1979) 88 *Yale LJ* 1299.

Wolfson, N, 'A Critique of Corporate Law' (1979) *Uni of Miami L Rev* 959.

Wolfson, N (1980) 34 *U Miami L Rev* 959.

Wright-Mills, S, *White Collar,* New York: Oxford University Press (1951).

Yablon, 'Overcompensating: The Corporate Lawyer and Executive Pay' (1992) 92 *Colum L Rev* 1867.

Zeitlin, M, 'Corporate Ownership and Control: The Large Corporation and The Capitalist Class' (1973-4) 79 *Am J Sociology* 1073.

Index